Comprehensive School Counseling Programs

K-12 Delivery Systems in Action

Colette T. Dollarhide
The Ohio State University

Kelli A. Saginak
University of Wisconsin, Oshkosh

PEARSON

Boston ◆ New York ◆ San Francisco
Mexico City ◆ Montreal ◆ Toronto ◆ London ◆ Madrid ◆ Munich ◆ Paris
Hong Kong ◆ Singapore ◆ Tokyo ◆ Cape Town ◆ Sydney

Senior Series Editor: *Virginia L. Blanford*
Series Editorial Assistant: *Matthew Buchholz*
Marketing Manager: *Erica DeLuca*
Production Editor: *Mary Beth Finch*
Editorial Production Service: *Omegatype Typography, Inc.*
Composition Buyer: *Linda Cox*
Manufacturing Buyer: *Linda Morris*
Electronic Composition: *Omegatype Typography, Inc.*
Interior Design: *Omegatype Typography, Inc.*
Cover Administrator: *Joel Gendron*

For related titles and support materials, visit our online catalog at www.ablongman.com.

Between the time website information is gathered and then published, it is not unusual for some sites to have closed. Also, the transcription of URLs can result in typographical errors. The publisher would appreciate notification where these errors occur so that they may be corrected in subsequent editions.

ISBN-10: 0-205-40441-3
ISBN-13: 978-0-205-40441-4

Library of Congress Cataloging-in-Publication Data

Dollarhide, Colette T.
  Comprehensive school counseling programs : K–12 delivery systems in action / Colette T. Dollarhide, Kelli A. Saginak. — 1st ed.
       p. cm.
  Includes bibliographical references and index.
  ISBN 0-205-40441-3
  1. School counseling—United States. I. Saginak, Kelli A. II. Title.

LB1027.5.D55 2008
813'.6—dc22

                                                                            2006047970

Printed in the United States of America

10   9   8   7   6   5   4   3   2   1   11   10   09   08   07

This book is dedicated to my family:
Jerry Dollarhide; Shiloh, Jason,
James Wesley, and Cadence Colette Wende;
Charles W. Reding, Jr., and Carol Reding; Kathy Guffey,
Mike Reding, and Tricia Bartley; my beloved nieces;
and to the memory of my mother,
Kathleen Colette Scherr Reding.

—CD

♦ ♦ ♦

I dedicate this book to my children:
Andrea, Riley, and Avery;
to the children of the world;
and to the dedicated school counselors
who devote their work to
guiding, counseling, and advocating
*for **all** children.*

—KS

About the Authors

Colette T. Dollarhide, Visiting Professor with The Ohio State University, earned her master's and doctorate in counseling and educational psychology from the University of Nevada, Reno. She earned her bachelor's degree in political science from California State University at Fullerton. For the past eight years, her main teaching and research focus has been school counseling, but she has taught career counseling, college student development, theories and techniques of counseling, foundations of school counseling, special issues in school counseling (at elementary, middle, and secondary school levels), counseling through play, ethics, consultation, group counseling, pedagogy in counselor education, and practica and internships. She has co-authored a textbook on secondary school counseling, and she writes about school counseling leadership, supervision, and the work of school counselors. Dr. Dollarhide has presented papers at national ACES and ASCA conferences and at state conferences on topics in school counseling, supervision, and leadership. Currently she is the President-Elect of C-AHEAD. Her editorial work includes six years as a reviewer for CES as well as service as co-editor for a first-ever CES special section on school counselor supervision.

Kelli A. Saginak, Assistant Professor in the Department of Counselor Education at the University of Wisconsin Oshkosh, earned a master's degree in counseling from Rollins College and a doctorate in counselor education from Idaho State University. Her involvement with schools as a teacher, counselor, prevention specialist, and consultant extends more than twenty years. As a counselor educator for almost nine years, she has specialized in school counseling, group counseling, lifespan development, consultation, and clinical experiences. Dr. Saginak has published and presented on a variety of subjects, including experiential group counseling and group leadership development, school counseling leadership, systemic change and resistance to change, and service-learning in counselor education. She enjoys writing grants with student and community partners, and working collaboratively with schools on service-learning projects. Her current research focuses on school counselor leadership, group leadership development, and service-learning in counselor education.

◆ CONTRIBUTORS

Charles Lindsey, Assistant Professor of Counselor Education at the University of Wisconsin Oshkosh, earned a master's degree in counseling and personnel services from the University of Maryland, and a Ph.D. in counselor education and supervision from Ohio University. He is a licensed professional counselor and school counselor in Wisconsin, a professional clinical counselor in Ohio, and a national certified counselor. His counseling experience includes work in crisis services, a cardiac rehabilitation program, outpatient community mental health clinics, and school systems. His scholarly interests include outcome research implementation, looking at the role of spirituality in counseling and supervision, developing innovative and student-centered pedagogic approaches, and qualitative research.

Phyllis Robertson, Assistant Professor at Western Carolina University in Cullowhee, North Carolina, serves as Advisor in the school counseling program, teaches core curricula, and supervises practicum students in the school and community counseling programs. Prior to her appointment, she was a middle school counselor for ten years and an elementary counselor for five years in a public school setting. Her research interests include professional issues affecting school counselors, working with children with disabilities, and multicultural counseling training and competency development.

Robert I. Urofsky, Assistant Professor and school counseling program coordinator in the Leadership, Counseling, Human and Organizational Development Department at Clemson University, has experience as a school counselor and is president-elect of the South Carolina School Counselor Association. He serves on the editorial board for the *Journal of Counseling and Development*. His research interests include ethics in counseling, the school counselor's role in educational reform, and leadership and school counseling.

Contents

SECTION FOUR: The Activities within Comprehensive School Counseling Programs   123

CHAPTER 7
Counseling for All Partners   124

CHAPTER 8
Educating and Advocating with All Partners   146

SECTION FIVE: The ASCA National Model in Action: Comprehensive School Counseling Programs   **223**

CHAPTER 11
The ASCA National Model in the Elementary School, *by Charles Lindsey*   224

CHAPTER 12
The ASCA National Model in the Middle School, *by Phyllis K. Robertson*   238

CHAPTER 15
Emerging Issues for Schools and Students,
with Robert I. Urofsky 300

CHAPTER 16
Personal and Professional Issues 326

APPENDIXES

Preface

This book is intended as both a textbook and professional development resource for school counselors whose work transcends educational levels and who will benefit from a K–12 perspective on comprehensive school counseling. Although this includes pupil services directors and principals who supervise school counseling programs, the primary readers are assumed to be counselors-in-training or currently practicing counselors.

The profession of school counseling is evolving very quickly, with new philosophies and new approaches to the way the work should be accomplished. Numerous entities, including the American School Counselor Association (ASCA), the DeWitt-Wallace Foundation, and the National Board for Professional Teaching Standards (NBPTS), have sparked debate among advocates of competing perspectives. There is need for a resource that integrates these various perspectives with a developmental view of the needs of children at all three levels of education.

In addition, the field of counseling is advancing as new problems that affect children emerge. Although traditional therapy is not typically conducted in the schools, school counselors are nonetheless charged with helping to facilitate the academic, career, personal and social development of all children, including those with mental health issues. In the continuum of prevention/intervention/treatment, school counselors must be educated in the ways that their work influences students, families, and entire school environments.

School counseling as a profession is at a crossroads. Old attitudes and old paradigms are still manifest in many schools, which makes new visions seem revolutionary. These new ideas are not radical; they are commonsense solutions to new problems. And they are practiced in many schools. The American School Counselor Association has articulated a coherent model for comprehensive school counseling programs, called the ASCA National Model®. This National Model is presented as the foundation of this book, and various delivery systems that align with the ASCA National Model are presented. One approach, the Domains/Activities/Partners (DAP) Model, will be used as the structure for exploring the activities of school counselors within the National Model. Both of these models are commonsense, and they are attainable—but only when a critical mass of practitioners believes it is possible to change. That is the reason for this book—to promote a change in our profession and in our schools that will enable all students to be successful.

This book is written with love—love for children, love for schools, and love for counselors-in-training, who we hope will benefit from the perspectives within. We are passionate about the need for all our children to have access to qualified counselors and quality comprehensive school counseling programs. In too many schools, the old answers to old problems are all that children are offered, and we find this troubling and tragic. It is troubling that educational professionals have not bothered to keep up with new thinking in their chosen profession, and it is tragic that their lack of commitment will have an effect on the lives of their students. It is our hope that this book and the vision of what school counseling *can be* will help generate new energy for the school counseling profession.

◆ CURRICULAR AND PROFESSIONAL FOUNDATIONS

Two organizations have defined professional standards for school counselors—one for professionals-in-training in terms of curricular expectations for training programs, and the other for professionals in the field. The first, the Council for Accreditation of Counseling and Related Educational Programs (CACREP), represents the field's premier accrediting agency. The second, the American School Counselor Association (ASCA), is the national association for school counselors. This book has been written to reflect both the training and the professional standards applicable for school counselors.

- ◆ Inside the front cover of this book, you will find a "snapshot" of the standards material (for both the 2003 ASCA School Counselor Performance Standards and the 2001 CACREP Standards for School Counseling Programs) that appears in each chapter of this book.
- ◆ Preface Table 1 provides a list of all the ASCA School Counselor Performance Standards (2003) and identifies the book chapters in which each standard is addressed.
- ◆ Preface Table 2 provides a list of all the CACREP Standards for School Counseling Programs (2001) and identifies the book chapters in which each standard is addressed.

We hope that instructors using this text will find these tables convenient for organizing course content and helpful in increasing their confidence that this book provides school counselors-in-training with content for reflection on each standard. (New CACREP Standards are due out in 2008, and information about those will be added in future editions.)

◆ INSTRUCTOR SUPPLEMENTS

myhelpinglab is the online destination designed to help students in Counseling and Psychotherapy make the transition from their academic coursework to their professional practice. The online content consists of video clips of authentic practitioner/client sessions, video interviews with professionals in the field, an interactive case archive, and a licensing center with valuable information for students who are beginning their in-service career. For a demonstration of the website and to find out how to package student access to this website with your students' textbooks at no additional cost, go to www.myhelpinglab.com.

◆ ACKNOWLEDGMENTS

No book is ever the sole intellectual property of the author or authors. There are countless people who serve as inspiration, whose thoughts influence the authors, whose presence makes the authors' lives more livable and more meaningful.

To acknowledge their many contributions, I would like to thank

- Mary Maples and Tom Harrison of the University of Nevada, Reno, who were there at the start of my journey in counseling and counselor education
- Norm Gysbers of Missouri, whose unflagging energy has transformed school counseling "services" into school counseling programs
- The many professionals in the American School Counselor Association, whose continuing work to shape and refine the profession reflect dedication, vision, and creativity
- All those whose works are cited in this book

I would be remiss if I did not give special acknowledgment to my colleague and co-author. Kelli Saginak is a constant source of inspiration, creativity, and energy. She helped me articulate and refine many of the ideas that are expressed in our first book, *School Counseling in the Secondary School: A Comprehensive Process and Program,* which now have provided the foundation for this book. Her faith in our collaboration on the first book provided fuel for its completion, and now I am blessed with this opportunity to collaborate with her again. She is a very special colleague indeed.

I would also like to thank those who made my life livable and meaningful: my beloved family named in the dedication and my colleagues.

—CD

I am pleased to acknowledge the following individuals whose contributions, support, and encouragement made this book possible:

- The Department of Counselor Education at the University of Wisconsin Oshkosh
- Jillian Schofield, graduate assistant, devoted researcher, and school counselor
- Colette Dollarhide, my co-author, inspiration, and friend
- Alan Saginak, my husband and lifelong companion

—KS

We would both like to thank our editors at Allyn & Bacon: Virginia Lanigan and Ginny Blanford. Finally, we are grateful to the reviewers of this book for their helpful suggestions: Hande Briddick, South Dakota State University; Laurie Carlson, Colorado State University; Tracy Leiubaugh, Ohio University; Amy Milson, University of Iowa; Phyllis Mogielski-Watson, Purdue University Calumet; Bob Nielson, North Dakota State University; Steve Rainey, Kent State University; Joe Ray Underwood, Mississippi State University; Karen Rowland, Valdosta State University; Pat Schwallie-Giddis, George Washington University; and David Spruill, Louisiana State University.

TABLE P.1 ◆ ASCA School Counselor Performance Standards (2003) and Book Content

ASCA School Counselor Standards	Book Chapters
Standard 1: The professional school counselor plans, organizes and delivers the school counseling program.	
1.1 A program is designed to meet the needs of the school.	1, 6
1.2 The professional school counselor demonstrates interpersonal relationships with students.	1, 3, 6
1.3 The professional school counselor demonstrates positive interpersonal relationships with educational staff.	2, 6
1.4 The professional school counselor demonstrates positive interpersonal relationships with parents or guardians.	3, 6
Standard 2: The professional school counselor implements the school guidance curriculum through the use of effective instructional skills and careful planning of structured group sessions for all students.	
2.1 The professional school counselor teaches school guidance units effectively.	8
2.2 The professional school counselor develops materials and instructional strategies to meet student needs and school goals.	8
2.3 The professional school counselor encourages staff involvement to ensure the effective implementation of the school guidance curriculum.	8
Standard 3: The professional school counselor implements the individual planning component by guiding individuals and groups of students and their parents or guardians through the development of educational and career plans.	
3.1 The professional school counselor, in collaboration with parents or guardians, helps students establish goals and develop and use planning skills.	7, 8, 9
3.2 The professional school counselor demonstrates accurate and appropriate interpretation of assessment data and the presentation of relevant, unbiased information.	7, 8, 9
Standard 4: The professional school counselor provides responsive services through the effective use of individual and small-group counseling, consultation and referral skills.	
4.1 The professional school counselor counsels individual students and small groups of students with identified needs and concerns.	7
4.2 The professional school counselor consults effectively with parents or guardians, teachers, administrators and other relevant individuals.	9
4.3 The professional school counselor implements an effective referral process with administrators, teachers and other school personnel.	7
Standard 5: The professional school counselor provides system support through effective school counseling program management and support for other educational programs.	
5.1 The professional school counselor provides a comprehensive and balanced school counseling program in collaboration with school staff.	2, 3, 4
5.2 The professional school counselor provides support for other school programs.	10

TABLE P.1 ◆ (Continued)

Standard 6: The professional school counselor discusses the counseling department management system and the program action plans with the school administrator.

6.1	The professional school counselor discusses the qualities of the school counselor management system with the other members of the counseling staff and has agreement.	5
6.2	The professional school counselor discusses the program results anticipated when implementing the action plans for the school year.	5

Standard 7: The professional school counselor is responsible for establishing and convening an advisory council for the school counseling program.

7.1	The professional school counselor meets with the advisory committee.	10
7.2	The professional school counselor reviews the school counseling program audit with the council.	10
7.3	The professional school counselor records meeting information.	10

Standard 8: The professional school counselor collects and analyzes data to guide program direction and emphasis.

8.1	The professional school counselor uses school data to make decisions regarding student choice of classes and special programs.	5, 10
8.2	The professional school counselor uses data from the counseling program to make decisions regarding program revisions.	5, 10
8.3	The professional school counselor analyzes data to ensure every student has equity and access to a rigorous academic curriculum.	5, 10
8.4	The professional school counselor understands and uses data to establish goals and activities to close the gap.	5, 10

Standard 9: The professional school counselor monitors the students on a regular basis as they progress in school.

9.1	The professional school counselor is accountable for monitoring every student's progress.	10
9.2	The professional school counselor implements monitoring systems appropriate to the individual school.	10
9.3	The professional school counselors develop appropriate interventions for students as needed and monitors their progress.	10

Standard 10: The professional school counselor uses time and calendars to implement an efficient program.

10.1	The professional school counselor uses a master calendar to plan activities throughout the year.	10, 11, 12, 13
10.2	The professional school counselor distributes the master calendar to parents or guardians, staff and students.	10
10.3	The professional school counselor posts a weekly or monthly calendar.	10, 11, 12, 13
10.4	The professional school counselor analyzes time spent providing direct service to students.	10

Standard 11: The professional school counselor develops a results evaluation for the program.

11.1	The professional school counselor measures results attained from school guidance curriculum and closing the gap activities.	5, 10

(continued)

TABLE P.1 ◆ (Continued)

11.2 The professional school counselor works with members of the counseling team and with the principal to clarify how programs are evaluated and how results are shared.	5,10
11.3 The professional school counselor knows how to collect process, perception and results data.	5, 10

Standard 12: The professional school counselor conducts a yearly program audit.

12.1 The professional school counselor completes a program audit to determine the degrees to which the school counseling program is being implemented.	5, 10
12.2 The professional school counselor shares the results of the program audit with the advisory council.	5, 10
12.3 The professional school counselor uses the yearly audit to make changes in the school counseling program and calendar for the following year.	5, 10

Standard 13: The professional school counselor is a student advocate, leader, collaborator and a systems change agent.

13.1 The professional school counselor promotes academic success of every student.	2, 10, 15
13.2 The professional school counselor promotes equity and access for every student.	2, 10, 15
13.3 The professional school counselor takes a leadership role within the counseling department, the school setting and the community.	2, 10
13.4 The professional school counselor understands reform issues and works to close the achievement gap.	2, 10, 15
13.5 The professional school counselor collaborates with teachers, parents and the community to promote academic success of students.	2, 9, 10
13.6 The professional school counselor builds effective teams by encouraging collaboration among all school staff.	2, 10
13.7 The professional school counselor uses data to recommend systemic change in policy and procedures that limit or inhibit academic achievement.	10, 15

TABLE P.2 ◆ 2001 CACREP Standards for School Counseling Programs and Book Contents

CACREP Standards for School Counseling Programs	Book Chapters
A.1 history, philosophy, and current trends in school counseling and educational systems;	1, 2
A.2 relationship of the school counseling program to the academic and student services program in the school;	2, 4
A.3 role, function, and professional identity of the school counselor in relation to the roles of other professional and support personnel in the school;	2, 16
A.4 strategies of leadership designed to enhance the learning environment of schools;	10
A.5 knowledge of the school setting, environment, and pre-K–12 curriculum;	1, 2
A.6 current issues, policies, laws, and legislation relevant to school counseling;	14, 15, 16
A.7 the role of racial, ethnic, and cultural heritage, nationality, socioeconomic status, family structure, age, gender, sexual orientation, religious and spiritual beliefs, occupation, physical and mental status, and equity issues in school counseling;	3, 4
A.8 knowledge and understanding of community, environmental, and institutional opportunities that enhance, as well as barriers that impede student academic, career, and personal/social success and overall development;	2, 3, 4
A.9 knowledge and application of current and emerging technology in education and school counseling to assist students, families, and educators in using resources that promote informed academic, career, and personal/social choices; and	15
A.10 ethical and legal considerations related specifically to the practice of school counseling (e.g., the ACA Code of Ethics and the ASCA Ethical Standards for School Counselors).	14
B.1 advocacy for all students and for effective school counseling programs;	8
B.2 coordination, collaboration, referral, and team-building efforts with teachers, parents, support personnel, and community resources to promote program objectives and facilitate successful student development and achievement of all students;	2, 10
B.3 integration of the school counseling program into the total school curriculum by systematically providing information and skills training to assist pre-K–12 students in maximizing their academic, career, and personal/social development;	4, 5
B.4 promotion of the use of counseling and guidance activities and programs by the total school community to enhance a positive school climate;	2, 6
B.5 methods of planning for and presenting school counseling-related educational programs to administrators, teachers, parents, and the community;	3, 8
B.6 methods of planning, developing, implementing, monitoring, and evaluating comprehensive developmental counseling programs; and	10
B.7 knowledge of prevention and crisis intervention.	4
C.1a use, management, analysis, and presentation of data from school-based information (e.g., standardized testing, grades, enrollment, attendance, retention, placement), surveys, interviews, focus groups, and needs assessments to improve student outcomes;	10
C.1b design, implementation, monitoring, and evaluation of comprehensive developmental school counseling programs (e.g., the ASCA National Standards for School Counseling Programs) including an awareness of various systems that affect students, school, and home;	3, 4, 6, 10

(continued)

TABLE P.2 ◆ (Continued)

C.1c	implementation and evaluation of specific strategies that meet program goals and objectives;	10
C.1d	identification of student academic, career, and personal/social competencies and the implementation of processes and activities to assist students in achieving these competencies;	3, 4
C.1e	preparation of an action plan and school counseling calendar that reflect appropriate time commitments and priorities in a comprehensive developmental school counseling program;	5, 10, 11, 12, 13
C.1f	strategies for seeking and securing alternative funding for program expansion; and	15
C.1g	use of technology in the design, implementation, monitoring and evaluation of a comprehensive school counseling program.	15
C.2a	individual and small-group counseling approaches that promote school success, through academic, career, and personal/social development for all;	3, 7
C.2b	individual, group, and classroom guidance approaches systematically designed to assist all students with academic, career and personal/social development;	3, 7, 8
C.2c	approaches to peer facilitation, including peer helper, peer tutor, and peer mediation programs;	7
C.2d	issues that may affect the development and functioning of students (e.g., abuse, violence, eating disorders, attention deficit hyperactivity disorder, childhood depression and suicide);	3, 4
C.2e	developmental approaches to assist all students and parents at points of educational transition (e.g., home to elementary school, elementary to middle to high school, high school to postsecondary education and career options);	7, 8
C.2f	constructive partnerships with parents, guardians, families, and communities in order to promote each student's academic, career, and personal/social success;	3, 7, 8, 9
C.2g	systems theories and relationships among and between community systems, family systems, and school systems; and how they interact to influence the students and affect each system, and	3, 9
C.2h	approaches to recognizing and assisting children and adolescents who may use alcohol or other drugs or who may reside in a home where substance abuse occurs.	4
C.3a	strategies to promote, develop, and enhance effective teamwork within the school and larger community;	2, 9
C.3b	theories, models, and processes of consultation and change with teachers, administrators, other school personnel, parents, community groups, agencies, and students as appropriate;	9
C.3c	strategies and methods of working with parents, guardians, families, and communities to empower them to act on behalf of their children; and	3, 7, 8, 9
C.3d	knowledge and skills in conducting programs that are designed to enhance students' academic, social, emotional, career, and other developmental needs.	3, 5, 6, 7, 8

SECTION ONE

Introduction

CHAPTER

1

THE PROFESSION OF SCHOOL COUNSELING

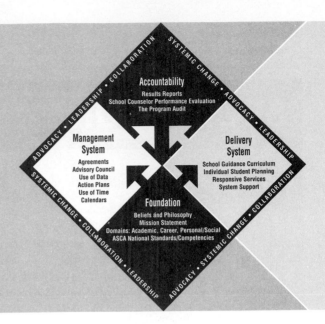

◆ LEARNING OBJECTIVES

By the end of this chapter, you will

1. Examine the professional and personal competencies and qualities that are needed by school counselors
2. Examine and understand various philosophies of counseling to begin to articulate your own philosophy of counseling
3. Examine and understand various philosophies of education to begin to articulate your own philosophy of education
4. Examine and understand various philosophies of school counseling to begin to articulate your own philosophy of comprehensive school counseling
5. Understand how the national association defines comprehensive school counseling programs
6. Understand the importance of the expectations and standards as defined by the national association for professional school counselors
7. Examine the differences between the three levels of educational progression and understand the school counselor's main activities at each level

DOMAINS / ACTIVITIES / PARTNERS MODEL

	Academic Development ▼	Career Development ▼	Personal/ Social Development ▼			
Counseling	1a	1b	1c	5	6	7
Educating and Advocacy	2a	2b	2c	8	9	10
Consulting	3a	3b	3c	11	12	13
Leadership and Coordination	4a	4b	4c	14	15	16
	Students			Parents and Caregivers	Colleagues in Schools	Colleagues in Community

DOMAINS

ACTIVITIES

PARTNERS IN THE PROCESS

CASE STUDY ◆ Mrs. Grundy's Retirement

Mrs. Grundy saw herself as everyone's "mother" in the middle school. The principal was usually a nice man, but when he lost his temper, he was prone to yelling at the kids in a red-faced fit of rage. Mrs. Grundy would hear the yelling, float in to calm the tempest, soothe the principal's ego and dry the student's tears, and send both parties on their way. This was how she thought of her job, as an angel of peace and harmony in the middle school. She would wait in her office until there was a crisis; then she would handle it. This is what she was good at.

This was her last week on the job, and she sighed as she thought about the last 40 years in the schools. She started out in the high school, spending her days scheduling students and handling emergencies. The stress of that job was horrible, so she opted to come to the middle school when the district developed a counseling job there. Now she was in her element—she did some scheduling and waited for the next crisis. She walked around making others feel good about themselves and their day, she lent a sympathetic ear when a parent was upset, and she knew all the students by name as she passed them in the halls. When one of her students returned to become a teacher in the school, she knew it was time to retire.

She looked up as Tracy, the new counselor and her replacement, came in the office. The principal had scheduled training for Tracy this week so that Tracy could enter the job smoothly. After exchanging pleasant greetings, Tracy could hardly wait to get to work. "I'm ready! Show me your program—I'm excited about some ideas I have for groups to help the kids. . . ."

"What program?" Mrs. Grundy interrupted. "You don't have time for any programs. You'll barely have time for lunch. You'll have things to do and kids in here all day long with one problem after another, problems you need to handle in five minutes or less. Programs won't work here."

"Oh. OK. I imagine that you have a lot to show me, with your experience here for so many years."

"No, not really. It'll take me an hour to show you where everything is—the computer and the master schedule. You'll know everything you need in a day. The biggest part of the job is handling Mr. Runyon's tantrums. If you can handle him, you have this job under control."

"But what about going into classrooms? Working on school climate issues? Consulting with other. . . ."

"Nope. You don't need to worry about any of that." Mrs. Grundy smiled, thinking of how young and naïve Tracy was. She would learn the limits of the job, with time. She would be shaped just as Mrs. Grundy had been, by the emotional demands of the school and those in it.

Tracy felt confused. She wondered why she needed a master's degree in counseling to be a scheduling secretary and a babysitter for a man-sized child.

CHALLENGE QUESTIONS

What do you see as the nature of Mrs. Grundy's job as she defines it? Are there limitations or problems with her definition? What are they? How do you think the principal and teachers perceive Mrs. Grundy? How would they define the job of the school counselor as they see Mrs. Grundy do the job? Which of those professionals would you imagine approves of the way she does her job? If you were Tracy, what questions would you have for Mrs. Grundy? What would you say to Mrs. Grundy about the job? How much of Mrs. Grundy's job is appropriate for the middle school, given the developmental needs of middle schoolers?

◆ OVERVIEW OF THIS BOOK

This book is designed to provide you with a structure from which you will be able to design, implement, and evaluate your own comprehensive school counseling program for any educational level. Focusing on elementary, middle, and secondary schools, this book is not a cookbook for programming; it is an opportunity to reflect on why school counselors do what they do, how school counselors should function, and in what ways school counselors can create comprehensive programs to accomplish what they should. In this discussion, you, the reader, will be challenged to personalize your learning and to develop your own understanding of how you want to practice the art and science of comprehensive school counseling. You will also be challenged to examine the examples of school counseling you may have experienced in your K–12 education, to separate your prior understanding of school counseling from some new visions of school counseling.

To help you do that, this book is written in the first person, directly to you, to connect with your heart and soul as well as your intellect. As you will see, the best school counselors are able to integrate and balance their intellectual understanding of school counseling, young people, and schools, with their empathic, intuitive understanding of learning, growth, and the conditions that facilitate healthy development. We need, therefore, to discuss both the professional skills and the personal qualities of effective school counselors.

The ASCA School Counselor Performance Standards addressed in this chapter are

Standard 1: The professional school counselor plans, organizes and delivers the school counseling program.

1.1   A program is designed to meet the needs of the school.
1.2   The professional school counselor demonstrates interpersonal relationships with students.

The CACREP Standards for School Counseling Programs addressed in this chapter are

A.1   history, philosophy, and current trends in school counseling and educational system;
A.5   knowledge of the school setting, environment, and pre-K–12 curriculum.

Reflection Moment ◆

Think about school counselors you have known in your K–12 education. Call to mind the image of the best school counselor you have known. How did that school counselor facilitate your learning, growth, and development? Now call to mind the image of the worst or least effective school counselor you have known, or recall stories of the worst school counselors others have known. How did that counselor, either actively or through a sort of "benign neglect," detract from the development of students? As you read this text, keep both the Super-Counselor and the Anti-Counselor in mind. Juxtapose those "role models" with your reading and reflection.

◆ ◆

◆ PROFESSIONAL COMPETENCIES AND PERSONAL QUALITIES OF SCHOOL COUNSELORS

In preparing to be effective school counselors, we must be prepared to demonstrate various professional skills and abilities and various personal qualities. Let's examine the professional skills first, looking at professional competencies and tests of professional competence. A good place to begin this exploration is with accreditation standards.

According to the 2001 Standards of the Council for Accreditation of Counseling and Related Educational Programs (CACREP) (Council for Accreditation of Counseling and Related Educational Programs, 2000), school counselors must be able to demonstrate significant professional knowledge and skills. These competencies comprise the essence of comprehensive school counseling. As you advance through your graduate program, you must remain aware of these competencies so that you can integrate them into your professional repertoire. In general, school counselors must be able to use data to improve student outcomes; design, implement, and evaluate comprehensive developmental school counseling programs, using a systems view of students' lives; design activities to help students attain academic, career, and personal/social competencies; and know legal and ethical standards and practices of counseling and school counseling. In addition, school counselors must be able to design and implement a school counseling calendar and must know strategies for integrating the school counseling program into the full school curriculum, strategies for seeking alternative funding, and ways to use technology in the comprehensive school counseling program.

The specific professional skills that school counselors must demonstrate include individual and small-group counseling; skills in individual, group, and classroom developmental curriculum; and skills in multicultural counseling issues. School counselors must understand and address conditions that impede the development and functioning of students, including assisting students with transitions, and techniques for prevention and early intervention of mental health challenges. School counselors partner with parents, families, and communities to promote the holistic development of all students using leadership, advocacy, and consultation strategies to enhance the school climate and promote effective teamwork across all systems.

As you can see, your skills in counseling, your understanding of young people, your learning about schools and families as systems, and your in-depth knowledge of comprehensive school counseling programs will all be required to attain the professional competencies of a school counselor. These skills are echoed in the School Counselor Performance Standards that are articulated as a part of the ASCA National Model (American School Counselor Association, 2003a). This professional organization for school counselors represents the interests of professional school counselors in this country. You will see that each chapter begins with the ASCA Performance Standards and the CACREP Standards that are addressed in that chapter and serve as the template for the design of this book.

External Tests of Professional Competencies

Currently, as accountability and outcomes assessments are increasingly emphasized, tests may be used in a number of ways to document professional attainment in school counseling. At the entry level, tests may be used to document the professional competencies of aspiring school counselors as a prerequisite for state licensure/certification as a school counselor. One example is the Praxis test in School Guidance and Counseling, published by ETS (Educational Testing Service). (More information on the test and the fees will be available from their website at www.ets.org). At the mid-professional level, a test may be used to document the development of advanced or refined skills, as in the evaluation process for school counselors offered by the National Board of Professional Teaching Standards (NBPTS). This voluntary process of documentation of professional development enables school counselors to validate their professional attainment in the same way that teachers may choose to obtain their national professional teacher credential. (More information about the process, tests, and fees will be available from their website at www.nbpts.org).

In addition, many school counselors choose to become a Nationally Certified Counselor (NCC) and a Nationally Certified School Counselor (NCSC) through the National Board of Certified Counselors (NBCC). With the successful completion of the National Counselor Exam (NCE), payment of the required fees, and two years of full-time (or equivalent) experience, a school counselor may obtain the national school counselor certification status. (More information about the test and fees will be available from their website at www.nbcc.org). Being a Nationally Certified School Counselor is a laudable accomplishment; however, there is no current way to obtain school counseling licensure that is acceptable in all states. Each state defines its own requirements for licensure, and if you relocate to another state, you must contact that state's department of education to learn about requirements.

The desire of the profession to recognize and document professional competence is not borne out of a distrust of the counseling profession, but rather from a desire to ensure that only the best professionals work in our schools. This then begs the question: How do schools define the "best" professionals? Do former teachers make better school counselors? Do all school counselors have to have teaching experience?

The perception has been (and in some states, continues to be) that former teachers make the best school counselors (Farwell, 1961; Fredrickson & Pippert, 1964; Hudson, 1961; Rochester & Cottingham, 1966; Tooker, 1957). Studies of the perceptions of administrators suggested that teaching experience was *not* a predictor of a counselor's success (Beale, 1995; Dilley, Foster, & Bowers, 1973; Olson & Allen, 1993). However, teachers themselves might still perceive counselors with teaching experience as more effective (Quarto, 1999). Rather than accept this conclusion fatalistically, school counselors should accept that it is their expertise in academic issues that will establish their connection with the academic mission of the school and give them credibility within the school. Professional school counselors must develop this expertise for this reason.

Recent research suggests that teachers and nonteachers both face challenges in their professional development. In a study done by Peterson, Goodman, and Keller (2002), the challenges faced by interns who had not been teachers were compared with those faced by former teachers. They found that both groups faced challenges in the transition to becoming professional school counselors, but they faced different challenges. Teachers had to relinquish their old credibility (place in the school hierarchy), power (counselor role is less directive with fewer "perks" of prep time and breaks), and assumptions about education (need to learn about more age cohorts, need to learn how to negotiate for students' time out of class). Nonteachers had to learn about the school environment and culture, the various stressors placed on all educators, and how to negotiate with teachers. The researchers' conclusions were that both teachers and nonteachers experienced a steep learning curve and had to make significant adjustments to fit in this new role.

Reflecting on the insights offered by Peterson et al. (2002), aspiring school counselors who do not have teaching experience could gain such experience through substitute teaching or working as a teacher's aide in the classroom. Additionally, aspiring school counselors who have been teachers might shadow a school counselor to learn more about the reality of the counselor's role, reflecting on the differences and similarities with the teacher's role.

Reflection Moment ◆

Where are you in the development of your professional competencies? What do you need to do to develop and/or refine these competencies? (Ideas to attain these competencies include graduate coursework, attending workshops and/or courses on topics relevant to youth, reading the professional literature, joining professional associations, and attending professional conferences.) Are you preparing yourself now for the exams of professional licensure? If you are not currently a teacher, how will you develop your experience in the classroom? Substitute teaching can help tremendously to develop your empathy for teachers;

it may be viewed positively by principals in the hiring process. Some states are moving toward the portfolio as documentation of the attainment of these professional competencies, and many principals and hiring committees in schools value portfolios as a way to evaluate the candidate's abilities. Consider starting a portfolio now to document your professional development. What would you insert into such a portfolio? Ideas for portfolio artifacts will be presented at the end of each chapter.

◆ ◆

◆ PERSONAL QUALITIES OF A SCHOOL COUNSELOR

In addition to the professional competencies listed above, professional school counselors are also well served by personal qualities that enhance their ability to be effective. These personal qualities provide school counselors with passion for their work, energy, and resistance to burnout. An exhaustive list would be impractical, but below are some of the most notable qualities.

Creativity and Imagination

Students, parents, teachers, administrators, and other professionals will bring questions, perspectives, issues, experiences, and challenges to us that we have never before encountered. Furthermore, as society changes over time, the needs of our students will change. We must have the creativity to respond to their various needs in an appropriate, ethical, and effective manner and the ability to imagine and design new approaches to old problems.

Flexibility

School counselors must be flexible in how they view their time, their activities, their students, and their students' needs over time. School counselors move from one activity to the next with little time to regroup, meaning that they need to move fluidly from one role to the next and from one activity to the next. Furthermore, school counselors address the needs of many different kinds of people (students, parents, teachers, administrators, school board members, and community members, to name a few), each with his or her own unique cultural, intellectual, emotional, and developmental signature. Highly flexible school counselors will be more fluid in response to those various needs. As needs change over time, flexible counselors will find themselves more comfortably adapting to new ways of looking at school situations.

Courage and Belief

School counselors address situations every day that challenge their courage and belief in others and in themselves, as well as in counseling itself. Daily we meet students engaging in dangerous risk-taking, irate parents who don't understand why the counselor can't fix their child, and school board members who threaten to cut the counseling program because they don't understand what counselors do. Having courage in the face of these challenges comes from knowing that counselors make a difference, and that, while the larger pattern of meaning might not be immediately visible, all things do happen for a reason. This is not to say that school counselors must adopt a fatalistic worldview. A good example of courage and belief in the value of what we do is found in the story of the young girl who, when the tide was out, threw stranded starfish back into the sea. She knew she couldn't save them all, but she did what she could to make a difference for one at a time. She had the courage to try to help and the faith to know that it mattered. School counselors can't "save" any students, but they know they make a difference for those whose lives they touch. Knowing that school counselors make a difference in the lives of students is a powerful antidote to apathy and burnout.

Passion

Passion is not a word that is used in many counseling books. However, passion is a wonderful word that describes the feeling of profound commitment, the type of commitment and meaning described in existentialism (Frankl, 1984). The best counseling professionals are passionately and profoundly committed to clients, to the clients' best interests, and to their own personal and professional excellence. For counselors who work in the schools, this means that they are passionately committed to their students and to education. For some professionals, this might be a daunting challenge; if you've never worked in a school or around young people, how do you know you have that passion for kids and for schools? The answer is to find a way to work with kids in schools to see if there is "passion" in working with students in that setting.

Where do creativity, flexibility, courage, belief, and passion come from? After reading this book, thinking about the case studies in each chapter, reflecting on the questions posed throughout the text, and integrating the text with insights from your own life and experience, you will have the answers to that question.

Reflection Moment ◆

How would you rate yourself on the preceding personal qualities? Reflect on the most important task or accomplishment of your life. In the completion of this task or accomplishment, how did each of the listed personal qualities manifest themselves? In what ways did you demonstrate your creativity, flexibility, courage, belief or faith, and passion? How did each quality help you in your task or accomplishment? How would you document these qualities in a professional portfolio?

◆ ◆

◆PHILOSOPHIES OF COUNSELING

Imagine yourself outside on a cold, clear, moonless winter night, far from the lights of a city. When you look up, you see millions upon millions of points of light. How would you describe what you see?

Astronomers would talk about black holes, galaxies, and light years of distance; historians would contemplate how mariners navigated using the stars. Classical Greek scholars would describe the mythical origins of various constellations (Zimmerman, 1964), whereas astrologers would talk about those same constellations as related to personalities and birth signs. The Onondaga people would tell you that the stars are the Spiritual Beings of the Sky World (Wall & Arden, 1990). Poets would find divine inspiration; physicists would find inspiration from the possibility of discovering life somewhere else in the universe. And each of these persons would recommend that, to truly understand the points of light in the midnight sky, you need to study, as they have, in their philosophy, their discipline, and their culture.

We can use the example of how various people might describe the stars to understand how various people describe counseling. In this culture, it is generally agreed that the points of light in the sky are stars (as opposed to beliefs that the lights are millions of spacecraft, or evil demons, or campfires on the roof of the world). Similarly, we agree on certain qualities of a helping relationship that we call counseling (Brammer & McDonald, 1999; Corey, 1996; Cormier & Hackney, 1987; Hutchins & Cole, 1992; Kottler, 1991, 1993; Krumboltz & Thoresen, 1976; Meier & Davis, 1997; St. Clair, 1996). These qualities bind various theories of the counseling process into a constellation that we can map and navigate.

Counseling is a helping relationship, in which the primary focus is on the psychological healing, growth, change, and development of the client, with the goal that the client will be able to establish and maintain healthy relationships with self and others. The relationship is intentional, meaning that the counselor engages the client in activities that are thoughtfully chosen for their potential to help the client heal, grow, and develop.

Counseling is a unique profession. It shares some common theoretical underpinnings with other disciplines such as psychology, psychiatry, and social work, but it is unique in its focus on developmental issues, interpersonal and intrapersonal relationships, and therapeutic milieu (Hanna & Bemak, 1997). As a profession, counseling is ethical, meaning helping behaviors are exhibited that adhere to moral, ethical, and professional guidelines as defined by the profession and the law (American Counseling Association, 1995; American School Counselor Association, 1998; Blackwell, Martin, & Scalia, 1994; Canon & Brown, 1985; Christopher, 1996; Corey, Corey, & Callanan, 1993; Herlihy & Corey, 1996; Huber & Baruth, 1987; Van Hoose & Kottler, 1988).

Counseling is both an art and a science, requiring intellect and intuition (Nystal, 1993). Intellectually, counselors need to understand various theories of change and the stages of development and maturation. Intuitively, counselors need to listen to the inner voice that whispers when to speak, when to be silent, when to intervene, and when to let go. Furthermore, to be ethical and effective, counselors must be sensitive to the values of the client's contexts of significance, as defined by the client and suggested by the client's culture, family system, gender, generation, abilities, health, and other diversity and values markers (Dollarhide & Haxton, 1999; Nichols & Schwartz, 1991; Sue & Sue, 1990).

Recall the various descriptions of the stars. Every time a counselor meets a client for the purpose of engaging in an intentional helping relationship, what will best facilitate change can be described in a variety of contexts based on theoretical orientation or philosophy. Some counselors would describe what they do in spiritual or intuitive terms, and other counselors would describe what they do in scientific or intellectual terms. Each theory describes change and those strategies that facilitate change: behavioral (Ellis, 1973), existential (Frankl, 1984), Rogerian (Carkhuff, 1987), Alderian (Dinkmeyer, Dinkmeyer, & Sperry, 1987), reality therapy (Glasser, 1965), and others.

How you see counseling is determined by your theoretical orientation, the lens of your philosophy. Whereas we can generally agree that the points of light in the night sky are indeed stars, descriptions of the stars vary widely. The profession of counseling generally agrees that the goal of counseling is to facilitate psychological healing, growth, change, and development to empower clients to experience healthy relationships with self and others. To be an effective counselor, you must have a method of bringing that healing, growth, change, and development to fruition with the client.

One useful way to conceptualize how to facilitate change with the client is to use the principles of learning, dealing with ambiguity, and reflective judgment. These are the same principles of learning described by Social Learning Theory (Bandura, 1977) and epistemological development (Dollarhide & Scully, 1999; Kegan, 1982; King & Kitchener, 1994; Perry, 1981). These theories constitute a description of counseling that includes both a model of the process of counseling and the process of change and growth, and using the language of learning, lends itself well to the educational setting.

In essence, both Social Learning Theory and counseling based on epistemological development begin at the same point—that counseling and learning are parallel constructs. If the point of counseling is to help clients learn how to develop and maintain healthy relationships with themselves and with others, then counseling strategies that use learning paradigms will be successful. In Social Learning Theory, that learning is the result of direct experiences, observation of models and vicarious experiences, and verbal persuasion (Bandura, 1977), which modifies the client's perception of self-efficacy and expectations of outcomes. From more positive perceptions of self-efficacy and more accurate expectations of outcomes, clients can choose healthier behaviors and attitudes. In counseling based on epistemological theory (Dollarhide & Scully, 1999), clients learn how to choose healthier behaviors and attitudes when they are allowed to encounter, struggle with, and resolve ambiguous life questions that have no clear answers. The counseling process entails allowing the client maximum freedom to explore existential questions, such as: What is the meaning of my life? What is my life direction? How do I establish healthy relationships? The counselor helps the client move from looking outside oneself for the answers to these questions, to looking within oneself for the answers, to ultimately, understanding how to look within for future answers.

Reflection Moment ◆

What is your theory of counseling? How adaptable is that theory for use with children, adolescents, and young adults, recalling that verbal abilities and insight develop over time? How adaptable is that theory for use in the schools, considering that time for one-on-one counseling is often limited? What can you foresee as challenges in using your theory? What can you foresee as advantages in using your theory?

◆ ◆

◆ PHILOSOPHIES OF EDUCATION

To understand education, we must first understand the rationale for the design of educational experiences. These experiences are defined by the philosophy of education of state departments of education, superintendents, principals, parents, teachers, and district personnel. The style of the educational experience could be characterized by two basic camps on either side of a "pedagogical and philosophical divide" (Olson, 1999, p. 25): *progressive* versus *traditional* education. According to Olson, in its simplest form, traditional philosophy holds the primacy of subject matter, mastery of content, and preservation of the existing national cultural heritage. Progressive philosophy, on the other hand, has been characterized by primacy of the child, active learning, recognition of students' individual differences, the drive to relate school to real life, the "broad mission to address health, vocational, social and community issues" (p. 26), and an agenda that includes transforming the national cultural heritage. Each approach has significant problems as well as significant strengths.

What we see in schools today are the various combinations of a number of subtexts within the progressive movement, as well as the swing of the cultural values pendulum back and forth between progressive agendas and return-to-basics traditionalism (Olson, 1999). From 1873 through 1918, the pedagogical progressive movement was in full swing, emphasizing learning environments that were more informal and pupil-oriented and pedagogical approaches emphasizing active learning through meaningful, comprehensive projects and interdisciplinary teaching. The progressive view was that schools should fit the natural development and interests of children and should encourage self-expression through the arts—that children are "creative beings" who should be "nurtured, rather than disciplined, shaped, and controlled" (Olson, 1999, p. 26).

The next educational movement came into its own during the Great Depression and was called the social progressive, or social reconstructionist, movement. The educational reform agenda at this time included addressing the social ills created by laissez-faire capitalism and by the perceived inability of the family or community to provide for the basic needs of children. According to Olson, the legacy of this movement is manifested by professionals who bring health and other social services into the schools and in the move to involve schools in community issues (p. 29).

The third strand in the progressive movement also has had long-reaching influence on education. Called the administrative progressive movement, this philosophy arose from the need to organize education to be more cost-effective in times of rapid growth in enrollment (Olson, 1999). It falls into the progressive philosophical camp because its proponents' rationale was the desire to help students adapt to society, rather than transforming society, by scientifically measuring students' abilities, grouping students based on ability, and then individualizing instruction by those groupings. Scientific testing and ability grouping (also known as *tracking*) were the legacies of this movement.

During the Korean War and the McCarthy era, progressive schools were criticized heavily for creating school environments without goals or educational standards, in which low performance was excused and from which students emerged without demonstrable social morals (Olson, 1999). Critics charged that without a solid academic foundation, students from disadvantaged backgrounds would remain disadvantaged and social inequities would be perpetuated. With the launch of Sputnik in 1957, progressive education was given less emphasis as the call arose for more math, science, and foreign language education. Also known as academic rationalism (Eisner, 1985), this criticism evolved into the belief that the major purpose of schools is to "foster intellectual growth of the student in those subject matters most worthy of study" (p. 66).

In the 1960s and 1970s, the progressive movement enjoyed a temporary resurgence, with many notable contributions to the debate about pedagogy, including Bruner's article on discovery learning (Bruner, 1961). However, the pendulum swung back toward traditional educational approaches in the late 1970s with the back-to-basics movement, which brought minimum competency testing, increases in course requirements, and a reliance on standardized tests (Brown & Peterkin, 1999; Olson, 1999).

As you can see, the debate over educational reform has continued for over a century, with ongoing conversations about the best environments and pedagogy for educating young people. Current thinking about learning and the educational process has emerged from various disciplines. From psychology and counseling came Adlerian schools (Dubelle & Hoffman, 1984, 1986), the application of Reality Therapy to schools and adolescents (Glasser, 1965), and personality styles translated into education (Berens, 1988). The constructivist movement from psychology was brought into schools, holding that students need to construct meaning for themselves in order to learn. The implications of this educational strategy have been explored from kindergarten to college teaching (Palmer, 1998). From learning styles literature came various ways of conceptualizing learning: Gardner's Eight Intelligences (Gardner, 1983; Lazear, 1999), various models of learning preferences (Dunn & Griggs, 1988), and various ways of understanding thinking, including gender as a learning construct (Clinchy, 1989; Golderberger, Clinchy, Belenky, & Tarule, 1987).

Many educators have examined various pedagogical approaches espoused by different educational traditions and have opted to incorporate teaching methods that energize both teaching and learning. Cooperative learning, where students are encouraged to work together on projects (Gibbs, 1995; Slavin, 1994), and learning centers, where students move physically to a location in the room designed for group activities, have transformed many classrooms into highly mobile, interactive learning environments. New strategies for helping students acquire knowledge include manipulatives for math and abstract concepts, extensive creative writing strategies such as mindmapping and clustering (Rico, 1983), and socially reinforcing strategies such as Tribes (Gibbs, 1995), all of which are designed to assist students in the acquisition and retention of knowledge, skills, and attitudes.

Public schools of today, however varied they are in terms of philosophy, all answer to the federal and state governments in terms of accountability and funding. In 2001, the No Child Left Behind (NCLB) Act was passed, and the Elementary and Secondary Education (ESEA) Act was reauthorized (U.S. Department of Education, 2001). In this legislation, the "primary purpose [is] the intent to close the achievement gap between disadvantaged students and their peers" (Dahir, 2004) through annual progress assessments in reading, math, and science (U.S. Department of Education, 2001). Information on the progress of individual students, plus information on the progress of the student body of the individual school, will go to parents to facilitate their decision making. Based on this progress, then, schools are evaluated and rated, and remediation efforts are outlined for schools that do not show satisfactory progress. For a full exploration of the issues of this legislation, visit the U.S. Department of Education's website at www.ed.gov/nclb and the National Education Association (NEA) website at www.nea.org/esea.

We will now leave our examination of philosophies of education, but we will see these philosophies reemerge in our next chapter on schools.

Reflection Moment ◆

Think back on the various classrooms you've been in. Have you ever been in a traditional classroom? How did it feel? Have you been in a more nontraditional, more informal classroom? How did that feel? In which class did you feel more motivated to learn?

Describe the purpose of education. What are schools supposed to do? What, exactly, is your philosophy of education? Based on that philosophy of education, describe what a school would look like that followed that philosophy. What would that school do? What would teachers do? What would counselors do?

◆ ◆

◆ PHILOSOPHIES OF SCHOOL COUNSELING

If you pick up a book, open it to the middle, and begin reading, you will get to the end of the book never truly understanding the relationships among the characters, the true depth of the story, or the journey of the main character. The drama and characters are seen in a smaller frame of time and understanding, becoming flattened and two-dimensional in the process. Without context, events, people, and places become oversimplified stereotypes, seen though a lens focused on current experience. However, if you read the entire book and spend time reflecting on the story, you would have the context within which to understand the ending, and you might better understand the insights within the story that could help you in your own life journey.

In the same way, it would be a mistake to attempt to understand school counseling as it is today in this country without also examining school counseling of yesterday. As you read these philosophies, think about how each is still evident in schools today, and how this "clash of the philosophies" can result in conflicting definitions of the job of the school counselor.

Guidance/Careers Emphasis

The development of school counseling is linked to the development of secondary education. Until the late 1800s in the United States, education was defined in terms of reading and writing, necessary to achieve pious living through reading the Bible. Education about life—learning about jobs, relationships, and duty to one's community—was seen primarily as the responsibility of the family (Hine, 1999). Organized education was more common at the elementary ages than in adolescence, because the work produced or wages earned by older children often was needed for family survival (Hine). However, with the advent of the Industrial Revolution, the nature of education changed.

The Industrial Revolution brought the need for higher-level skills. Awareness of these skills was articulated in the mission of the first high school in the country, Boston English High School, established in 1821 "to give a child an education that shall fit him [sic] for an active life, and shall serve as a foundation for eminence in his [sic] profession, whether Mercantile or Mechanic" (Hine, 1999, p. 144). But the social ills that came with the Industrial Revolution—poverty, ethnic slums, corruption, and moral decay—generated awareness of the power of the schools as a tool for social remedies (Olson, 1999; Schmidt, 1999) that fueled the birth of the school counseling profession in the early 1900s.

Two persons are primarily credited with the emergence of school counseling, then known as vocational guidance. Jesse B. Davis, principal of a high school in Grand Rapids, Michigan in 1907, began a program in his school to include guidance lessons in English composition classes to "help students develop character, avoid problem behaviors, and relate vocational interests to curriculum subjects" (Schmidt, 1999, p. 7). A year later, Frank Parsons, who is credited as the "father of guidance," issued a report of his Vocational Bureau, in which the term "vocational guidance" first appeared. In this report, Parsons called for vocational guidance to be provided by "trained experts" and offered in all public schools (Gysbers & Henderson, 2000, p. 4). In response, Boston elementary and secondary schools hired vocational counselors from their teaching staff and charged them, in addition to their regular teaching duties, with the following partial list of responsibilities:

1. To gather and maintain occupational information, including making arrangements with local librarians for the shelving of books about vocations
2. To arrange and present lessons in occupations and encourage teachers to connect their curriculum to vocations
3. To interview pupils "who are failing, attempt to find the reason, and suggest a remedy"
4. To use cumulative records and intelligence tests when advising children
5. To encourage students to remain in school
6. To "recommend conferences with parents of children who are failing or leaving school" (Gysbers & Henderson, 2000, p. 5)

It is easy to see the connection between these duties and the duties of current professionals in school counseling. For the nascent profession, this was the genesis of professional identity, training, and definition. Vocational guidance in schools grew around the country (Gysbers & Henderson, 2000). The emphasis of the secondary school as preparation for vocations, college attendance, and productive citizenship emerged as the rallying point for the passage of compulsory attendance legislation. This served to maintain focus on careers as the outcome of schooling and directive guidance as the activity by which those outcomes were guaranteed (S. B. Baker, 2000). Many school administrators, teachers, and counselors still hold these beliefs.

Further reinforcing the directive guidance function of school counselors was the need to classify young men into various activities within the military during World Wars I and II. Educational and vocational psychometrics, or mental measurement, grew in importance with the development, widespread validation, and acceptance of group-administered intelligence tests (S. B. Baker, 2000). "Psychometrics offered school guidance not only the tools for assessment but also corresponding respectability because the tools seemed so precise and scientific" (p. 4). Bolstered by the administrative progressive movement (Olson, 1999) discussed earlier, advising students on ways to reach their potential by identifying their limitations became the cement that hard-set advisement and directive guidance as the role of counselors during the 1930s and 1940s. Called "trait and factor" guidance, this approach was characterized by testing students' intelligence, interests, and abilities, then using that information to advise them about vocational and adjustment issues (S. B. Baker, 2000).

Challenged as too narrow, too restrictive, and inadequate to address students' developmental issues, emphasis on test-and-tell, directive guidance waned in popularity during the late 1940s and 1950s as the mental health emphasis emerged.

Mental Health Emphasis

As criticism mounted concerning the emphasis on "guidance" and "advisement," conversations were occurring in the educational and psychological arenas that would culminate in the second direction of school counseling. The writings of John Dewey in the 1920s caused many education professionals to reexamine their philosophy based on a more student-centered, progressive view of the role of education (Olson, 1999), and the writings of Carl Rogers in the 1940s and 1950s caused many mental health professionals to reexamine their philosophy based on a more holistic view of the relationship between guidance counselors and students (Schmidt, 1999). According to Schmidt, "This focus moved the profession away from the counselor-centered perspectives of earlier times and emphasized a growth-oriented counseling relationship as opposed to an informational and problem-solving one" (p. 11). At this time, mental health services and counseling became "the central secondary school guidance function, with all other functions in supplementary roles" (S. B. Baker, 2000, p. 6). As you can see, school counseling was practiced only in high schools; it had not yet reached the middle school or elementary schools.

The agenda of the social progressive movement in education was welcome, because it gave counselors greater awareness of their role in facilitating the development of all students in terms of their social, emotional, educational, and vocational needs. The emphasis on the role of the counselor as the mental health provider of the school was incorporated into the training of many school counselors during the 1950s and 1960s—when the National Defense Education Act of 1958 was funding the training of record numbers of school counselors (S. B. Baker, 2000, p. 6). It is the legacy of the mental health emphasis of this era that many counselors still hold the view that their primary role is to be the mental health provider for the school (Smith & Archer, 2000). However, in the 1960s, conversations emerged in the professional counseling literature challenging the focus of counselors on the limited number of students who needed crisis counseling and therapeutic services (S. B. Baker, 2000; Schmidt, 1999). In this reevaluation of the profession, and in discussions about the emerging role of middle school and elementary school counselors, there was increased advocacy for "developmental rather than remedial goals for elementary and secondary school guidance" (S. B. Baker, 2000, p. 8), leading to the third wave in defining what school counselors do: developmental guidance.

Developmental Guidance

During the late 1960s and through the 1970s, school counselors became increasingly aware of the need to prevent problems by providing educational activities that promote healthy adjustment, social awareness, interpersonal problem solving, and vocational development (Wittmer, 2000), moving school counseling solidly into elementary and middle schools. And if the foundation unit of education is the classroom, what better venue to provide this preventative programming than in the classroom itself? As Wittmer stated, "The question becomes, who does the most good? The school counselor who works with 25 children (using a large group guidance approach) in a six-week, one hour per week unit on improving self-concept, or the school counselor who spends six hours with one child in crisis? Although the latter is important (and may even be more fun for some), it is obvious that the school counselor using the former approach meets the needs of more students and does much more good in the long run" (Wittmer, 2000, pp. 4–5).

While some authors use the term "developmental guidance" to refer to all activities of a school counselor (Gysbers & Henderson, 2000), other authors cite the terms "guidance" and "development" as archaic (S. B. Baker, 2000). According to Baker, the term "developmental guidance" is limited, denoting a focus on classroom interventions more often associated with elementary school counseling programs. Furthermore, the strong association between the term "guidance" and the role of the counselor (Schmidt, 1999) suggests that the responsibility for guiding young people is the sole purview of the counselor, a fallacy that continues to trap counselors in inappropriately directive relationships with students (such as overreliance on test results) and in inappropriate administrative tasks (such as enrollment management). Hoyt (1993) also found that, when surveyed, American School Counselors Association leaders expressed the preference for the term "counseling" rather than "guidance" when referring to the program offered by the school counselor.

Reflection Moment ✦

Take a moment and reflect on your experience as a student interacting with your school counselor. Based on what that person did and said, can you identify her or his philosophy of school counseling? Did that person adopt an "expert" stance, provide directive guidance, and focus more on your career development than on your personal, social, or academic development? Or did that person assume a more therapeutic posture toward you, focusing more on your mental health? Did your school counselor(s) come to the classroom to present lessons and facilitate discussions about personal adjustment, academic success, or career development? Can you see a connection between when a counselor was trained in school counseling and his or her philosophy of school counseling?

✦ ✦

Comprehensive School Counseling Programs (CSCP)

So, what's the correct way of defining school counseling? There is no one absolute way of defining school counseling. What we see in today's school counseling is a field manifesting a "number of themes, all having varying degrees of influence across training programs and among counselors. The newer activist, developmental, service-oriented, and eclectic themes mixed with remnants of the trait and factor, adjustment, administrative, and counseling themes that were [are] still very much alive" (S. B. Baker, 2000, p. 9).

However, in the mix of various philosophies, it is possible to articulate a path that outlines what school counselors need to be able to know, feel, and demonstrate. It is called *comprehensive school counseling* (or developmental school counseling) (Paisley & Hubbard, 1994; Paisley & Peace, 1995), and it brings together the various roles and responsibilities with which school counselors are charged. In this book, we will use the National Model from ASCA, the professional association of school counselors, as our template for examining comprehensive school counseling programs (CSCPs). Let's first explore the documents that ASCA developed to describe what school counselors do (Role Statement) and to describe appropriate outcomes of comprehensive school counseling programs (the National Standards).

ASCA Role Statement and National Standards.   School counselors have joined together in a national association, the American School Counselor Association (ASCA), which has defined the role of the professional school counselor. "The professional school counselor is a certified/licensed educator who addresses the needs of students comprehensively through the implementation of a developmental school counseling program. . . . They are specialists in human behavior and relationships who provide assistance to students through four primary interventions: counseling (individual and group); large group guidance; consultation; and coordination" (American School Counselor Association, 1999).

ASCA (1999) goes on to define each of the four functions. Counseling is defined as "a confidential relationship in which the counselor meets with students . . . to help them resolve or cope constructively with their problems and developmental concerns." Large group guidance is defined as "a planned, developmental program of guidance activities designed to foster students' academic, career, and personal/social development" provided for all students. Consultation is defined as "a collaborative partnership in which the counselor works with parents, teachers, administrators, school psychologists, social workers, visiting teachers, medical professionals and community health personnel in order to plan and implement strategies to help students be successful in the educational system." Finally, coordination is defined as "a leadership process in which the counselor helps organize, manage, and evaluate the school counseling program."

To further describe what school counselors do, ASCA stated that "Above all, school counselors are student advocates who work cooperatively with other individuals and organizations to promote the development of children, youth, and families in their communities. . . . They work on behalf of students and their families to insure that all school programs facilitate the educational process and offer the opportunity for school success for each student" (ASCA, 1999).

What is school success? The National Standards for Student Academic, Career, and Personal/Social Development present guidelines for school counseling programs across the country (ASCA, 2003a; Campbell & Dahir, 1997). These standards outline goals for school counseling programs, establish school counseling as essential and integral to the educational mission of all schools, promote access by all students, and describe the key competencies all students should be able to demonstrate by the end of their K–12 experience. (See Appendix B for the complete text of the ASCA National Standards addressing student academic, career, and personal/social development.)

As summarized in Figure 1.1, the National Standards highlight three content areas that summarize the developmental themes of schools. There are reasons behind the order in which these content areas are presented. Competencies in academic development, as the primary mission of education, confirm that school counselors are integral to the mission of the school and district in which the counselor functions. Competencies in career development, the transition from school to contributing member of society, represent outcomes of education as defined by society. Competencies in personal and social development answer the need for young people to function in an informed citizenry addressing the challenges of modern living. This holistic approach to students provides the caring

FIGURE 1.1 ◆ Summary: National Standards for Student Academic, Career, and Personal/Social Development

I. Academic Development

Standard A: Students will acquire the attitudes, knowledge, and skills that contribute to effective learning in school and across the lifespan.

Standard B: Students will complete school with the academic preparation essential to choose from a wide range of substantial postsecondary options, including college.

Standard C: Students will understand the relationship of academics to the world of work, and to life at home and in the community.

II. Career Development

Standard A: Students will acquire the skills to investigate the world of work in relation to knowledge of self and to make informed career decisions.

Standard B: Students will employ strategies to achieve future career success and satisfaction.

Standard C: Students will understand the relationship among personal qualities, education and training, and the world of work.

III. Personal/Social Development

Standard A: Students will acquire the attitudes, knowledge, and interpersonal skills to help them understand and respect self and others.

Standard B: Students will make decisions, set goals, and take necessary action to achieve goals.

Standard C: Students will understand safety and survival skills.

---

environment critical for development and has been linked to academic and personal success of students.

Each standard is accompanied by student competencies that define the standard. For example, Standard A under Academic Development states that "Students will acquire the attitudes, knowledge, and skills that contribute to effective learning in school and across the life span." This standard involves three global competencies: improve academic self-concept, acquire skills for improving learning, and achieve school success. Each global competency is then further specified in language that allows counselors to evaluate the success of their students and their program in terms of attaining that competency (see Appendix B).

ASCA National Model.   In 2003, ASCA published its National Model (American School Counselor Association, 2003a) as a means of helping practicing school counselors design and implement a comprehensive school counseling program (CSCP). This model "consists of four interrelated components: foundation, delivery systems, management systems, and accountability. Infused throughout the program are the qualities of leadership, advocacy and collaboration, which lead to systemic change" (American School Counselor Association, 2003b, p. 165). A summary of each of these components follows; a complete description of the National Model is explored in Chapter 5.

1. The foundation of the model consists of beliefs and philosophy, a mission statement, and a reminder that the ASCA National Standards are the competencies that all

students should develop as a result of being in a school with a comprehensive school counseling program (CSCP).

2. The delivery system consists of a) the guidance curriculum designed to provide developmentally appropriate lessons to help students achieve the competencies; b) individual student planning for academic goals and future plans; c) responsive services of counseling, consultation, referral, and peer helping; and d) system support of program management and administration.

3. The management system consists of agreements between the principal and professional counselor outlining how the counselor's time will be allocated, an advisory council, the use of data, action plans, appropriate use of time, and the use of calendars to inform everyone of the program.

4. Accountability refers to results reporting, performance standards for the professional school counselor, and a program audit that collects information about the program to guide future action.

These documents—the National Model, the Role Statement, and the National Standards—outline a system of program expectations, program delivery, counselor competencies, and student competencies by which school counselors can prioritize, design, and evaluate the counseling activities in the school. As a statement of national scope, it is important that every counselor become familiar with these documents, and it is for this reason that these documents form the foundation of this book. It is vital that school counselors are knowledgeable about how the profession defines its role and the standards of effective programs and then apply those standards to design, implement, and evaluate the CSCP in their schools and districts.

◆ SCHOOL COUNSELING ACROSS ELEMENTARY, MIDDLE, AND SECONDARY SCHOOLS: AN OVERVIEW

As we saw in the previous discussion on the National Model, school counselors in comprehensive school counseling programs work with all students in the school, providing all services in an environment of leadership, advocacy, and collaboration, with the goal of achieving systemic change and improvement. Exactly what that "work" looks like will vary depending on a variety of factors. From the broadest source of variation to the most specific, these could include regional preferences, state department of education mandates, community and attendance zone issues, and building characteristics. Until now, we have been discussing school counseling as a whole, without making local/state distinctions or distinctions among the three educational levels. As a professional, you must attend to state and district mandates; you need to consult your state department of education for regulations and/or legislation and consult your district policy to understand local requirements and expectations.

The distinctions among school counseling activities at different grade levels are hard to identify; however, we can see distinctions among the three levels of educational progression: elementary, middle school, and secondary school. As we will explore in depth in Chapter 2 in our discussion of developmentally appropriate education, schools should be built around an understanding of the development of young people; this understanding should include balanced consideration of academic, social, and emotional needs. As an introduction to the profession of school counseling, let's look at developmentally appropriate, comprehensive counseling at the three levels of elementary, middle, and secondary schools (Myrick, 1993). (First, though, a disclaimer: Different districts, for a variety of reasons, will configure schools in ways that are meaningful to that district. The following discussion will use grade levels that are most commonly associated with the three levels of schools: elementary, middle, and high schools.)

Elementary counseling encompasses the largest span of a young person's development. This span of development requires counselors to be sensitive to the needs of primary grade students (pre-kindergarten through third grade) as well as the needs of intermediate grade students (fourth through sixth grades). Elementary students in the primary grades are characterized by their strong ties to primary caregivers, the development of social skills, adjustment to nonhome environments and challenges, high need for physical activity, and rapid cognitive development (Charlesworth, 1996). Elementary students in the intermediate grades are characterized by the development of same-sex peer relationships, integration and solidification of prior learning, development of fine motor skills, and exploration of nonfamily adult relationships (Schickedanz, Schickedanz, Forsyth, & Forsyth, 1998). From these insights into development, it is easy to see why counselors in the elementary grades focus on building healthy self-concept, learning to get along with peers, developing morality and values, achieving personal independence, and developing healthy attitudes toward social groups (Snyder, 2000).

Both the focus of each activity and the amount of time devoted to each activity change according to the developmental level of the student. Overall, elementary counselors provide (1) behavioral counseling, with an emphasis on play and art in counseling, (2) small group counseling focusing on issues and skills specific to elementary development, (3) classroom guidance in self-concept and adjustment issues, and (4) consultation for parents and teachers (Schmidt, 1999). The focus is more on personal/social development and academic development than on career development (Dollarhide, 2000). According to Gysbers and Henderson (2000), elementary counselors ideally spend approximately 35 to 45 percent of their time in developmental guidance delivered in the classroom, with individual responsive services (counseling, consultation, and referrals) comprising approximately 30 to 40 percent of the counselor's time. Within this broad framework, elementary counselors adjust the amount of time providing individual counseling, depending on the level of language development and capacity for insight of the child (Schmidt, 1999). This would suggest that counselors generally spend more time counseling with intermediate students than with primary graders, due to the older students' greater abilities to understand themselves and their choices.

The middle school student is characterized by "transescence," being caught between childhood and adolescence (B. B. Baker, 2000). This educational phase involves multiple transitions: the transition from small neighborhood elementary schools to larger, more diverse middle or junior high schools, and the transition from childhood to adolescence. Young people at this stage of development struggle with their self-esteem, focus on their status relative to peers, begin to experiment with various behaviors, and develop formal thought processes (Schickedanz, Schickedanz, Forsyth, & Forsyth, 1998). It is at this point that many young people begin to exhibit the signs of troubles to come: eating disorders; unhealthy sexual choices; smoking, drug, and alcohol use; and lack of interest or motivation in schools (Schickedanz et al., 1998), increasing the need for counselors to be proactive and aware of each student's unique challenges.

To address these developmental needs, middle school counselors have to be as flexible and spontaneous as their students are. Typical activities include insight-oriented and rational individual counseling; group counseling (which, given the transescent's focus on peers, is usually highly effective); peer helping and mediation programming; transitional services to ease students from elementary to middle school and then from middle to high school; developmental curriculum on change, sexuality, healthy choices, and conflict resolution; and consultation with teachers, and to a lesser degree, with parents (Schmidt, 1999). Middle school counselors generally distribute their time equitably across issues addressing personal/social development, career development, and academic development (Dollarhide, 2000). Other ways that middle school counseling will vary from elementary school counseling include more emphasis on crisis counseling and management and more developmental curriculum involving drug and alcohol education and prevention (B. B. Baker, 2000), realities shared by secondary school counselors.

The developmental issues of young people in secondary schools involve the search for identity, independence, self-definition, meaningful relationships, and ways to make a unique contribution to the world. In response, school counselors need to become more aware of their roles as student advocate and environmental assessor, working to enhance the climate of mutual respect in secondary schools. Coy and Sears (2000) identify the primary activities for secondary school counselors as individual counseling, group guidance, group counseling, career development and information services, placement, consultation, and coordination. Similarly, Schmidt (1999) found that counseling, decision making about postsecondary options, providing college information, and helping with class schedules were the most important counseling services as identified by students, parents, and teachers. The focus of secondary counselors often shifts away from personal/social development, to focus instead on career and academic development (Dollarhide, 2000).

It is our hope that this preview of the work of school counselors will help you envision the profession as you explore school counseling in more depth in the coming chapters.

Reflection Moment ✦

Can you see the different ways that school counselors function at various levels? With which age group do you see yourself functioning most effectively?

✦ ✦

CASE STUDY REVISITED ✦ Integration

Now that you have read this chapter, go back and reread Mrs. Grundy's Retirement. Reflect on and answer the following questions:

1. What is Mrs. Grundy's philosophy of counseling? Of education? Of school counseling? How can you tell?
2. What do we know about Tracy's philosophy in each of these areas?

3. What actions would you recommend for Tracy that might help her develop a proactive, professional relationship with her new colleagues?
4. How would you rate Mrs. Grundy's effectiveness in terms of the ASCA Role Statement and Model? How would you imagine her students might rate on the ASCA National Standards?
5. What is appropriate about Mrs. Grundy's activities, given the nature of middle schools? What is inappropriate about those activities?

APPLICATION

(Some of these activities, indicated with the note "Possible Portfolio Artifact," might be worth including in your professional portfolio)

1. In a Reflection Moment in this chapter, you have been challenged to think about the development of a professional portfolio to document the professional competencies and personal qualities that will make you an employable school counselor. Outline what you would insert into such a portfolio.
2. Use the Internet to research the requirements of your state for school counseling licensure/ certification. Outline a plan for completing those requirements.
3. What is your philosophy of counseling and your theoretical orientation? (Possible portfolio artifact) Do you need to adapt that orientation for use in the schools? How, specifically, will you accomplish that? Where can you go to get additional information and/or practice in using your theory?
4. Schools don't have signs on them that identify their philosophy of education, but you can make some educated guesses about which philosophy or philosophies guided the design of the school and its programs. Visit a local school to see if you can identify the legacy of each of the educational philosophies discussed in this chapter. Interview the principal to identify his or her philosophical orientation(s) in the answers to the questions: "What does this school provide to its students? Why does this school exist? Why are those results important?"
5. Conduct an Internet search using "education" and "schools" as keywords. How many hits do you get? Outline a strategy for selecting descriptors that will help you access more meaningful sites. Visit those sites and record the web addresses for future access. Why did you select the sites you did? What does that say about your philosophy of education?
6. This chapter addresses various philosophies of school counseling, from career guidance, to mental health, to developmental guidance, to comprehensive school counseling. Which one is most consistent with your own philosophy of school counseling? In what ways? Which one is the least similar? In what ways? Write out your philosophy of school counseling. (Possible portfolio artifact)
7. Interview two school counselors about their philosophies of school counseling. How do they define their jobs? How similar or dissimilar are those perspectives from the national perspective as presented in this chapter? Discuss your reactions to this experience.
8. Search the Internet using "school counseling" as your keyword. How many hits do you get? Visit a couple of those sites, recording them for sharing with the class. What did you find there? How well did those sites fit the picture you have in your mind about school counseling? How well do the programs described at those sites conform to the ASCA National Model? (Possible portfolio artifact)
9. Visit the U.S. Department of Education's website and the NEA website to outline all the issues in the debate about No Child Left Behind. Based on your reading, what are your conclusions about the efficacy of the legislation? Interview a school counselor and a principal to learn about the effect(s) this legislation has had on that school.

SUGGESTED READINGS

American School Counselor Association (1999). *The role of the professional school counselor*. Alexandria, VA: Author. Retrieved May 31, 2000, from www.schoolcounselor.org/role.htm. This resource, provided by ASCA, outlines the role and expectations of professional school counselors.

American School Counselor Association (2003). *The ASCA National Model: A framework for school counseling programs*. Alexandria, VA: Author. This resource outlines the National Model with performance expectations and sample forms that will make the transition to the National Model feasible for every school. This is the seminal statement from the profession about the ideal structure of school counseling programs.

Campbell, C. A., & Dahir, C. A. (1997). *Sharing the vision: The national standards for school counseling programs*. Alexandria, VA: American School Counselor Association. Every school counselor must be aware of the national standards for counseling programs and should use these standards in designing their programs.

Dahir, C. A., Sheldon, C. B., & Valiga, M. J. (1998). *Vision into action: Implementing the national standards for school counseling programs*. Alexandria, VA: American School Counselor Association. The companion resource for the implementation of the national standards.

Gysbers, N. C., & Henderson, P. (2000). *Developing and managing your school guidance program* (3rd ed.). Alexandria, VA: American Counseling Association. This resource addresses the programmatic concerns of initiating change in the school system to move toward coherent school counseling programs.

Hahn, T. N. (1991). *Peace is every step*. New York: Bantam; Hoff, B. (1982). *The Tao of Pooh*. New York: Penguin; Hoff, B. (1982). *The Te of Piglet*. New York: Penguin. These three resources are recommended to help the reader to think outside the box of linear, Western society, with the hope that reflection on these readings will increase flexibility, creativity, and access to intuition.

McWhirter, J. J., McWhirter, B. T., McWhirter, A. M., & McWhirter, E. H. (1998). *At-risk youth: A comprehensive response for counselors, teachers, psychologists, and human service professionals*. Pacific Grove, CA: Brooks/Cole. A must-read for school counselors, this book provides wonderful insights about risk factors, issues facing youth, and issues facing educational professionals who work with youth.

REFERENCES

American Counseling Association. (1995). *Code of ethics and standards of practice*. Alexandria, VA: Author.

American School Counselor Association. (1998). *Ethical standards for school counselors*. Alexandria, VA: Author.

American School Counselor Association (1999). *The role of the professional school counselor*. Alexandria, VA: Author. Retrieved May 31, 2000, from www.schoolcounselor.org/role.htm.

American School Counselor Association (2003a). *The ASCA National Model: A framework for school counseling programs*. Alexandria, VA: Author.

American School Counselor Association (2003b). The ASCA National Model: A framework for school counseling programs; Executive Summary. *Professional School Counseling, 6,* 165–168.

Baker, B. B. (2000). Middle school counseling in the new millennium: A practitioner's perspective. In J. Wittmer (Ed.), *Managing your school counseling program: K–12 developmental strategies* (2nd ed.; pp. 49–55). Minneapolis, MN: Educational Media.

Baker, S. B. (2000). *School counseling for the twenty-first century* (3rd ed.). Upper Saddle River, NJ: Merrill.

Bandura, A. (1977). *Social learning theory*. Englewood Cliffs, NJ: Prentice-Hall.

Beale, A. V. (1995). Selecting school counselors: The principal's perspective. *School Counselor, 42,* 211–217.

Berens, L. V. (1988). *Please understand me: Empowering students of the 90's*. Huntington Beach, CA: Temperament Research Institute.

Blackwell, T. L., Martin, W. E., Jr., & Scalia, V. A. (1994). *Ethics in rehabilitation: A guide for rehabilitation professionals*. Athens, GA: Elliott & Fitzpatrick.

Brammer, L. M., & McDonald, G. (1999). *The helping relationship: Process and skills* (7th ed.). Boston: Allyn and Bacon.

Brown, O. S., & Peterkin, R. S. (1999). Transforming public schools: An integrated strategy for improving student academic performance through districtwide resource equity, leadership accountability, and program efficiency. *Equity and Excellence in Education, 32*(3), 37–52.

Bruner, J. S. (1961). The act of discovery. *Harvard Educational Review, 31,* 31–32.

Campbell, C. A., & Dahir, C. A. (1997). *Sharing the vision: The national standards for school counseling programs.* Alexandria, VA: American School Counselor Association.

Canon, H. J., & Brown, R. D. (Eds.). (1985). *Applied ethics in student services.* San Francisco: Jossey-Bass.

Carkhuff, R. R. (1987). *The art of helping* (6th ed.). Amherst, MA: Human Resource Development Press.

Charlesworth, R. (1996). *Understanding child development* (4th ed.). Albany, NY: Delmar.

Christopher, J. C. (1996). Counseling's inescapable moral visions. *Journal of Counseling & Development, 75,* 17–25.

Clinchy, B. (1989). On critical thinking and connected knowing. *Liberal Education, 75*(5), 14–19.

Corey, G. C. (1996). *Theory and practice of counseling and psychotherapy* (5th ed.). Pacific Grove, CA: Brooks/Cole.

Corey, G. C., Corey, M. S., & Callanan, P. (1993). *Issues and ethics in the helping professions.* Pacific Grove, CA: Brooks/Cole.

Cormier, L. S., & Hackney, H. (1987). *The professional counselor, a process guide to helping.* Englewood Cliffs, NJ: Prentice-Hall.

Council for Accreditation of Counseling and Related Educational Programs (2000). *The 2001 standards: CACREP accreditation standards and procedures manual.* Alexandria, VA: Author.

Coy, D., & Sears, S. (2000). The scope of practice of the high school counselor. In J. Wittmer (Ed.), *Managing your school counseling program: K–12 developmental strategies* (2nd ed.; pp. 56–67). Minneapolis, MN: Educational Media.

Dahir, C. A. (2004). Supporting a nation of learners: The role of school counseling in educational reform. *Journal of Counseling and Development, 82,* 344–353.

Dilley, J., Foster, W., & Bowers, I. (1973). Effectiveness ratings of counselors without teaching experience. *Counselor Education and Supervision, 13,* 24–29.

Dinkmeyer, D. C., Dinkmeyer, D. C., Jr., & Sperry, L. (1987). *Adlerian counseling and psychotherapy* (2nd ed.). Columbus, OH: Merrill.

Dollarhide, C. T. (2000, April). *How do school counselors allocate their time?* Paper presented at the meeting of the Tri-County School Counselors Consortium, Whitewater, WI.

Dollarhide, C. T., & Haxton, R. (1999). Generations Theory: Counseling using generational value systems. *The CACD Journal, 19,* 21–28.

Dollarhide, C. T., & Scully, S. (1999). The counseling/learning model: Using epistemological theory in college counseling. *The Journal of the Pennsylvania Counseling Association, 2,* 3–18.

Dubelle, S. T., & Hoffman, C. M. (1984). *Misbehavin':* *Solving the disciplinary puzzle for educators.* Lancaster, PA: Technomic.

Dubelle, S. T., & Hoffman, C. M. (1986). *Misbehavin' II: Solving more of the disciplinary puzzle for educators.* Lancaster, PA: Technomic.

Dunn, R., & Griggs, S. A. (1988). *Learning styles: Quiet revolution in American secondary schools.* Reston, VA: National Association of Secondary School Principals.

Ellis, A. (1973). *Humanistic psychotherapy: The rational emotive approach.* New York: McGraw-Hill.

Eisner, E. W. (1985). *The educational imagination: On the design and evaluation of school programs* (2nd ed.). New York: Macmillan.

Farwell, G. F. (1961). The role of the school counselor. *Counselor Education and Supervision, 1,* 40–43.

Frankl, V. E. (1984). *Man's search for meaning* (rev. ed.). New York: Washington Square.

Fredrickson, R. H., & Pippert, R. R. (1964). Teaching experience in the employment of school counselors. *Counselor Education and Supervision, 4,* 24–27.

Gardner, H. (1983). *Frames of mind: The theory of multiple intelligences.* New York: Basic.

Gibbs, J. (1995). *Tribes: A new way of learning and being together.* Sausalito, CA: Center Source Systems.

Glasser, W. (1965). *Reality therapy: A new approach to psychiatry.* New York: Harper & Row.

Golderberger, N. R., Clinchy, B. M., Belenky, M. F., & Tarule, J. M. (1987). Women's ways of knowing. In P. Shaver & C. Hendrick (Eds.), *Sex and gender.* London: Sage Publications.

Gysbers, N. C., & Henderson, P. (2000). *Developing and managing your school guidance program* (3rd ed.). Alexandria, VA: American Counseling Association.

Hanna, F. J., & Bemak, F. (1997). The quest for identity in the counseling profession. *Counselor Education and Supervision, 36,* 194–206.

Herlihy, B., & Corey, G. (1996). *ACA ethical standards casebook* (5th ed.). Alexandria, VA: American Association for Counseling and Development.

Hine, T. (1999). *The rise and fall of the American teenager.* New York: Bard.

Hoyt, K. B. (1993). Guidance is not a dirty word. *The School Counselor, 40,* 267–273.

Huber, C. H., & Baruth L. G. (1987). *Ethical, legal, and professional issues in the practice of marriage and family therapy.* New York: Merrill.

Hudson, G. R. (1961). Counselors need teaching experience. *Counselor Education and Supervision, 0,* 24–27.

Hutchins, D. E., & Cole, C. G. (1992). *Helping relationships and strategies* (2nd ed.). Pacific Grove, CA: Brooks/Cole.

Kegan, R. (1982). *The evolving self: Problem and process in human development.* Cambridge, MA: Harvard University Press.

King, P. M., & Kitchener, K. S. (1994). *Developing reflective judgment.* San Francisco: Jossey-Bass.

Kottler, J. A. (1991). *The compleat therapist.* San Francisco: Jossey-Bass.

Kottler, J. A. (1993). *On being a therapist* (rev. ed.) San Francisco: Jossey-Bass.

Krumboltz, J. D., & Thoresen, C. E. (Eds.). (1976). *Counseling methods.* New York: Holt, Rinehart and Winston.

Lazear, D. (1999). *Eight ways of teaching: The artistry of teaching with multiple intelligences* (3rd ed.). Arlington Heights, IL: SkyLight Training & Publishing.

Meier, S. C., & Davis, S. R. (1997). *Elements of counseling* (3rd ed.). Pacific Grove, CA: Brooks/Cole.

Myrick, R. D. (1993). *Developmental guidance and counseling: A practical approach* (2nd ed.). Minneapolis, MN: Educational Media Corporation.

Nichols, M. P., & Schwartz, R. C. (1991). *Family therapy concepts and methods* (2nd ed.). Boston: Allyn and Bacon.

Nystul, M. S. (1993). *The art and science of counseling and psychotherapy.* New York: Merrill.

Olson, L. (1999, April 21). Tugging at tradition: Lessons of a century. *Education Week,* pp. 25–29, 30–31.

Olson, M. J., & Allen, D. N. (1993). Principals' perceptions of the effectiveness of school counselors with and without teaching experience. *Counselor Education and Supervision, 33,* 10–21.

Paisley, P. O., & Hubbard, G. T. (1994). *Developmental school counseling programs: From theory to practice.* Alexandria, VA: American Counseling Association.

Paisley, P. O., & Peace, S. D. (1995). Developmental principles: A framework for school counseling programs. *Elementary School Counseling & Guidance, 30*(2), 85–93.

Palmer, P. (1998). *The courage to teach: Exploring the inner landscape of a teacher's life.* San Francisco: Jossey-Bass.

Perry, W. G., Jr. (1981). Cognitive and ethical growth. In A. Chickering (Ed.), *The modern American college.* San Francisco: Jossey-Bass.

Peterson, J., Goodman, R., & Keller, T. (2002, October). *A comparison of school counseling students with and without teaching background: Perceptions of the internship experience.* Paper presented at the meeting of the Association for Counselor Education and Supervision, Park City, UT.

Quarto, C. J. (1999). Teachers' perceptions of school counselors with and without teaching experience. *Professional School Counseling, 2,* 378–383.

Rico, G. L. (1983). *Writing the natural way: Using right-brain techniques to release your expressive powers.* Los Angeles: Tarcher.

Rochester, D. E., & Cottingham, H. F. (1966). Is teaching experience necessary? Counselor educators speak out. *Counselor Education and Supervision, 5,* 175–181.

Schickedanz, J. A., Schickedanz, D. I., Forsyth, P. D., & Forsyth, C. A. (1998). *Understanding children and adolescents* (3rd ed.). Boston: Allyn and Bacon.

Schmidt, J. J. (1999). *Counseling in schools: Essential services and comprehensive programs* (3rd ed.). Boston: Allyn and Bacon.

Slavin, R. E. (1994). *A practical guide to cooperative learning.* Boston: Allyn and Bacon.

Smith, S. L., & Archer, J. (2000). The developmental school counselor and mental health counseling. In J. Wittmer (Ed.), *Managing your school counseling program: K–12 developmental strategies* (2nd ed.; pp. 68–74). Minneapolis, MN: Educational Media.

Snyder, B. A. (2000). Managing an elementary school developmental counseling program: The role of the counselor. In J. Wittmer (Ed.), *Managing your school counseling program: K–12 developmental strategies* (2nd ed.; pp. 37–48). Minneapolis, MN: Educational Media.

St. Clair, M. (1996). *Object relations and self psychology.* Pacific Grove, CA: Brooks/Cole.

Sue, D. W., & Sue, D. (1990). *Counseling the culturally different* (2nd ed.). Somerset, NJ: Wiley and Sons.

Tooker, E. D. (1957). Counselor role: Counselor training. *Personnel and Guidance Journal, 36,* 263–267.

U.S. Department of Education. (2001). *The No Child Left Behind Act.* Washington, DC: Author.

Van Hoose, W. H., & Kottler, J. A. (1988). *Ethical and legal issues in counseling and psychotherapy.* San Francisco: Jossey-Bass.

Wall, S., & Arden, H. (1990). *Wisdomkeepers: Meetings with Native American spiritual leaders.* Hillsboro, OR: Beyond Words.

Wittmer, J. (2000). Section One: Developmental school counseling: History, reconceptualization, and implementation strategies. In J. Wittmer (Ed.), *Managing your school counseling program: K–12 developmental strategies* (2nd ed.; pp. 1–34). Minneapolis, MN: Educational Media.

Zimmerman, J. E. (1964). *Dictionary of classical mythology.* New York: Bantam.

CHAPTER

2

SCHOOLS: SOCIAL INSTITUTIONS

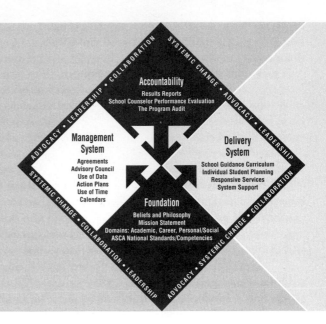

◆ LEARNING OBJECTIVES

By the end of this chapter, you will

1. Define and describe an effective school
2. Identify the qualities of effective schools
3. Describe the qualities of ineffective schools and those conditions that lead to unhealthy environments
4. Define and describe a developmentally appropriate school
5. Identify the qualities of developmentally appropriate educational programs
6. Identify the ways that school counselors partner with other professionals in schools

7. Describe healthy relationships with partners in the school and ways to collaborate with them
8. Describe Adelman and Taylor's vision of collaboration
9. Understand the rationale for leadership by the school counselor to address closing the achievement gap
10. Understand the need to monitor achievement, equity, and access to resources

DOMAINS / ACTIVITIES / PARTNERS MODEL

ACTIVITIES	DOMAINS					
	Academic Development ▼	Career Development ▼	Personal/ Social Development ▼			
Counseling	1a	1b	1c	5	6	7
Educating and Advocacy	2a	2b	2c	8	9	10
Consulting	3a	3b	3c	11	12	13
Leadership and Coordination	4a	4b	4c	14	15	16
	Students			Parents and Caregivers	Colleagues in Schools	Colleagues in Community

PARTNERS IN THE PROCESS

CASE STUDY ◆ Mr. Bass: A Fish out of Water

Jesse Bass was sure of his counseling skills with children; as a successful private therapist, he had worked with many troubled families with children. He had established his reputation as an expert in depression and was able to publish and present at many conferences. He was eager to extend his knowledge and expertise into the local schools.

He contacted several schools and gave his contact information and a summary of his background to the school counselors. One high school counselor in particular, Cissy Parks, was very excited to meet him, indicating that she had a sophomore named Cody who needed some therapy for depression. He was exhibiting all the behaviors of depression and was engaging in self-mutilation, a practice that, Ms. Parks admitted, frightened and revolted her. When Cody's parents called to ask Ms. Parks for the names of community therapists, Mr. Bass's name was at the top of the list. They interviewed Mr. Bass and selected him as Cody's therapist.

Mr. Bass invited Cody to share experiences from his day-to-day life in the school, and learned that Cody was the regular target of several school bullies—some of whom appeared to be teachers. An artistic and sensitive student, the primary source of pain in his life was the isolation and ridicule he experienced every day in the classroom, from the derision of peers to outright abuse from several teachers. When describing his interaction with students, Cody reported being physically pushed and slapped in the halls between classes, being laughed at in class, and having his things stolen. He described teachers who used sarcasm, used him as an example of stupidity, and gave his work lower grades than comparable work of other students. Mr. Bass called Ms. Parks to discuss the school situation to explore possible interventions with the students and teachers.

"Oh, Mr. Bass, you don't take his stories *seriously*, do you? Do you think we hire teachers who are abusive to students? That's ridiculous. It is true that not every teacher will like every student, but that's life. Cody's going to have to learn how to work with people who don't coddle him *someday,* and he might as well begin now. If you ask me, you need to treat *him,* because you can't change the school."

CHALLENGE QUESTIONS

How do you feel about Ms. Parks' comments to Mr. Bass? Is it possible to change a school? If it is possible, would you want to? What would you do if you were Ms. Parks? What would you do if you were Mr. Bass? What are some of the possible interventions that could help the student? If things do not change for this student, what do you see as some of the possible outcomes?

◆ WHAT MAKES EFFECTIVE SCHOOLS?

In the previous chapter, you had a chance to think about your philosophy of education. What is the purpose of education, and how well do schools accomplish their purpose? The research into effective schools suggests some ways to think about which educational philosophies, in which combinations, have implications for helping students learn what they need to know as adults.

Effective Schools

Occasionally, educators want to infuse progressive learning strategies into their schools and classrooms, only to find that parents, caregivers, or school board members have different educational philosophies—different ideas of how learning experiences should be designed (Lewis, 1994). Our jobs as counselors involve helping these stakeholders to understand the development of young people, learning, education, and what constitutes excellent schools. Understanding how to facilitate excellent schools can only come from understanding how schools function as organizational entities and understanding what qualities culminate in effective schools.

Professionals in schools today face tremendous expectations as well as tremendous challenges. Usually, school districts are governed by an elected body from the community, which makes all policy, financial, and educational decisions (Simon, 1999). Funding for schools comes primarily from state and local taxes; taxes paid by the community or communities in the school district for school support must be approved by the voters in that community or communities (Newman, 1994). School district board members are accountable to those voters for expenditures and outcomes for all school programs.

Education professionals are accountable to the parents/guardians of students and to the school board. With certain variations, professionals in schools are expected to

- ◆ Interact positively with the community
- ◆ Maintain high educational expectations
- ◆ Maintain test scores in crucial academic areas
- ◆ Provide special assistance to students with special physical, academic, and emotional needs
- ◆ Provide early screening and intervention for young students entering kindergarten
- ◆ Provide transportation to and from the school to within a reasonable and safe distance from the student's residence

The ASCA School Counselor Performance Standards addressed in this chapter are

1.3 The professional school counselor demonstrates positive interpersonal relationships with educational staff.

5.1 The professional school counselor provides a comprehensive and balanced school counseling program in collaboration with school staff.

13.1 The professional school counselor promotes academic success of every student.

13.2 The professional school counselor promotes equity and access for every student.

13.3 The professional school counselor takes a leadership role within the counseling department, the school setting and the community.

13.4 The professional school counselor understands reform issues and works to close the achievement gap.

13.5 The professional school counselor collaborates with teachers, parents and the community to promote academic success of students.

13.6 The professional school counselor builds effective teams by encouraging collaboration among all school staff.

The CACREP Standards for School Counseling Programs addressed in this chapter are

A.1 history, philosophy, and current trends in school counseling and educational systems;

A.2 relationship of the school counseling program to the academic and student services program in the school;

A.3 role, function, and professional identity of the school counselor in relation to the roles of other professional and support personnel in the school;

A.5 knowledge of the school setting, environment, and pre-K–12 curriculum;

A.8 knowledge and understanding of community, environmental, and institutional opportunities that enhance, as well as barriers that impede student academic, career, and personal/social success and overall development;

B.2 coordination, collaboration, referral, and team-building efforts with teachers, parents, support personnel, and community resources to promote program objectives and facilitate successful student development and achievement of all students;

B.4 promotion of the use of counseling and guidance activities and programs by the total school community to enhance a positive school climate; and

C.3 **(a)** strategies to promote, develop, and enhance effective teamwork within the school and larger community.

◆ Communicate with parents/guardians/caregivers regularly

◆ Respond to parents' and caregivers' concerns

◆ Provide a safe, exciting, fun, invigorating learning environment

◆ Provide language assistance as needed

◆ Provide limited health services and screening for problems

◆ Provide limited mental health services and screening for problems

◆ Instill respect for the traditions and symbols of the country, state, and/or community

◆ Instill core values that transcend cultures, such as honesty, caring, respect, responsibility, and justice

◆ Provide education in fundamental behaviors such as problem solving, friendship building, and decision making

◆ Other requirements as determined by local school boards, state law, federal mandate, the community, and society as a whole

If these expectations are not met, it is easy to blame others. Parents and caregivers blame teachers, teachers blame parents and schools, schools blame the school board, the school board blames the community and parents, and everyone blames society, movies, music, and the media. If it takes a village to raise a child, then we are all accountable for the education our young people receive in our schools. Communities must be willing to fund excellent schools; schools must be willing to listen to the needs of the students, families, and the community; and parents and caregivers must be willing to participate in the educational processes of all children. Counselors can be a crucial link in the chain of excellence and achievement, facilitating communication and understanding among all stakeholders in the process of educating young people.

A broad synthesis of research, incorporating ideas emerging from youth development and resiliency literature, protective factors research, and developmental assets literature, yields eight outcomes desired by society for young people. According to UCLA's School Mental Health Project/Center for Mental Health in Schools [SMHP] (1999; p. 5), these eight outcomes are

1. Academics, which includes connection to and commitment to learning, motivation for learning and self-learning, and feelings of academic competence
2. Healthy and safe behavior, which includes the ability to make good decisions about how to establish and maintain good physical health and a healthy lifestyle, solve interpersonal conflicts and problems as a means of managing stress, delay gratification, and resist impulses and unhealthy peer/social pressures
3. Social-emotional functioning, which includes the ability to relate interpersonally in a culturally appropriate manner; understand, express, and manage emotions; experience generally positive feelings about oneself, others, and the world; experience a sense of social and emotional competence and connection with others; and experience a sense of hope for the future
4. Communication, which includes basic communication skills and the ability to understand social cues and the perspectives of others
5. Character/Values, which includes personal, social, and civic responsibility, honesty and integrity, and the ability to monitor one's own choices to maintain congruence between values and behaviors
6. Self-direction, which describes the ability to evaluate life situations and make effective long-term decisions that are appropriately autonomous and self-responsible
7. Vocational and other adult roles, which include those skills and attitudes that facilitate locating, securing, and maintaining employment, community involvement, intimate adult relationships, and other adult roles
8. Recreational and enrichment pursuits, which include engaging in behaviors and activities that improve quality of life, permit expression of creativity, and reduce stress

Given these eight outcomes as desired for young people, an effective school would provide the environment in which progress toward these outcomes is evident. According to

Travers, Elliott, and Kratochwill (1993), effective schools are characterized by connections among staff, teachers, students, and caregivers; consistently fair decision making and discipline; an environment of encouragement for academic and personal achievement; teaching that blends both the basics and methods that facilitate discovery; realistic but high expectations for all; and high accountability for learning (p. 16). In this effective school setting, two principles emerge of primary importance: a caring environment and an emphasis on holistic development (SMHP, 1999, p. 5).

These two conditions are the result of collaborative efforts among schools, communities, and caregivers to provide a school environment in which young people feel welcome and respected; in which there are opportunities to make connections with caring adults and peers; in which information and counseling is provided to help them determine what it means to care for self and others; and in which opportunities and expectations are present that encourage them to contribute to the community through service and advocacy (Pittman, n.d.). These caring conditions and holistic factors do not appear magically; they are the result of hard work, determination, and the focus of the school and community on those elements that nurture young people. And research is clear that when these *support* elements are in place, there are substantial gains in *academic* achievement. Counselors are instrumental in advocating for environments of respect and caring, and counselors share enormous responsibility for the holistic development of students. How do they accomplish this? By understanding schools: what makes them work and ways they fail.

Reflection Moment ◆

What was the educational environment in which you grew up? What was the purpose you ascribed to education when you were a K–12 student? Torture? Play? Can you separate out those elements of school that nurtured you and those that didn't to help you in thinking about the material to come in this chapter?

◆ ◆

How Do We Know That a School Is Effective?

Imagine that you are in a school. What do you see around you? What do you smell, hear, see? Take a moment to experience that school.

When people imagine an elementary school, the images typically include the sound of young peoples' voices, laughter, bright colors of clothes and bulletin boards, and the smell of peanut butter, apples, and crayons. The emotions generated by these images are usually positive. In contrast, when asked to imagine a high school, the images are darker, more somber, less vibrant. Typical responses include crowded hallways, darker colors, angry voices, slamming lockers, a dusty-smoky smell. Why? Secondary school students are no less vibrant, no less creative, no less happy than elementary students—or are they?

To understand school counseling, we must understand both the promise of effective schools and the reality of dehumanizing schools. We must be able to understand what contributes to, and what impedes, the development of our students. Because counselors are charged with facilitating the academic, career, and personal/social development of students, it is essential that counselors be willing to confront, as appropriate, those elements that impede students' development. Conversely, counselors need to empower themselves to advocate for those elements that contribute to students' development. You will be able to understand why those images of high school darken in comparison to elementary school if you understand the extent to which schools respond to the developmental needs of students.

School counselors see the full spectrum of students, with a wide range of needs. Some students seem to sail through school. They love going to school, they love learning, they feel energized by their teachers, their peers, the subjects they study. Their lives are blessed with strong families, strong career goals, and strong social skills. For these students, the school counselor may be the person who challenges them to stretch, encourages their potential, and cheerleads for them in academics and beyond. But such students are rare.

Other students don't fare well, struggling with social skills, academic skills, or life challenges. Many young people's physical, social, or emotional needs may not always be met. But many education professionals still struggle with why students fail. Don't all schools meet the educational needs of students? Just as family systems research has found that the way you were parented can determine, to a large extent, the way you will parent, so it is with education. The way we were schooled, if unquestioned, translates into the way we school our young people.

The problem is that not everyone learns the same way. If you're one of those unfortunate students whose learning needs do not match what the school can provide, school after school, teacher after teacher, year after year, failure after failure, you learn one thing. You might not learn math, or reading, or history, but you'll learn one lesson very well—that you don't belong in school, that you're stupid, useless, worthless, a waste of time for everyone. So you find ways to avoid being there, or ways to avoid facing yet another failure, or ways to make everyone think you know when you don't. Then perhaps you will find ways to make other people pay for making you feel bad, ways to settle the score a little, ways to make others wish they weren't there, either.

Does this sound familiar? It should. We read about these students in the newspapers every day. Their pain becomes more obvious as time passes, their spirits more subdued each year as their self-esteem wears down. The person who started out as an energetic, bubbly kindergartner has come to high school expecting to fail.

What can counselors do to help? The answer may be found in the literature about developmentally appropriate schools, but to understand what is developmentally appropriate, let's first look at what dehumanizing schools look like.

Dehumanizing Schools. Schools, as a reflection of the society in which they were created, evolved ways of dealing with children based on models used in other sectors of society—namely, business. The model of efficiency of the 1860s through the 1930s was the factory, and schools evolved classrooms where everyone did the same thing at the same time (sit in rows, no talking, eyes forward) (Perry, 1992; Sheldon & Biddle, 1998), and everyone was expected to progress at the same rate based on chronological age (Morrison, 1997). The expressed goals of schooling, as described in the Cardinal Principles of Secondary Education written in 1918, were to teach health, a command of fundamental processes, worthy home membership, citizenship, ethical character, vocational preparation, and worthy use of leisure time (as cited in Morrison, 1997). The unexpressed goal of schooling was to instill a common morality, which came to mean nondenominational Christian (Newman, 1994, p. 149).

The process of learning involved rote memorization (Newman, 1994) of information deemed appropriate by the social mores of the time (Morrison, 1997). The relevance of the data was unquestioned—it was in the book, so it must be learned. Recitation, drills, and evaluation of recall in the form of objective tests were the norm (Shaffer, 1999).

Classes were controlled by the adult, in what is known as "teacher-centered" instruction. Teachers were required to maintain order, cover a body of material, and demonstrate that students have learned (Newman, 1994). A significant advantage of teacher-centered instruction is control, and as class sizes got bigger in the post–World War II baby boom, control became more and more important. In the eyes of school boards, schools were measured by test scores and cost-effectiveness (Newman, 1994).

What drove the factory model was competition: To establish and maintain the U.S. as the industrial giant of the world, we needed to train factory workers. What drove the need to control was fear—fear of the sheer numbers of students, fear of losing our competitive edge, fear that young people could not be trusted to make sound decisions. What drove education-by-memorization and teacher-centered classrooms was the "banking" model of learning (Sheldon & Biddle, 1998); the learner was an empty vessel, passively awaiting wisdom from the all-knowing expert in the front of the classroom who was the exclusive source of knowledge. Knowledge could not be gained by discovery, self-teaching, or intuition, but only after such grace was earned by many hours of hard work, sacrifice, and discipline.

The implicit curriculum of the factory model of education, according to Eisner (1985), is compliance with authority rather than initiative, dependence on others to provide answers, extrinsic motivation, and competitiveness with classmates. The intellect is nurtured at the expense of the affect; learning about the arts is no more than play that one earns when the serious endeavor of schooling has been finished. He likens the school to a hospital environment, stamped with routine, sameness, sterility, and lack of privacy. "Schools are educational churches, and our gods, judging from the altars we build, are economy and efficiency. Hardly a nod is given to the spirit" (Eisner, 1985, p. 97).

The spirit is nurtured when it is in contact with caring others, but as Lipsitz (1984) pointed out, "Schools are peculiar social agencies, charged by society with socializing youth into that society *while excluding them from it*" (emphasis added) (p. 7). She goes on to add that teachers and administrators represent all adults to young people who act out their ambivalence about adults, one another, and themselves. Perhaps it is this acting out that causes schools to exclude young people from any meaningful involvement. The search for identity, the struggle between dependence and independence, the quest for a life vision—all these developmental tasks are painful to watch.

It is easy to see how the schools described above would create places where the spirit, if not outright crushed, is at least substantially bruised. These are dehumanizing institutions, and young people who have endured 12 (or more) years of such institutionalization do not usually emerge whole. The price they pay is their creativity, initiative, flexibility, autonomy, and trust in themselves as change agents for tomorrow's world.

Yet if we agree that schools are charged with helping students to become citizens of tomorrow's world, we need workers who possess those very characteristics that factory-model schools are designed to eradicate (Sheldon & Biddle, 1998). Recall that in the definition of effective schools, the two most salient features of effective schools are a caring environment and a holistic orientation to the development of students. It is from the synthesis of the needs of tomorrow's world with the research into effective schools that the concept of developmentally appropriate education has emerged.

Reflection Moment ◆

If you are like most people, there were elements of your educational past that did not work well for you. What were those elements? School as a whole, one particular school, one teacher, one other student? What could have helped you to deal with those negative elements?

◆ ◆

Developmentally Appropriate Schools.   It would be inaccurate and unfair to claim that there was nothing of educational value to be gained from traditional schools. Among some positive lessons that are learned in a structured setting are punctuality, persistence, delayed gratification (Eisner, 1985), and the need to obey the rules, respect authority, and become good citizens (Shaffer, 1999). It is also true that some lessons, such as abstract concepts, are easier to learn in a structured, lecture-oriented setting (Shaffer, 1999). As we shall see, developmentally appropriate education incorporates these benefits of structured education and extends the range of learning experiences to reduce structure, as determined by students' developmental needs.

First coined to describe educational strategies for use with preschool age children (Travers, Elliott, & Kratochwill, 1993), developmentally appropriate education (also known as open classrooms [Eggen & Kauchak, 1994]) refers to educational experiences that are tailored to the developmental needs of students in terms of social skills, emotional maturation, and academic strengths and challenges. According to Eggen and Kauchak (1994), developmentally appropriate education provides balance among academic, social, and emotional goals, in a well-organized classroom that includes an emphasis on peer and teacher interaction, active learning strategies, and intrinsically interesting learning activities. They characterize developmentally appropriate methodology as utilizing discovery, group projects, independent thinking, and reflection; motivation is intrinsic and based on curiosity; classroom organization is designed for individualized instruction and small-group interaction; and the educator's role is perceived as that of director and facilitator, rather than exclusively that of presenter (p. 111).

The key to understanding what makes these educational strategies "developmentally appropriate" is that the entire learning environment and all learning activities within that environment are designed based on what is most conducive to the learning of those particular students. Balanced consideration is given to the students' social, emotional, and academic needs; cooperation, rather than competition, drives peer interactions, and initiative, rather than blind compliance, is fostered.

According to Eggen and Kauchak (1994), open classrooms were criticized when educators misunderstood how to apply these concepts and allowed students to do whatever they wanted in class. The quality of learning suffered in those classrooms. As school counselors, we must be concerned for the holistic development of the student, so we must know how well students learn in developmentally appropriate classrooms.

Research into the academic efficacy of various pedagogies suggests that students will actually learn *more* in a developmentally appropriate learning environment (Charlesworth, 1996; Schickedanz, Schickedanz, Forsyth, & Forsyth, 1998; Travers, Elliott, & Kratochwill, 1993). The reasons students learn better involve how and why students learn. Since developmentally appropriate education allows for natural curiosity and intrinsic motivation to be expressed, students may learn better because they enjoy what they are learning. Studies have shown that intrinsically motivated learners retain memorized material longer, demonstrate a stronger understanding of both memorized and more complex material, and demonstrate greater creativity and cognitive flexibility (Sheldon & Biddle, 1998, p. 166). Furthermore, open classrooms allow students to learn in the way that is most natural to them, as "active, autonomous agents who learn better by being actively involved in education" (Shaffer, 1999, p. 611).

There is evidence that developmentally appropriate education, or open classrooms, provide additional developmental benefits in the social and emotional domains (Shaffer, 1999). Students in such classrooms expressed more positive attitudes about school, they were more self-directed, they displayed greater ability to cooperate with their classmates, and they exhibited fewer behavioral problems.

Hence, in any well-functioning academic setting, academic expectations and accountability for learning are high, but there is also a connection between educators and students, an environment of encouragement, and teaching that blends structure and discovery (Travers, Elliott, & Kratochwill, 1993). It would appear that developmentally appropriate education fits these conditions for effective schools. Given the preponderance of evidence in support of developmentally appropriate educational strategies, it is hard to argue for a return to "factory model" schools.

While developmentally appropriate education is not a guaranteed panacea for all the ills of schools and society, it does hold the promise of helping young people find their way to functional adulthood (Paisley & Peace, 1995). The essence of developmentally appropriate education is summarized by Fay and Funk (1995): "All effective systems allow people to learn from the results of their own decisions" (p. 26). It is only through making decisions, and learning from the results, that young people attain functional adulthood. Developmentally appropriate schools provide healthier systems for nurturing young people because the central premise of the system is profoundly simple: *Respect.*

In their book about educational psychology, Travers, Elliott, and Kratochwill (1993) advise new teachers that, to help students attain psychosocial maturity, teachers should treat them as *"almost adults* [emphasis authors']; that is, providing them with independence, freedom, and respect" (p. 105). The Grolier-Webster International Dictionary defines *respect* as "to hold in high estimation or honor; to treat with consideration; to avoid interfering with or intruding upon" (p. 817). As counselors, you are trained to respond to other people with unconditional positive regard and respect for their values, attitudes, and experiences. Is it possible to hope that an entire institution can view students with respect?

The answer is a resounding "yes." *Respect is the foundation of all healthy relationships,* and students need all professionals who work in our schools to view them with positive regard and respect. We may not accept individual behavior within the boundaries of responsibility, accountability, and mutually respectful choices in a community, but we value each young person as a human being, with all the creativity, potential, beauty, and hope that any human being possesses. We respect their potential and their reality, and, as counselors, we hold onto our belief in their potential in the face of sometimes very painful reality. Recall from Chapter 1 that the necessary personal qualities of school counselors were described as creativity and imagination, flexibility, courage, belief, and passion. Here is where your belief and courage will be called into play.

As professionals, school counselors must be able to maintain the belief that young people will rise to our high expectations, and if they don't, that it is their life path to learn their life lessons another way. In any case, we must respect them as having a right to their opinions, talents, interests, and feelings—and help them learn appropriate and responsible ways to express those opinions, talents, interests, and feelings (Fay & Funk, 1995) in the context of a learning community. This is how we educate our young people into responsible citizenry in our society.

If we do not respect young people, we fall back into the factory model of schools, back into teacher-centered education, and back into the trap of the banking model of learning. Without respect, we revert to the "adult control → student acting out → more control → more acting out" cycle of interaction. With respect for young people and their developmental needs, we break that cycle, and opt instead for a more responsible and responsive school environment. We build a more holistic system, teaching healthier values, attitudes, and ways of relating.

Reflection Moment ◆

What experiences have you had in a developmentally appropriate environment? How did those experiences feel?

◆ ◆

◆ EFFECTIVE RELATIONSHIPS WITHIN EDUCATIONAL COMMUNITIES

When we examine the implications of various philosophies of education, we have some sense of why school professionals often disagree about how to best help kids. Because these philosophies of education translate directly into the relationships we develop and nurture in an attempt to help our students learn, we can see how a school professional's philosophy of education can lead to effective or ineffective working relationships. But you may be asking yourself, "Aren't we all here to help kids?" Understanding how our partners interact will help you appreciate the school counselor's relationship with our partners in education.

School counselors, as we will see, are charged with a large task: the academic, social/emotional, and career development of students (Dahir, Sheldon, & Valiga, 1998). While it is natural that new professionals will feel tremendous professional pride, when such pride results in the belief that "the counselor is the only one who works with kids" or "the counselor only conducts one-on-one counseling," the counselor is creating a situation that is fraught with problems.

The national average student-to-counselor ratio is 561 to 1 ("$20 Million Set Aside," 2000). With that ratio, no one person alone (emphasis on "alone") can attend to all the academic, career, and personal/social needs of all the students in a school, even a small school. Not only does it take an entire community to raise a child, it takes an entire community to educate a child.

Community, in this context, refers both to the community outside a school and the community within a school. Essential elements of students' lives, including the primary support system, caregivers and family, exist outside of school. To be effective on behalf of students, school counselors must be able to engage caregivers and families—to develop rapport, develop trust, make referrals, educate, consult, and counsel, if need be. In many schools, school counselors provide direct services to caregivers, teaching parenting and communication skills, economic survival skills (such as resume writing and interviewing), consulting on the needs of students, and providing direct counseling through one-on-one sessions and support groups. (See Chapters 7–10 for an in-depth discussion of ways that counselors work with caregivers.)

In addition, counselors must be able to work effectively with other members of the outside community. For example, counselors must have effective working relationships with social agencies, health providers, and other mental health providers to facilitate referrals. Since counselors are also charged with the career development of students, effective relationships with employers will facilitate career exploration programming. Effective relationships with community leaders will enable the counselor to be an effective advocate for schools and for children and may facilitate the exploration of external funding for schools and for school counseling programs.

The school system itself is also a community, and within that community are professionals with whom partnerships are essential. Effective partnerships with school board and central administration members, as well as with building-level administrators such as principals and directors, result in an increased districtwide awareness of and appreciation for the school counseling program. These partnerships yield respect, trust, communication, resources, and more effective services for students.

Other pupil services professionals (or student services professionals, depending on local terminology) are also essential. Many authors have written extensively on the need for greater collaboration among pupil services professionals such as school psychologists, school social workers, school counselors, and school nurses. Together, the pupil services team of counselors, psychologists, social workers, and nurses represent the expertise and training needed to support the learning of young people, to ensure that good physical health, good psychological health, and solid support systems enable young people to be successful—to become healthy and resilient learners. The pupil services team facilitates the personal/social development of students.

Finally, no discussion of effective partnerships within schools would be complete without a discussion of the need to partner with teachers. Counselors are experts in both the change process and the learning process—these processes are the foundation of each theory of counseling. Using our expertise to help students learn can only go so far without the primary partner in the learning process: the teacher. Many teachers are already aware of and appreciate the role that counselors play in schools, but not all are. It is essential that counselors work with teachers to facilitate effective referrals, problem solving, and communication with students, families, and administrators about students, their lives, and their challenges. In the next section, we will examine a progressive and visionary approach to respectful collaboration that connects schools with the larger community.

Reflection Moment ◆

What are your perceptions of the professions of school administrator, school psychologist, school social worker, and school nurse? Have you had any experience with members of these professions? Were those contacts positive or negative? What will you do to learn more about these professions to enable you to interact effectively with the professionals you will meet in the future?

◆ ◆

Adelman and Taylor Model of Collaboration

Pioneers in the discussion of systemic collaboration among all partners are Howard Adelman and Linda Taylor (Adelman & Taylor, 1994, 1997, 1998; Taylor & Adelman, 2000). This researcher/practitioner team outlined a model of collaboration that effectively involves all stakeholders in the process of educating young people.

The foundation of their approach includes three observations. First, school professionals do not integrate functions well. The school psychologist, the school social worker, the school nurse, and the school counselor have many overlapping duties and professional goals (helping students function in school). Yet these professional services are fragmented and seldom coordinated. Some professionals feel territorial ownership; the importance of one's own role overshadows those of the other school professionals (Adelman & Taylor, 1994). Second, compounding this fragmentation, school professionals often feel threatened by the intrusion of community professionals in the school setting, creating alienation from community resources and isolating school professionals and students (Adelman & Taylor, 1998). Third, the needs of the vast majority of students have not been considered in the design of programs and services.

Adelman and Taylor (1998) describe the typical student population within a school as a continuum. At one end there are those few students who come to school "motivationally ready and able" to learn for that hour (Adelman & Taylor, 1998, p. 146). They experience no barriers to their learning; they engage in the instructional component of the school (defined as classroom teaching and enrichment activities) and consequently experience the desired outcome of the instructional component (learning).

At the other end are those high-needs students who are "avoidant, very deficient in current capabilities, have a disability, or major health problems" (Adelman & Taylor, 1998, p. 146). It is in response to these students that most school support services are designed. But the very intensity of these needs consume much of the school professionals' time, leaving little time for the needs of any other students.

The vast majority of students fall in the middle, and these are the students whose needs are not being met. In any given hour, many of these students are "not very motivated, lacking prerequisite knowledge and skills, possess different learning rates and styles, and experience minor vulnerabilities" such as emotional upsets, concerns about home functioning, minor health concerns, and so on (Adelman & Taylor, 1998, p. 146). For these students, their barriers to learning may be addressed in a piecemeal manner by the school professionals who happen to notice, but student support services are not designed to address the needs experienced by these students.

From this awareness of student needs, Adelman and Taylor (1994, 1998; Taylor & Adelman, 2000) proposed the need for an "enabling component" that supports and enhances instruction built by collaboration among all educational professionals with support from the community. To implement this concept, schools must rethink how services are provided and programs are designed. Taylor and Adelman (2000) view collaboration as multidisciplinary, interdisciplinary, and transdisciplinary. To them, collaboration entails combining resources, programs, professionals, and volunteers to integrate services and programs to meet the needs of all students.

Adelman and Taylor call for school counselors to be prepared to carry out new roles in this restructuring process, including increased coordination of programs and services within schools and communities, focus on learner support activities related to broad awareness of barriers to learning, and assuming leadership over the change process (Taylor & Adelman, 2000). They cite the Memphis School District as one example in which school counselors have been assigned leadership roles in "creating readiness for systemic change; mapping, analyzing, and redeploying relevant school resources; and working to strengthen connections between school, home, and other community resources" (p. 306).

It is clear that this model of coordination and collaboration is very broad-based, suggesting how services can be meshed, how collaboratives can be transdisciplinary, and how schools can be transformed into caring, respectful places.

Reflection Moment ✦

What are some models for collaboration that you have seen that parallel what Adelman and Taylor propose?

✦ ✦

Leadership Role to Close the Gap and Monitor Achievement, Equity, and Access

While Adelman and Taylor's vision of school/community collaboration may be ambitious, there is no doubt that professional school counselors in comprehensive school counseling programs need to be proactive in many schoolwide efforts. Monitoring the school climate for respect is one profound example of the effect of the school counselor in the affective reality of the school. But school counselors also have systemic, wide-reaching leadership responsibilities in the academic reality of the school, as school counselors are charged with monitoring student achievement, ensuring equity across student groups, and promoting access to educational resources (ASCA, 2003).

This responsibility is shared by multiple professionals in the school, but it is critical that the school counselor take leadership in these efforts. As we will see in many chapters in this book, school counselors are leaders of the heart of the school, and as such, are charged with monitoring the learning conditions of the school, most especially for those students who, by demographic, economic, or cultural characteristics, might be vulnerable in the school environment. Leadership activities with the student system (students, parents, families), the school systems (teachers, administrators, staff, other student service professionals), and the community, ensure dialogue on multiple fronts about the conditions that could impede the students' achievement and the resources that could enhance access and achievement. School counselors have access to schoolwide information (i.e., grades, behavior statistics, test scores) and must monitor that data to alert school professionals and families of the progress of students. With multiple professionals watching out for students and counselors leading and advocating for equity, the achievement gap will narrow. Without this leadership of systemic interventions for students, the achievement gap widens and students who may have limited access to resources fall further behind.

CASE STUDY REVISITED ◆ Integration

Now that you have read the chapter, go back and reread Mr. Bass: A Fish out of Water. Reflect on and answer the following questions:

1. Based on what Mr. Bass learned from the student, how would you describe the school environment in terms of this chapter?
2. Based on Ms. Parks' comment, what can you tell about the relationship between Ms. Parks and other school professionals?
3. If you were Ms. Parks, what would be your response to Mr. Bass? What can Ms. Parks do to help the student?
4. Considering the premise that respect is the foundation of all healthy relationships, in what way(s) is lack of respect evident in this case study?
5. Using the Adelman and Taylor approach to providing services to students, what would you do to change the school environment and to improve educational and counseling services to students?
6. How would leadership activities with all the systems (family, school, and community) help resolve this situation? What are some activities you might consider in this case?

APPLICATION (Possible portfolio artifacts are noted)

1. Given what you know about developmentally appropriate education, select your favorite school subject and design a developmentally appropriate classroom, describing how each developmentally appropriate strategy would be woven into your "ideal" classroom. (Possible portfolio artifact)

2. Visit a local school. When you walk through the halls, see if you can identify the following:
   a. What remnants of the factory model still exist in the school?
   b. What evidence of teacher-centered education and the banking model of learning did you see?
   c. What evidence of developmentally appropriate education did you see?
   d. What evidence of respect for students did you see?
   e. What evidence of respect for faculty, staff, and administration did you see?
   f. Now interview that school counselor about the respect in the building. What could that person do to make the school a more respectful environment?

3. Outline a plan for learning more about each of the professions presented in the discussion about relationships with other school professionals. What distinguishes school counselors from school social workers and from school psychologists? Why do some schools hire one profession over another? (For example, why would a school hire a school social worker over a school counselor?) Obtain job descriptions and identify those job duties that are unique to each.

4. Based on question 3 above, outline a plan for collaborating with each of the student service professionals. What are the activities you would envision for each based on question 3? (Possible portfolio artifact)

5. Evaluate your education using the concepts of this chapter:
   a. On a scale of 1 to 10, with 1 being the most restrictive, highly structured educational environment and 10 being the most developmentally appropriate educational environment, rate each year of your education.
   b. For each year, rate how much you learned using a letter grade.
   c. For each year, list the most respectful and least respectful aspects of your education. One a scale of 1–10, with 1 being overall

disrespected and 10 being overall respected, rate each year in terms of how you felt as a member of that learning community.

    d. Give each year a letter grade for its overall contribution to the person you are today.

    e. What patterns do you see?

6. Use the Internet to visit home pages for local schools. Look for evidence that allows you to rate the amount of collaboration among educational professionals.

7. Interview a local school counselor about collaborating with other school professionals. Personalities aside, what are all the advantages of collaboration? What are the disadvantages?

8. Contact your state's department of education to talk with the school counseling consultant about what that person has seen in the field in terms of collaboration among school professionals. What are some of the best examples of collaboration that person has seen in the state?

9. Visit a local school and talk to the counselor about achievement data collected in that school. How useful is it? If you were the school counselor, what ideas would you have to explore the achievement gap in that school? Outline a general plan for collaborating with the families, school personnel, and the community about achievement. (Possible portfolio artifact)

SUGGESTED READINGS

Adelman, H. S., & Taylor, L. (1998). Reframing mental health in schools and expanding school reform. *Educational Psychologist, 33*(4), 135–152; and Taylor, L., & Adelman, H. S. (2000). Connecting schools, families, and communities. *Professional School Counseling, 3,* 298–307. These two resources outline Adelman and Taylor's model of school-community collaboration, and represent a vision of the next step in creating seamless systems of support for children.

Fay, J., & Funk, D. (1995). *Teaching with love and logic.* Golden, CO: Love & Logic Press. The Love and Logic resources are invaluable to those working with children and are highly recommended for school professionals.

Anyone working with children must have a depth of understanding about childhood development, so any of the references that address development and/or educational psychology is also highly recommended.

REFERENCES

$20 million set aside for school counseling. (2000, January). *Counseling Today, 42,* 1, 19.

Adelman, H. S., & Taylor, L. (1994). Pupil services and education reform. Paper presented at the "Safe Schools, Safe Students: A Collaborative Approach to Achieving Safe, Disciplined, and Drug-Free Schools Conducive to Learning" Conference, Washington, DC, October 28–29, 1994. ERIC No. 383955. Retrieved April 18, 2000 from http://webnf2.epnet.com (the EBSCO database).

Adelman, H. S., & Taylor, L. (1997). Addressing barriers to learning: Beyond school-linked services and full service schools. *American Journal of Orthopsychiatry, 67,* 408–421.

Adelman, H. S., & Taylor, L. (1998). Reframing mental health in schools and expanding school reform. *Educational Psychologist, 33*(4), 135–152.

ASCA. (2003). *The ASCA National Model: A framework for school counseling programs.* Alexandria, VA: Author.

Charlesworth, R. (1996). *Understanding child development* (4th ed.). Albany, NY: Delmar.

Dahir, C. A., Sheldon, C. B., & Valiga, M. J. (1998). *Vision into action: Implementing the National Standards for School Counseling Programs.* Alexandria, VA: American School Counselor Association.

Eggen, P., & Kauchak, D. (1994*). Educational psychology: Classroom connections* (2nd ed.). New York: Merrill.

Eisner, E. W. (1985*). The educational imagination: On the design and evaluation of school programs* (2nd ed.). New York: Macmillan.

Fay, J., & Funk, D. (1995). *Teaching with love and logic.* Golden, CO: Love & Logic Press.

Grolier-Webster international dictionary of the English language. (1975). New York: Grolier.

Lewis, A. C. (1994). Expectations for schools. *Education Digest, 60*(4), 72–74.

Lipsitz, J. (1984). *Successful schools for young adolescents.* New Brunswick, NJ: Transaction Books.

Morrison, G. S. (1997). *Teaching in America.* Boston: Allyn and Bacon.

Newman, J. W. (1994). *America's teachers: An introduction to education* (2nd ed.). New York: Longman.

Paisley, P. O., & Peace, S. D. (1995). Developmental principles: A framework for school counseling programs. *Elementary School Counseling & Guidance, 30*(2), 85–93.

Perry, N. (1992). *Educational reform and the school counselor.* (Report No. EDO-CG-92-25). Washington, DC: Office of Educational Research and Improvement. (ERIC Document Reproduction Service No. ED 347 491). Retrieved April 18, 2000, from http://webnf2.epnet.com (the EBSCO database).

Pittman, D. (n.d.). *Preventing problems or promoting development: Competing priorities or inseparable goals.* Retrieved April 18, 2000, from www.iyfnet.org/document.cfm/22/general/51.

Schickedanz, J. A., Schickedanz, D. I., Forsyth, P. D., & Forsyth, C. A. (1998). *Understanding children and adolescents* (3rd ed.). Boston: Allyn & Bacon.

School Mental Health Project/Center for Mental Health in Schools [SMHP]. (1999, Fall). Promoting youth development and addressing barriers. *Addressing Barriers to Learning,* 1–8.

Shaffer, D. R. (1999). *Developmental psychology: Childhood and adolescence* (5th ed.). Pacific Grove, CA: Brooks/Cole.

Sheldon, K. M., & Biddle, B. J. (1998). Standards, accountability, and school reform: Perils and pitfalls. *Teachers College Record, 100*(1), 164–180.

Simon, C. A. (1999). Public school administration: Employing Thompson's Structural Contingency Theory to explain public school administrative expenditures in Washington State. *Administration & Society, 31,* 525–542.

Taylor, L., & Adelman, H. S. (2000). Connecting schools, families, and communities. *Professional School Counseling, 3,* 298–307.

Travers, J. F., Elliott, S. N., & Kratochwill, T. R. (1993). *Educational psychology: Effective teaching, effective learning.* Madison, WI: Brown & Benchmark.

SECTION TWO

Comprehensive School Counseling Programs

CHAPTER

3

SIX QUALITIES OF COMPREHENSIVE SCHOOL COUNSELING PROGRAMS, PART 1

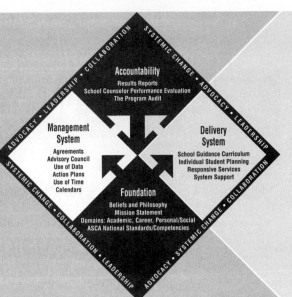

◆ LEARNING OBJECTIVES

By the end of this chapter, you will be able to

1. Know the six qualities of a comprehensive school counseling program (CSCP)
2. Understand and articulate the issues and prototypes in student development in a holistic CSCP

3. Understand and articulate the issues and prototypes in student development in a systemic CSCP
4. Demonstrate an understanding of how these prototypes apply in a case study

DOMAINS / ACTIVITIES / PARTNERS MODEL

ACTIVITIES	DOMAINS Academic Development	Career Development	Personal/ Social Development	Parents and Caregivers	Colleagues in Schools	Colleagues in Community
Counseling	1a	1b	1c	5	6	7
Educating and Advocacy	2a	2b	2c	8	9	10
Consulting	3a	3b	3c	11	12	13
Leadership and Coordination	4a	4b	4c	14	15	16

Students

PARTNERS IN THE PROCESS

CASE STUDY ◆ Mr. Paulson Counseling Ty

Mr. Paulson was finishing up some paperwork before the bell rang to start the day, when Ty came into the office. "Mr. Paulson, can I see you today?" he asked.

"Yeah, Ty. Sure. What's up? Do you want to meet now?" He gestured to the chair by his desk when he saw Ty's face. "Have a seat."

Paulson paused to keep himself from swearing. "What happened to your face? Who did this to you?" Instinctively he began to reach up to the young man's face, but withdrew his hand when Ty pulled away.

"You know, man. The streets are a bitch." Ty paused. "That's not why I'm here. I'm getting pressure at home to get another job to help out more with the bills. I hate working at the burger place, but I do it to help out my mom. Now how am I gonna get the grades to get into college if I'm working two jobs? I'm already struggling in my science class and Miss Epps tells me I'm barely pulling a C. Now this.

"Maybe I should just give up the college thing anyway. Everyone tells me that I won't make it, because I don't know what I want to study. They think it's a waste of time. But I wanted to go just to get the hell out of the city. I don't think I'll have any life at all if I stay here. There aren't any jobs here, the ones that are here don't pay anything, and I don't want to live with my mom the rest of my life.

"And then there's this," he says as he points to the cuts and bruises on his face. "I'm sick of being beat up because I'm not cool—I work and go to school and don't want to make trouble. I'm just not going to take it anymore. Mom wants me to turn the other cheek, but how can I ever call myself a man if I don't stand up for myself and what I believe in?"

CHALLENGE QUESTIONS

What are your reactions as you picture Ty? What questions came to your mind? What would you like to say to Ty? Where would you begin in your conversation with him? What do you think Mr. Paulson should do?

What do you see as Ty's biggest challenges? What will be the most helpful for him right now? In the long run? Are those different issues or not?

If Mr. Paulson does nothing to help Ty, where do you see this young man's future path taking him?

You now have some perspective in terms of the history and development of the fields of counseling, education, and school counseling. You have also had a chance to think about what works and what doesn't work in school and how a school climate of respect benefits students and staff alike. Now we will turn our attention to what you need to know to design and implement a Comprehensive School Counseling Program, or CSCP. To be comprehensive, a school counseling program must be

◆ *Holistic*, addressing the question "What do school counselors focus on with students?" The answer: All aspects of the student's development.

◆ *Systemic*, addressing the question "Who do school counselors work with?" The answer: All persons with whom the student interacts and all systems of significance in the student's life.

◆ *Balanced*, addressing the question "How do they do their work?" The answer: By balancing their time in the primary activities of the school counselor—namely, counseling, educating and advocacy, consultation, and leadership and coordination.

◆ *Proactive*, addressing the question "Why do school counseling programs exist?" The answer: To mitigate the effects of any experiences that may compromise the development of the students through primary, secondary, and tertiary prevention.

◆ *Infused into the academic curriculum*, addressing the question "How will kids access the program?" The answer: By infusing the CSCP into all aspects of the school experience, from presentations of the developmental curriculum in appropriate classes, to group and individual counseling, to events for parents and faculty that help everyone to understand students better.

◆ *Reflective*, addressing the question "How do we know we make a difference?" The answer: By being accountable to our schools, our students, and ourselves for the information about the impact our work has on the lives of our students.

These six questions, and the six qualities for comprehensive school counseling programs that answer these questions, will be essential for implementing a program in the school that truly benefits all children. For each of these six qualities, we will examine the issues that school counselors address within that topic. Next, we will present various "prototypes," or templates, which can be used to design the *content* of your CSCP. (In Chapters 5 and 6, we will present the *form* or structure of your program in terms of the ASCA National Model (2003) and the various models for delivery systems within the National Model.) In order to address each of these qualities, we will examine the first two qualities, holistic and systemic, in this chapter, then we will turn our attention to the other four qualities in the next chapter.

The ASCA School Counselor Performance Standards addressed in this chapter are

1.2 The professional school counselor demonstrates interpersonal relationships with students.

1.4 The professional school counselor demonstrates positive interpersonal relationships with parents or guardians.

5.1 he professional school counselor provides a comprehensive and balanced school counseling program in collaboration with school staff.

The 2001 CACREP Standards for School Counseling Programs addressed in this chapter are

A.7 the role of racial, ethnic, and cultural heritage, nationality, socioeconomic status, family structure, age, gender, sexual orientation, religious and spiritual beliefs, occupation, physical and mental status, and equity issues in school counseling;

A.8 knowledge and understanding of community, environmental, and institutional opportunities that enhance, as well as barriers that impede student academic, career, and personal/social success and overall development;

B.5 methods of planning for and presenting school counseling-related educational programs to administrators, teachers, parents, and the community;

C.1 **(b)** design, implementation, monitoring, and evaluation of comprehensive developmental school counseling programs (e.g., the ASCA National Standards for School Counseling Programs) including an awareness of various systems that affect students, school, and home;

C.1 **(d)** identification of student academic, career, and personal/social competencies and the implementation of processes and activities to assist students in achieving these competencies;

C.2 **(a)** individual and small-group counseling approaches that promote school success, through academic, career, and personal/social development for all;

C.2 **(b)** individual, group, and classroom guidance approaches systematically designed to assist all students with academic, career, and personal/social development;

C.2 **(d)** issues that may affect the development and functioning of students (e.g., abuse, violence, eating disorders, attention deficit hyperactivity disorder, childhood depression and suicide);

C.2 **(f)** constructive partnerships with parents, guardians, families, and communities in order to promote each student's academic, career, and personal/social success;

C.2 **(g)** systems theories and relationships among and between community systems, family systems, and school systems, and how they interact to influence the students and affect each system;

C.3 **(c)** strategies and methods of working with parents, guardians, families, and communities to empower them to act on behalf of their children; and

C.3 **(d)** knowledge and skills in conducting programs that are designed to enhance students' academic, social, emotional, career, and other developmental needs.

◆ CSCPs ARE HOLISTIC

The overall development of young people depends on so many factors: biological, social, familial, and educational, to name a few. Because the school environment is the context in which school counselors work, we focus on those developmental domains in which we have influence. Those domains are academic development, career development, and personal/social development. Think of this chapter as a roadmap. In Chapters 1 and 2, we discussed the outcomes of excellent education: That is our destination. To get to that destination, our students must maximize their personal potential in each area: academic success, career success, and personal/social success. The first part of this chapter is designed to help you understand where students are headed with their development and how to help your students achieve the most within each domain. In the second part of the chapter, we will examine the systems that affect the development of students.

Academic Development

There is no doubt that the mission of the school is academic development—the lifelong ability to acquire and use new information, new insights, and new ways of seeing and interacting with the world. Addressing academic development as the first domain is a confirmation of the partnership between school counselors and the educational mission of the institution. Being an effective partner in the educational process requires that counselors be able to effectively help students with that mission. Issues that arise in this domain are many, and include helping students "close the gap" in achievement across cultural and economic lines, attaining academic success and confidence, the challenges in helping students plan their education (especially in the middle and high schools), academic mediation (when the teacher's style of teaching and the student's style of learning do not match), and other impediments to learning as outlined in the previous chapter's discussion of Adelman and Taylor. These are all issues that counselors attend to in this domain.

Prototypes.   The following prototypes are presented to give you an overview of ways to think about the learning of young people. They are not the only ways to conceptualize academic development but are presented as a means of thinking about how young people learn and ways to help students be more successful academically.

Learning Styles.   In the most basic prototypes of learning, academic success or failure is a result of input (the relative efficiency of various ways individuals acquire and attend to information to be stored) and output (the relative efficiency of various ways individuals recall and communicate the information they have stored). Notice the almost mechanical "feel" to the prototype; this is not accidental. The closest metaphor for these prototypes is the computer; intellectual processes that allow information to be acquired, stored, and retrieved with minimal loss are considered the most elegant and efficient.

One way of conceptualizing learning preferences involves internal versus external orientation. For some students, information about the world comes from external reality, accessed through the five senses of touch, taste, sight, sound, and smell. For others, information about the world comes from the internal world of perception, intuition, and connections. Both the Myers-Briggs Type Indicator (Briggs & Myers, 1998) and the

Keirsey-Bates (Berens, 1988; Keirsey, 1974) capture this most basic orientation to learning in the S/N continuum. In this score, the "S" represents "sensing," the external orientation, in which the student trusts information that comes from the external world through the five senses. Conversely, the "N" represents "iNtuition" [sic], in which the score represents a preference for information that is discovered, intuited, or inferred. Helping students learn requires an understanding of how the student is oriented to what is to be learned. For those with an external orientation, information that is outside of self and acquired from an expert other would be more readily accepted. Conversely, for those students with an internal orientation, discovery and intuitive insights are more trusted and valued.

Another way of thinking about learning is described by Dunn, Dunn, and Price (1996) and Dunn and Griggs (1988). Providing a comprehensive inventory of learning modalities, their Learning Styles Inventory (LSI) assesses a wide variety of conditions in which learning takes place. First, the assessment gives students a chance to reflect on the physical environment in which their learning is maximized: ambient noise level, lighting, temperature, physical environment (formal with chair and table or informal with places to recline), preferences of intake of food during studying, the time of day that they prefer to study, and the amount of mobility they need to feel alert while studying. Second, students are assessed on their qualities, such as their motivation level, persistence level, responsibility for learning, and need for structure in directions and assignments. Third, students are asked to reflect on social influences that affect their learning, in terms of whether they learn better alone or with peers or whether they learn better with authority figures present (and if so motivated, whether they are parent motivated or teacher motivated). Next, students respond to preferred sensory input(s) to define the unique sensory constellation to which they ascribe effective learning: auditory, visual, tactile, or kinesthetic (also known as experiential, in which the whole body is used to learn), and if they prefer variety or consistency of stimuli. In the LSI, each score is represented on a continuum. Furthermore, group summaries can be generated to give counselors, teachers, and administrators information relative to the learning styles and needs of groups, classes, or entire schools. The purpose of presenting this information is not to promote the use of the LSI; rather, Dunn, Dunn, and Price (1996) and Dunn and Griggs (1988) present an important way to help students think about their best learning by reflecting on a variety of factors that enhance their ability to perform well academically.

Multiple Intelligences.   The traditional definition of intelligence as a univariate construct, the "individual's capacity or innate potential for learning," has been challenged for a number of years (Travers, Elliott, & Kratochwill, 1993, p. 231). What has replaced this elementary definition of a complex construct are various models, both psychometric and practical (Esters & Ittenbach, 1999).

Based on the work of Howard Gardner (Gardner, 1983; Gardner & Hatch, 1989; Lazear, 1999), one practical and useful model for understanding academic development involves understanding the concept of multiple intelligences. According to Gardner, an intelligence involves the ability to solve a problem or create something that has meaning in a particular context, and it is this view of intelligence as related to *context* that is unique and powerful. Gardner asserts that individuals possess the full spectrum of intelligences, but that we have natural strengths that bring one or more of these strengths into use more often than the others. Furthermore, the issue of context becomes important in that we choose to access certain intelligences based on context and situation.

This perspective on intelligence is particularly useful for understanding why a student learns (motivation and predilection for learning), how a student learns (acquisition and retention of information), as well as how a student manifests that learning has taken place (performance on academic tasks). In other words, when you understand an individual's unique constellation of intelligences, you can understand why that student is interested in certain subjects, how the student learns, and how the student might prefer to demonstrate her or his understanding of the subject learned.

The intelligences include verbal/linguistic intelligence, logical/mathematical intelligence, visual spatial intelligence, bodily/kinesthetic intelligence, musical/rhythmic intelligence, interpersonal intelligence, intrapersonal intelligence, and naturalist intelligence (Lazear, 1999). Information about the individual's unique intelligence constellation can be obtained through conversation with the student, through discussions of what the student finds interesting, how he or she learns things, and what he or she does for fun. You don't need a formal assessment to understand which intelligences the student possesses and uses.

There are many ways that multiple intelligences can be helpful when students struggle with academic issues. Counselors could use multiple intelligences as a context in which to mediate conversations between students and teachers about ways to individualize learning and teaching strategies. In addition, counselors can use multiple intelligences in counseling and educating students, as will be discussed in Chapters 7 and 8.

Reflection Moment ◆

What were your academic issues in school? What were your grades like? Did you study hard, or did you play hard? What were your life priorities? What were your "easy" subjects, and which ones really challenged you? Ask significant others what they remember from their school days. Compare your hardest and easiest courses with theirs. Talk about what made those courses seem hard or easy. See if you can identify their intelligence constellation. How would you have wanted to be treated if you came to someone for help with a hard course that they thought was easy? What are the implications for your counseling style?

◆ ◆

Career Development

As we saw in Chapter 1, career development has been the historical "home" of the school counselor, especially at the secondary level. It is an important part of what school counselors do at every level, and you will find that much of your day as a school counselor will be spent dealing with career issues. Some issues in this domain include fear of making a "mistake" in career selection and the effect of rapid world changes on confidence in career predictions. In addition, some parents and teachers are reluctant to begin career discussions early in a student's life; conversely, some adults pressure students to decide too early. Other students struggle with pressure from adults to be practical in their career decision making rather than following dreams, and sometimes parents and others push students into college as a means of "guaranteeing" success.

Prototypes
Overview of the Career Process.   What does the career decision process look like, both in terms of the process itself and in terms of the outcomes? From a whole-life perspective (Dollarhide, 1997), the process of making viable career decisions involves seven steps (Dollarhide, 2000):

Step 1: Understanding of self (knowledge of one's likes, dislikes, abilities, skills, gifts, challenges, values, needs, dreams, lifestyle goals, personality, interests).

Step 2: Understanding of the world of work (knowledge of career paths, job titles, salary levels, employers, employment environments, occupational projections, training requirements).

Step 3: Reality testing (firsthand experience through employment, volunteering, internships, cooperative education jobs, lab experiences, job shadowing)

Step 4: Commitment (making a decision, with relative confidence, in the face of uncertainty).

Step 5: Career preparation (accessing formal or informal training for the job or occupation).

Step 6: Placement/career entrance (using job-seeking skills, filling out applications, writing cover letters and resumes, participating in interviews, then accessing opportunities in the chosen occupation).

Step 7: Evaluation and renewal (as the individual matures throughout life, the core self changes in terms of likes, dislikes, values, and other variables outlined in Step 1. Concurrently, there are changes in the work world. Individuals continuously evaluate their level of career satisfaction, and will begin again at Step 1 when their level of career satisfaction reaches a low-point threshold of tolerance. If they still like the tasks of the occupation, they may decide to change employers. If they dislike the tasks, they may decide to change occupations entirely.)

In terms of outcomes, Henderson (2000) studied persons who were happy at work and found striking similarities among those studied. The first finding was that they were "notably similar in their particularly dogged commitment to follow their interests, their competencies, and what they enjoyed doing. Consequently, their careers tended to follow a *positive meandering path*" (emphasis added) (p. 309). This metaphor feels particularly empowering, and will help students and families feel less pressure to make the right choice right now.

Henderson's second finding (2000) has implications for our discussion of the personal/social domain; she found significant attributes that characterized the study participants who were happy at work. These attributes include

1. A positive sense of self (defined as self-confidence, self-understanding, intuition, and imagination, among others)
2. Self-determination (defined as "independent strategies in choice and action that determine successful . . . approaches to experiences, all characterized by measures of rational thinking and self-responsibility," p. 315)
3. Energy (defined as enthusiasm, goal-directed motivation, and forward focus)
4. Strength of character (defined as the ability to tolerate ambiguity and uncertainty, self-advocacy, resilience, and tenacity)
5. Positive relationships with others (defined as strategies of behavior and communication, such as humor, openmindedness, and active listening, that build positive relationships with others)
6. Positive orientation to the world (defined as positive attitude, optimism, and curiosity that provides a "hopeful and practical approach to functioning in the world," p. 315)

These individuals, because of their overall positive life orientation, would be well equipped to make life work, no matter how inconvenient some details might be. The point is not that these people had perfect jobs or perfect lives; the point is that these findings can help students and families understand what personal qualities and characteristics could lead students to find their "bliss," no matter what life has in store for them.

Positive Uncertainty.   Gellatt (1991, 1996) presents one response to the dilemma of decision making in times of uncertainty and rapid change. Dubbed "positive uncertainty," he suggests a personal decision-making philosophy or paradigm to help people both "imagine and create possibilities" (1996, p. 391). In this paradigm, people are urged to balance two opposing perspectives simultaneously. To maximize adaptability and flexibility while maintaining focus on a desired life/career outcome, positive uncertainty would urge being "focused and flexible" about life and career goals (p. 391). To maximize learning while maintaining awareness of career information, this philosophy would maintain being "aware and wary" about what is known, since "facts" change all the time (p. 391). To maximize the power of dreams while remaining grounded, people are urged to "be objective and optimistic" about one's beliefs (p. 391). Finally, to maximize the power of creativity while engaging in reality testing, Gellatt would suggest being "practical and magical" in one's career behavior (p. 391). In essence, Gellatt (1996) sums it up:

> Developing future sense involves becoming a dreamer and a doer, combining pie-in-the-sky and feet-on-the-ground strategies, balancing achieving goals with discovering them, balancing useful facts and fantasy, balancing reality testing and wishful-thinking, balancing responding to change and causing change. This involves a reinvention of career development. (pp. 392–393)

The implications for students? Keep dreaming those big dreams, and never eliminate the possible to settle for the probable.

The Career Portfolio.   One tool for facilitating the career development process is the career portfolio, in which students systematically explore their career ideas and understanding of self. There are a variety of ways such portfolios can be constructed, from highly individualized to highly structured.

In this portfolio, students document their self-knowledge in terms of personal qualities, personal skills, decision-making processes, and various competencies. They document their educational development, including things they know about their own learning, their plans for after high school, and various competencies. Finally, they document the results of their career exploration and planning, including the results of any career assessments taken and various career competencies. The final document is a personal career plan, in which students synthesize their self-knowledge, awareness of the world of work, career assessment information, training options, and skills into a viable list of career and training options that seem workable. The emphasis is on the word "options." The goal isn't to force students to make a career choice; the goal is to empower students to identify options that will focus further exploration.

Career Clusters.   Career Clusters is also a popular way of conceptualizing the ways to merge education with eventual careers. Promulgated by the National Association of State

Directors of Career Technical Education Consortium (2006, (www.careerclusters.org/16clusters.htm), the sixteen clusters are

1. Agriculture, Food, and Natural Resources
2. Architecture and Construction
3. Arts, AV Technology, and Communications
4. Business, Management, and Administration
5. Education and Training
6. Finance
7. Government and Public Administration
8. Health Science
9. Hospitality and Tourism
10. Human Services
11. Information Technology
12. Law, Public Safety, Corrections, and Security
13. Manufacturing
14. Marketing, Sales, and Service
15. Science, Technology, Engineering, and Mathematics
16. Transportation, Distribution, and Logistics

In some schools, the curriculum is organized around the career clusters, so that both college-bound and non–college-bound students will graduate ready for whatever their post-graduate plans may be.

Reflection Moment ◆

Recall your career journey. Were you intentional, focused, and deliberate, or did your career follow a "positive meandering path"? Do you know, with certainty, how your career path will unfold? (What do you want to do when *you* grow up?) What is the most empowering thing anyone said to you about your career path? What is the most destructive thing anyone said to you about it? What can you do now to avoid ever inflicting that same disappointment and disillusionment on any of your students?

◆ ◆

Personal/Social Development

The third domain which forms the foundation of holistic comprehensive school counseling programs is the development of personal and social skills. This is an area in which many counselors feel especially comfortable, because it is the domain in which counseling itself is focused. Some examples of issues in this domain include the search for identity, relationship development, development of acceptance of others, skills for coping with change and adversity, and the search for rites of passage into adulthood.

Prototypes
Identity Achievement. Marcia (as cited in Craig, 1996) referred to the resolution of the adolescent identity crisis as "identity achievement" (Craig, 1996, p. 439). This was defined as people who have made commitments to their careers and their own "individually

formulated moral code" (p. 439). It is easy to see how this development of personal identity, morality, and definition resonates with the concepts of intelligences and careers discussed in the previous sections. Working to help young people develop higher cognitive skills concurrently helps them to think critically about their choices and to reflect on their responsibility for choice. It also puts into perspective the risk-taking and experimentation with expression that young people exhibit during identity exploration (Craig, 1996, p. 453). Since experimentation is an essential part of choice, it might behoove school counselors to discuss the concept of safe risk-taking with families and school professionals. In this context, safe risk-taking would involve allowing young people safe expression of individuality without adult boundaries. For example, what does it hurt to allow a young person to wear a dark colored shirt in the summer sun, rather than a light colored one? That young person will learn that dark shirts do indeed get hot in the summer sun and will choose the light one next time. If life lessons are really only learned the hard way (Fay & Funk, 1995), then allowing young people to experience the consequences of their choices is the best way we can help young people learn about choice.

Identity Development for Students of Difference. Since identity development depends on how young people see themselves and how others see them, those qualities that cause them to see themselves as "less than" are intensely painful and embarrassing. Adults tell young people to be proud of their unique qualities; the reality is that such appreciation often comes much later in life. The journey toward accepting oneself and others can begin, however, in school, and the struggles of young people to accept their own Difference can be resolved in a way that allows for the appreciation of many Differences. (Since "diversity" has been used rather narrowly to refer to only racial difference, we will use "Difference" to refer to the full spectrum of uniquenesses: race, gender, religion, sexual orientation, ability status, culture, etc.) Many authors have addressed the unique challenges of one group of nondominant values holders, such as racial identity development (Atkinson, Morten, & Sue, 1989; Helms, 1994), disability identity development (Scheer, 1994), female identity development (Pipher, 1994), male identity development (Pollack, 1998) and gay and lesbian identity development (D'Augelli, 1994). Each of these theories has made a significant contribution to the understanding of the struggles of that particular population, and school counselors are urged to become familiar with the identity development theories that address the challenges of their students.

While each theory reflects the struggles of that particular population, many of these theories reflect some common experiences. In general, these theories of Difference identity development share these five common stages:

1. Unawareness of Difference: The Different person sees himself or herself as the same as others; is unaware that others think of him or her as different.
2. Awareness of Difference: The person begins to see that others view her or him as different and becomes aware that those of other groups are treated preferentially.
3. Anger at other groups: The person is now fully aware of prejudicial treatment from others. This can result in tremendous anger, frustration, and rejection of those who are a part of the "dominant" culture. At this stage, people of Difference will often associate with, and identify themselves exclusively with, others of their Difference category.

4. Awareness of commonalities: At some point, the Different person recognizes that there are some similarities between their views and the views of others in the "dominant" culture.

5. Integration of both the Different and dominant: At this stage, the Different person sees that there are ideas, persons, and concepts of value from other perspectives, and is able to integrate the best of the Different culture with the best of the dominant culture to become self-defining and tolerant of the Difference of others.

School counselors who are aware of the Differences of their students and who understand the theories of Different identity development can better understand the painful aspects of the process of identity development, such as rage, isolation, and the need to associate with those of their Difference category. Furthermore, knowing about identity development can help counselors communicate with students, by knowing when to help students connect with positive role models of their own Difference culture. Finally, counselors who use the insights gained from knowing identity development theories can help students integrate the best of both perspectives, teaching tolerance toward others in the process.

Self Esteem. Many educators have heard, ad nauseum, about self-esteem and the need to foster self-esteem in young people. In fact, some authors have criticized an overemphasis on self-esteem in the schools (Hewitt, 1998), charging that schools have fostered self-esteem (translated as passing every student with an A) at the expense of academics, hard work, and any lessons in dedication, persistence, or commitment. Branden (1994) examines self-esteem, defining it as two interrelated concepts: "the disposition to experience oneself as competent to cope with the basic challenges of life and as worthy of happiness" (p. 27). In that definition, it is easy to see that the foundation of self-esteem is competence or self-efficacy, and this comes from experiences in which meaningful challenges are met and dealt with effectively (Travers, Elliott, & Kratochwill, 1993). Branden then goes on to identify six foundations on which self-esteem is built, stressing that self-esteem is a process (meaning lifelong effort) and a practice (meaning that self-esteem must be actively earned). The six pillars of self-esteem (Branden, 1994, p. 66) are

1. The practice of living consciously, with awareness and intent
2. The practice of self-acceptance, with the intent of gentle and continuous self-improvement toward meaningful goals
3. The practice of self-responsibility, which means responsibility for choices, feelings, behaviors, priorities, values, and progress toward fulfillment of goals
4. The practice of self-assertiveness, which means being assertive about one's right to ask for what is needed in life
5. The practice of living purposefully, which entails self-discipline, clear thinking, and working hard
6. The practice of personal integrity, living up to one's own principles, values, and morals

School counselors understand that self-esteem is not a passing educational or pop-psychology buzz-word; rather, it is a very human need to feel competent to deal with life and worthy of the effort.

Goleman's Emotional Intelligence. In helping high school students to maximize their personal/social development, school counselors often struggle with how to help them learn emotional stability. Goleman (1995) addressed this using the construct of emotional intelligence.

> In the dance of feeling and thought, the emotional faculty guides our moment-to-moment decisions, working hand-in-hand with the rational mind, enabling—or disabling—thought itself. Likewise, the thinking brain plays an executive role in our emotions—except in those moments when emotions surge out of control and the emotional brain runs rampant. . . . How we do in life is determined by both—it is not just IQ, but *emotional* intelligence that matters. Indeed, intellect cannot work at its best without emotional intelligence. (Goleman, 1995, p. 26)

In essence, Goleman described emotional intelligence in terms of five domains: a) knowing one's emotions, b) managing one's emotions, c) motivating oneself, or "marshaling emotions in the service of a goal" (p. 43) to enable sustained attention, management of stress, and delayed gratification, d) recognizing emotions in others primarily through empathy, and e) understanding and managing relationships effectively, or understanding and managing the emotions of others. It is through these five elements of emotional intelligence that people learn about themselves, acquire goal-directed behaviors and attitudes, learn about others, and acquire leadership skills and interpersonal effectiveness. Goleman further discussed emotional intelligence in terms of "schooling the emotions" (p. 261), and identified ways that classroom guidance can address cooperation, problem solving, conflict resolution, empathy training, and impulse control through a curriculum called Self Science (Stone & Dillehunt, 1978).

Snyder's Concept of Hope.   Snyder (1994) provided a powerful metaphor for helping us understand how to help young people with a new definition of hope. This new definition states that "Hope is the sum of the mental willpower and waypower that you have for your goals" (Snyder, 1994, p. 5). In this context, goals are those objects or accomplishments that we desire that serve as "mental targets for our thoughts" (p. 5). To serve effectively as a motivating target, goals should be meaningful, important, and clearly articulated. To reach our goals, we access our willpower, which is defined as a "driving force" toward our goals, the "reservoir of determination and commitment that we can call on to help move us in the direction of the goal to which we are attending at any given moment" (p. 6). The final piece of the puzzle is waypower, defined as the mental roadmap that guides hopeful thought (p. 8). It is waypower, or planfulness, that is the "mental capacity we call on to find one or more effective ways to reach our goals" (p. 8).

In order to have hope, then, students would need 1) clearly articulated, meaningful goals, 2) a sense of willpower or energy to move them toward those goals, and 3) high waypower, or the mental flexibility needed to find alternative routes should the path be blocked. Snyder also addresses ways that hope can be nurtured in children, or, if hope is already mortally wounded, ways that hope can be rekindled (pp. 189–205). These suggestions include the following:

- ◆ Teach kids to have positive mental tapes
- ◆ Help them formulate clear short and long-term goals
- ◆ Praise them for determination
- ◆ Help young people accentuate strengths
- ◆ Discuss roadblocks as a normal part of life

◆ Help them articulate paths around roadblocks
◆ Help them see failures as learning experiences to improve future planning

It is possible that the concept of hope as presented by Snyder can help students to under-stand how to move forward with their lives and gives counselors new language to discuss goals, goal-related planning, and the energy or commitment needed to attain goals.

Reflection Moment ◆

Do you remember struggling with your identity? What sorts of things did you do to express your individuality? What was the reaction of adults to your forms of self-expression?

In what ways were you Different? How did that feel?

What was your level of self-esteem? Emotional intelligence? Hope? How did the events of your life affect your self-esteem, emotional intelligence, and hope? How did school impact your experience?

◆ ◆

CASE STUDY REVISITED ◆ Integration

Go back and reread Mr. Paulson's conversation with Ty.

1. There are examples in this conversation of Ty's struggle in all three domains. Find an exam-ple of each.
2. What prototypes from the chapter would you employ to talk with Ty about his struggles?
3. Because there are several issues with which Ty needs help, you might feel conflicted about where to begin with him. Where would you begin and why?
4. Ty is caught between the pacifism of his mother and the "tough it out" message from soci-ety and the streets. What does "being a man" mean to you? What does it mean to Ty? How can you help Ty honor his sense of emerging manhood (dignity) and increase his ability to ask for help dealing with the harassment and violence?

CASE STUDY CONTINUED ◆ Mr. Paulson Meets Ty's Mother

Later that day, Mr. Paulson called Ty's house to make an appointment to meet with Ty's mother. She was able to come to the school on her lunch break, so Mr. Paulson arranged to have the conference room at noon so that they could talk while they ate lunch. After exchanging greetings and getting settled with their sandwiches, Mr. Paulson explained why they were meeting.

"Thank you for coming in, Mrs. Bonté. I'm Calvin Paulson, Ty's counselor. Please call me Calvin. Ty came in this morning with some bruises on his face and concerns about school. I'd like to see what we can do together to help Ty deal with things."

Mrs. Bonté nodded. "I've been concerned about him. He's not been himself lately, more moody and irritable with everyone. What do you think's going on?"

"Well, he seemed upset with his needing to work more to help out at home. He said his grades are slipping, and he's not sure he can get into college. What can you tell me about what you see at home?"

Mrs. Bonté's eyes grew moist as she thought about her son. "He's such a good boy, always helping out with everything. He's my oldest, and he took over after his daddy died three years ago, helping out with his two younger brothers. I'm working all I can at my job, but I don't earn a lot. Ty watches his brothers, and that's no easy task—they like to needle him and pick fights with each other. I do know that Ty has his hands full until I get home.

"Ty usually starts dinner, then when I get home, he goes to his job. When he gets home from his work, he does his homework and studies until all hours of the night, because he wanted to get into college. Now he doesn't know what he wants to do, go to college or stay home and take care of me and the boys.

"I was sick for a couple of weeks and lost some hours at work; now I owe the doctor some money and all the bills are late. Ty insisted that he could work more hours or get a second job to help pay those bills, even though I told him I didn't want him to. His dad and I put some money aside so that the boys could go to college if they wanted. If I save that money for his schooling, I need his help for the bills, which means he won't be able to study as much and may not even get into college. If I use that money now for the bills, there won't be anything for his tuition." She sighed, feeling the weight of her worries.

"He's really having a tough time in his science class," she continued. "I don't know what it is about that teacher, that Ms. Epps. She seems to ride Ty pretty hard. He said that she seems mad at him all the time, but he's not sure what he did to cause it. Then there are problems with some of the kids on the block—some name-calling and pushing. I'm not sure what that's about, because he won't talk about that, either.

"I see him sinking, Calvin, and I don't know what to do about it. Look at all the things he's having trouble with—his brothers, the money worries, his job, his grades, Ms. Epps, the kids on the street. I don't know what to do to help him. I don't even know where to begin."

Reflection Questions ✦

Think about what you heard from Ty and now you've heard from his mother. Do you understand Ty better, now that you see the context of his life? When you first heard from Ty that he needed to work more to help his family with the bills, did you jump to any conclusions about his parents? (Be honest!) Now that you know more, do you feel more compassion for him and his family?

How many systems do you see influencing Ty in this situation? What systems support him? Which ones challenge him?

If you recall a basic truth, that each of us has power to influence the world, then what are the costs to all involved if you do nothing to intervene in these systemic problems?

✦ ✦

◆ CSCPs ARE SYSTEMIC

Recall the story in Chapter 1 of the little girl who threw stranded starfish back into the sea. It is true that we can help individual starfish by putting them back in the ocean, but if the water is polluted or poisonous, the starfish won't survive, in spite of our best efforts. Our work with students has to incorporate the environment and context in which our students live; otherwise the poison from that context will render our best efforts moot. This section of the chapter addresses the ocean of the starfish, the context of our students' lives.

Undeniably, the systems that surround children as they grow exert dramatic influences on development (Saginak, 2003). All young people are shaped developmentally by their environmental systems or context. It is in these contexts that young people learn the rules of living; values are acquired and explored and attitudes are shaped. It is also in these contexts that young people learn the rules of relating: to themselves, each other, their families, and society as a whole. These systems include broad and diffuse relationship webs, such as communities and cultures, as well as intermediate relationship webs, such as schools, to the most intimate of relationships, those with families and peers. The developmental resilience of young people will reflect the extent to which the systems in which they matured were healthy, respectful, and nurturing. This is where school counselors come in; they help young people understand and cope with the reality of the systems in which they are embedded.

The skills each child develops in response to his or her own unique systems context are as unique as the context. From community, culture, school, family, and peers, young people learn about the world, their place in the world, and by extension, themselves, in the process of socialization. According to Craig (1996), "socialization is the lifelong process by which individuals learn to become members of a social group, whether a family, a community, or a tribe. Becoming a member of a group involves recognizing and dealing with the social expectations of others. . . ." (p. 95). Each of these relationships teaches important social skills, and because of the connection between social "intelligence" (Goleman, 1995) and life success, it is no leap to state that systemic components in the CSCP are crucial to students' overall K–12 success. These systemic components are programmatic responses to the needs of communities, cultures, schools, families, and peer groups in which our students are embedded (Blustein & Noumair, 1996).

In a systemic view of development, it is essential that school counselors be mindful of two rules of systems:

1. All actions within a system affect all members of that system. Much like all elements of a mobile move when one element is touched, all parts of a system resonate if there is a disturbance anywhere in the system.
2. Young people can be profoundly affected by the values and attitudes that are directly or indirectly taught through that system.

Issues

Community. From the broadest perspective, young people are a part of a community—both geographic and sociological. Our geographic boundaries shrink every day; young people with access to the media are bombarded daily with messages about the state of the world and their place in that world, often to the detriment of the child. Excessive violence, gratuitous sexuality, and rampant consumerism are plainly visible in the ethos of the United States. Violence and sexuality are part of young people's everyday lives—from newscasts, to video games, to movies, music, and television talk shows.

Rampant consumerism is a product of our capitalist society. Regardless of family income, in this competitive, capitalistic society, it's not enough. Our market-driven, advertisement-saturated culture makes everyone feel inadequate; the goal of the marketing profession is to make us want things we don't have (Fox, 1994). It's little wonder that young people, who are painfully status- and self-conscious, feel the effects of peer pressure to have bigger, more, better, newer, biggest, newest, best. It's a race with no winners (except in the corporate world), and young people are played for all they are worth, because marketing an image to young people is big business.

In addition to the reality of our sociological community, we now see how technology is reducing our geographic community. Computers are both a gift and a curse in modern society. We can communicate around the world, access information, transact holiday shopping, and produce volumes of work in a fraction of the time it took a short decade ago. However, it is also a dangerous toy in the family den; through it, pedophiles access new victims, threats of violence are delivered, young people withdraw further from meaningful human contact, and new addictions are fostered.

Culture.   It would be a mistake to try to summarize all the multicultural literature in this book, and oversimplifying would be disrespectful of the members of those cultures. It would also be a mistake to assume that you, the reader, have not had any exposure to multicultural education. A synthesized theory of identity development was presented in the discussion of a holistic program, and identity development for persons of Difference is an important part of personal/social development. Recall that diversity can be experienced through cultural affiliation, gender, sexual orientation, socioeconomic class, being differently abled, or many other diversity constructs. Diversity is any aspect of our lives that makes us feel different from others; some experience this as negative, but others experience it as a positive influence.

It is crucial that school counselors are aware of how cultural values and attitudes are learned from the cultural context(s) of our lives (Payne, 2003). These cultural contexts can include, but are not limited to:

> *Attitudes of society in general*: Whispered or sotto voce comments, graffitti, television shows, movies, music, magazine ads (for example, that communicate a Eurocentric vision of beauty)
>
> *Attitudes of significant adults*: Jokes and comments made by family, teachers, and other significant adults
>
> *Attitudes of peers*: Teasing, bullying, or provocation or aggressive actions of peers

Schools.   In Chapter 2, we discussed schools as social institutions, and you were invited to consider dehumanizing schools and developmentally appropriate, effective schools. As we contemplate the effect of systems on our students, we must be aware of the values, messages, attitudes, and rules that are taught in our schools. We must examine how young people are taught to relate to each other, themselves, and the world around them. If the messages taught are "Don't trust anyone; they will hurt you"; "Don't trust yourself; you're stupid (lazy, crazy, incompetent . . .)"; "Don't try; it won't do any good"; or "Don't care; no one cares for you," then the cycle of pain, fear, hatred, and self-loathing will be perpetuated.

Families.   School counselors must also be aware of the influence of families, students' primary social context, on students' social, emotional, and cognitive development (Craig, 1996). These influences are two-directional and mutually reciprocal, with complicated and unpredictable interrelationships conveying rules, expectations, and experiences between members and across generations (Craig). Even within the same family, each person experiences the family unit and family events in a unique and idiosyncratic way (See Dinkmeyer, Dinkmeyer, and Sperry [1987] for a discussion of this concept in Adlerian counseling; see Hanna and Brown [1999] for a discussion of this concept in family systems counseling).

One of the primary roles of the family is as a socializing agent, as the family "interprets for the child the outside society and its culture. . . . Parents express their cultural values to their children in their attitudes toward such daily choices as food, clothing, friends, education and play" (Craig, 1996, p. 94). The challenge, especially in the current social reality of the United States, is that "the more diverse the social fabric [of society], the more pressure exists on the family system" (p. 94) to teach and perpetuate the family's unique values. The struggle of the family to teach these values determines the influence of the family system on the children directly, and on their schools indirectly.

The influence of families can range from positive, nurturing, motivating, and empowering (Schickedanz, Schickedanz, Forsyth, & Forsyth, 2001, p. 467), through ambivalent, neglectful, and overtly hateful and destructive (McWhirter, McWhirter, McWhirter, & McWhirter, 1998). When this influence is positive, children learn positive social skills. According to Hartup (as cited in Bee, 1997, p. 305), development of social skills and social relationships depends on both *vertical* and *horizontal* relationships. In vertical relationships, attachment is between the young person and someone with greater social knowledge, such as a parent, older child, or mentoring adult, and is characterized by reciprocity—when the child requests attention, the person with greater social power responds with nurturance. It is from this nurturance that the young person develops internal models of appropriate interaction and basic social skills. Different social skills are learned through horizontal relationships, in which social power is equal and interaction is egalitarian; it is from these relationships that young people learn cooperation, competition, and intimacy.

Unfortunately, when this learning is not possible, children are left with socially inadequate skills, or skills that foster domination and/or violence—a lesson many young people learn from their homes, where they witness violence daily (McWhirter, McWhirter, McWhirter, & McWhirter, 1998; Tolan & Guerra, 1998). In fact, violence that is witnessed most often by young people is relationship violence, in which one family member or "loved" one assaults another. When family stability is missing, we have good documentation of the negative effects (McWhirter, McWhirter, McWhirter, & McWhirter, 1998). Communitywide economic instability, stagnation, intolerance, poor health care (mental and physical), poor childcare, and a host of other problems can cause increased stress in the home. This stress often resonates with stress and vulnerability in the family system, increasing the risk for divorce, family violence, neglect, substance abuse and addiction, and mental health problems, which then resonate with increased stress on the children living in the home (McWhirter, McWhirter, McWhirter, & McWhirter, 1998).

These problems have a direct correlation with academic achievement, career development, and personal/social life functioning. For example, Noble (2000) found that students whose parents earn less than $36,000 a year or who have experienced three or more major problems at home (e.g., parental unemployment, chronic health problems, death, separation or divorce, or the need to work to help support the family) are more than twice as likely to be low academic achievers as high academic achievers (p. 15). According to Schickedanz, Schickedanz, Forsyth, and Forsyth, (2001), "[p]arents . . . can affect their children's cognitive performance by creating an environment that leads to positive emotions and mood states,

[as] [r]esearch demonstrates that a sad or angry mood leads to poorer performance at cognitive tasks like those children perform in school" (p. 467). These family stressors also have a direct correlation with more serious behaviors, such as school dropout, substance abuse and addiction, teenage pregnancy and risky sexual behaviors, delinquency, violence, and suicide (McWhirter, McWhirter, McWhirter, & McWhirter, 1998).

As families change, emotional support for children often becomes uncertain. Chaos in the family results in chaos in the student's life, and traditional support systems of extended family members are not always ready, willing, or available to pick up the slack. As a result, young people are often adrift emotionally, seeking significance and safety from others like themselves. The result is affiliation with other disenfranchised youth—a gang (McWhirter, McWhirter, McWhirter, & McWhirter, 1998), which we will examine next.

Peers.   According to Saginak (2003), it is through interactions with peer groups in addition to the family system that students develop a sense of identity and learn how to function as independent adults in society. "Peer groups help adolescents resolve internal conflicts and reduce anxiety by serving as sounding boards without arousing guilt or anxiety, respecting competencies as seen in social and athletic skills, and providing honest and critical feedback about behaviors and personal attributes" (p. 57). Peers model behaviors, teach values, and promote select attitudes—some to the benefit and some to the detriment of the student. "Just as peer groups can exert positive peer pressure such as leadership skills, they can also exert negative peer pressure in the form of deviance and antisocial behavior" (p. 59). There are a variety of peer groupings.

Cliques are small, socially cohesive groups of friends who share similar ages, socioeconomic status, interests, attitudes, and preferences (Dunphy, as cited in Muuss, 1988). They have the ability to exert extreme pressure on their members to maintain structure and organization (Saginak, 2003).

Crowds are larger social groups, usually made up of several cliques. They "are not as cohesive as cliques, individuals are not necessarily friends, and their value structures tend to be more varied than those of cliques" (Saginak, 2003).

Peer clusters are youth who tend to engage in deviant, antisocial behavior; they have a tendency to gravitate toward each other, forming peer clusters. These are small subsystems that are highly organized, maintain rigid boundaries, and are highly resistant to change. These groupings often enforce compliance through physical intimidation, eventually developing into gangs (Saginak, 2003).

Gangs are organized structured groups that form for a common purpose, usually involving unlawful or criminal behavior. "It is the breakdown of homes, schools, and communities that has lead to the prevalence of gangs in today's society. Many teens feel isolated in their families, misunderstood within their school buildings, and disengaged from their communities, and they are seeking connections elsewhere" (Saginak, 2003, p. 59).

Reflection Moment ◆

Think about the effects your community, culture, family, and peers have had on your development. What did you learn from each system? Take a moment and list five of your deepest, most closely held values. Now, one by one, examine which system(s) taught you that value, which system(s) challenged those values, and how you felt about yourself as you battled that system.

◆ ◆

Prototypes

Developmental Assets.   In an attempt to understand resilience in young people, the Search Institute has examined and conducted research to determine those conditions that allow young people to thrive. "All children and youth need a stable, positive sense of self and an ability to increasingly regulate themselves, a belief in their overall competence and skills at social problem-solving, and a connection to caring adults" (Starkman, Scales, & Roberts, 1999, p. 7). To accomplish these goals, the Institute has outlined 40 Developmental Assets, 20 "external" assets and 20 "internal" assets (see Table 3.1).

TABLE 3.1 ◆ Forty Developmental Assets

Category	Asset Name and Definition
	External Assets
Support	1. **Family support**—Family life provides high levels of love and support.
	2. **Positive family communication**—Young person and her or his parent(s) communicate positively, and young person is willing to seek advice and counsel from parent(s).
	3. **Other adult relationships**—Young person receives support from three or more nonparent adults.
	4. **Caring neighborhood**—Young person experiences caring neighbors.
	5. **Caring school climate**—School provides a caring, encouraging environment.
	6. **Parent involvement in schooling**—Parent(s) are actively involved in helping young person succeed in school.
Empowerment	7. **Community values youth**—Young person perceives that adults in the community value youth.
	8. **Youth as resources**—Young people are given useful roles in the community.
	9. **Service to others**—Young person serves in the community one hour or more per week.
	10. **Safety**—Young person feels safe at home, at school, and in the neighborhood.
Boundaries and Expectations	11. **Family boundaries**—Family has clear rules and consequences, and monitors the young person's whereabouts.
	12. **School boundaries**—School provides clear rules and consequences.
	13. **Neighborhood boundaries**—Neighbors take responsibility for monitoring young people's behavior.
	14. **Adult role models**—Parent(s) and other adults model positive, responsible behavior.
	15. **Positive peer influence**—Young person's best friends model responsible behavior.
	16. **High expectations**—Both parent(s) and teachers encourage the young person to do well.
Constructive Use of Time	17. **Creative activities**—Young person spends three or more hours per of Timeweek in lessons or practice in music, theater, or other arts.
	18. **Youth programs**—Young person spends three or more hours per week in sports, clubs, or organizations at school and/or in the community.

(continued)

TABLE 3.1 ◆ (Continued)

Category	Asset Name and Definition
	19. **Religious community**—Young person spends one or more hours per week in activities in a religious institution.
	20. **Time at home**—Young person is out with friends "with nothing special to do" two or fewer nights per week.

Internal Assets

Category	Asset Name and Definition
Commitment to Learning	21. **Achievement motivation**—Young person is motivated to do well in school.
	22. **School engagement**—Young person is actively engaged in learning.
	23. **Homework**—Young person reports doing at least one hour of homework every school day.
	24. **Bonding to school**—Young person cares about her or his school.
	25. **Reading for pleasure**—Young person reads for pleasure three or more hours per week.
Positive Values	26. **Caring**—Young person places high value on helping other people.
	27. **Equality and social justice**—Young person places high value on promoting equality and reducing hunger and poverty.
	28. **Integrity**—Young person acts on convictions and stands up for her or his beliefs.
	29. **Honesty**—Young person "tells the truth even when it is not easy."
	30. **Responsibility**—Young person accepts and takes personal responsibility.
	31. **Restraint**—Young person believes it is important not to be sexually active or to use alcohol or other drugs.
Social Competencies	32. **Planning and decision making**—Young person knows how to plan ahead and make choices.
	33. **Interpersonal competence**—Young person has empathy, sensitivity, and friendship skills.
	34. **Cultural competence**—Young person has knowledge of and comfort with people of different cultural/racial/ethnic backgrounds.
	35. **Resistance skills**—Young person can resist negative peer pressure and dangerous situations.
	36. **Peaceful conflict resolution**—Young person seeks to resolve conflict nonviolently.
Positive Identity	37. **Personal power**—Young person feels he or she has control over "things that happen to me."
	38. **Self-esteem**—Young person reports having a high self-esteem.
	39. **Sense of purpose**—Young person reports that "my life has a purpose."
	40. **Positive view of personal future**—Young person is optimistic about her or his personal future.

The external assets consist of the relationships and opportunities that are provided to young people, including Support, Empowerment, Boundaries and Expectations, and Constructive Use of Time. The internal assets, those values and skills young people develop that are used for self-governance, include Commitment to Learning, Positive Values, Social Competencies, and Positive Identity.

The Developmental Assets weave all systems together to create the solid fabric of support for students. Family, peers, school, and community are all connected in ways to facilitate healthy development for each child. In fact, Starkman, Scales, and Roberts (1999) report that the more assets a child experiences, the more likely it is that child will succeed in school and make healthy choices in terms of alcohol and drugs. Furthermore, "young people who are already vulnerable and at high risk of making poor health choices and being unsuccessful in school and other areas of life—because of abuse, violence, or other developmental deficits—experience an even greater positive impact from having developmental assets in their lives" (p. 13).

Because these assets can be directly correlated with academic success, schools have been very receptive to learning about the assets. The Search Institute has compiled these insights into numerous resources for schools (administrators, teachers, counselors, and other school professionals), parents, community leaders and churches, and students themselves, and has been actively promoting this message of hope and resilience.

Multisystemic Intervention. Taken from a community perspective, Laveman (2000) described "a community-based agency that counsels with adolescents who are at moderate to high risk of developmental defeat because their behavior either threatens their health or jeopardizes their future. . . . [This approach] teaches counselors how to trace consistent underlying patterns that are embedded in an adolescent's life across subsystem boundaries so that problems at home, school, or in the community can be viewed in a uniform manner and treated within the relational context of the family and community systems." This approach has great promise for helping young people make new choices because it views all problems as resonating in all areas of a person's life: home, school, friendships, and the community.

Using solutions-focused approaches, Laveman's (2000) approach empowers adolescents through collaboration, the expansion of strengths, the awareness of the reciprocity of effects between individuals and the systems of their lives, and empowering young people to take responsibility for their lives. All parts of the adolescent's life are involved in the change process, as counselors work to identify strengths and challenges in eight life domains: residential, family, social, educational, vocational, medical, psychological, and legal. In each domain, the question "What gets you into trouble?" is asked, and when the question yields a conflict-free area, the student is asked what he or she does differently in this area than in the conflict-filled areas. These insights are used to design interventions for those areas in which the student gets into trouble; these are distilled down into one- or two-word themes. The same process of distillation of themes is done for other troublesome life domains, so that the young person and all the partners in these domains can share in an understanding of the systemic issues at work. Interventions are then designed in each subsystem, agreed to by the client and the partners of that subsystem, with the final responsibility for follow-through falling on the adolescent.

Laveman's (2000) view is that individual actions and choices affect all systems in the individual's life; challenges in a family, a classroom, a school, or a friendship group affect all the other systems. Bringing together the major representatives of all these systems communicates to the student that these persons care about the student. When all the partners in a student's life—parents, teachers, counselors, and administrators, outside therapists and peers who are also involved—are seated around the same table, working toward the same goal, there is a powerful incentive for the student to make new choices.

Finding similar effects, but writing from a school perspective, Keys and Lockhart (1999) applied multisystemic insights to working with families, peers, community, and the school. They focused on and described the role of the school counselor in multisystemic interventions: "School counselors who function within a multisystemic paradigm expand the traditional definition of consultant and coordinator to reflect an emphasis on systemic change and collaborative relationships with families and the broader community" (p. 104). With this redefined view of the student and school counseling, school counselors must adopt five new ways of working:

1. School counselors must be a liaison between the school and the community, facilitating and coordinating a school's efforts to contact and access community resources and services.

2. School counselors must function as a member of the team of school and community professionals dedicated to the delivery of "wraparound services" for students and their families. This means that services are designed around the needs of the family and are not agency- or school-driven and confined. Examples of the membership of such integrated service teams include representatives from social services, law enforcement, education, juvenile justice, welfare, mental and physical health, nutrition, and substance abuse programs.

3. School counselors have the group facilitation skills, consultation skills, and collaboration skills to function as the group process facilitator in a multisystemic service view, which would include establishing a warm environment, facilitating group norms, monitoring the group process to facilitate productive contributions by all members, building consensus, negotiating conflicts, and other tasks.

4. School counselors should empower themselves as social advocates who work "to effect changes in policy, organizational structure, and service delivery practices" within both the school building and the larger school system (p. 106).

5. Finally, school counselors should view themselves as family advocates, who can connect families with services in the school and in the community.

These interventions can have a profound effect on the systems in which our students live, and we can see the far-reaching and important effects we can have on the lives of students, their families, the entire school, and whole communities.

Reflection Moment ◆

What are your reactions as you read about these new visions of schools, school counseling, and systemic change? Think about your feelings right now. Are you enthused? Overwhelmed? Are you able to visualize these new services? Many new counselors report that these prototypes of multisystemic services are hard to conceptualize because they don't have a firm grasp on what comprehensive school counseling is, much less this expanded vision of service delivery. If this is the case for you, file this information away in the back of your mind and let it stay there until you've worked for a year or two in the field. Then you can revisit these prototypes and see if any of them might work for your school.

◆ ◆

CASE STUDY REVISITED ◆ Integration

Now that you have both a developmental and systemic view of Ty's life, what ideas do you have for interventions to help with the situation? What are the systemic issues you see? What resources are available to help him (think in terms of the prototypes presented in the second half of this chapter)? Evaluate his situation in terms of the Developmental Assets. What interventions are suggested by that evaluation?

APPLICATION (Possible portfolio artifacts are noted)

1. Take each one of the developmental prototypes presented in this chapter and apply them to someone you know well: a relative, your significant other, a friend. Interview that person to see if you can determine which of the prototypes seem to "fit" the life of the person you interview.

2. Enroll in a big brother/big sister program, or volunteer to mentor a child. As you get to know the young person, examine the student's life to ascertain her or his level of development in each of the domains. Then see which of the prototypes in the first part of the chapter would help you understand ways that this young person might benefit from your mentoring relationship. (Possible portfolio artifact)

3. With that same young person you're mentoring, examine the systems in which the child is embedded. Which ones are healthy and which ones are unhealthy? Evaluate the young person's life using the Developmental Assets listed in this chapter, or visit the website at

www.search-institute.com. How might you intervene to increase the assets in his or her life? (Possible portfolio artifact)

4. Expand your own multiple intelligences. Take each of the multiple intelligences and look for lessons that address the three domains. For example, what lessons can be gleaned from social insects that might provide a prototype for a problem in the personal/social domain? (Possible portfolio artifact)

5. Take a drive through the residential area for an inner-city school. Look at the systemic issues in the community. Identify the resources that would be helpful for the families living in that area.

6. Do a literature search on one of the prototypes presented in this chapter (i.e., multiple intelligences, hope, self-esteem, identity development, career portfolios) to expand your understanding of that prototype. What are the way(s) you can use this expanded knowledge of the prototype(s) to help students? (Possible portfolio artifact)

SUGGESTED READINGS

Brandan, N. (1994). *The six pillars of self-esteem.* New York: Bantam. This book defines self-esteem in terms of intentional practices that reinforce a healthy life direction. Many practical suggestions for developing self-esteem are provided that can help school counselors design counseling and curricular experiences to foster self-esteem in students.

Brookfield, S. D. (1987). *Developing critical thinkers: Challenging adults to explore alternative ways of*

thinking and acting. San Francisco: Jossey-Bass. The book contains wonderful insights into ways to help young people develop their critical thinking skills. While not written as a counseling manual, this book has many implications, both for counseling and for the developmental curriculum.

Gellatt, H. B. (1991). *Creative decision making using positive uncertainty.* Los Angeles: Crisp. Many school counselors are faced with helping students make important decisions in the face of uncertainty, and Gellatt offers ideas for reframing this stressful situation into one that is intuitively engaging for both counselor and student.

Goleman, D. (1995). *Emotional intelligence: Why it can matter more than IQ.* New York: Bantam. This book helps counselors understand and articulate to faculty and staff why the developmental curriculum is important. It provides a holistic perspective of what constitutes a well-functioning person in this society.

Hanna, S. M., & Brown, J. H. (1999). *The practice of family therapy: Key elements across prototypes* (2nd ed.). Belmont, CA: Brooks/Cole. This book is helpful for school counselors to understand the process of family counseling.

Hansen, L. S. (1997). *Integrative life planning: Critical tasks for career development and changing life patterns.* San Francisco: Jossey-Bass. This author writes about life-career planning from a holistic, existential view; this philosophy can help counselors to retain that holistic foundation while engaging students in discussions about their future.

King, P. M., & Kitchener, K. S. (1994). *Developing reflective judgment: Understanding and promoting intellectual growth and critical thinking in adolescents and adults.* San Francisco: Jossey-Bass. Since intellectual development and academic maturity are goals of the comprehensive school counseling program, counselors will benefit from an understanding of what their students are working to attain. This book provides many insights that can help counselors design counseling and curricular experiences to help students develop intellectually.

Lazear, D. (1999). *Eight ways of teaching: The artistry of teaching with multiple intelligences.* Arlington Heights, IL: SkyLight Training and Publishing. This book offers educators practical ideas for engaging students of all ages in the learning process, by designing learning experiences tailored to each student's individual intelligence constellation.

Payne, R. K. (2003). *A framework for understanding poverty* (3rd ed.). Highlands, TX: aha! Process. This invaluable resource helps counselors understand the dynamics of poverty, a community and cultural issue.

Pipher, M. (1994). *Reviving Ophelia: Saving the selves of adolescent girls.* New York: Ballantine. This book describes the challenges of growing up female in this culture.

Pollack, W. (1998). *Real boys: Rescuing our sons from the myths of boyhood.* New York: Henry Holt. This book outlines the challenges of growing up male in this culture.

Snyder, C. R. (1994). *The psychology of hope.* New York: Free Press. Detailing research into the concept of "hope," this author provides a prototype of hope that is teachable to students. Each component is then discussed in detail, providing insights that can help counselors in counseling and educating students, faculty, and parents.

Starkman, N., Scales, P. C., & Roberts, C. (1999). *Great places to learn: How asset-building schools help students succeed.* Minneapolis, MN: Search Institute. Any of the resources of the Search Institute (www.search-institute.com) would be very helpful for counselors; this book provides direct insights for school professionals in the process of using Developmental Assets as an organizing foundation for educational programs and services.

REFERENCES

Atkinson, D. R., Morten, G., & Sue, D. W. (1989). *Counseling American minorities: A cross-cultural perspective.* Dubuque, IA: Brown.

Bee, H. (1997). *The developing child* (8th ed.). New York: Longman.

Berens, L. V. (1988). *Please understand me: Empowering students of the 90's.* Huntington Beach, CA: Temperament Research Institute.

Blustein, D. L., & Noumair, D. A. (1996). Self and identity in career development: Implications for theory and practice. *Journal of Counseling & Development, 74,* 433–441.

Branden, N. (1994). *The six pillars of self-esteem.* New York: Bantam.

Briggs, K. C., & Myers, I. B. (1998). *Myers-Briggs Type Indicator* (3rd ed.). Palo Alto, CA: Consulting Psychologists Press.

Craig, G. J. (1996). *Human development* (7th ed.). Upper Saddle River, NJ: Prentice Hall.

D'Augelli, A. R. (1994). Identity development and sexual orientation: Toward a prototype of lesbian, gay, and bisexual development. In E. J. Trickett, R. J. Watts, & D. Birman (Eds.), *Human diversity: Perspectives on people in context* (pp. 312–333). San Francisco: Jossey-Bass.

Dinkmeyer, D. C., Dinkmeyer, Jr., D. C., & Sperry, L. (1987). *Adlerian counseling and psychotherapy* (2nd ed.). Columbus, OH: Merrill.

Dollarhide, C. T. (1997). Counseling for meaning in work and life: An integrated approach. *Journal for Humanistic Education and Development, 35,* 178–187.

Dollarhide, C. T. (2000). Career process and advising: Tools for the advisor. *NACADA Journal, 19*(2), 34–36.

Dunn, R., Dunn, K., & Price, G. E. (1996). *Learning Styles Inventory.* Lawrence, KS: Price Systems, Inc.

Dunn, R., & Griggs, S. A. (1988). *Learning styles: Quiet revolution in American secondary schools.* Reston, VA: National Association of Secondary School Principals.

Esters, I. G., & Ittenbach, R. F. (1999). Contemporary theories and assessments of intelligence: A primer. *Professional School Counseling, 2,* 373–376.

Fay, J., & Funk, D. (1995). *Teaching with love and logic: Taking control of the classroom.* Golden, CO: Love & Logic Press.

Fox, M. (1994). *The reinvention of work: A new vision of livelihood for our time.* San Francisco: Harper.

Gardner, H. (1983). *Frames of mind: The theory of multiple intelligences.* New York: Basic.

Gardner, H., & Hatch, T. (1989). Multiples intelligences go to school: Educational implications of the theory of multiple intelligences. *Educational Researcher, 18*(8), 4–10.

Gellatt, H. B. (1991). *Creative decision making using positive uncertainty.* Los Angeles: Crisp.

Gellatt, H. B. (1996). Developing a future sense. In R. Feller and G. Walz (Eds.), *Career transitions in turbulent times: Exploring work, learning, and careers* (pp. 387–394). Greensboro, NC: ERIC Counseling and Student Services Clearinghouse.

Goleman, D. (1995). *Emotional intelligence: Why it can matter more than IQ.* New York: Bantam.

Hanna, S. M., & Brown, J. H. (1999). *The practice of family therapy: Key elements across prototypes* (2nd ed.). Belmont, CA: Brooks/Cole.

Helms, J. E. (1994). The conceptualization of racial identity and other "racial" constructs. In E. J. Trickett, R. J. Watts, & D. Birman (Eds.), *Human diversity: Perspectives on people in context* (pp. 285–311). San Francisco: Jossey-Bass.

Henderson, S. J. (2000). "Follow your bliss": A process for career happiness. *Journal of Counseling and Development, 78,* 305–315.

Hewitt, J. P. (1998). *The myth of self-esteem: Finding happiness and solving problems in America.* New York: St. Martin's Press.

Keirsey, D. (1974). *Please understand me.* Del Mar, CA: Prometheus Nemisis.

Keys, S. G., & Lockhart, E. J. (1999). The school counselor's role in facilitating multisystemic change. *Professional School Counseling, 3,* 101–107.

Laveman, L. (2000). The Harmonium Project: A macrosystems approach to empowering adolescents. *Journal of Mental Health Counseling, 22*(1), 17–23.

Lazear, D. (1999). *Eight ways of teaching: The artistry of teaching with multiple intelligences.* Arlington Heights, IL: SkyLight Training and Publishing.

McWhirter, J. J., McWhirter, B. T., McWhirter, A. M., & McWhirter, E. H. (1998). *At-risk youth: A comprehensive response for counselors, teachers, psychologists, and human service professionals.* Pacific Grove, CA: Brooks/Cole.

Muuss, R. E. (1988). *Theories of adolescence* (5th ed.). New York: Random House.

Noble, J. (2000). Students' educational achievement: What helps or hinders? *The ASCA Counselor, 38,* 14–15.

Payne, R. K. (2003). *A framework for understanding poverty* (3rd ed.). Highlands, TX: aha! Process.

Pipher, M. (1994). *Reviving Ophelia: Saving the selves of adolescent girls.* New York: Ballantine.

Pollack, W. (1998). *Real boys: Rescuing our sons from the myths of boyhood.* New York: Henry Holt.

Saginak, K. A. (2003). A systems view of adolescents: The student in context. In C. T. Dollarhide and K. A. Saginak (Eds.), *School counseling in the secondary school: A comprehensive process and program* (pp. 49–62). Boston: Allyn and Bacon.

Scheer, J. (1994). Culture and disability: An anthropological point of view. In E. J. Trickett, R. J. Watts, & D. Birman (Eds.), *Human diversity: Perspectives on people in context* (pp. 244–260). San Francisco: Jossey-Bass.

Schickedanz, J. A., Schickedanz, D. I., Forsyth, P. D., & Forsyth, G. A. (2001). *Understanding children and adolescents* (4th ed.). Boston: Allyn and Bacon.

Snyder, C. R. (1994). *The psychology of hope.* New York: Free Press.

Starkman, N., Scales, P. C., & Roberts, C. (1999). *Great places to learn: How asset-building schools help students succeed.* Minneapolis, MN: Search Institute.

Stone, K. F., & Dillehunt, H. Q. (1978). *Self Science: The subject is me.* Santa Monica, CA: Goodyear.

Tolan, P. & Guerra, N. (1998). *What works in reducing adolescent violence: An empirical review of the field.* Boulder, CO: Center for the Study and Prevention of Violence.

Travers, J. F., Elliott, S. N., & Kratochwill, T. R. (1993). *Educational psychology: Effective teaching, effective learning.* Madison, WI: Brown & Benchmark.

4

SIX QUALITIES OF COMPREHENSIVE SCHOOL COUNSELING PROGRAMS, PART 2

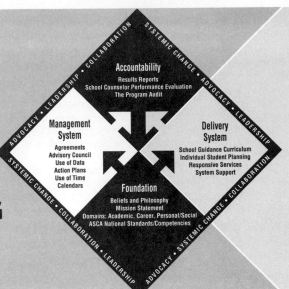

◆ LEARNING OBJECTIVES

By the end of this chapter, you will be able to

1. Understand and articulate the issues and prototypes to create a balanced CSCP
2. Understand and articulate the issues and prototypes to create a proactive CSCP
3. Understand and articulate the issues and prototypes in a CSCP that are infused into the academic agenda of the school
4. Understand and articulate the issues and prototypes to create a reflective CSCP
5. Demonstrate an understanding of how these prototypes apply in a case study

DOMAINS / ACTIVITIES / PARTNERS MODEL

	Academic Development ▼	Career Development ▼	Personal/ Social Development ▼			
Counseling	1a	1b	1c	5	6	7
Educating and Advocacy	2a	2b	2c	8	9	10
Consulting	3a	3b	3c	11	12	13
Leadership and Coordination	4a	4b	4c	14	15	16
	Students			Parents and Caregivers	Colleagues in Schools	Colleagues in Community

DOMAINS (spanning Academic Development, Career Development, Personal/ Social Development)

ACTIVITIES (left axis)

Students (spanning the first three columns)

PARTNERS IN THE PROCESS

CASE STUDY ◆ Mr. Paulson's Efforts

Mr. Paulson continued to think about Mrs. Bonté and Ty all day. This was his first year as a school counselor and he wanted to do the right thing, but wasn't sure what that was at this point. He figured that it was time to consult with his director of counseling.

The director of counseling for the high school, Bob Winters, had been with the school for over 25 years and had designed the program. Bob had seen many principals come and go, but the guidance service was still going strong. As a high school counselor, Bob learned that his job was primarily to schedule students, write the master schedule, coordinate the school-to-work program, coordinate the school's testing processes, secure information on scholarships and write recommendation letters, and help students get into college. When Calvin Paulson was hired, Bob finally had someone with whom he could share his burden, which he did gladly. Calvin and Bob shared the students evenly for scheduling, and Bob maintained much of the administrative work of which he was fond. Bob never really liked working with the students directly.

Knocking on Bob's door, Calvin asked for a couple of minutes of Bob's time. When he was invited in and seated, he gave a quick update. "I have this junior who is struggling in science, but wants to go to college. He's working hard to take care of his brothers and mom, to help pay bills when she got sick. He's a good kid, and I want to help. Mom is worried, too. The problem is that I'm not sure where to start. Do we have information on financial assistance for families? Or do you know of anyone I can call? Do you think I could meet with the family to...."

Bob cut him off at that point. "Whoa! Sorry, bucko, but I don't think that's really our job. We're not social services here—we're a school. And in this guidance office that's what we do—*guide* kids to college. We're just an add-on here; we don't have the authority to work with kids in their academics—science especially! You're not this kid's parent or this kid's social worker. And we sure as heck don't have time to do family counseling—we barely have time to do the things we are supposed to do, important things like scheduling and testing. That reminds me, here are the test packets for next week. You need to label each one with the student's name, student ID number, and home room...."

CHALLENGE QUESTIONS

Whose position do you identify with? Given what you've read to this point in this book, what reactions do you have to Mr. Winters' comments? If you were Mr. Paulson, what would your response be to Mr. Winters?

In the last chapter, we discussed two of the six qualities of a comprehensive school counseling program. Recall that, to be comprehensive, a school counseling program must be

◆ *Holistic*, addressing all aspects of the student's development;
◆ *Systemic*, addressing all persons with whom the student interacts and all systems of significance in the student's life;
◆ *Balanced*, addressing the primary activities of the school counselor—namely, counseling, educating and advocacy, consultation, and leadership and coordination;
◆ *Proactive*, addressing the effects of any experiences that may compromise the development of the students through prevention, intervention, and, sometimes, referral for treatment;
◆ *Infused into the academic curriculum,* addressing the extent to which the work of the CSCP is integrated into the general academic functions of the school; and
◆ *Reflective*, addressing accountability to our schools, our students, and ourselves for information about how our work influences students' lives.

To this point, we have discussed holistic and systemic issues in school counseling. In this chapter, we will discuss the need for balanced activities, proactive programming, ways to infuse the CSCP into the academic agenda, and what it means to be reflective. As with the last chapter, we will present the issues first, then we will present prototypes that can provide ideas for the content and focus of your CSCP—what that quality looks like in a comprehensive school counseling program.

◆ CSCPs ARE BALANCED

Issues. There are various ways to define "balance" in comprehensive school counseling programs, and each of these definitions helps us to understand how to conceptualize the work of the school counselor. In comprehensive school counseling programs, balance needs to be maintained

1. In terms of balanced concern for academic, career, and personal/social issues (Campbell & Dahir, 1997), which are the domains we will see in the Domains/Activities/Partners (DAP) model for a delivery system presented in Chapter 6
2. In terms of balance within the activities of the school counselor—namely, counseling, educating and advocacy, consulting, and leadership and coordination (Dollarhide & Saginak, 2003), which are the activities we will see in the DAP model presented in Chapter 6

The ASCA School Counselor Performance Standards addressed in this chapter are

5.1 The professional school counselor provides a comprehensive and balanced school counseling program in collaboration with school staff.

The CACREP Standards for School Counseling Programs addressed in this chapter are

A.2 relationship of the school counseling program to the academic and student services program in the school;

A.7 the role of racial, ethnic, and cultural heritage, nationality, socioeconomic status, family structure, age, gender, sexual orientation, religious and spiritual beliefs, occupation, physical and mental status, and equity issues in school counseling;

A.8 knowledge and understanding of community, environmental, and institutional opportunities that enhance, as well as barriers that impede student academic, career, and personal/social success and overall development;

B.3 integration of the school counseling program into the total school curriculum by systematically providing information and skills training to assist pre-K–12 students in maximizing their academic, career, and personal/social development;

B.7 knowledge of prevention and crisis intervention;

C.1 (b) design, implementation, monitoring, and evaluation of comprehensive developmental school counseling programs (e.g., the ASCA National Standards for School Counseling Programs) including an awareness of various systems that affect students, school, and home;

C.1 (d) identification of student academic, career, and personal/social competencies and the implementation of processes and activities to assist students in achieving these competencies;

C.2 (d) issues that may affect the development and functioning of students (e.g., abuse, violence, eating disorders, attention deficit hyperactivity disorder, childhood depression and suicide); and

C.2 (h) approaches to recognizing and assisting children and adolescents who may use alcohol or other drugs or who may reside in a home where substance abuse occurs.

3. In terms of balanced concern for all partners in the process—namely, students, parents, colleagues, and community (Dollarhide & Saginak, 2003; Keys & Lockhart, 1999), which are the partners we will see in the DAP model discussed in Chapter 6
4. In terms of balance between prevention goals (developmental goals) and intervention goals (also known as treatment or remediation) (Baker, 2000), which we will examine in terms of the need for proactive programs in a CSCP program

What happens when the school counseling program is not balanced in all these ways? Out-of-balance conditions in these four areas result in problems in the work of the counselor, which are easiest to identify in terms of out-of-balance activities. Numerous studies have been conducted into the work of the school counselor documenting the need for reevaluation of the priorities for various counselor activities. In their study, Burnham and Jackson (2000) examined how counselors allocated time within their programs. They found the majority of respondents (69 of 80) reported involvement with nonguidance activities. Of their 80 respondents, 65 percent reported being involved with student records, 56 percent with scheduling, 49 percent with transcripts, 44 percent with office sitting, 38 percent with bus duty, and 28 percent with attendance. Overall, their respondents reported time spent in nonguidance activities ranging from 1 percent to 88 percent of their time, with an average amount of time being 25 percent. This means that fully one-fourth of their respondents' time was spent on nonguidance work. Clearly, balance within the activities of the program will reduce the likelihood that time will be siphoned off for nonguidance activities.

Prototype

Balanced Counselor Activities.   Balanced concern for the domains and partners has been discussed in the previous chapter, as we examined the ways that CSCPs focus on the needs of individual students and on the needs of the systemic influences of community, peers, and family. Balanced concern for prevention and intervention, in terms of the content of programs offered in the CSCP, will be discussed in the next section of this chapter. This leaves the question of balance within the activities of the CSCP to discuss.

Let's focus on the activities of the school counselor, which have been described in the literature in very consistent terms. Baker (2000) describes appropriate activities as counseling, proactive developmental curriculum programming, consulting, referral and coordination, providing information, enhancing transitions, and assessment. Similarly, Schmidt (1999) defines a comprehensive school counseling program as consisting of "counseling, consulting, coordinating, and appraisal services offered in response to the identified needs, goals, and objectives . . . given priority as the result of adequate assessment and analysis of students', parents', and teachers' needs . . . as a series of processes that include planning, organizing, implementing, and evaluating" (p. 39).

In this book, we will use the Domains/Activities/Partners model (Dollarhide & Saginak, 2003) to highlight how services should be delivered (see Chapter 6 for a complete discussion of this and other models for the delivery system). The Domains/Activities/ Partners model highlights the primary activities as *counseling, educating and advocacy, consulting*, and *leadership and coordination.* Counseling refers to individual and group counseling, as well as making referrals as a means of bringing closure to counseling relationships. It is the most essential activity that students indicate they want from the school counselor (Hutchinson & Bottorff, 1986; Wiggins & Moody, 1987).

Educating refers to providing the developmental curriculum, facilitating transitions, advisement, placement, and assessment and appraisal. Advocacy refers to activities that educate with passion, those activities that enhance others' empathy for students, schools, families, the comprehensive school counseling program, and better human relationships.

Consulting refers to problem solving, referring, enhancing communications, and mediation. Leadership involves developing and maintaining the vision of the comprehensive school counseling program and promoting the importance of a developmentally appropriate learning environment. Coordination refers to the management of logistics to bring programs to the partners of the school counselor. Leadership and coordination include public relations, committee service, schoolwide programs, and accountability for the work of the professionals in the CSCP.

It is important to know that balance among these activities does not mean "equal time." It refers to the need to balance activities based on the needs of the partner being helped.

Reflection Moment ◆

Have you ever found yourself in a professional situation where your sense of balance was at odds with those of the leadership of the program? How did that feel? What did you do to address that out-of-balance situation?

◆ ◆

CASE STUDY ◆ Integration

Mr. Paulson is in a school guidance program (the term "guidance" is used very intentionally there). Based on what Mr. Winters said, what are the ways in which this program is out of balance?

CASE STUDY CONTINUED

Mr. Paulson wonders where the school system has failed Ty. Or has it? Ty stated that he is interested in college, but he is making choices under stress that are likely to limit his academic and vocational opportunities. Mr. Paulson wonders what he could have done to be more helpful to Ty. Has Ty ever worked with a counselor on his choices? Has he ever had any classroom lessons on stress and stress management? And what did Ty mean when he said he "is just not going to take it any more"? Is he headed for a violent confrontation with the people in the neighborhood? How can that be prevented?

◆CSCPs ARE PROACTIVE

Issues. Being "proactive" means the counselors in a CSCP work to prevent problems before they become serious impediments to the success of the student. But because school counselors do not control all aspects of the students' lives, being proactive also means working to mitigate challenges to the students' success; these efforts involve intervention and treatment, also known as secondary prevention and tertiary intervention.

To understand what is meant by the terms of prevention, intervention, and treatment, school counselors must understand the concept of being "at-risk." McWhirter, McWhirter, McWhirter, and McWhirter (1998, p. 7) define at-risk in terms of risk from "dangerous future events" (substance use, abuse, and addiction; early sexual behavior and/or unplanned pregnancy; early departure from school; criminal and/or violent behaviors). They identify five categories on a continuum of risk status (p. 8):

Minimal Risk. Students with positive socioeconomic demographics; positive family, school, and interpersonal interaction; and limited psychosocial and environmental stressors (McWhirter et al., 1988, p. 8). These students would benefit from prevention programming to help them maintain healthy choices in case of future challenges.

Remote Risk.   Students with negative socioeconomic demographics; less positive family, school, and peer interaction; and some psychosocial and environmental stressors (McWhirter et al., 1988, p. 8). These students also would benefit from prevention programming to help them maintain healthy choices in the face of their challenges.

High Risk.   Students with negative socioeconomic demographics; negative interpersonal interaction; numerous psychosocial/environmental stressors; and development of personal at-risk markers: negative attitudes, emotions, and skills deficiencies (McWhirter et al., 1988, p. 8). These students would benefit from intervention programming to help them change their attitudes and to help them improve their coping skills.

Imminent Risk.   Students with negative socioeconomic demographics; negative interaction with others; numerous psychosocial and environmental stressors; development of personal at-risk markers: negative attitudes, emotions, and skills deficiencies; and the development of dangerous unhealthy behaviors (McWhirter et al., 1988, p. 8). These students also would benefit from intervention programming to help them focus on their choices and their responsibility to change, and to help them improve their life skills.

At-Risk Activity.   Students with negative socioeconomic demographics; overall negative interactions; numerous psychosocial and environmental stressors that escalate into more high-risk behaviors; development of personal at-risk markers, such as negative attitudes and skills deficiencies that place them solidly in the at-risk category (McWhirter et al., 1988, p. 8). This includes the development of gateway behaviors and activities that put them at risk for other categories of risk behaviors (McWhirter et al., 1988, p. 8). For these students, treatment would be warranted.

These authors caution that professionals working with adolescents not use the term "at-risk" to denote students or families doomed to failure; rather, the term is to be used to describe students who are "at-risk" in terms of their context. It is important to remember that risk status is usually related to poverty, racism, and the limited economic opportunities in impoverished communities. The term "at promise" suggests a more optimistic and empowering view of the stressors in the environment; the student is "at promise" for resilience and coping.

In terms of the search for identity, some students have relatively stable internal parameters, boundaries beyond which they will not go because they know at least that much about themselves. "Drugs are not me," or "Piercing that part of my body grosses me out." Proactive prevention programming can help these students to maintain healthy choices. These are students who are at minimal and remote risk.

Other students may be suffering from what Marcia (as cited in Craig, 1996) described as "identity diffusion," in which the young person lacks a sense of direction or motivation to determine a life direction. To avoid dealing with their identity crisis, these young people seek activities that provide immediate gratification, or they experiment "in a random fashion with all possibilities" (p. 439). These students don't know who they are, who they want to be, or where they belong. Counselors will see them as a result of their lack of motivation (excessive absenteeism or chronic truancy), as a result of their method(s) of immediate gratification (unwanted pregnancy, substance abuse and/or addiction, poor impulse control in the classroom, excessive risk-taking), or as a result of their bizarre behaviors as they experiment with the style of the month. Intervention can help these students, who can be thought of as being at high risk and imminent risk.

Finally, for still others, the identity crisis has been resolved; the problem is that the student despises the self she or he has found. These students engage in seriously self-destructive behaviors, such as self-cutting, self-mutilation, eating disorders, suicidal behaviors and risk-taking, and substance abuse. The differences between identity diffusion and identity loathing are the intensity of the self-inflicted damage and the intentionality of the act of self-destruction. Treatment is warranted for these students, who clearly are involved in at-risk activity.

Prototype. School counselors must be able to see the connection between risk status, behavioral manifestations, and comprehensive counseling programmatic responses. These responses are categorized into three levels: prevention, intervention, and treatment (McWhirter et al., 1998).

Prevention. The prevention level includes programmatic responses that are designed to enhance resilience and prevent at-risk characteristics. Examples of prevention efforts are schoolwide programs for excellence, character education, the developmental curriculum delivered in the classroom, and working toward an environment of respect and inclusion.

Intervention. The intervention level includes programmatic responses that are designed to arrest the deterioration of existing at-risk characteristics, or to mitigate against the effects of psychosocial or educational stressors. Examples of these responses include individual counseling, group counseling, family interventions and home visits, consultation with teachers, consultation with parents, and conflict mediation between teachers and students.

Treatment. The treatment level includes programmatic responses that are designed to address fully developed at-risk behaviors. In some cases, counselors can adequately address the treatment needs of students through groups and one-on-one counseling, but often, students who need treatment are best served by mental health professionals in the community. Outside counseling for students who need treatment does not imply that counselors are not trained to provide such assistance to students. Rather, outside therapy for students who need treatment reflects the intensity of treatment (often students in treatment need several sessions each week), and the necessity of medications to assist with the therapeutic process (which counselors are not authorized to prescribe).

A close examination of the at-risk categories and the accompanying descriptions suggests there are specific connections between what students are experiencing and their danger for at-risk behaviors. Examining both resilience and risk can lead to important insights for counselors. According to McWhirter et al. (1998, p. 83), there are five characteristics—the "five Cs of competency"—that discriminate young people who are at high risk from those who are at low risk. The five characteristics are (a) critical school competencies (basic academic skills and academic survival skills), (b) a concept of self and self-esteem, (c) positive communication skills, (d) effective coping abilities, and (e) control (decision-making skills, delay of gratification, and purpose in life). These five characteristics can serve as a template to understand the differences between prevention, intervention, and treatment. Prevention efforts would be undertaken to enhance or increase students' acquisition of the five Cs of competency. Intervention efforts would begin as counselors notice students struggling in one or more competency, or if the counselor became aware that the student was moving from a lesser risk category into high or imminent risk. Finally, treatment efforts would begin as counselors notice students exhibiting serious struggles that indicate the student is in the at-risk activity category.

As you may have already noticed, the "five Cs of competency" (McWhirter et al., 1998, p. 83) resonate with the three developmental domains of academic, career, and personal/social development, as well as with the Developmental Assets discussed in the previous chapter. Now that you have had a chance to reflect on the levels of at-risk status and differences between prevention, intervention, and treatment, let's look at why CSCPs must be integrated into the academic curriculum, the fifth quality of a CSCP.

Reflection Moment ◆

What was your risk status when you were young? Did that status change over time? If so, what caused it to change? How will these insights help you when you become a school counselor?

◆ ◆

CASE STUDY REVISITED ◆ Integration

Using the at-risk continuum, identify where Ty would be placed in terms of his risk status and explain your reasoning. What comprehensive counseling programmatic response—prevention, intervention, or treatment—would you recommend for Ty?

Assess Ty in terms of the 5 Cs of competency. With which competencies does Ty need help? What would you do to help him develop, refine, or enhance those competencies?

CASE STUDY CONTINUED

Mr. Paulson thought about Ty's struggle in his science class. Since Mr. Paulson's arrival in this school, he had not really had the chance to meet the faculty. Perhaps he might go to Ms. Epps' office and introduce himself. Maybe it was time to become familiar with the academic side of the school, so that if Ty gave him permission to talk with Ms. Epps about his college plans, she might be open to talking about ways Ty could bring up his grade. It couldn't hurt to try, right? He decided to visit Ms. Epps in her office.

As he walked toward the science wing of the school, he tried to compose the best approach. The last thing he wanted was to come across as accusing Ms. Epps of anything, of being too hard or unfair. He'll just see how receptive she might be to the developmental agenda and to the expertise he has to offer in terms of student development.

After he introduced himself, she insisted that he come in and have a seat. Right away, he could tell she would become a strong ally to the school counseling office. "Tell me what I can do to help you teach your kids," he began.

She jumped right into that offer. "In my previous school, the counselors would come to our classes and teach various topics that met our standards and also met theirs," she offered. "They would present on healthy choices in terms of drugs or cigarettes, for example, when we talked about biology. I'd love to have you come to my classes so that they are getting more than just academics. Do you have any groups going for students? I have a couple of kids who I need to refer to you...."

"This is wonderful!" thought Calvin. "Perhaps I will be able to help more kids than just Ty," and he smiled as Ms. Epps talked about her concerns for her kids.

◆ CSCPs ARE INTEGRATED INTO THE ACADEMIC AGENDA

Issues.   ASCA (2003) enjoins all counselors to design programs that reach all students, yet it is clear that, in some schools, the school counseling program is considered an extra "service" or an "add-on." In this view, school counseling is not comprehensive; it does not reach all students. As you will recall from Chapter 1, there are multiple philosophies of school counseling, and each focuses on one or two functions of a school counselor. In the guidance/career emphasis, school counselors were administrators who provided career direction and college information; in the mental health emphasis, school counselors remain in their offices providing "therapy"; in the developmental guidance emphasis, school counselors worked hard to get into the classrooms. Now, in the Comprehensive School Counseling Program movement as represented in the ASCA National Model (ASCA, 2003), school counselors are full partners in the educational activities of the entire school.

Prototype
Curricular and Programmatic Integration.   Derived from the National Standards for Student Academic, Career, and Personal/Social Development (guidelines for school counseling programs across the country [ASCA, 2003; Campbell & Dahir, 1997]) most states have developed their own state-level standards. These state-level standards comprise the developmental curriculum for which school counselors are responsible, just as teachers are responsible for the academic curriculum. (See Appendix B for the complete text of the ASCA National Standards for Student Academic, Career, and Personal/Social Development.)

As a professional school counselor, you are responsible for delivering this curriculum, as will be discussed in detail in Chapter 8. In addition, infusion with the academic agenda means that school counselors are not penalized for asking to see students as appropriate; it means that the school counseling program is viewed as essential for students' development by our partners in the schools. So infusion is a broad concept, addressing the extent to which the CSCP is viewed as integral to the educational process by administrators and faculty; and it is specific to include the extent to which teachers allow students out of class to see the counselor and the extent to which counselors are allowed access to students during the course of the day to provide prevention and intervention programming.

Specific ways to infuse the CSCP prevention and intervention activities are as varied as the schools that are served. Based on the counselor's ability to communicate a vision of a comprehensive school counseling program, allies can be recruited from school boards, administration, other student support professionals, teachers, staff, janitors—and these allies can be integral to the counselor's efforts to reach out to all students.

Reflection Moment ◆

What is your reaction when thinking about how to talk to teachers about the possibility of using classroom time to deliver the developmental curriculum? In Chapter 8, you will be challenged to think about how to integrate the developmental curriculum with the academic curriculum using multiple intelligences. Many states have developed a "crosswalk" that connects the developmental curriculum with the academic curriculum of the state. How would you use such a document to support your request for classroom time?

◆ ◆

CASE STUDY REVISITED ◆ Integration

What if Ms. Epps had not been receptive to Mr. Paulson? What could he have said that would not have violated Ty's confidentiality?

CASE STUDY CONTINUED

Later that day, Calvin was still pondering what else he could do to help Ty, while absently applying labels to the test packets, when Bob popped his head into Calvin's office. "By the way," he said casually, "don't forget that I will need your performance evaluation for this year on my desk by the end of the week. I will meet with the principal next week to discuss it; then we'll meet with you to give you our feedback on ways to improve for this next year."

Calvin shuddered involuntarily. He wondered how he would ever document his work with a student like Ty, a "work in progress." But then, aren't all students still "in progress"? Shaking off his worry about Ty, he said to Bob, "Do you have an example that I can use to look at while I write mine?"

Mr. Winters shook his head. "No, this is the first year we've had to do them. Just write up what you've done this year in a paragraph or two. Don't be real specific; keep it general. You don't want to make me look bad."

◆CSCPs ARE REFLECTIVE

Issues.   Reflection involves spending time thinking about the efficacy of your efforts as a school counselor and the efficacy of your CSCP. Evidence of this reflection, which is an ethical and moral mandate, comes in the form of examination and documentation of your work.

It has been a challenge for school counselors to document their work. After all, counseling is confidential, isn't it? How do you document that this student is passing third grade, that one is getting along better with her friends, that boy decided not to commit suicide, and a student you counseled two months ago is finally turning his attitude around and coming to school? Besides, where will you find the time to collect all that information? School counselors work very hard as it is, and now they have to count everything they do on top of it all? The problem is that for years, counselors have been stumped by these questions.

Professional reflection results in accountability. Many authors discuss the need to be accountable (Baker, 2000; Schmidt, 2000), and there is no question that school counselors must be accountable to their schools, their communities, and to their students for their comprehensive school counseling programs and for their own contribution to the program. School counselors are accountable for their time, for the quality of their work, and for the quality of the program overall as evaluated on the basis of needs and outcomes (Hutchinson & Bottorff, 1986). For example, Baker (2000) indicated that school counselors are professionally and morally bound to evaluate (gather information about one's programs and services) and be accountable (report the results of the evaluation) (p. 300). Schmidt (1999) also called upon school counselors to "identify your role in the school, account for the time you allot to specific activities, and measure whether or not these services make a difference in the lives of students, parents, and teachers" (p. 275). In fact, it is so important that the American School Counselor Association has devoted one entire element of the National Model (2003) to the accountability system. We will discuss this in detail in Chapters 5, 10, and 15.

But accountability is often misunderstood to mean that school counselors must bite the yearly bullet to pull data together and write a self-evaluation, something to be avoided like the plague. The challenges of collecting meaningful data on the efficacy of school counseling interventions is significant, especially, as Akos (2005) points out, when youngsters' developmental progress is not easily attributable to anything done in the schools. Expand your definition of accountability so that you can envision a process of effective management, needs and outcomes assessment, reflection, and program improvement. Management of the program is more than being accountable for the results of the program—it is a continuous process. As a part of leadership and coordinating activities, counselors need to manage, evaluate, and improve their comprehensive school counseling program—in essence, effectively lead the program—and this starts with reflection.

Prototype

Reflection on Quality of Program and on Counselor Performance.   Reflection is both an internal and external process. When counselors reflect on the quality of their work, and then take responsibility for that work, they effectively manage their program. What, exactly, does it mean to "manage" a program? According to Hersey, Blanchard, and Johnson (1996) management consists of the functions of *planning, organizing, motivating,* and *controlling*—functions that are consistent across all types of organizations and all levels. Planning is defined as setting goals and objectives and developing "work maps" showing how goals and objectives are to be accomplished. Organizing involves bringing together resources to accomplish the goals and objectives derived from the planning process. Motivating involves working effectively with the human resources available to meet those goals and objectives, and controlling refers to the use of feedback and results "to compare accomplishments with plans and to make appropriate adjustments where outcomes have deviated from expectations" (p. 11).

Are these terms foreign or familiar to you? If all this sounds very businesslike, that's because it is. We are looking at functions that are not the source of passion for most school counselors, functions that may be contrary to the counselor's preference to work with people (not data) and in which counselors seldom receive training (Baker, 2000). We don't know any counselors who jump out of bed in the morning and exclaim, "Yippee! Today I get to plan, organize, and control my school counseling program. Get out of my way, world, here I come!" Don't despair, however; the efforts to manage and account for your work and the outcomes of your program efforts are very worthwhile.

The importance of personal, professional, and programmatic reflection is elaborated and explored in Chapter 5, in which the ASCA National Model will be discussed in terms of the Management System, data collection and analysis, and Accountability. This Model contains explicit directions and formats for the collection and analysis of data for program evaluation and improvement and for counselor evaluation and improvement.

In spite of the fact that these terms may seem unfamiliar, you have done these activities. Unless you have a maid who does all your shopping and cooking for you, believe me, you have done each of these functions. When you made out your shopping list, you were planning. When you went to the store, bought your groceries, then brought them home and put them away, you were organizing. When you cooked the meal and thought about whether it tasted good to you, you were assessing. When you decided to cook it again next month or throw away that recipe, you were evaluating and using that information to engage in planning. When you bragged to your friends that you cooked beef Wellington and it was delicious, you were accounting for your time. Not so frightening now, is it? Reflection is the first step toward responsibility and accountability for the work of the counselor and the program.

Now that you have the foundation of a comprehensive school counseling program, it is time to examine what the national association, the American School Counselor Association (ASCA), has to say about comprehensive school counseling programs. The next chapter is devoted to the ASCA National Model for School Counseling Programs, in which we will look in detail at school counseling's foundation, management system, delivery system, and accountability as defined at the national level.

Reflection Moment ◆

Some counselors believe their time is too precious to waste it on gathering data and information about the outcomes of their work and then don't understand how their programs get cut. Can you see how accountability and program survival are connected? How do you think school counselors can collect important outcomes information about the CSCP from the students, parents, school colleagues, and community colleagues with whom they work?

◆ ◆

CASE STUDY REVISITED ◆ Integration

If the program and the professionals are not adequately, fairly, and completely evaluated, what are the risks to the program and the professionals? Based on what Mr. Winters said, what concerns do you have about Calvin Paulson's evaluation? If you were to evaluate the program in that school, what grade would you give it for its programmatic responses to Ty's situation?

APPLICATION (Possible portfolio artifacts are noted)

1. Outline what "balance" means to you. Now apply that definition to a CSCP. What qualities do you look for to determine if something is "balanced"? How do you know if a program is balanced? Visit a school and interview the school counselor to determine if the program is balanced. Now interview the principal to see what that person's definition of balance is. What would you do about any differences you hear in those definitions?

2. Using a real elementary-age child or a fictional child from a movie or book, practice identifying that young person's risk status. Now view that person through the 5 Cs of competency. Outline a prevention-intervention-treatment plan for that young person to reduce their risk status. (Possible portfolio artifact)

3. Using a real middle-school-age child or a fictional pre-adolescent child from a movie or book, practice identifying that young person's risk status. Now view that person through the 5 Cs of competency. Outline a prevention-intervention-treatment plan for that young person to reduce their risk status. (Possible portfolio artifact)

4. Using a real high-school-age adolescent or a fictional adolescent from a movie or book, practice identifying that young person's risk status. Now view that person through the 5 Cs of competency. Outline a prevention-intervention-treatment plan for that young person to reduce their risk status. (Possible portfolio artifact)

5. Select a local school and visit the CSCP to design an outcomes evaluation plan. First, learn about their most "important" top three activities. Second, design a means to capture outcomes data from each of these three activities. Finally, share your evaluation plan with the school counselor to obtain that person's reaction. How doable are your ideas? (*Note:* Do not be disappointed with the reaction. For some people, it is hard to rethink their work to include new activities.) Share your evaluation plan with your classmates. Do they have ideas to improve your plan? Do you have ideas to improve theirs?

6. Conduct an Internet search of school counseling program websites. First, is the program balanced? Second, what are their prevention-intervention-treatment activities? What evidence to you see that their school counseling program is integrated with the academic agenda of the school? Finally, what evidence can you find of their self-evaluation efforts?

7. Design the "perfect" comprehensive school counseling program, outlining all six of the qualities of a comprehensive program as described in these two chapters. Now design a flyer or brochure for your ideal program: one for the students and one for the adult partners (parents, teachers, and administrators). (Possible portfolio artifact)

SUGGESTED READING

Hersey, P., Blanchard, K. H., & Johnson, D. E. (1996). *Management of organizational behavior: Utilizing human resources* (7th ed.). Upper Saddle River, NJ: Prentice Hall. This book, written for business professionals, gives a wonderful overview of leadership and management practices.

REFERENCES

Akos, P. (2005). The unique nature of middle school counseling. *Professional School Counseling, 9*, 95–103.

American School Counselor Association (2003). *The ASCA National Prototype: A framework for school counseling programs.* Alexandria, VA: Author.

Baker, S. B. (2000). *School counseling for the twenty-first century* (3rd ed.). Upper Saddle River, NJ: Merrill.

Burnham, J. J., & Jackson, C. M. (2000). School counselor roles: Discrepancies between actual practice and existing prototypes. *Professional School Counseling, 4*(1), 41–49.

Campbell, C. A., & Dahir, C. A. (1997). *Sharing the vision: The national standards for school counseling programs.* Alexandria, VA: American School Counselor Association.

Craig, G. J. (1996). *Human development* (7th ed.). Upper Saddle River, NJ: Prentice Hall.

Dollarhide, C. T., & Saginak, K. A. (2003). *School counseling in the secondary school: A comprehensive process and program.* Boston: Allyn and Bacon.

Hersey, P., Blanchard, K. H., & Johnson, D. E. (1996). *Management of organizational behavior: Utilizing human resources* (7th ed.). Upper Saddle River, NJ: Prentice Hall.

Hutchinson, R. L., & Bottorff, R. L. (1986). Selected high school counseling services: Student assessment. *The School Counselor, 33*, 350–354.

Keys, S. G., & Lockhart, E. J. (1999). The school counselor's role in facilitating multisystemic change. *Professional School Counseling, 3*, 101–107.

McWhirter, J. J., McWhirter, B. T., McWhirter, A. M., & McWhirter, E. H. (1998). *At-risk youth: A comprehensive response for counselors, teachers, psychologists, and human service professionals.* Pacific Grove, CA: Brooks/Cole.

Schmidt, J. J. (1999). *Counseling in schools: Essential services and comprehensive programs* (3rd ed.). Boston: Allyn and Bacon.

Wiggins, J. D., & Moody, A. H. (1987). Student evaluations of counseling programs: An added dimension. *The School Counselor, 34*, 353–361.

SECTION THREE

The Form of Comprehensive School Counseling Programs: The ASCA National Model and Models of Delivery Systems

5

THE ASCA NATIONAL MODEL

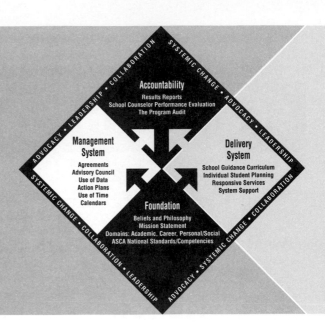

◆ LEARNING OBJECTIVES

By the end of this chapter, you will

1. Understand the rationale for a National Model
2. Understand and be able to articulate the ASCA National Model in general
3. Understand and be able to articulate the Themes of advocacy, leadership, collaboration, and systemic change
4. Be able to discuss the Model Elements of Foundation, Delivery System, Management System, and Accountability
5. Be able to apply the Model in theory and in practice

CASE STUDY ◆ Cadence's Big Decision

Cadence was very excited that she had finally made a decision about what she wanted to do with her life. After completing her degree in elementary education, she realized that her passion was not in the classroom—it was working with the children to help them with problems. She had a chance to talk with the school counselor, Kayli, when she was doing her student teaching, and learned a lot about the counselor's job. Cadence then invited Kayli to do some classroom developmental guidance in her room and decided that the combination of classroom guidance, plus one-on-one and group counseling, gave her the perfect opportunity to combine all the things she loved most into one profession.

The problem was that when she mentioned it to someone, she was often met with a negative reaction. These reactions were disheartening; after all, she was talking about starting a graduate program, in which the investment of time and resources would be substantial. She wanted to understand these reactions so that she could feel confident in her decision.

Her cooperating teacher said that counselors are just extra baggage to the school—what was needed were more teachers. One of her fellow students at the university said he thought counselors didn't contribute to the students' lives at all, that counseling was just "playing head games." A parent of one of her students said that she thought counselors shouldn't be allowed to work with kids, that all they did was interfere with the parents' rights to discipline their own children. And Cadence's own mother said that she had no idea what counselors did in schools except work with kids who were really sick. None of these comments were consistent with what Cadence had learned from the counselor at her school, so she went back to talk to Kayli about these reactions.

"It's not a well-understood profession," Kayli shared. "There are numerous ways to define the work a school counselor does, and it's hard to get consensus about what a counselor *should* do. Everyone wants to have a say in what school counselors should do—from teachers, to administrators, to parents, to the public."

"Isn't there anyone who speaks for the school counseling profession, who can make definitive statements about what school counselors are all about?"

"Yes, it's the professional association, and they have made such a definitive statement, called the ASCA National Model. But they face two challenges: how to inform teachers, administrators, and parents about this Model and how to reach those school counselors who aren't members of the professional association. We have a coherent forum to advocate for the profession, to help everyone understand what school counselors do and why they do it, but we need more people willing to get involved to spread the word."

"Sounds exciting!" Cadence said, wondering how political advocacy fit into the job of a school counselor. This was turning into a tougher decision than she thought.

CHALLENGE QUESTIONS

What are the images you have of the job of a school counselor? Given what you have read so far in this book, what do you know about what counselors do and why they do it? What do you believe they *should* do?

◆ THE PROFESSIONALIZATION OF SCHOOL COUNSELING

What is a "profession"? According to Grolier's (1975), it is "a vocation requiring specialized training in a field of learning, art, or science; a body of persons engaged in a calling or vocation. . . ." (p. 761). With specialized training in a discipline, persons in that vocation define their work within a professional identity, and in the process, develop a commonly shared set of rules and norms for the profession. These rules and norms evolve into codified ethics and standards of practice by which persons in that profession are expected to abide and by which persons in the profession are held accountable. Sometimes these standards and expectations are translated into law (as in legislation protecting confidentiality between doctor-patient, lawyer-client, and priest-penitent); other times these standards and expectations are enforced by the profession alone. (See Chapter 14 for a full discussion.)

The process of professionalization for the counseling profession in general is not new, but for some counseling specialties, the process has been more recent. This latter description applies to school counseling. As we saw in Chapter 1, comprehensive school counseling evolved as recently as the 1980s (American School Counselor Association, 2003), and Comprehensive School Counseling Programs (CSCPs) emerged in the literature in the late 1990s. The necessity of CSCPs is still being debated in many communities around the country. Just because the profession of school counseling recognizes their worth does not mean that the general public agrees.

The huge challenge posed for the profession of school counseling is how to promote consistent norms and expectations among those the profession serves. After all, as the job and definition of the school counselor changed over the years, so have the experiences of those being served by the school counselor. The parents of today's students were in the schools twenty, thirty, or more years ago, and all they know about the job of a school counselor is what they saw in those schools years ago. How will they know that the profession has evolved unless current school counselors educate them?

As a result, today's school counselors have challenges ahead of them. They must remain current with their profession, and this means being committed enough to the

The ASCA School Counselor Performance Standards addressed in this chapter are

Standard 6: The professional school counselor discusses the counseling department management system and the program action plans with the school administrator.

6.1 The professional school counselor discusses the qualities of the school counselor management system with the other members of the counseling staff and has agreement.

6.2 The professional school counselor discusses the program results anticipated when implementing the action plans for the school year.

Standard 8: The professional school counselor collects and analyzes data to guide program direction and emphasis.

8.1 The professional school counselor uses school data to make decisions regarding student choice of classes and special programs.

8.2 The professional school counselor uses data from the counseling program to make decisions regarding program revisions.

8.3 The professional school counselor analyzes data to ensure every student has equity and access to a rigorous academic curriculum.

8.4 The professional school counselor understands and uses data to establish goals and activities to close the gap.

Standard 11: The professional school counselor develops a results evaluation for the program.

11.1 The professional school counselor measures results attained from school guidance curriculum and closing the gap activities.

11.2 The professional school counselor works with members of the counseling team and with the principal to clarify how programs are evaluated and how results are shared.

11.3 The professional school counselor knows how to collect process, perception and results data.

Standard 12: The professional school counselor conducts a yearly program audit.

12.1 The professional school counselor completes a program audit to determine the degrees to which the school counseling program is being implemented.

12.2 The professional school counselor shares the results of the program audit with the advisory council.

12.3 The professional school counselor uses the yearly audit to make changes in the school counseling program and calendar for the following year.

The CACREP Standards for School Counseling Programs addressed in this chapter are

B.3 integration of the school counseling program into the total school curriculum by systematically providing information and skills training to assist pre-K–12 students in maximizing their academic, career, and personal/social development;

C.1 **(e)** preparation of an action plan and school counseling calendar that reflect appropriate time commitments and priorities in a comprehensive developmental school counseling program; and

C.3 **(d)** knowledge and skills in conducting programs that are designed to enhance students' academic, social, emotional, career, and other developmental needs.

profession to be an active, involved member of the professional association. It is through active involvement that members remain true to their life vocation, the calling to work effectively with children and families in schools.

◆ THE ASCA NATIONAL MODEL

As an extension of those professional rules and expectations, ASCA has published a number of documents. You will recall that we discussed those recent publications in Chapter 1, when we visited the ASCA Role Statement (American School Counselor Association, 1999) and National Standards for Student Academic, Career, and Personal/Social Development (Campbell & Dahir, 1997; see also Appendix B). In these documents, the profession has attempted to define the job of the school counselor and the expected outcomes of a CSCP in terms of students' knowledge, skills, and abilities. In the most recent publication, the ASCA National Model and the School Counselor Performance Standards are presented (American School Counselor Association [ASCA], 2003).

It is important to note that every school counselor should be knowledgeable about the National Model from the original source, not just from secondary sources like this one. Reading this chapter will not substitute for personal examination of and reflection on the original publication. (A copy of the Model can be ordered directly from ASCA at www.schoolcounselor.org.)

Overview of the Model

As you can see from the graphic at the beginning of the chapter, the National Model reflects the Themes, Elements, and flow that are the essence of school counseling. The *Themes* are Leadership, Advocacy, Collaboration, and Systemic Change. As we will see in the next section, these themes constitute the environment in which school counselors conduct their work. The *Elements* of the model include Foundation, Delivery System, Management System, and Accountability, which give structure to the day-to-day work of the school counselor. Finally, the *flow* of the model indicates the directionality of the elements and the manner in which feedback moves through the program elements to ensure the highest efficacy of the school counselor's work.

The Themes

The Themes of the model are critical for understanding the context, or environment, of the school counselor's work. These themes highlight the systemic nature of the work and provide a template for understanding the importance of these four topics. They surround the diagram of the day-to-day work of the school counselor, as they would in the field. Leadership, Advocacy, and Collaboration result in Systemic Change, which then results in the need for new efforts in Leadership, Advocacy, and Collaboration to bring about more Systemic Change in a cycle of systemic institutional renewal.

Leadership.   Leadership will be discussed in greater detail in the next chapter and Chapter 10, but we will examine it briefly here. The National Model states that "School counselors serve as leaders who are engaged in systemwide change to ensure student success" (ASCA, 2003, p. 24). According to Bolman and Deal (1997), leadership involves four "frames" or contexts for leadership: structural leadership (ensuring that the organization you lead is effective), human resource leadership (inspiring others to follow), political leadership (working with others who hold power in the setting you lead), and symbolic leadership (leading using a vision). Taking a chronological, prescriptive view, Kouzes and Posner (1995) describe leadership in a five-step template: challenge the process, inspire a shared vision, enable others to act, model the way, and encourage the heart. It is possible to create a template for leadership that combines the contexts in which leadership must take place (adapted from Bolman & Deal, 1997) with the chronological view of leadership proposed by Kouzes and Posner. This view of leadership captures many elements of vision, growth, and dynamic environmental interaction necessary for the evolution of the profession of school counseling and the improvement of schools for all children. Examples of leadership include chairing a committee on campus climate, serving as an advisor to a student group, and serving on a schoolwide student issues committee.

Advocacy.   The role of advocacy, the second theme, is described by ASCA: "School counselors advocate for students' educational needs and work to ensure these needs are addressed at every level of the school experience. . . . School counselors work as advocates to remove systemic barriers that impede the academic success of any student" (ASCA, 2003, p. 24). To "advocate," as defined by Grolier Webster (1975), is "to plead in favor of, as of a cause, policy, etc.; to defend by argument; to recommend publicly; to support or vindicate" (p. 17). When you advocate, you are attempting to persuade someone to embrace your point of view; you are teaching them about your perspective on a given subject. Because you are "pleading," "defending," "supporting," you are doing this educating with some emotion; advocacy is educating with passion. True leadership involves passion, enthusiasm, and advocacy, which means that leadership and advocacy are linked. School counselors are advocates for students, families, teachers, and schools; they use their pivotal position to enhance understanding of the issues involved in healthy development of both individuals and systems.

Collaboration.   Grolier Webster (1975) defines "collaborate" as working together with others, cooperating. Drew (2004), in his discussion of conditions that help students graduate, elaborates further, defining collaboration as the building of interdependent systems to achieve a common goal that cannot be achieved by each entity working alone. ASCA (2003) highlights the role of collaboration in the Model, stating that "School counselors build effective teams by encouraging genuine collaboration among all school staff to work toward the common goals of equity, access, and academic success of every student" (p. 25). Examples of collaboration include serving on the administrative council for the school, working with teachers to develop and deliver the developmental curriculum, and working with parents on a fund-raising project for the parent-teacher association.

Systemic Change.   Taken together, leadership, advocacy, and collaboration culminate in systemic change: "Collaborating as leaders within the school, counselors have access to quantitative and qualitative data from the school and relevant community sources. They use these data to advocate for every student, ensuring equity and access to a rigorous curriculum, which maximizes postsecondary options. Systemic change occurs when policies and procedures are examined and changed in light of new data" (ASCA, 2003, p. 25). Examples of systemic change are visible when efforts toward leadership, advocacy, and collaboration bear fruit—when more parents come to parent programs and classes and are more involved in the school, when school administration changes a policy because the counselor's efforts have shown it to be detrimental to the educational process.

Reflection Moment ◆

Reflect on Richard Long Harkness's famous quote: "What is a committee? A group of the unwilling, picked from the unfit, to do the unnecessary." What is your reaction? What has been your experience with committees? Now reflect on what ASCA has presented in terms of the Themes of the Model. It is through the work of committees, task forces, and other work groups that school counselors accomplish systemic change. How does that affect the view of committees as seen by Harkness?

◆ ◆

The Elements

The Elements of the Model, which constitute the body of the model, outline the structures that school counselors must have in place to do their work. In order to accomplish this important work, school counselors must have a solid Foundation, they must have Management and Delivery Systems, and they must have Accountability. In this section, we will examine each of these elements, as ASCA has provided both descriptive (what could be) and prescriptive (what should be) information about each element.

The Foundation.   The foundation of a solid comprehensive school counseling program (CSCP) includes beliefs and philosophies, a mission statement, and the ASCA National Standards for Student Academic, Career, and Personal/Social Development (Appendix B). This foundation addresses our beliefs about the profession, the values embedded in our work, and our philosophy about who we are and what we contribute to the lives of the students and our partners in the educational process.

The Model highlights our collaborative role in the school by building the foundation on a collaborative process based within an advisory board or advisory council. This advisory board consists of partners with whom the school counselors must collaborate (students, parents or guardians, colleagues in the school, and colleagues in the community). Once the partners have been assembled, school counselors lead discussions, as outlined below, to articulate beliefs, assumptions, values, and philosophy. In a systematic way, each topic is explored.

Beliefs.   ASCA begins the process of building this foundation with a private exploration, on the part of each participant, of fundamental beliefs on a wide range of topics. General topics include student achievement, support for students, understanding of learning styles, and the importance of reaching every student. Specific to school counseling, topics include the role of the CSCP in supporting the mission of the school, educational reform and the counselor's role, and the role of all partners (students, parents and guardians, colleagues in the school, and colleagues outside of the school) in the CSCP (p. 28). After this private reflection, a group discussion ensues to help all members of the advisory council understand each other.

Assumptions.   When applied to the CSCP, these beliefs are the underlying basis for the assumptions about the CSCP. It is through the examination of assumptions that school counseling teams (the advisory council and the professional counselors) create a consensus that translates into the philosophy statement of the program. ASCA provides some example assumptions, including those that parallel Chapters 3 and 4 of this book:

♦ A CSCP reaches every student
♦ Is comprehensive in scope
♦ Is preventative in design
♦ Is developmental in nature
♦ Is integral to the educational process (p. 28)

Values.   While not explicit in the Model, the discussion of values is also integral to the development of a philosophy statement. Values represent what we believe to be important, what we hold most dear. The difference between values and beliefs is that beliefs are cognitive; they are usually derived and experienced intellectually and are expressed as "I think." Values, on the other hand, are derived and experienced affectively and are usually expressed as "I feel." Values relative to this process could include for all advisory council members:

♦ What is most important: academic, career, or personal/social development?
♦ What is the second most important?
♦ Who is the most important partner: students, parents and caregivers, colleagues in the schools, or colleagues in the community?
♦ Who is the second? Third?

For the professional counselors:

♦ Why did I become a school counselor? What do I dream of accomplishing professionally? Personally?
♦ Where do I want to see my program go? What is my vision of the future of my CSCP? What is my ideal role in that ideal CSCP?

Although developed privately, discussions about these values, coupled with the discussion of assumptions, can help team members understand the unique perspectives of each member.

Philosophy.   The philosophy statement is developed by consensus, and addresses six topics (ASCA, 2003, pp. 28–29):

1. A set of beliefs motivating program innovations
2. A set of values visible to all
3. A set of principles guiding professional contributions
4. Statement of professional conduct
5. Statement committing counselors to continuous professional growth
6. Source of collective power

Furthermore, ASCA (2003, p. 29) states that, at a minimum, the philosophy statement should

1. Indicate a shared belief system about the ability of all students to achieve
2. Address every student
3. Address student developmental needs and focus on primary prevention
4. Address the school counselor's role as an advocate for every student
5. Identify persons to be involved in the delivery of program activities

6. Specify who will plan and manage the program
7. Use data to drive program decisions
8. Define how the program will be evaluated and by whom
9. Include ethical guidelines or standards

From this point, the work team will develop a *mission statement*. The mission statement, the second part of the Foundation, is developed from the work done relative to beliefs, assumptions, values, and philosophy. This statement "describes the program's purpose and provides the vision of what is desired for every student," "aligns with and is a subset of the school or district's mission," and "should be clear, concise, and specific as to the program's intent and what the program will contribute" (ASCA, 2003, p. 30). Furthermore, the mission statement should

1. Be written with students as the primary clients
2. Advocate for the equity, access, and success of every student
3. Be written for every student
4. Indicate the content and competencies to be learned
5. Show linkages with the school, district, and state department of education mission statements
6. Indicate the long-range results desired for all students (ASCA, 2003, p. 30)

Finally, the ASCA National Standards for Student Academic, Career, and Personal/Social Development (Campbell & Dahir, 1997) are included as part of the Foundation of the Model, as it outlines the competencies of knowledge, attitudes, and skills that students should attain as a result of being in a school with a CSCP. (The document, originally titled "National Standards for School Counseling Programs," has been renamed to more accurately reflect the content of the standards.) The domains of academic, career, and personal/social development remain the "broad developmental areas" (ASCA, 2003, p. 32) within which school counseling programs make their contribution to the success of each student. For each domain, measurable goals are to be defined for each school year to provide data for program and systemic improvement efforts. Just as each state has established academic competencies to determine academic success, these National Standards outline developmental competencies to assist school counselors in determining the developmental success of students. It is this data that inform the school counselor's leadership, advocacy, and collaboration efforts to bring about program improvement and systemic change. Just as philosophy statements need to be linked from schools, districts, and states to the philosophy of the CSCP, so too will counselors work to link the National Standards with existing school, district, and state competencies. These standards are included in this book as Appendix B.

The Delivery System.   The delivery system is the template that is used to define what school counselors actually do. The delivery system described by ASCA in the National Model is based on Gysbers and Henderson (2000); however, as we will see in Chapter 6, there are other templates to consider. In this chapter, however, we will examine the Gysbers and Henderson template as presented in the National Model.

There are four parts to the Gysbers and Henderson (2000) model as it is presented in the National Model: the school guidance curriculum, individual student planning, responsive services, and system support. Each of these parts is further broken down to provide direction to the delivery of the CSCP to students.

School Guidance Curriculum. The "guidance" curriculum identifies the responsibility of the counselors to provide a "written instructional program that is comprehensive in scope, preventative and proactive, developmental in design, coordinated by school counselors, and delivered, as appropriate, by school counselors and other educators" (ASCA, 2003, p. 40). This curriculum consists of learning opportunities, designed for the development of knowledge, skills, and attitudes, that are derived from the National Standards and district standards. Since counselors are responsible for the planning, designing, implementing, and evaluation of this curriculum, their responsibilities make them accountable for documenting the learning that results. According to the National Model, the guidance curriculum may be delivered in any of the following venues: classroom instruction, small-group discussions, presentations to parents and guardians, large-group assemblies, and collaborative planning and coordinating of instruction with other school personnel.

Individual Student Planning. In these activities, school counselors work to ensure that all students have future plans and make progress toward attainment of personal, educational, and postsecondary and occupational goals. In this area of service delivery, counselors help students to define their academic, career, and personal goals; make plans on the basis of those goals; and transition to the next phase of their development in the attainment of those goals. Activities through which counselors provide these services include individual or small-group appraisal and individual or small-group advisement. Topics addressed in these settings could include financial aid, graduation requirements, course selection information, and test score interpretation and analysis addressing abilities, interests, skills, and achievement.

Responsive Services. Even in the best school imaginable, students will still need counselors to respond to immediate needs that arise. These needs include academic issues such as academic failure or retention; career issues such as career counseling for postsecondary life; and personal/social issues such as crisis counseling and suicide prevention, support during painful or difficult personal transitions (death of family member, divorce of parents), or unhealthy choices (sexual activity, substance use/abuse/addiction). These responsive services are provided through such strategies as individual and small-group counseling, consultation, peer facilitation, and referrals to community resources.

System Support. School counselors, as members of the school community, contribute in important ways to support the school's educational mission. Through professional development, school counselors provide in-service training to colleagues and keep their own professional development current through membership in professional associations and contributions to the literature about school counseling. Through consultation, collaboration, and teaming, school counselors consult with parents and school colleagues, provide community relations support and outreach, and serve on advisory councils and district committees. Through program management and operations, school counselors maintain the management system for the program, analyze data needed for planning, and engage in "fair share" (p. 44) activities commensurate with other professionals in the school.

The Management System. The Management System includes information school counselors need in order to effectively manage a comprehensive school counseling program. Topics covered by this section of the Model include Management Agreements, Advisory Council, the Use of Data, Action Plans, Use of Time (for CSCP activities and non-CSCP activities) and Calendars.

Management Agreements.   A vital part of the effective functioning of any organization is the structure that undergirds program efforts. For a program to be effective, everyone involved in the program must understand the roles, expectations, and priorities of all activities in the program. It is through management agreements that these are articulated and disseminated, that assignments are made through careful analysis of the data and a carefully designed action plan. The document must be negotiated with and supported by administration from both the building and the district to be considered viable. Topics that should be included in these agreements would include

- Assignment of students to counselors to ensure access to the CSCP
- The person(s) who will provide each program activity within the CSCP and a schedule for those activities
- The amount of time to be devoted to each aspect of the delivery system
- How counselors will be compensated for work beyond the regular work day
- The budget available for materials and supplies to implement the program
- The need for professional development to ensure the best possible CSCP
- The structure for the support services for the CSCP

Advisory Council.   Advisory councils provide critical "support, input and recommendations for program development and improvement" (ASCA, 2003, p. 47). Introduced as a part of the process for establishing the Foundation of the CSCP, an "advisory council is a representative group of persons appointed to both advise and assist the school counseling program" (ASCA, 2003, p. 47).

Use of Data.   ASCA maintains that a CSCP is data-driven, and as such, derives from the "careful analysis of student needs, achievement, and related data" (p. 49; Stone & Dahir, 2007). The types of data school counselors collect include

- Student progress data:
  - Student achievement data, defined as data that measure students' academic progress, such as standardized test data, GPAs, SAT or ACT scores, promotion and retention rates, and so on
  - Achievement-related data, defined as data derived from behavior correlated with academic achievement, such as discipline referral patterns, suspension rates, attendance rates, homework completion rates, and so on
  - Standards- and competency-related data, defined as data measuring student mastery of the ASCA's National Standards, such as percentage of students with four-year plans on file, percentage of students who apply conflict resolution skills, and so on
- Disaggregate data, separated by demographic variables such as gender, ethnicity, socioeconomic status, vocation, language spoken at home, special education, grade level, and teachers.
- Program evaluation data, or data collected to document the impact of the CSCP, would include
  - Process data, documenting how a program is conducted, including statements like "I provided group counseling to five groups from grade 5, totaling 45 students, in which I addressed anger management."
  - Perception data, answering the question "What do people think they know, believe, or can do?" and measured through pre-post surveys, documentation, skill

demonstrations, or evaluation forms. An example of perception data from the personal/ social domain could include a statement such as "Ninety-eight percent (44 of 45) of students in an anger management group reported that they learned how to recognize anger triggers."

◆ Results data, documenting the impact of an activity or program through results, including statements such as "As a result of the group counseling, none of those students has been referred for fighting, resulting in a 25 percent reduction in discipline referrals for fighting in the school."

The Model highlights the need for data to be collected and analyzed over time, documenting the change for students over one semester, one year, and over a number of years, to identify and understand trends. Analysis of data need not be complicated; rather, statistics that are understandable and measurable repeatedly are most useful for planning and evaluation (Stone & Dahir, 2007). Furthermore, most of the data needed for understanding trends within the school are already compiled in the data system for the school and/or the district, so the management of the data need not be an impediment to this process. As highlighted in the Model, activities that document how all students, regardless of income, gender, or ethnicity, are assisted through the CSCP will close the educational gap for students and emphasize the vital nature of the work of school counselors.

Action Plans.   Each CSCP must have a timeline for the provision of two specific components of the program: the developmental curriculum and the activities for closing the achievement gap in the school. These Action Plans are designed by the counselors, then are negotiated with and approved by the administration of the school. The first document, the Action Plan for the Developmental Curriculum, is based on the ASCA National Standards (Competencies and Indicators), found in Appendix B of this book. For these Action Plans, a chart is developed that details the topic, the domain and standard related to that topic, the curriculum materials to be used, the dates of delivery of the curriculum, the number of students to be impacted, the class or subject in which the curriculum will be provided, an overview of the evaluation method(s), and the contact counselor. For the Action Plans that detail the Closing-the-Gap activities, the Plan contains everything listed above, with the addition of the disaggregated data relative to achievement of various populations that justify the programmatic interventions listed.

Use of Time.   Though the careful documentation of counselor time, it is possible to identify activities that do not contribute directly to the goals of the CSCP. ASCA recommends that school counselors spend a majority of their time providing direct services to students; and although everyone contributes to activities required to maintain an institution (such as serving on committees or providing lunchroom supervision), it is crucial that counselors maintain their responsibilities in such a way that their primary focus is always on the goals of the CSCP.

Calendars.   ASCA further highlights the appropriate use of time through the Model's inclusion of calendars as a means of maintaining focus on program goals as well as a means of communication and accountability. A three-tiered approach to scheduling can assist CSCPs to maximize each counselor's time and efforts: an annual calendar highlights activities for yearlong planning of presentations, collaboration and services for parents, and the delivery of the developmental curriculum; a monthly calendar serves as a reminder for upcoming events and themes; and a weekly calendar provides flexibility and account-ability. Together, these tools define how services within the program will be delivered.

The Accountability System.   In this section of the National Model, data collected as a part of the Management System are compiled, evaluated for program improvement, and prepared for dissemination. With this part of the process, accountability is ensured, the program improves, and the value of the CSCP is communicated to building and district administration. Several processes highlight fully accountable programs: results reports, school counselor performance standards, and the program audit.

Results Report.   As data are collected relative to program efficacy, they are compiled and maintained for dissemination to administration, parents, and teachers, as well as for pro-gram evaluation and improvement. One forum for this compilation is the Results Report, in which the following is included:

◆ Grade level
◆ Lesson content area, located by ASCA Domain/Standard
◆ Curriculum or materials used
◆ Process data, such as methods of delivery (small-group topics and number offered, classroom subjects and number of presentations), dates, and number of students
◆ Short-term perception data, such as pre-post tests of knowledge
◆ Intermediate and long-term results data, such as attendance, test scores, graduation rates or other measures of behaviors
◆ The implications of the results on the school and the counseling program

In addition, the impact of the results of such efforts will be tracked over time and compiled for presentation to administration. In this report, demographics, graduation rates, discipline and attendance data, test scores, and other data are used to document progress of students in each of the domains of school counseling and are "analyzed in relation to progress made toward school-wide mission and achievement goals" (p. 62). As a summary document, the Impact-Over-Time Report contains

◆ Student demographics, such as enrollment data, gender, ethnicity, grade levels, lan-guages, students on free-and-reduced lunch
◆ Academic achievement data, such as test scores, grade point averages, and dropout and graduation rates
◆ Career development data, such as numbers in career programs of work exploration, job shadowing, and job mentoring, or number of students who have identified a career direction or career cluster
◆ Personal/social development data, such as climate survey results, substance use data, and school crime/violence data
◆ Parent and guardian involvement: Number of parents at conferences, workshops, and events.

The goal of the Impact-Over-Time Report is to put the Results Report within the context of the entire school, to highlight the growth of students in each domain over time. As each year passes, the same data is collected to allow administration and the CSCP staff to understand the changing nature of students and their challenges in education. As the Results Report for the year highlights the school counselor's efforts of that year, the Impact-Over-Time report shows accountability for the year as well as being a planning tool for the coming year.

School Counselor Performance Standards.   The Performance Standards for school counselors, as seen in Appendix C, outline the professional activities and expectations as defined by the profession. (These standards form the skeleton of this book.) It is recommended that these standards be used in the yearly evaluation process, both for counselor self-evaluation and for administrative counselor evaluations. Professional development and learning opportunities result from careful analysis and reflection on skills and conceptual deficits.

The Program Audit.   The National Model document provides counselors with the audit format and process to be used in the design and continuous improvement evaluation of the comprehensive school counseling program. In summary, the Audit document provides a definition of each component of the National Model and then provides a template for determining the extent to which the program meets each component (ASCA, 2003, pp. 110–120). The intended use of the tool is to document four critical areas for program evaluation and improvement:

◆ The major strengths of the program
◆ The areas in need of improvement
◆ Short-range goals for improvement
◆ Long-range goals for improvement

The results of the Program Audit, along with the counselor evaluations and the Results Reports, all provide administrators with information to assess the health and viability of the CSCP. Furthermore, accountable programs subject to active evaluation and continuous improvement are more likely to engender parent and teacher support, which is more likely to result in administrative support. Positive growth and effective public relations are the outcomes.

Reflection Moment ◆

What concerns do you have as you look at the National Model? Is it comforting to know that there is an outline of the professional expectations, or is it intimidating to think about all the expectations placed on you as you enter your new profession? Recall the daunting process of applying for graduate school, and reflect on what you heard were the expectations of graduate students. How did you manage your anxiety around that process? What did you learn from that experience that you can use now?

◆ ◆

The Flow

Look again at the National Model on page 88. The black-and-white graphics were carefully chosen to communicate the flow of information and data through the four elements of the comprehensive school counseling program. As you can see, the Foundation, comprising beliefs and philosophy, mission statement, and ASCA National Standards for Students, feeds into the Management System (the nuts-and-bolts of managing the CSCP) and the

Delivery System (the day-to-day activities of the CSCP). In turn, both the Management System and the Delivery System feed into Accountability process, as data collected from program management duties and from the delivery of the CSCP flow together for evaluation, program improvement, and dissemination. Finally, you will notice that the white arrows into the Accountability block create a black arrow pointing from Accountability to Foundation, as the results of the reports and the evaluation process are used to further refine the mission statement and assess progress toward the students' attainment of the ASCA National Standards for Students. The border around the Model that contains the words "Systemic Change–Advocacy–Leadership–Collaboration" reflects the environment of the work school counselors do in terms of the Themes discussed earlier in this chapter.

CASE STUDY REVISTED ◆ Integration

Go back and reread the opening case study, then answer the following questions:

1. When you read the discussion between Cadence and Kayli, what would you say in response to each of the following arguments?
   a. Counselors are just extra baggage to the school—what is needed are more teachers.
   b. Counselors don't contribute to the students' lives at all; counseling is just "playing head games."
   c. All counselors do is interfere with the parents' rights to discipline their own children.
   d. Counselors only work with kids who are really sick.
2. Would the National Model help Cadence with her decision? How would you use the National Model to help Cadence decide whether to become a school counselor?
3. How will the Themes of the Model (namely, Leadership, Advocacy, Collaboration, and Systemic Change) relate to Kayli's conversation with Cadence?

APPLICATION (Possible portfolio artifacts are noted)

1. In your opinion, does the National Model bring school counseling into greater focus as a profession, or do you think it is a lot of talk that won't help school counselors? Discuss your answer with your classmates. Debate both positions in class.
2. You will be teaching a class on the National Model for various audiences. Reflecting the values and priorities that you believe belong to each audience group, write out your lecture notes for each of the following:
   a. Teachers
   b. Administrators
   c. Parents (Possible portfolio artifact)
3. What are your reactions to the Themes of systemic change, advocacy, leadership, and collaboration? What are the advantages to school

counselors that these are formally a part of the National Model, and what are the disadvantages?
4. What are your concerns about the School Counselor Performance Standards? In what way(s) does your current graduate program prepare you for these activities? In what areas will you need to enhance your skills to meet those Standards?
5. What are your concerns about your ability to follow the National Model? (The most often cited concerns involve lack of confidence in one's skills [of data collection and analysis, of advocacy, of leadership], and the amount of time [for the collection and analysis of the data, for advocacy, for collaboration].) What can you do to manage your concerns about all these topics? Design a stress reduction plan for yourself.

6. Create a skills inventory from the activities you see in the National Model, using the Counselor Performance Standards. Rate yourself on the skills inventory; then have a peer rate you. Design a professional development plan for improving your skills in those areas in which you perceive a deficit. (Possible portfolio artifact)

7. Wouldn't it be fun to be able to conduct a program audit for a school counseling program? Obtain a copy of the National Model with the Program Audit forms; then contact a school counselor to see if such work is possible at the level you plan to work as a professional. (Possible portfolio artifact)

8. Contact and interview a school counselor about data collection in that school and for that program. What kinds of data are collected by that program? What are the gaps you see in data collection in terms of the National Model? What does data collection actually involve? (Possible portfolio artifact)

9. In a group with three other students, each of you taking one Element of the Model, design a comprehensive school counseling program. What would a program look like that meets all the standards? (Possible portfolio artifact)

10. Use the Internet to locate and examine several school counseling websites. Rate what you see of the programs in terms of the National Model. To what extent do you see evidence of the Themes and Elements as outlined in the National Model?

SUGGESTED READINGS

Every professional school counselor must be familiar with the standards and expectations of the profession as articulated by the American School Counselor Association. The most important resources follow. Contact ASCA via the Internet to obtain a copy of each of the documents.

American School Counselor Association. (1999). *The role of the professional school counselor.* Alexandria, VA: Author.

American School Counselor Association. (2003). *The ASCA national model: A framework for school counseling programs.* Alexandria, VA: Author.

Campbell, C. A., & Dahir, C. A. (1997). *Sharing the vision: The national standards for school counseling programs.* Alexandria, VA: American School Counselor Association.

Stone, C. B., & Dahir, C. A. (2007). *School counselor accountability: A MEASURE of student success* (2nd ed.). Upper Saddle River, NJ: Pearson.

REFERENCES

American School Counselor Association. (1999). *The role of the professional school counselor.* Alexandria, VA: Author.

American School Counselor Association. (2003). *The ASCA national model: A framework for school counseling programs.* Alexandria, VA: Author.

Bolman, L. G., & Deal, T. E. (1997). *Reframing organizations: Artistry, choice, and leadership* (2nd ed.). San Francisco: Jossey-Bass.

Campbell, C. A., & Dahir, C. A. (1997). *Sharing the vision: The national standards for school counseling programs.* Alexandria, VA: American School Counselor Association.

Drew, S. F. (2004). The power of school-community collaboration in dropout prevention. In J. Smink and F. P. Schargel (Eds.), *Helping students graduate: A strategic approach to dropout prevention* (pp. 65–78). Larchmont, NY: Eye on Education.

Grolier Webster, Inc. (1975). *The new Grolier Webster international dictionary of the English language.* New York: Author.

Gysbers, N. C., & Henderson, P. (Eds.). (2000). *Developing and managing your school guidance program* (3rd ed.). Alexandria, VA: American Counseling Association.

Kouzes, J. M., & Posner, B. Z. (1995). *The leadership challenge: How to keep getting extraordinary things done in organizations.* San Francisco: Jossey-Bass.

Stone, C. B., & Dahir, C. A. (2007). *School counselor accountability: A MEASURE of student success* (2nd ed.). Upper Saddle River, NJ: Pearson.

6

MODELS FOR DELIVERING COMPREHENSIVE SCHOOL COUNSELING PROGRAMS

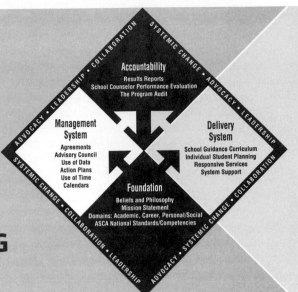

◆ LEARNING OBJECTIVES

By the end of this chapter, you will

1. Gain an understanding of four additional delivery system models for implementing comprehensive school counseling programs (in addition to Gysbers and Henderson's model discussed in the previous chapter)

2. Understand the difference between prescriptive and nonprescriptive models for comprehensive school counseling programs

3. Review relevant research on comprehensive school counseling programs

DOMAINS / ACTIVITIES / PARTNERS MODEL

	Academic Development ▼	Career Development ▼	Personal/ Social Development ▼			
Counseling	1a	1b	1c	5	6	7
Educating and Advocacy	2a	2b	2c	8	9	10
Consulting	3a	3b	3c	11	12	13
Leadership and Coordination	4a	4b	4c	14	15	16
	Students			Parents and Caregivers	Colleagues in Schools	Colleagues in Community

DOMAINS

ACTIVITIES

PARTNERS IN THE PROCESS

CASE STUDY

Molly DeRosa landed her ideal school counseling position. Fresh out of graduate school, and after interviewing with several school districts, Molly accepted a position with a district that valued school counselors and was committed to comprehensive school counseling programs. The district was in the beginning stages of designing a K–12 comprehensive school counseling program that would be implemented in all buildings, and it hired Molly to lead the way in the design of the new districtwide program. Molly's graduate program had thoroughly educated her in the ASCA National Model and provided her with opportunities to receive hands-on training in how to implement, manage, and evaluate comprehensive school counseling programs. Her school district was depending on her to provide the leadership necessary to move the district's school counseling program into the twenty-first century—to a comprehensive school counseling program.

One of Molly's first priorities was to assess the district's current school counseling program to determine what pieces were in place by conducting a districtwide audit: an assessment of the program pieces already in place, those which were "under construction," and those program components that were either in need of redesign or did not exist. The district's current school counseling program lacked a philosophical basis, mission, and organizational structure and was implemented inconsistently across groupings and buildings. The administration and school board supported comprehensive school counseling yet struggled with a district description and overall guiding mission statement. The school counselors were involved in a variety of activities across buildings and concentrated most of their efforts on assisting students with personal issues and providing services. They were aware of a need to involve students in more career exploration activities and lacked the means to implement such activities. Overall, how the counselors were using their time in relation to a district mission and rationale for school counseling was unknown. The individual schools had been able to produce some data and evaluation outcomes, but they were not linked to any specific program goals and objectives. Most of the evaluation data was subjective and anecdotal from parents, teachers, and students who voiced their appreciation and respect for the school counselors in such remarks as, "Our school counselors are wonderful! They help us feel good about ourselves, encourage our children, and assist the schools in many ways."

The challenge facing Molly was how to pull all of these pieces together and decide on a delivery model that would best suit the needs and goals of the district's school counseling programs. Would it be one delivery system model? Would it require more than one model, a combination perhaps, to fit with the district's definition, mission, and rationale for school counseling? How would it vary from building to building? Would one delivery system work best in one building and another in another building? What are the district's philosophy, rationale and mission of school counseling? She would definitely need to review current delivery systems to make an informed decision for her district. This was going to be a lengthy, time-consuming process.

CHALLENGE QUESTIONS

Based on your reading of Chapter 5, how do you think ASCA would advise Molly? If you were Molly, how would you decide which delivery model is most appropriate for implementing a comprehensive school counseling program in her district? Will Molly need to rely on one delivery system or will a combination of models work best for the needs of the district? What are the additional delivery systems models available for implementing a comprehensive school counseling program?

Comprehensive school counseling delivery models organize school counseling programs and provide school counselors with frameworks from which to implement, manage, and evaluate their school counseling programs. Chapter 5 provides an overview of the ASCA National Model (2003) and the foundation of this textbook. Models of delivery that follow the ASCA National Standards rely on Gysbers and Henderson's (2000) Comprehensive Guidance Program Model to organize their comprehensive school counseling programs, as this model is subsumed within the National Model. However, additional delivery models exist to assist school counselors in organizing, implementing, managing, and evaluating their comprehensive school counseling programs.

Various models of delivering comprehensive school counseling are grounded in "philosophical assumptions," essential program components, and specific goals and objectives (Brown & Trusty, 2005, p. 80). Each model outlined in this chapter aligns with the ASCA National Standards for School Counseling (2003), specifically the three domains of academic development, career development, and personal/social development. The models also support the mission of The Education Trust (2003) by promoting high academic achievement for all students. The differences among these models is how each one articulates their specific goals and objectives around the three domains for all students. Is the focus on developing competencies? Or is increasing knowledge the area of concentration? Perhaps changing behaviors and attitudes is most important. In most cases the goals and objectives of these delivery models focus on all of these areas (Brown & Trusty, 2005) for all students.

Specifically how school counselors meet their program goals and objectives lies on a continuum of implementation strategies. Some school counselors may rely mainly on

The ASCA School Counselor Performance Standards addressed in this chapter are

Standard 1: The professional school counselor plans, organizes and delivers the school counseling program.

1.1 A program is designed to meet the needs of the school.

1.2 The professional school counselor demonstrates interpersonal relationships with students.

1.3 The professional school counselor demonstrates positive interpersonal relationships with educational staff.

1.4 The professional school counselor demonstrates positive interpersonal relationships with parents or guardians.

The CACREP Standards for School Counseling Programs addressed in this chapter are

B.4 promotion of the use of counseling and guidance activities and programs by the total school community to enhance a positive school climate;

C.1 **(b)** design, implementation, monitoring, and evaluation of comprehensive developmental school counseling programs (e.g., the ASCA National Standards for School Counseling Programs) including an awareness of various systems that affect students, school, and home; and

C.3 **(d)** knowledge and skills in conducting programs that are designed to enhance students' academic, social, emotional, career, and other developmental needs.

classroom and large-group guidance, whereas other school counselors may devote a majority of their time to individual and small-group counseling programs. Still other school counselors may implement more schoolwide counseling programs such as teacher-advisor, peer facilitation, and mediation programs to meet the specific goals and objectives of the school counseling program. Choice of strategies generally evolves from district philosophy and mission, as well as needs assessment and ongoing program evaluation.

Each delivery model places emphasis on data derived from needs assessments and program evaluations as a means of determining how and if the school counseling program is meeting its goals and objectives (Brown & Trusty, 2005). Data from these sources informs decisions, recommendations, and, in essence, fuels school counseling programs. Data and knowledge are vital to ensuring that all students have access to resources and are receiving essential services to increase academic achievement and close gaps between groups (The Education Trust, 2003).

Delivery models generally fall into one of two categories: *prescriptive* or *nonprescriptive*. Prescriptive models tend to rest on clear assumptions as to the role and function of school counselors and school counseling programs. Based on specific guidelines, prescriptive models tend to detail specific "do's and don'ts" for school counselors. Specific prescriptive guidelines may include the use of a calendar, what percentage of a school counselors' time should be spent in specific areas, and what activities school counselors should be engaging in. Nonprescriptive models rely more on aligning the role and function of school counselors and school counseling programs with the needs of the school and the student body. Specific assumptions and "do's and don'ts" are not characteristic of nonprescriptive models, meaning school counselors are freer to use their time and delivery strategies as deemed appropriate (Brown & Trusty, 2005).

Reflection Moment ◆

Based on what you know about yourself, which category, prescriptive or nonprescriptive, fits more with your personality and school counseling style? Do you prefer a more detailed and specific organizational structure, or do you prefer to have more freedom and flexibility within your organizational structure?

◆ ◆

◆ MODELS OF DELIVERY SYSTEMS

The Essential Services Model

Based on the *trait-and-factor approach* (Brown & Trusty, 2005), the essential services model evolved out of differential psychology and studies concerned with the "measurement of human traits and environments" (p. 82). School counselors may well recall the traditional career planning process of assessing students' values, interests, skills, and abilities and using the results to assist students in locating an occupation that matched their assessment (Brown & Trusty, 2005). The original components of the essential services model included counseling, educational and occupational information, student appraisal, and placement (Brown & Trusty, 2005; Gibson, Mitchell, & Higgins, 1983; Williamson, 1939). Schmidt (2003) presented an updated version of the essential services model based on the components of counseling, consulting, coordinating, and appraising. These four broad categories make up the essential components of comprehensive school counseling programs and provide a framework for school counselors to design their roles and functions (Brown & Trusty, 2005).

The counseling component includes such activities as individual counseling, group counseling, student counseling, and parent and teacher counseling (Schmidt, 2003). Individual counseling may be developmental in nature and focus on assisting students in problem solving, decision making, "relationships, and self-development" through a variety of modalities such as play therapy, "nonverbal interactions, and modeling techniques" (p. 80). Schmidt (2003) advocates for group counseling as an essential service and recognizes that school counselors often shy away from relying on groups because of the disruption created for teachers. School counselors are encouraged to collaborate with teachers to design creative ways to promote group counseling and maintain a reasonable instructional schedule (Schmidt, 2003). The component of parent and teacher counseling recognizes that often school counselors are approached by parents and teachers for assistance with personal problems and concerns. Whereas school counselors are expected to listen fully and empathize with individuals' troubles, they should make every effort to refer parents and teachers to the appropriate community services. Schmidt (2003) views this type of service to parents and teachers as a "combination of counseling and consulting processes" (p. 83).

Consulting activities include information services, instructional services, problem-solving services, and other school services (Schmidt, 2003). School counselors serve as resources for information, concerning for example, community and school resources, career opportunities, educational opportunities, and financial assistance. Instructional services describe classroom guidance, parent education, and teacher in-services. Interestingly, Schmidt (2003) places classroom guidance under the component of consulting and agrees that school counselors do not play a major role in the delivery of classroom guidance. Problem-solving activities involve parent-teacher conferences, administrative conferences, and student services team conferences. Other school services might include developing guidance curriculum, individual student planning, school climate initiatives, and special events and projects.

The component of coordination focuses on activities involving data collection and sharing, referrals and follow-up, and schoolwide events (Schmidt, 2003). Data collection concerns itself with test administration, test results, and student records. Referrals and follow-up include activities that require school counselors to network and connect with community agencies and private practitioners. Schoolwide events could be activities such as student recognition assemblies, career awareness campaigns, teacher-advisor programs, and peer-helper programs.

Appraising emphasizes student evaluation and environmental evaluation (Schmidt, 2003). Student evaluation activities are concerned with tests, inventories, observations and interviews, and group assessment. Environmental evaluation activities involve assessment of school climate, families, and peer groups.

Designing an essential services comprehensive school counseling program involves planning, organizing, implementing, and evaluating. Activities include assessing the current program; seeking input and support for change; assessing the needs of students, parents, and teachers; determining resources; assigning responsibilities; marketing the program; scheduling services; balancing time; providing services; and evaluating outcomes. Schmidt (2003) places assessment as a priority in the planning process "because assessment is the fuel for counseling and consultation" (Brown & Trusty, 2005, p. 82).

The Essential Services model has served as a basis for comprehensive school counseling for decades. The model typically does not account for all of the activities of a school counselor; however, the four components of counseling, consulting, coordinating, and appraising, generally considered as interdependent activities, target all students' personal/social, educational, and career development needs (Brown & Trusty, 2005).

Reflection Moment ◆

What are your reactions to the Essential Services Model? What aspects of the model are more meaningful for you? What pieces of the model are not as appealing?

◆ ◆

Developmental Guidance and Counseling Model

Developmental guidance (Myrick, 1987, 1993) focuses on those developmental learning behaviors, tasks, skills, and experiences necessary for children and adolescents to be successful in school and in life. It is based on the assumption that "human nature moves individuals sequentially and positively toward self-enhancement" (Myrick, 1987, p. 31). As children and adolescents move through the consecutive stages of development, they require certain skills, behaviors, and attitudes for successful transition from one stage to the next. Likewise, young people naturally encounter challenges and problem situations as they mature and develop. Developmental guidance promotes students' learning about themselves and others before problem situations occur and provides the necessary skills to deal with those situations in advance (Myrick, 1987, 1993).

Developmental guidance is organized around a planned, sequential developmental curriculum that complements the existing academic curriculum. Teachers and counselors collaboratively and cooperatively integrate the developmental curriculum into the regular academic curriculum. The development of specific life skills are included in the developmental curriculum to assist in preparing students for adulthood (Myrick, 1993). The developmental guidance curriculum is generally organized around eight specific objectives. They are (1) understanding the social environment, (2) understanding self and others, (3) understanding attitudes and behavior, (4) decision making and problem solving, (5) interpersonal and communication skills, (6) school success skills, (7) career awareness and educational planning, and (8) community pride (Myrick, 1993).

In addition to these eight program objectives, seven principles of developmental guidance provide direction to program implementation and evaluation. Developmental guidance (1) is for all students; (2) has an organized and planned curriculum; (3) is sequential and flexible; (4) is an integrated part of the total educational process; (5) involves all school personnel; (6) helps students learn more effectively and efficiently; and (7) includes counselors who provide specialized counseling services and interventions (Myrick, 1993).

Developmental guidance programs depend on the collaboration and participation of everyone working together to promote students' personal, academic, and social growth (Myrick, 1987, 1993). One of the most successful approaches to directly involving teachers in the personal development of students places the teacher as an advisor to a group of 15 to 20 students who become their advisees (Myrick & Myrick, 1990). Teacher-advisors work with their advisees on a more personal level, build closer relationships, and serve as "everyday advocates" (Gonzalez & Myrick, 2000, p. 243) for their assigned students. This type of program is often referred to as an advisory program, a mentoring program, or a teacher-advisor program (TAP).

This concept of teacher-advisor programs (TAP) was first introduced into the middle schools (Daresh & Pautsch, 1981). Modeled after elementary schools, TAP programs organize students under a team of teachers and assign a homeroom teacher who meets with the students regularly and serves as advisor to the students (Alexander & George, 1981). Homeroom provides a time when developmental guidance lessons and units are presented and processed with all students. Guidance units generally focus on getting acquainted, study skills and habits, self-assessment, communication skills, decision making and problem solving, peer relationships, motivation, conflict resolution, wellness, career development, educational planning, and community involvement (Myrick, 1993). Florida and Wisconsin have well-respected TAP programs. Examples are Green Bay, Wisconsin's program entitled "Our Time"; in Florida, Hillsborough County's "Quality Time"; Orlando's "IMPACT"; and Sarasota's "Prime Time" programs (Gonzalez & Myrick, 2000).

Teachers are not expected to take all the responsibility for a developmental guidance program; counselors are central to developmental guidance programs. Counselors serve as resources for the teachers and work collaboratively with the teachers on an ongoing basis. Counselors help co-lead guidance lessons or may be invited in as guests. Counselors develop special units based on their assessment of the specific needs of students. A highlight of TAP is the time it allows for counselors to meet with students on an individual basis or in small groups without interrupting the regular academic schedule (Myrick, 1993).

The existence of a school guidance committee solidifies the counselor-teacher relationship and provides a practical solution for creating a collaborative, team environment between counselors and teachers. The guidance committee meets regularly to identify students' needs and concerns, brainstorm ideas, review curriculum, design prevention programs, explore strategies for specific interventions, and examine data and evaluation measures (Myrick, 1993).

The role and function of counselors in developmental guidance programs expand across a diverse array of activities and services. Counselors are developmental guidance specialists, facilitators, and providers of basic and essential counselor interventions. Their expertise in developmental theory and counseling theory makes them invaluable resources in designing age-appropriate developmental guidance curriculum, individual student interventions, and schoolwide prevention and intervention strategies.

Counseling interventions in developmental school counseling programs consist of the six basic counseling tools: individual counseling, small-group counseling, large-group guidance, peer facilitator training and projects, consultation, and coordination of guidance services. These basic interventions are general recommendations and provide the role and function of school counselors in developmental school counselor programs (Myrick, 1993).

Peer facilitator programs as a counseling intervention is unique to developmental guidance. This popular counselor intervention trains peer facilitators in basic helping skills to enable them to assist other students. Although parents and other adults have great influences on children, it is peers who are most influential during the school years. Most youngsters would rather turn to a peer/friend than a parent, teacher, or other adult when encountering a problem (Myrick, 1993). Some examples of peer facilitator programs include peer tutoring to students in school suspension; tutoring students who have missed extended amounts of school due to special circumstances; tutoring students in specific subjects; and peer mediation. Extensive training and supervision are absolute necessities when students are assisting other students, and counselors serve as process monitors, consultants, and supervisors in peer programs.

All comprehensive school counseling programs are accountable: What are the objectives of our school counseling program? Are we meeting those goals and objectives? How can we improve in how we are going about meeting our goals and objectives? Accountability procedures are instrumental in all comprehensive school counseling programs. As described in Chapter 5, the four essential phases of program evaluation are planning, designing, implementing, and evaluating.

Implementing a comprehensive developmental school counseling program relies on a series of implementation strategies. They are: (1) administrative understanding and support; (2) selecting a school guidance advisory committee; (3) developing and writing a philosophy statement; (4) needs survey; (5) developing and writing a program rationale; (6) setting goals, objectives, and developing strategies for implementation; and (7) accountability (Wittmer, 1993).

Developmental guidance and counseling is a comprehensive preventative delivery model grounded in a well-planned, developmentally appropriate guidance curriculum that is integrated with the existing academic curriculum for all. A majority of the program goals and objectives depend on classroom guidance; however, developmental guidance programs also include specialized counseling services and interventions. This model relies on all school personnel as part of the total education process aimed at helping students learn more effectively and efficiently (Myrick, 1993).

Reflection Moment ◆

What are your reactions to developmental guidance and counseling? What aspects of the model are more meaningful for you? What pieces of the model are not as appealing?

◆ ◆

Results-Based Program Delivery Model

Instead of asking, "What do counselors do?" a results-based systems approach asks, "What do students learn, and how are students different as a result of what they learn?" Goals, standards, and competencies define the ways that students are prepared for success. Accountability focuses on outcomes, more clearly stated as student results. These statements describe a systems approach to building a results-based school counseling program.

Results-based guidance or "new guidance" offers a guarantee that all students will acquire the competencies to be successful in school and in their transition into higher education, employment, or a combination thereof. Student competencies are articulated based on research that reveals student needs (Johnson & Johnson, 2003) and focus on the academic, career, and personal/social needs of students. Counselors work as teams with students, parents, school personnel, social workers, psychologists, nurses, and specialists to meet the needs of students (Johnson & Johnson, 2003)—especially those traditionally "left behind."

This acute focus on those who have been underserved by our educational system has been promoted by The Education Trust, a nonprofit organization dedicated to educational reform through accountability and data analysis. According to Reese House, director of the new National Center for Transforming School Counseling, the emphasis is on providing "practicing school counselors with the data and knowledge to lead schools efforts to raise achievement of all students and close the gap between groups once and for all" (The Education Trust, 2003).

Program evaluation reflects the number of students who demonstrate the competencies learned and achieved (Johnson & Johnson, 2003). Based on the identified student competencies, program evaluation might ask, "How many high school juniors achieved proficiency in postsecondary planning as a result of tenth-grade career planning workshops?" Counselors are then evaluated on their success in providing guidance competencies. School counselors use the research on student needs and select, design, and implement programs that achieve results.

School counselors are positioned to provide the management and leadership for the school counseling program. They are instrumental in maintaining the vision of the school counseling program and monitoring its direction aimed at meeting students' needs. Continuous and ongoing evaluation, combined with constant analysis of disaggregated data, provide systemic management to the school counseling program and accountability for the progress of all students (Johnson & Johnson, 2003).

This systems-oriented delivery model is proactive and preventive and designed to reach all students as an integral part of the academic curriculum. School counselors' skills and knowledge are expanded beyond counseling and crisis interventions. Developmental age-appropriate programming as part of the educational component assists students with acquiring lifelong problem-solving and decision-making skills (Johnson & Johnson, 2003).

Program elements are congruent with the school district's philosophy, curriculum, and other educational programs. The elements are (1) mission (vision, purpose); (2) philosophy (guiding principles); (3) conceptual model of guidance (framework for students goals and competencies based in research); (4) goals (desired results); (5) competencies (developed proficiencies); (6) management system (data flow schedule); (7) results agreements (the responsibility statements of each support team member); (8) needs assessment/data (the gap between desired results and results that are being achieved); (9) results plans (the plan for how results will be achieved); (10) monitoring system (the assurance that each student acquires specific academic, career, and personal/social competencies); (11) advisory council (the representatives of those groups affected by the program who will review results and make recommendations); and (12) master calendar of events (the communication tool for programs offered) (Johnson & Johnson, 2003; Johnson, Johnson, & Downs, 2006).

A results-based delivery model gives professional direction while providing school counselors with the flexibility to use their time as best suited to meet the needs of their school counseling program and the students (Johnson & Johnson, 2003). Each element serves an individual purpose, and when combined, creates a comprehensive program based on results to achieve results. Schools and districts are free to design and deliver curriculum, manage and implement programs, and use their resources and allocations to achieve the results that best meet the needs and desired results for their students (Johnson, Johnson, & Downs, 2006).

Reflection Moment ✦

What are your reactions to the results-based program delivery model? What aspects of the model are more meaningful for you? What pieces of the model are not as appealing?

✦ ✦

The Domains/Activities/Partners Model

The Domains/Activities/Partners (DAP) Model (Dollarhide & Saginak, 2003) provides school counselors with both a systemic and systematic way of thinking about their role and function with an organizing strategy for a comprehensive school counseling program (CSCP). The DAP Model emphasizes student-focused activities that result in student competencies and success through collaborative partnerships among counselors, students, parents, colleagues in the schools, and colleagues in the community (Dollarhide, 2003). Collaboration between all of the partners in the education process is crucial "to the success of our students, our programs, and our schools" (p. 93).

To ensure comprehensive school counseling, school counselors must have a systematic way of understanding their work in order to design programmatic interventions, prioritize conflicting demands on time, and evaluate both their effectiveness and that of their program (ASCA, 2003; S. B. Baker, 2000; Gysbers & Henderson, 2000; Schmidt, 1999). To that end, we have designed a model that serves a variety of purposes. It increases the emphasis on students while concurrently reducing the emphasis on nonstudent-focused activities and provides a systematic way of thinking about the work of the school counselor that fits with the ASCA National Model. As you can see from Figure 6.1, this new model could serve as the delivery system of the National Model.

The DAP model outlines the domains of student competencies that focus the work of the counselor and the program, the activities in which school counselors engage to facilitate the students' success in those competencies, and the partnerships that are crucial to the success of our students, our programs, and our schools. As you can see from Figure 6.1, the shading indicates the primary activity with that partner. While the domains define our work with students, each activity is nonetheless applicable to each partner in the model. Figure 6.2 gives a description of each square in the model to help you conceptualize how each activity with each partner in the model would appear in practice.

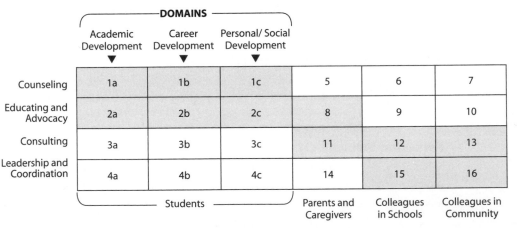

FIGURE 6.1 ◆ Domains/Activities/Partners Model (shading indicates primary activities with that partner)

FIGURE 6.2 ◆ Domains/Activities/Partners Model, Detail

Italics indicate primary activities with that partner.

1a: *Academic counseling with students*
1b: *Career counseling with students*
1c: *Personal/social counseling with students*
2a: *Educating students about academic issues (developmental guidance) and advocating academic excellence with students*
2b: *Educating students about career issues and advocating pursuit of career dreams*
2c: *Educating students about personal/social issues and advocating personal/social excellence*
3a: Consulting with students about academic issues (i.e., how to work with certain teachers)
3b: Consulting with students about career issues (i.e., how to get along with authority figures, employers)
3c: Consulting with students about personal/social issues (i.e., how to get along better with family members)
4a: Leading and coordinating academic events for students (i.e., study skills workshops or presentations)
4b: Leading and coordinating career activities for students (i.e., career fairs, school-to-work programs)
4c: Leading and coordinating personal/social activities for students (i.e., serving as the advisor of a student group)
5:      Counseling with parents and caregivers, as appropriate, then referrals
6:      Counseling with colleagues in schools, as appropriate, then referrals
7:      Counseling with colleagues in the community, as appropriate, then referrals
8:      *Educating parents and caregivers about developmental issues of students, and advocating on behalf of students and schools.*
9:      Educating colleagues in schools about developmental issues of students and advocating on behalf of students and schools.
10:     Educating colleagues in the community about developmental issues of students and advocating on behalf of students and schools.
11:     *Consulting with parents and caregivers about problems with students or the school.*
12:     *Consulting with colleagues in schools about developmental issues of students or the family.*
13:     *Consulting with colleagues in the community about developmental issues of students, the school, or the family.*
14:     Leadership in making the school a respectful place for parents and coordinating services for parents as appropriate (i.e., assisting with a parent resource room).
15:     *Leadership in making the school a respectful place for students and coordinating information for the school and district administrators about the school counseling program; administrative tasks as appropriate.*
16:     *Leadership in making others aware of the needs of the school community and coordinating efforts of community colleagues who support the school (i.e., coordinating the mental health staffing for students who are in therapy in the community).*

The Domains.   The three domains of the DAP model align with the ASCA National Standards domains—academic, career, and personal/social development (ASCA, 2003). These three domains and associated student competencies, combined with those competencies outlined by the school/district, define a school counselor's work. Consistent with the ASCA National Standards for Student Academic, Career, and Personal/Social Development (ASCA, 2003; Campbell & Dahir, 1997), the Domains of the model consist of the student competencies promulgated in that document. Counselors designing programs for their school and district would insert those competencies (see Appendix B), and those prioritized within their district, to define the primary focus of their comprehensive school counseling program. Even though the National Standards for Student Academic, Career, and Personal/Social Development only address the Domains within the Student Partner column, they are the most important priority of the comprehensive school counseling program.

The Activities.   The four activities most appropriate for school counselors, as advocated by ASCA, are counseling, educating and advocating, consulting, and leadership and coordination (ASCA, 2003; Dollarhide, 2003). Figure 6.2 describes each unit of the model and how the model might be implemented and appear in practice (Dollarhide, 2003). The DAP model, more so than other delivery models, aligns completely with the ASCA National Standards and the National Model. Over the last twenty years, appropriate school counselor activities have been described as counseling, developmental curriculum programming, consulting, referral, coordinating, providing information (advising), enhancing transitions, assessment/appraisal, and system support of public relations, committee service, and community outreach (ASCA, 1999; S. B. Baker, 2000; Gysbers & Henderson, 2000; Schmidt, 1999). We have synthesized these insights into four activities: counseling, educating and advocating, consulting, and leadership and coordination. We believe that these four terms incorporate the activities of the other models, in that

1. *Counseling* refers to individual and group counseling, peer facilitators, the use of assessment in the counseling process, as well as making referrals as a means of bringing closure to counseling relationships. It is listed first as the foundation of the comprehensive school counseling philosophy and as the most essential activity that students indicate they want from the school counselor (Hutchinson & Bottorff, 1986; Wiggins & Moody, 1987). This activity is outlined in detail in Chapter 7.

2. *Educating* refers to developmental curriculum, facilitating transitions, advisement, placement, and assessment and appraisal. In addition, this term, more than the term "guidance," accurately describes what counselors do in the schools, as well as clearly describing how comprehensive school counseling allies with the mission of the school. *Advocating* refers to activities that educate with passion, those activities that enhance others' affective understanding of, and empathy for, students, schools, families, the comprehensive school counseling program, and better human relationships. It includes, as ASCA (2003, 1999) points out, championing what is best for students, their families, schools, and the community, and is one of the Themes of the ASCA National Model. These activities are discussed in Chapter 8.

3. *Consulting* refers to problem solving, referring, enhancing communications, and mediation. We feel this activity is a hybrid between counseling and educating, requiring specialized skills that are unique. Chapter 9 discusses this activity.

4. *Leadership* involves several areas: developing and maintaining the vision of the comprehensive school counseling program and promoting the importance of a developmentally appropriate learning environment. In addition, this is one of the Themes of the ASCA National Model (ASCA, 2003). *Coordination* and collaboration refer to the management of logistics to bring programs to the partners of the school counselor. Leadership and coordination are connected, as they include management activities to provide information to the school and the district about the program, general outreach and public relations, school/professional/community committee service, and programs that reach a large audience of students. Furthermore, making these activities an explicit part of the Delivery System provide for both the Themes of the ASCA National Model (Collaboration and Systemic Change) and the Management System and Accountability to be explicit in the activities of the school counselor. Chapter 10 explores these activities in detail.

The Partners.   It is vital that you understand why the concept of "partnership" is used in discussing the people involved in the comprehensive school counseling program. First, it is important to reinforce the collegial, collaborative, and egalitarian nature of the relationships counselors must develop with everyone in the school setting. Second, it serves to reinforce the active nature of the participation in school counseling programs as counseling, educating/advocating, consulting, and leading/coordinating are all active, intentional behaviors, both for the counselor and for others in the process. Third, it is important for counselors to remember that it takes a whole community to raise a child. Similarly, it takes an entire community to educate healthy and resilient young people; no one person can do it alone. So no one school counselor, no matter how talented and dedicated that person may be, can be the only helping professional for our students. We must reach out and establish these broad, inclusive partnerships for the students' benefit. The work of the school counselor could not happen without our partners in the process. In addition, the National Model includes Systemic Change as one of the themes, and the Management System and Accountability both incorporate the work counselors do with colleagues in the schools. By considering all these individuals our partners, we explicitly include these individuals as part of our work.

Similarly, school counselors have responsibilities to all of our partners. Just as the profession has articulated the National Standards for Student Academic, Career, and Personal/Social Development, there is also the need to understand our program goals with our adult partners. These goals have been proposed in Appendix D as a beginning for conversations about our work with our adult partners.

Our primary partner is the student. At its most fundamental level, school counseling would not occur without students; their development is the very essence of the comprehensive school counseling program. By calling them partners in the process, we hope to convey that they, too, are stakeholders in the program; their involvement in the program, in many cases, is voluntary, and so we can't take for granted that they will avail themselves of the services we have to offer. We must actively solicit their continued involvement.

Our second partners are parents and caregivers. We must remember that they, too, have a stake in the school counseling program (Schmidt, 1999). Involvement of the student is contingent on parental approval (depending on the age and circumstance), so we cannot forget that, by extension, parents impact whether we have students with whom to work. Their involvement is essential (Colbert, 1996).

Our third partners are our colleagues in the schools. Teachers, administrators, school social workers, school psychologists, school nurses, and the administrative staff are very involved with how our program functions and how effective we can be. By extension, this includes professionals from other schools, at the district level, and in the school counseling profession as a whole.

Finally, we have partners in the community. From the mental health professional who provides therapy, to the physician who provides medication, to the local businessperson who provides jobs, these stakeholders need to be included in the school counseling program as their work may have implications for individual students and/or the school.

Reflection Moment ❖

What are your reactions to the Domains/Activities/Partners (DAP) Model? What aspects of the model are more meaningful for you? What pieces of the model are not as appealing?

❖ ❖

Partners and the Advisory Board.   As was outlined in the National Model, the process of building a comprehensive program begins with building the foundation of an agreed-upon philosophy and mission statement. This begins with convening a working advisory board. In conjunction with the discussion of partners, it is important to also provide some information about how to operationalize the concept of "partner" into insights in building your advisory board.

The size of the group will need to be carefully considered to maximize the ability for members to meet as a group over several sessions. This advisory committee should consist of representatives of each group of partners:

1. *Students.* Select student representatives from all areas, not just the areas that are already well represented in school structures. As an example from a secondary school setting, select students from honors groups, athletics, the vo-tech program, frequent detention attendees, music, theater, and other student venues. The point is, at every educational level, to include students from across the spectrum in terms of ability, family income, language in the home, grade level, and school involvement.

2. *Parents and caregivers.* Select parent and caregiver representatives from all economic strata of your attendance area, including those who are in shelters and/or homeless (Strawser, Markos, Yamaguchi, & Higgins, 2000). Include parents and guardians from a variety of neighborhoods, not just those in the parent-teacher associations.

3. *Colleagues in the schools.* Select representatives from teachers, aides, administrators, and other student services professionals. Go outside your school building to invite counselors from other schools, including your feeder schools (if any) and counselors from the schools to which your students progress. In addition, you may want to invite representatives from the district level of administration, perhaps including the director of pupil services and even a representative from the school board itself.

4. *Colleagues in the community.* Invite representatives from employers, community mental health providers, medical professionals, and so on. In addition, you may wish to invite colleagues from other social service agencies with which you interact.

There are several purposes of this group. First, they will assist you in the design of the comprehensive school counseling program. Second, they will guide you as you implement the program. Third, they will assist you in the assessment and evaluation of your program as time passes, so it is imperative that your advisory group comprises people who are committed to and understand developmentally appropriate schools, young people, and school counseling. Finally, they will help you design programs for the adult partners in terms of the activities of the DAP model.

◆UPCOMING CHAPTERS

This chapter introduced and highlighted other delivery models used to implement comprehensive developmental school counseling programs. These models provide school counselors with effective services, goals and objectives, and components and activities necessary in the design of a CSCP. The differences in the models are philosophically based, and varying degrees of alignment with the ASCA National Model are evident. The similarity of the models is the priority placed on the three domains of personal/social, academic achievement, and career development advocated by the ASCA National Model and supported by state boards of education, school districts, buildings, and communities.

Upcoming chapters will further explore the activities of the DAP Model, and specific chapters are dedicated to "real-life" examples of school counseling programs across the nation. Chapters 7–10 correspond with each of the activities, and within each chapter, the activity relative to each partner is discussed. Chapter 7 focuses on counseling with all partners. Specifically this chapter provides an understanding of developmentally appropriate individual, group, and peer facilitated counseling interventions with students, understanding and applying a systems perspective in working with adult partners, and relevant ethical issues. In Chapter 8 educating and advocating with all partners is explored in depth, specifically in relation to student competencies, developmental curriculum, creating respectful and developmentally appropriate classroom environments, and educating and advocating with adult partners. Consultation with all partners is the focus of Chapter 9. In this chapter consultation is examined as an effective means of working with all partners using a variety of consultation processes including a generic process model of consultation and personal philosophy of consultation. Chapter 10 discusses leadership and coordination with all partners and the importance of the activities of the ASCA National Model including leading an advisory council, managing the system, and accountability practices.

Chapters 11–13 highlight actual school counseling programs that utilize the ASCA National Model. Chapter 11 introduces Ford Elementary School in Tucson, Arizona. Sequoia Middle School located in Fontana, California, a suburb of Los Angeles, is presented in Chapter 12. Chapter 13 highlights Wakefield High School in Raleigh, North Carolina. Each of these schools demonstrates how comprehensive school counseling is implemented using the various delivery models.

CASE STUDY REVISTED ◆ Integration

Now that you've read the chapter, answer the following questions:

1. What is Molly's greatest challenge?
2. What three questions could you ask Molly to encourage her thinking about the delivery model(s) most appropriate for the district's school counseling program?
3. Given what you know about delivery models, which model(s) would you employ for implementing comprehensive school counseling? Provide a rationale.

APPLICATION (Possible portfolio artifacts are noted)

1. Develop a mission statement for a school counseling program.
2. Develop a rationale for a school counseling program.
3. Design an age-appropriate developmental guidance curriculum that focuses on one of the goals of developmental guidance. (Possible portfolio artifact)
4. Research the current delivery models. What are some similarities? What are some differences? Which of the models or which parts of the models would you use in the design of a comprehensive school counseling program?
5. In small groups, outline the strengths and weaknesses of the current delivery models. Create a delivery model based on research and what you have learned about the current models.

SUGGESTED READINGS

School counselors are encouraged to be knowledgeable about current delivery models for implementing comprehensive school counseling programs. The following recommended readings will provide important resources for deciding which delivery model(s) are most appropriate for attaining the goals of your building's school counseling programs.

American School Counselor Association. (2003). *The ASCA National Model: A framework for school counseling programs.* Alexandria, VA: Author.

Baker, S. B. (2000). *School counseling for the twenty-first century* (3rd ed.). Upper Saddle River, NJ: Merrill.

Brown, D., & Trusty, J. (2005). *Designing and leading comprehensive school counseling programs: Promoting student competence and meeting student needs.* Belmont, CA: Brooks/Cole.

Dollarhide, C. T., & Saginak, K. A. (2003). *School counseling in the secondary schools: A comprehensive process and program.* New York: Allyn and Bacon.

[The] Education Trust. (2003). Transforming school counseling. Available at www2.edtrust.org/EdTrust/Transforming+School+Counseling/main.

Gysbers, N. C., & Henderson, P. (2000). *Developing and managing your school guidance program*

(3rd ed.). Alexandria, VA: American Counseling Association.

Myrick, R. D. (1993). *Developmental guidance and counseling: A practical approach* (2nd ed). Minneapolis, MN: Educational Media Corp.

Paisley, P. O., & Hubbard, G. T. (1994). *Developmental school counseling programs: From theory to*

practice. Alexandria, VA: American Counseling Association.

Schmidt, J. J. (2003). *Counseling in the schools: Essential services and comprehensive programs* (4th ed.). Boston: Allyn and Bacon.

Sink, C. (2005). *Contemporary school counseling: Theory, research, and practice.* Boston: Lahaska Press.

REFERENCES

Alexander, W. M., & George, P. S. (1981). The exemplary middle school. In R. D. Myrick (Ed.), *Developmental guidance and counseling: A practical approach* (2nd ed). Minneapolis, MN: Educational Media Corp.

American School Counselor Association. (1999). *The role of the professional school counselor.* Alexandria, VA: Author.

American School Counselor Association. (2003). *The ASCA National Model: A framework for school counseling programs.* Alexandria, VA: Author.

Baker, S. B. (2000). *School counseling for the twenty-first century* (3rd ed.). Upper Saddle River, NJ: Merrill.

Brown, D., & Trusty, J. (2005). *Designing and leading comprehensive school counseling programs: Promoting student competence and meeting student needs.* Belmont, CA: Brooks/Cole.

Campbell, C. A., & Dahir, C. A. (1997). *Sharing the vision: The national standards for school counseling programs.* Alexandria, VA: American School Counselor Association.

Colbert, R. D. (1996). The counselor's role in advancing school and family partnerships. *School Counselor, 44*(2), 100–104.

Daresh, J. C., & Pautsch, T. R. (1981). A successful teacher-advisor program. *Middle School Journal, 14*(3), 3–13.

Dollarhide, C. T. (2003). Comprehensive school counseling program and the domains/activities/partners model. In C. T. Dollarhide & K. A. Saginak (Eds.), *School counseling in the secondary schools: A comprehensive process and program.* New York: Allyn and Bacon.

Dollaride, C. T., & Saginak, K. A. (2003). *School counseling in the secondary schools: A comprehensive process and program.* New York: Allyn and Bacon.

[The] Education Trust. (2003) Transforming school counseling. Retrieved on May 22, 2006, from www.2.edtrust.org/EdTrust/Transforming+School+Counseling/main.

Gibson, R. I., Mitchell, M. H., & Higgins, R. E. (1983). Development and management of counseling programs and guidance services. In D. Brown & J. Trusty (Eds.), *Designing and leading comprehensive school counseling programs: Promoting student competence and meeting student needs* (pp. 78–106). Belmont, CA: Brooks/Cole.

Gonzalez, G. M., & Myrick, R. D. (2000). The Teacher as Student Advisors Program (TAP): An effective approach for drug education and other developmental activities. In J. Wittmer (Eds.), *Managing your school counseling program: K–12 developmental strategies.* (pp. 243–252). Minneapolis, MN: Educational Media Corp.

Gysbers, N. C., & Henderson, P. (2000). *Developing and managing your school guidance program* (3rd ed.). Alexanderia, VA: American Counseling Assocation.

Hutchinson, R. L., & Bottorff, R. L. (1986). Selected high school counseling services: Student assessment. *The School Counselor, 33,* 350–354.

Johnson, S., & Johnson, C. D. (2003). Results-based guidance: A systems approach to student support programs. *Professional School Counseling, 6*(3), 180–184.

Johnson, S., Johnson, C., & Downs, L. (2006). *Building a results-based student support program.* Boston: Lahaska Press.

Myrick, R. D. (1987). *Developmental guidance and counseling: A practical approach.* Minneapolis, MN: Educational Media Corp.

Myrick, R. D. (1993). *Developmental guidance and counseling: A practical approach* (2nd ed). Minneapolis, MN: Educational Media Corp.

Myrick, R. D., & Myrick, L. (1990). *The teacher advisor program: An innovative approach to school guidance.* Ann Arbor: University of Michigan, ERIC Counseling and Personnel Services.

Schmidt, J. J. (1999). *Counseling in the schools: Essential services and comprehensive programs* (3rd ed.). Boston: Allyn and Bacon.

Schmidt, J. J. (2003). *Counseling in the schools: Essential services and comprehensive programs* (4th ed.). Boston: Allyn and Bacon.

Strawser, S., Markos, P. A., Yamaguchi, B. J., & Higgins, K. (2000). A new challenge for school counselors: Children who are homeless. *Professional School Counseling, 3*, 162–171.

Wiggins, J. D., & Moody, A. H. (1987). Student evaluations of counseling programs: An added dimension. *The School Counselor, 34*, 353–361.

Williamson, E. G. (1939). How to counsel students: A manual of techniques for clinical counseling. In D. Brown & J. Trusty (Eds.), *Designing and leading comprehensive school counseling programs: Promoting student competence and meeting student needs* (pp. 78–106). Belmont, CA: Brooks/Cole.

Wittmer, J. (1993). Implementing a comprehensive developmental school counseling program. In J. Wittmer (Eds.), *Managing your school counseling program: K–12 developmental strategies* (pp. 191–200). Minneapolis, MN: Educational Media Corp.

SECTION FOUR

The Activities within Comprehensive School Counseling Programs

CHAPTER

7

COUNSELING FOR ALL PARTNERS

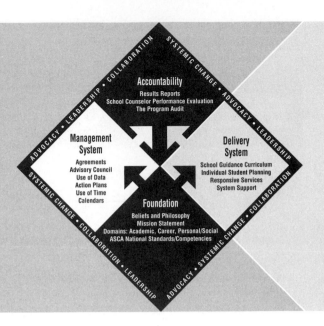

◆ LEARNING OBJECTIVES

By the end of this chapter, you will

1. Understand how counseling may be perceived by colleagues in the school setting; design ways to communicate with them about the nature of counseling and how important it is for students
2. Understand the concept of developmentally appropriate counseling
3. Understand how to use multiple intelligences when developing theoretically congruent counseling interventions
4. Evaluate when counseling is warranted for effective intervention and when referral is warranted for effective treatment
5. Be able to evaluate the advantages and disadvantages of group counseling

6. Be able to articulate the difference between structured and process groups in the schools
7. Understand and articulate the issues involved with peer facilitators
8. Discuss the ethical issues of using assessment instruments in counseling and identify various assessment instruments for counseling in each domain
9. Understand systems perspectives and be able to articulate why school counselors need to work with the adult partners
10. Be able to apply systems thinking when analyzing counseling as an appropriate intervention with an adult partner

DOMAINS / ACTIVITIES / PARTNERS MODEL

ACTIVITIES	DOMAINS					
	Academic Development ▼	Career Development ▼	Personal/ Social Development ▼			
Counseling	1a	1b	1c	5	6	7
Educating and Advocacy	2a	2b	2c	8	9	10
Consulting	3a	3b	3c	11	12	13
Leadership and Coordination	4a	4b	4c	14	15	16
	Students			Parents and Caregivers	Colleagues in Schools	Colleagues in Community

PARTNERS IN THE PROCESS

CASE STUDY ◆ Phillipe and the Anger Monster

Dovey read the note from the second-grade teacher, Ms. Miller, without surprise. For the third time this month, one of her students was acting aggressively on the playground, resulting in another fight. Ms. Miller, who had witnessed the confrontation, described the student, Phillipe, as bossing other students, refusing to play cooperatively, and finally, as the one to hit first when the other children refused to comply with his demands for the basketball. As an elementary school counselor for twelve years, Dovey had worked with many students who seemed unable to control anger, just like Phillipe. Knowing there were only so many of these episodes the principal would tolerate before asking the family to find another school for the boy, Dovey wanted to help this child find some way to channel his anger besides bullying and fighting.

Dovey called Phillipe into her office at the next recess. Because of Phillipe's age, Dovey used play materials to allow him to "play out" some of his issues, rather than attempt to engage him in traditional counseling. She used reflection to track his play scenarios and found his affect expressed through play to be profoundly aggressive, angry, and violent, after which he would become tearful and sad. After meeting with him almost daily for two weeks, she decided that his anger was not abating after play-counseling sessions, which she found to be unusual. There did not seem to be consistent themes when she asked him who the "bad guys" were in his play, but the "victims" of his play violence were always "little boys." Her attempts to explore real events behind the play were unproductive, as Phillipe would always state at the end of a session that he was "OK" and wanted to go back to class. Meanwhile, the fighting on the playground continued.

Not surprisingly (as people who have been in the schools would attest), there were several second- and third-grade boys this year who had been involved in fighting, and Dovey decided that Phillipe and some of these other boys might benefit from a group counseling experience. This would give them all a chance to learn about anger management skills and to explore some of the sources of their anger. She obtained permissions from the parents, and started a group to help these youngsters learn about the "anger monster" and how to make the "anger monster" smaller.

CHALLENGE QUESTIONS

1. What are your reactions to Phillipe's playground behavior? Consider that all anger comes from *fear* and *pain*. Reflecting on this, what changes in your reaction? Does that help you to reframe his behavior in more compassionate terms?
2. What experiences do you have with alternative methods of counseling? Where can you go to learn more about counseling methods with young children? With middle school students? With high school students?
3. How do you think the group experience will work for Phillipe?
4. How might you use older peers to help him?
5. What questions do you wish to answer about Phillipe's life situation? What are your tentative hypotheses about the systems of his life—his classroom, his home, his neighborhood?

◆ COUNSELING WITH STUDENTS

The work we do with students is a partnership—a symbiotic relationship that exists because our work helps them to achieve the outcomes of education and their full cooperation gives our profession its unique position as a member of the education team. Our partnership with students begins with the foundation of our profession: counseling. We are school counselors, not registrars, not bus monitors, not vice principals. As the basis of everything we do, the profession of counseling provides guiding philosophies, ways of viewing students, and ways of helping students.

The importance of counseling as an essential part of a counselor's job is reinforced when examining student needs. When students were surveyed to measure how they perceived school counselors, the counselors in schools with the highest ratings reported that they devoted 71 to 72 percent of their time in individual and group counseling (Wiggins & Moody, 1987). Furthermore, when students were asked what services they needed in high school, 89 percent responded that they needed career counseling, and 60 percent indicated that they needed personal counseling (Hutchinson & Bottorff, 1986). Sadly, only 40 percent said they received career counseling, and only 21 percent said they received any personal counseling. These studies serve as reminders that students value counseling. The value of this activity is indicated in the DAP Model, as this activity is considered one of the primary activities.

Counseling is not just for students who are "troubled," nor does counseling only enhance a student's personal/social functioning. According to ACT, "students who see themselves as competent and effective, with a realistic view of themselves and their abilities, are more than three times more likely to be high achievers as low achievers. . . . Students who have a low level of motivation to succeed, or who have a high level of anxiety about their schoolwork or home environment are five to six times as likely to be low achievers as high achievers" (Noble, 2000, p. 15). The domains of academic development, career development, and personal/social development resonate with each other; counseling for concerns in one area can improve a student's functioning in all areas. But

The ASCA School Counselor Performance Standards addressed in this chapter are

Standard 3: The professional school counselor implements the individual planning component by guiding individuals and groups of students and their parents or guardians through the development of educational and career plans.

3.1 The professional school counselor, in collaboration with parents or guardians, helps students establish goals and develop and use planning skills.

3.2 The professional school counselor demonstrates accurate and appropriate interpretation of assessment data and the presentation of relevant, unbiased information.

Standard 4: The professional school counselor provides responsive services through the effective use of individual and small-group counseling, consultation and referral skills.

4.1 The professional school counselor counsels individual students and small groups of students with identified needs and concerns.

4.3 The professional school counselor implements an effective referral process with administrators, teachers and other school personnel.

The CACREP Standards for School Counseling Programs addressed in this chapter are

C.2 **(a)** individual and small-group counseling approaches that promote school success, through academic, career, and personal/social development for all;

C.2 **(b)** individual, group, and classroom guidance approaches systematically designed to assist all students with academic, career and personal/social development;

C.2 **(c)** approaches to peer facilitation, including peer helper, peer tutor, and peer mediation programs;

C.2 **(e)** developmental approaches to assist all students and parents at points of educational transition (e.g., home to elementary school, elementary to middle to high school, high school to postsecondary education and career options);

C.2 **(f)** constructive partnerships with parents, guardians, families, and communities in order to promote each student's academic, career, and personal/social success;

C.3 **(c)** strategies and methods of working with parents, guardians, families, and communities to empower them to act on behalf of their children; and

C.3 **(d)** knowledge and skills in conducting programs that are designed to enhance students' academic, social, emotional, career, and other developmental needs.

there are many misconceptions about counseling, and this is where we will begin in our discussion of counseling.

Misconceptions of Counseling

It is easy to see how misconceptions about counseling could exist; for many adults, their only experiences with counselors were the career guidance counselors or the mental health counselors they knew in their high school days. (Refer to Chapter 1 to recall the historical context of school counseling.) Because of that training in either the career guidance or mental health models of school counseling, school counselors functioned very differently than counselors of today—but our colleagues and the parents of our students don't know that.

Adding to this misunderstanding are movies and public events that portray counselors in general as charlatans (or worse, criminals), and counseling as ineffective or manipulative, or even as brainwashing. It is important that counselors are sensitive to the questions and concerns that arise about counseling and are proactive in helping others understand the nature of counseling.

Letters to parents and teachers at the beginning of each year help to introduce the nature and scope of the comprehensive school counseling program in general and school counseling activities specifically. Follow-up communication reminds them of the work you do with students, parents, colleagues in the school, and colleagues in the community. Furthermore, professional accountability as outlined in the National Model demands that school counselors communicate regularly with administrators, both at the building and the district levels, about the activities of the counselors and of the CSCP as a whole. This can help alleviate misunderstandings.

Developmentally Appropriate Counseling

Most counseling training programs teach basic counseling skills using the template of adults to help counselors-in-training learn about empathy, unconditional positive regard, active listening, and other counseling competencies. It is up to counselor trainees to generalize those skills to the unique populations with whom they will practice those skills in a professional counseling context. This means that now is your opportunity to take the foundation counseling skills you know and modify those skills to counsel young people.

Children and adolescents have unique developmental and contextual realities, as we explored in our discussion of the characteristics of comprehensive school counseling programs in Chapters 3 and 4. To apply all these insights to counseling with K–12 students, we should be mindful of the following guidelines:

1. Young people need to be active because they possess a shorter attention span than adults.
2. Young people are still developing their own moral compass and intellectual, critical thinking skills. This means they are still developing their ability to tap their inner reality or insight.
3. Young people may not have the emotional intelligence to be able to identify their emotions, the source of their emotions, or words to describe their experience of their emotions.
4. Young people need to feel free to choose, while concurrently needing help articulating their framework (value system) by which to evaluate alternatives.
5. Young people need help developing strategies for generating and evaluating alternatives, making a commitment to an identifiable alternative, and then understanding the consequences of the choices they make. They are still refining their ability to draw cause-and-effect connections.

These important insights into the developmental realities and needs of students yield implications for both the manner in which we counsel young people and the content of our counseling. In terms of the *manner* in which we counsel students, we need to be aware of their activity level and attention span. We also need to be aware that they may have limited ability to understand themselves—limited insight. They may not be able to identify their feelings, or they may not have language to describe what they are experiencing. Most importantly, students must feel that their counselors trust them to make good decisions and believe in them.

In terms of the *content* of counseling, counselors must be aware that young people may need help articulating their own value system (the framework for evaluating alternatives) before conversations can take place about the alternatives themselves. The autonomy this dialogue teaches, and the respect this conveys, goes far in developing trust between the counselor and the student.

In addition, young students are still learning how to make decisions, practicing the process of identifying goals, articulating alternatives, evaluating alternatives, making a choice, and then designing a plan to implement that choice. Developing a counseling approach that emphasizes and teaches the process of decision making, in addition to the focus on the product of the decision making, helps students develop an important competency. Furthermore, it is very important that counselors understand that young people need help evaluating the consequences of their choices. These young students are still developing their abilities to understand cause and effect, so evaluating alternatives in terms of possible consequences is particularly challenging. For example, many researchers believe that adolescents engage in high-risk behavior because they see themselves as invulnerable, living the myth of "It won't happen to me" (Craig, 1996, p. 453). Helping young students understand that it can happen to them may be a hard sell, but without addressing this, young people are not effectively or realistically assessing the consequences of their choices (Ponton, 1997). Although the outcome of some choices have nonlethal consequences (i.e., Should I go out for the soccer team?), the consequences of others are life and death or are life altering (i.e., Should I drink alcohol?). This means that school counselors need to be able to assess

- ◆ The student's attention span
- ◆ The student's level of insight
- ◆ The student's level of emotional intelligence (ability to identify emotions, the source of emotions, or his or her experience of emotions)
- ◆ The student's clarity of values
- ◆ The student's level of decision-making strategies
- ◆ The student's ability to understand cause and effect relative to his or her choices.

Reflection Moment ◆

Recall a time when you needed help making a decision. If the alternatives were clear, how did it feel if the person you asked for help doubted your ability to evaluate your alternatives? Conversely, if your alternatives weren't clear, how did it feel to have a helper who assumed it was all so clear and so simple? These are common experiences. The point is to become more sensitive to how you help young people in terms of their decision making.

◆ ◆

Prevention, Intervention, and Treatment: When to Counsel and When to Refer

As you will recall from Chapter 4, prevention efforts are often associated with classroom developmental curriculum and schoolwide efforts to improve the school environment. Intervention efforts are often associated with individual counseling, group counseling, and parent-student-teacher-administration consultation and mediation. Treatment is called for when the student's issues are chronic, deeply traumatic, or deeply seated in the personality, such as issues of chronic depression, survival of abuse or violence, or severe anger management. In terms of this chapter, we are focused on counseling, which is usually classified as prevention and/or intervention.

In general, counselors try to enhance the positive elements of a student's life and mitigate the effect of negative elements through prevention efforts. Counseling is preventive in the attempt to mitigate the negative effects of some aspect of the student's life, usually in terms of one or two meetings. If the issues are more troublesome, counselors work primarily with short-term and medium-term issues that arise for students through intervention, referring for treatment outside the school as needed. Intervention involving short-term issues may be addressed in four to eight counseling meetings (which could last from ten to thirty minutes, depending on the situation) and usually involve predictable developmental issues (such as relationship issues, transition issues). Intervention involving medium-term issues could require a counselor's involvement (counseling, consulting with teachers, acknowledging the student with an encouraging smile) for a semester and involve issues that often resolve themselves as the student matures and as time passes (such as relationships or grief). Deep-level issues are those for which the student may require lifelong recovery work and are those issues for which the counselor would provide immediate intervention and support, with referral for treatment (such as substance addition, suicidal behaviors, depression).

Treatment consisting of in-depth, intensive, or medication-assisted therapy, however, is most often not conducted in schools. When students are in need of treatment, most school counselors refer those students to mental health therapists in the community (Smith & Archer, 2000). For example, if it is discovered that a student is severely depressed due to years of sexual abuse, that student may need medications, frequent sessions, and intensive recuperative therapy to address the depression and begin healing old scars from the abuse. The community therapist and the school counselor would collaborate so that the school counselor

1. Knows what medication(s) the student is taking
2. Would be available if the student experienced a crisis during school
3. Would assist in the coordination of IEP (individualized education plan) meetings or other efforts aimed at ensuring academic, career, and personal/social success
4. Would provide individual counseling for academic, career, and personal/social issues
5. May want to include the student in any groups currently meeting for students with similar issues

Functioning as a Professional, Ethical Counselor

Often, students will use minor friendship concerns, scheduling, careers, or minor academic concerns to mask their real reason to talk to the counselor. As an ethical professional counselor, you must be aware of this and be prepared to work with students on a deeper level if their issues warrant it. The general rule is to be open to all issues, be sensitive to nonverbal cues, and be constantly assessing all areas of the student's functioning for those times the student needs more attention than the presenting issue might warrant. It is crucial that counselors give the time and attention needed to students who come to see them; not providing adequate care is unethical and unprofessional. Furthermore, not devoting adequate time and attention to students will damage the trust needed to make effective use of the counselor's time and expertise. Students of color, in particular, might find the counselor's office to be a threatening place, especially if the counselor represents a different culture or socioeconomic background than the student (Wittmer, 2000). As the student establishes trust in both the person of the counselor and the process of counseling, the real reasons for the visit will be revealed.

Students also need to know that the counselor has a breadth of knowledge about student issues and what it means to be a young person, called "withitness" (Gordon, 1997). Students need to know that you're not going to "freak out" when you hear their problems. No counselor can know everything there is to know about every issue of every student, but counselors need to be knowledgeable enough about most issues to listen effectively for underlying themes and concerns, facilitate effective assessment and intervention, and help put the student at ease that help is possible. The case of an unplanned pregnancy can illustrate the embarrassment of sharing the "secret," the need for the counselor to be able to deal rationally with the "emergency," the need for the counselor to understand his or her own personal perspectives on the issue of teenage sexuality and parenting, and the need to be informed about options available in the community (Kiselica & Pfaller, 1993).

To be effective, you need to understand both the process of helping your students (your theoretical orientation and strategies) and the product of healing that you hope for your students (your insights into the student's issues). All of this is interrelated; how issues relate to each other and how you address various issues is shaped by your theoretical orientation. Let this serve as another reminder that you must, as an ethical counselor, be able to articulate and practice within your theoretical orientation.

Furthermore, an ethical school counselor must be sensitive to multicultural issues. Wittmer (2000) points out that culturally skilled counselors know how crucial culture is to a student's identity development and know how to preserve the dignity of both the student and his or her culture. Since most counselors are trained in the traditional Euro-American worldview, there are often large gaps in understanding different cultures that need to be identified and addressed, either by additional professional development and training, or by addressing it explicitly with the student ("I don't know what it has been like to grow up in your culture. Tell me what growing up has been like for you."). Even what we think we know about another culture must be respectfully explored with each student of that culture.

◆ INDIVIDUAL COUNSELING

Every counselor will select the theoretical orientation that works for him or her, and you will want to focus on those theories that lend themselves well to the school environment. Given that students don't often have much time for one-on-one sessions and that schools are not perceived to be the best setting for intensive psychotherapy, school counselors usually adopt a theoretical orientation that works well within time constraints (Smith & Archer, 2000). Three counseling approaches that are often practiced by school counselors are Adlerian therapy, solutions-focused or brief therapy, and reality therapy. You are urged to find out more about these approaches.

Using Multiple Intelligences in Counseling

Additional insights into how to work effectively with school students can be found in the concept of multiple intelligences. You can see in Table 7.1 that Gardner and Lazear described each learner as a unique constellation of eight intelligences (Lazear, 1999). These intelligences, as listed in Chapter 3, include verbal, mathematic/logical, artistic, musical, naturalist, interpersonal, intrapersonal, and kinesthetic strengths. If you know a student's strengths, you have important information that can be very useful in designing counseling interventions. For example, the use of journaling, art, music, and poetry has been advocated for years as effective ways to work with counseling students, regardless of theoretical orientation (Cormier & Hackney, 1999; Hutchins & Vaught, 1997). Effective counselors would naturally look for counseling methods that fit with the strengths of the student. Using Lazear (1999; pp. 142–145) and Corey (2004) as a springboard, the following list suggests some counseling strategies based on multiple intelligences and theoretical foundations:

1. *Verbal/linguistic intelligence:* Journaling, making up jokes, poetry, storytelling (Adlerian, person-centered)
2. *Logical/mathematical intelligence:* Creating formulas to show relationships between events (such as A → B → C from Rational Emotive Behavior Therapy, or REBT), creating logic/pattern games, syllogisms (Harrison, 2000)
3. *Visual/spatial intelligence:* Guided imagery (Image Psychology [Parker, 1998]), art (Kahn, 1999)
4. *Bodily/kinesthetic intelligence:* Situation sculpting (Psychodrama, family sculpting), sports, role playing, Ropes courses and outdoor challenge experiences
5. *Musical/rhythmic intelligence:* Music or sounds, rapping, singing new words to an existing song (REBT)
6. *Interpersonal intelligence:* Insight counseling, group counseling
7. *Intrapersonal intelligence:* Insight counseling, metacognition techniques, emotional awareness
8. *Naturalist intelligence:* Archetypal pattern recognition of human nature, caring for plants and animals, natural world insights (e.g., social animals, pack behavior, insect colonies, flocking of birds and schooling of fish; rock formations and geologic forces; plants; weather phenomena), counseling outdoors while taking a walk with the student

This list is by no means exhaustive. As a counselor, you will develop your own ideas of counseling strategies that will be helpful with your students, but these ideas might help you identify strategies that will engage the student more fully in the counseling process.

TABLE 7.1 ◆ Multiple Intelligences

Verbal/linguistic intelligence is responsible for the production of language and all the complex possibilities that follow, including poetry, humor, storytelling, grammar, metaphors, similes, abstract reasoning, symbolic thinking, conceptual patterning, reading, and writing. This intelligence can be seen in such people as poets, playwrights, storytellers, novelists, public speakers, and comedians.

Logical/mathematical intelligence is most often associated with what we call scientific thinking or inductive reasoning, although deductive thought processes are also involved. This intelligence involves the capacity to recognize patterns, work with abstract symbols (such as numbers and geometric shapes), and discern relationships and/or see connections between separate and distinct pieces of information. This intelligence can be seen in such people as scientists, computer programmers, accountants, lawyers, bankers, and of course, mathematicians.

The logical/mathematical and verbal/linguistic intelligences form the basis for most systems of Western education, as well as for all forms of currently existing standardized testing programs.

Visual spatial intelligence deals with the visual arts (including painting, drawing, and sculpting); navigation, mapmaking, and architecture (which involve the use of space and knowing how to get around in it); and games such as chess (which require the ability to visualize objects from different perspectives and angles). The key sensory base of this intelligence is the sense of sight, but also the ability to form mental images and pictures in the mind. This intelligence can be seen in such people as architects, graphic artists, cartographers, industrial design draftspersons, and of course, visual artists (painters and sculptors).

Bodily/kinesthetic intelligence is the ability to use the body to express emotion (as in dance and body language), to play a game (as in sports), and to create a new product (as in invention). Learning by doing has long been recognized as an important part of education. Our bodies know things our minds do not and cannot know in any other way. For example, our bodies know how to ride a bike, roller-skate, type, and parallel park a car. This intelligence can been seen in such people as actors, athletes, mimes, dancers, and inventors.

Musical/rhythmic intelligence includes such capacities as the recognition and use of rhythmic and tonal patterns, and sensitivity to sounds from the environment, the human voice, and musical instruments. Many of us learned the alphabet through this intelligence and the A-B-C song. Of all forms of intelligence, the consciousness altering effect of music and rhythm on the brain is probably the greatest. This intelligence can be seen in advertising professionals (those who write catchy jingles to sell a product), performance musicians, rock musicians, dance bands, composers, and music teachers.

Interpersonal intelligence involves the ability to work cooperatively with others in a group as well as the ability to communicate, verbally and nonverbally, with other people. It builds on the capacity to notice distinctions among others such as contrasts in moods, temperament, motivations, and intentions. In the more advanced forms of this intelligence, one can literally pass over into another's perspective and read his or her intentions and desires. One can have genuine empathy for another's feelings, fears, anticipations, and beliefs. This form of intelligence is usually highly developed in such people as counselors, teachers, therapists, politicians, and religious leaders.

Intrapersonal intelligence involves knowledge of the internal aspects of the self, such as knowledge of feelings, the range of emotional responses, thinking processes, self-reflection, and a sense of or intuition about spiritual realities. Intrapersonal intelligence allows us to be conscious of our consciousness; that is, to step back from ourselves and watch ourselves as an outside observer. It involves our capacity to experience wholeness and unity, to discern patterns of connection within

(continued)

TABLE 7.1 ◆ (Continued)

the larger order of things, to perceive higher states of consciousness, to experience the lure of the future, and to dream of and actualize the possible. This intelligence can be seen in such people as philosophers, psychiatrists, spiritual counselors and gurus, and cognitive pattern researchers.

Naturalist intelligence involves the ability to discern, comprehend, and appreciate the various flora and fauna of the world of nature as opposed to the world created by human beings. It involves such capacities as recognizing and classifying species, growing plants and raising or taming animals, knowing how to appropriately use the natural world (e.g., living off the land), and having a curiosity about the natural world, its creatures, weather patterns, physical history, and so on. In working with and developing the naturalist intelligence one often discovers a sense of wonder, awe, and respect for all the various phenomena and species (plant and animal) of the natural world. This intelligence can be seen in such people as farmers, hunters, zookeepers, gardeners, cooks, veterinarians, nature guides, and forest rangers.

From *Eight Ways of Teaching: The Artistry of Teaching with Multiple Intelligences* (3rd ed.), by David Lazear. © 1999 by Skylight Professional Development. Reprinted by permission of LessonLab, a Pearson Education Company, www.lessonlab.com.

Reflection Moment ◆

What is your theoretical orientation? In the chapter Case Study, did Dovey counsel Phillipe using one of the multiple intelligences outlined in this section? Which one?

◆ ◆

◆GROUP COUNSELING

Research into the efficacy of group counseling indicates recent changes in the ways counselors perceive group counseling in the schools. In 1993, Carroll found that elementary school counselors did not feel that they had adequate skills in group counseling; they would have liked more training in groups in their graduate programs. By 1996, Dansby found that counselors generally felt "that small group work should be a vital part of any counseling program, that their programs would be more effective if they led more groups, and that they felt adequately trained to implement group counseling" (pp. 233–234).

Group counseling involves primary intervention (Dansby, 1996; Johnson & Johnson, 2000), and for some students, it may be the most therapeutic intervention they will experience. The intent of conducting group counseling is that participants will be able to learn about themselves, other people, life tasks, and authentic ways of relating in a safe, confidential setting. While there are similarities between group counseling and group educating, we will emphasize that group counseling, as we mean it in this chapter, has a therapeutic and intervention focus. Educating a large group (15+) of students will be considered in the next chapter on educating and advocacy.

The importance of group counseling in schools cannot be overemphasized (Fleming, 1999). In fact, Keys, Bemak, and Lockhart (1998) suggested that group counseling is more effective than individual counseling to address the needs of students, most especially at-risk students. This contention is supported through research into violent youths, which suggests that peer-group interventions are effective in redirecting peer values, confronting antisocial behaviors, teaching problem-solving skills, and encouraging prosocial behaviors (Bemak & Keys, 2000; Tolan & Guerra, 1994).

Almost any topic a student will bring you could constitute a meaningful group experience. These topics can be addressed in either structured or process group formats.

Structured versus Process Groups

To understand group counseling, it is important to understand that there is a difference between structured groups and process groups. Structured groups refer to group experiences in which the counselor takes direct leadership of the group, including identifying goals, presenting material with an assumed values orientation, selecting activities, and directing interaction. Often, structured group exercises (i.e., role playing, behavior rehearsal, didactic experiences) and curricular materials are used to move the group intentionally toward certain conclusions and insights involving a psychoeducational goal (Goldstein, 1999). For this reason, structured groups are often criticized for being too prescriptive (Keys, Bemak, & Lockhart, 1998). In spite of this criticism, structured groups continue to yield excellent results for students. Examples of structured group topics include decision making; friendship skills; stress and anger management; drugs, tobacco, and alcohol resistance; metacognitive skills (Brigman & Goodman, 2001); study skills; planning for college; and career exploration. As you can see from each of these topics, the outcome of the group is predetermined; each topic has a clear learning goal.

In contrast, process groups rely on the learning that emerges from the group interaction and spontaneous experiences that occur as the members learn to negotiate the natural progression of all relationships: forming (working through trust issues), storming (working through authenticity issues and interpersonal dissonance), norming (creating shared norms and rules for the group), performing (addressing the therapeutic topic or issue that brings members to the group), and adjourning (saying goodbye at the end of the experience) (Tuckman & Jensen, as cited in Kline, 2003). Furthermore, process groups do not have a clearly predetermined goal; each member comes to the group to explore her or his own choices, and there is often a greater emphasis on the support that groups can provide. In fact, what is commonly referred to as "support groups" are process groups. Examples of such process groups in schools would include groups for sexual orientation (Street, 1994), career counseling, learning issues such as attention deficit disorder, self-concept or self-esteem, changing families (divorce, blended families, nontraditional families), loss and grief, self-discipline, fears, support for addiction recovery, diversity support, and support for students who are being treated in the community for suicide risk and depression.

The extent of structure or the extent of process within the group is best conceptualized as a continuum, with highly structured on one end and highly process-focused on the other. In the middle are groups that are blended. Perhaps the counselor has structure in the overall view of the group, but allows processing to be the main vehicle for change within each meeting. An excellent example of a blended group is presented by Muller (2000), in which she describes a group counseling experience for African American high school females to foster positive identity development. For each meeting, the facilitators have a stimulus experience or question to start the session, but then allow group interaction to guide the processing of that experience. It is always advisable that group leaders have activities planned for each meeting, in case the members are uncomfortable with sharing feelings or ideas (Posthuma, 1999). While silence is not a problem per se, some students might find extensive silence disconcerting, and chances of acting up increase as dissonance increases.

It is hoped that you will be able to see that many topics could be presented as either a structured group or a process group. For example, a topic like truancy could be a process group if the group is designed to allow members to clarify their values relative to attendance, explore their own attendance challenges, make choices about future behavior, and support each other in continuing those new behaviors. The same topic could be presented as a structured group if the intent is to teach the importance of regular attendance, emphasize strategies for reducing truancy, and then support members in truancy-reducing behaviors.

Advantages and Disadvantages of Group Counseling

There are numerous advantages to providing services to students through a group counseling format. The first advantage involves developmental appropriateness; as young people develop, they become more peer-oriented. It makes sense that counseling formats involving peers will meet with success (Ball & Meck, 1979). Group counseling harnesses that natural peer orientation to interest students in becoming involved in a group, engages them in values exploration and clarification, motivates them to attend, empowers them in the change process, and supports them while they try new behaviors.

A second advantage of group counseling involves efficiency. Conducting group counseling allows counselors to reach more students than is possible through one-on-one counseling. Students with similar issues will learn together, brainstorm ideas for growth for each other, and support each other as they struggle together. Furthermore, it connects students who may otherwise have little contact with each other and assures students who feel isolated by their problems that they are not alone in their suffering, providing significant therapeutic benefits; studies into the efficacy of groups have documented significant benefits for members (LaFountain & Garner, 1996; Nassar-McMillan & Cashwell, 1997; Zinck & Littrell, 2000).

Finally, there is a call in the literature for more systems awareness in our work in schools (Bilynsky & Vernaglia, 1999; Dansby, 1996; Fontes, 2000; Geroski & Knauss, 2000; Keys, Bemak, & Lockhart, 1998; Taylor & Adelman, 2000). Students come to schools as both products of, and producers of, change within the multiple systems of their existence. Working with students in group counseling allows counselors to expand their awareness of each student; what better way to see how students interact in their systems than to witness it firsthand?

However, group counseling is not for all students, nor is it for all issues. One of the most important limitations of group counseling is the issue of confidentiality. No matter how emphatically the counselor insists that all members respect confidentiality, some breaches may occur. Additional concerns involve the special relationship between schools, parents and other caregivers, and the school counselor in terms of the limits of confidentiality for health, safety, and legal reasons. In some cases, mandated reporting and/or informing parents of problems could result in serious trust issues with group members if those situations are not addressed in advance.

Furthermore, scheduling difficulties can seriously interfere with a counselor's ability to schedule groups, especially if there is no schoolwide study hall or period for such student-driven activities. Dansby (1996) found that lack of time and scheduling problems as well as difficulty getting students out of class were the top two sources of interference that hindered group counseling efforts. Clear communication about group counseling is a necessity for successful group counseling activities.

Reflection Moment ◆

Have you ever had a group counseling experience as a member? As a facilitator? As a leader? Most counselors have had a course in group counseling in their graduate program, but one course may not give you a chance to fully explore your group leadership/facilitation skills. How comfortable are you with groups? With which ages and which issues would you be comfortable leading a group? How can you expand your comfort zone?

◆ ◆

◆ PEER FACILITATORS

We must not neglect the powerful benefits that result when young people are actively involved in the counseling program. By this, we do not mean involvement as a student—we mean involvement as a peer helper (Foster-Harrison, 1995). In this program, older students would be selected and trained to act as peer facilitators, assisting the counselor in the logistics and management of a variety of services, including peer tutoring, peer mediation, peer helping, peer programs to help orient new students to the school, and peer facilitation of groups. Peer facilitators would need to be carefully screened for appropriateness with the counseling program (but those students with the best academic records are not always the most appropriate for peer training), persons to be helped, the specific counseling topic (academic subject, careers, adjustment issues for new students), and other factors. Special training would be provided in the helping process, listening, the basics of confidentiality, and facilitation of interaction. Most importantly, special attention would be paid to teaching peer helpers about the limits of their competence, so that the professional counselor would be involved immediately if there were any problems. It is crucial that these peer helpers are carefully supervised and monitored; even a well-trained peer facilitator is not qualified to conduct a group alone (Fleming, 1999).

A program of peer facilitation, with carefully selected, trained, and screened peer facilitators, can provide benefits for the counselor, the peer facilitator, and other students. For the counselor, the benefits of having peer facilitators are numerous; the peer facilitator can provide feedback about the progress of students being helped, serve as a role model to other students, and assist with some of the logistics of running the program, such as helping with scheduling and publicity. For the peer facilitator, this provides an opportunity to develop helping and leadership skills—a powerful way for the young person to "try on" roles connected with school-related and helping professions. One of the important ways that young people can develop and extend their "social interest" (to use an Adlerian term) is to help others, a powerful intrinsic motivator. Finally, there are benefits to the student population as a whole; peer helpers provide a safe method of connecting with the counselor in cases where trust is an issue, and it empowers students to see themselves, like the peer facilitator, as capable. In a recent study, students who had worked with a peer counselor were found to have a decrease in discipline referrals, improved attitudes toward school, improved school attendance, and improved grades ("Peer Counselors Help Kids . . . ," 2000).

◆ASSESSMENT IN THE COUNSELING PROCESS

Many authors agree that assessment and appraisal of students are important counselor functions (Baker, 2000; Gysbers & Henderson, 2000; Loesch & Goodman, 2000; Schmidt, 1999). But the extent of the counselor's involvement with student assessment and appraisal is a subject of debate in the profession. Some authors would consider assessment and appraisal to be major activities in the comprehensive school counseling program (Loesch & Goodman, 2000; Schmidt, 1999), whereas other authors argue that school counselors use assessment and appraisal as components of other, more important activities, such as counseling (Baker, 2000) and individual planning (Gysbers & Henderson, 2000).

First, it is essential that you obtain an in-depth understanding of assessment instruments and concepts; this is usually accomplished by the completion of a discrete course in assessment or appraisal in the graduate program. As you will note in the ethics statements of both the American Counseling Association and the American School Counseling Association (Appendix A), you are required to know the purposes, nature, results, reliability, validity, limitations, and appropriateness of any instrument you administer, and you must be able to communicate those clearly to students and parents. Furthermore, you must be able to understand the differences between formal and informal assessment strategies, so that you are able to use informal assessment strategies, such as card sorts, case histories, and behavioral observation checklists, as professionally as the formal assessment instruments. A comprehensive discussion of these important concepts will not be attempted here; rather, the purpose of this discussion is to help you integrate information from that appraisal course with the comprehensive school counseling program as outlined in this text.

Second, it is important that school counselors are aware of the criticisms of certain instruments that are often used in the schools. For example, instruments that are not presented in a student's native language will yield results that are highly suspect. Similarly, instruments that are administered in adverse conditions, such as overcrowded, noisy rooms, or under conditions contrary to those of the norming population are suspect. The use of assessment instruments in ways for which they are not designed (such as confusing aptitude tests for achievement tests) will invalidate the results. And counselors must maintain a healthy skepticism about some dear and long-held myths of education, such as the concept of intelligence as a hard-and-fast, measurable characteristic (when, in fact, the concept of intelligence should be viewed as very plastic and fluid and might better be understood in terms of multiple intelligences).

School counselors most often use assessments in the counseling function within the three domains. Within the academic domain, assessments can help students to know their learning styles and strengths, which can then be helpful in academic planning, such as the Learning Styles Inventory (Dunn, Dunn, & Price, 1996). Aptitude tests, purportedly measuring a student's ability to achieve in certain areas, might also be helpful in a student's academic development. Such instruments would include the General Vocational Aptitude Battery (available from the U.S. Employment Service), the Armed Services Vocational Aptitude Battery or ASVAB (available from the U.S. Department of Defense), the Differential Aptitude Test or DAT (available from The Psychological Corporation), and the Scholastic Aptitude Test or SAT. Tests that can be used to help assess a student's verbal and nonverbal functioning include the Peabody Picture Vocabulary Test and the Slosson Intelligence Test (these instruments must be carefully considered in terms of appropriateness for different ages of students).

Within the domain of career development, there are many instruments and computer programs that can help students further their self-knowledge and match that self-exploration with information about the world of work. These instruments include the Self Directed Search (available from Psychological Assessment Resources), the Strong Interest Inventory (available from Consulting Psychologists Press), and the Kuder General Interest Survey (available from Science Research Associates). Computer programs such as DISCOVER and SIGI are also designed to help students evaluate and understand their interests, lifestyle choices, and possible career options.

In the personal/social domain of development, counselors often use assessments to help students understand themselves better, such as the Myers-Briggs Type Indicator (MBTI, available from Consulting Psychologists Press). This instrument comes with a high school form and is often used to help students with career decision making.

◆ COUNSELING WITH ADULT PARTNERS

CASE STUDY CONTINUED ◆ Phillipe and the Anger Monster

As the group progressed, Dovey continued to meet with Phillipe. Dovey observed him in the classroom to see how he interacted with his peers and to see how the classroom environment "fed" his anger monster. There did not seem to be anyone in the class who picked on him or bullied him, but Dovey knew it was important to understand all the systems in which Phillipe interacted, so she knew these observations were not wasted.

As the group drew to a close, she continued to meet with him one-on-one. As he played out his anger, he often was able to talk a little more in the sad period after the angry play. About a month after their first meeting, he finally shared that his family was "full of anger monsters" and that he had trouble sleeping at night. Dovey called his home and asked for a meeting with his mother.

Phillipe's mother arrived in the school and sat down to talk to Dovey. "I know he's an angry little guy, but I don't know how to help him."

"Is there anything going on at home that might cause him to be angry?" Dovey gently asked.

Tears welled in her eyes. "Phillipe's dad moved out last week. We're getting a divorce," and she cried quietly.

Systems Thinking: Families, Schools, and Communities

As a whole, educational professionals know the environmental factors needed for healthy development. We touched on these in Chapter 2, in which we discussed schools as systems, and again in Chapter 3, in which we outlined the systems in which students live. We looked at the developmental assets as conditions that support students in their development (Search Institute, 1996). The top six support assets are identified as family support, positive family communication, supportive adult relationships, a caring neighborhood, a caring school climate, and parental involvement in schooling.

When those developmental assets are missing, we have good documentation of the negative effects (McWhirter, McWhirter, McWhirter, & McWhirter, 1998). Communitywide economic instability, stagnation, intolerance, poor health care (mental and physical), poor childcare, and a host of other problems can cause increased stress in the home. This stress often resonates with stress and vulnerability in the family system, increasing the risk for divorce, family violence, neglect, substance abuse and addiction, and mental health problems, which then resonate with increased stress on the children living in the home. This increased stress in the children then resonates with the stressors of the schools: overcrowding, insufficient funding, anxiety over testing, unhealthy school environments, unhappy staff, and other problems. All these problems can erode students' efforts to learn, grow, and prosper (McWhirter, McWhirter, McWhirter, & McWhirter, 1998).

These problems have a direct correlation with academic achievement, career development, and personal/social life functioning. For example, as noted in Chapter 3, Noble (2000) found that students whose parents earn less than $36,000 a year or who have experienced three or more major problems at home (e.g., parental unemployment, chronic health problems, death, separation or divorce, or the need to work to help support the family) are more than twice as likely to be low academic achievers as high academic achievers (p. 15). These stressors also have a direct correlation with more serious behaviors, such as school dropout, substance abuse and addiction, teenage pregnancy and risky sexual behaviors, delinquency, violence, and suicide (McWhirter, McWhirter, McWhirter, & McWhirter, 1998).

As you will recall from Chapter 3, systems thinking is a way of seeing and addressing these problems from a holistic, naturalistic perspective. It views all students as members of interlocking and dynamic systems of social interactions, which then informs intervention efforts aimed at those systems. You will recall from Chapter 5 that the National Model does indeed compel counselors to attend to systemic issues.

Does this mean that school counselors provide counseling for anyone who walks through the door? Most emphatically, no. Does this mean that school counselors provide family systems counseling? No, family systems counseling is a therapeutic treatment approach that requires specialized training. But we cannot ignore the pain of our families, schools, or communities. There are ways we can help, and problem-solving, intervention-level counseling for families, school colleagues, and community colleagues might be appropriate, depending on the situation.

Selection of Counseling as an Intervention

How might such systemic problems come to the school counselor's attention? Problems in the student's family might come to your attention in a case of child abuse, with an irate parent, or with a parent's request for assistance, for example. Problems in the school with colleagues might come to your attention when a teacher needs to process his or her frustration about students in the class, or when a colleague shares some personal issues with you. Problems in the community might come to your attention when an employer complains about your students in a work program, when the community identifies a problem with your students, or when a community colleague shares some personal issues with you. These experiences suggest that the adult partner is struggling with our students and may need help meeting the competencies for adult partners (Appendix D), and therefore deserves our attention.

The full range of actions available to school counselors vary from counseling, to educating, to consulting, to leadership and coordination. Although educating, consulting, and coordinating are the primary ways that counselors work with adult partners, counseling is always an option if warranted. In deciding whether to provide counseling as an intervention, these are the most essential issues:

1. A student-focused problem. The time and effort of counseling is justified if you believe that the problem is directly related to the development of your student(s).
2. Time considerations. Although there are scheduling implications for working with adult partners, there is also support for the efficacy and timeliness of family counseling in the resolution of school problems (Hinkle, 1993; Stone & Peeks, 1986; Wells & Hinkle, 1990).
3. Training in family systems counseling if you are providing family systems counseling. This is an ethical issue (Hinkle, 1993; Magnuson & Norem, 1998). It is important, however, to distinguish family systems counseling (systemic counseling approach with unique training requirements) from counseling with an individual parent, spouse, teacher, or other adult (individual counseling approach consistent with school counselor training). You do not need specialized training to provide counseling for a family member, parent, colleague in your school, or colleague in your community.
4. Administrative support. There are many studies that document the need, efficacy, and processes of systemic interventions. For administrators, the frame in which you present this part of your comprehensive school counseling program must include
   a. Needs assessment data that document the importance of this part of the program for your students
   b. Program evaluation data that support the effectiveness of this intervention as a contributor to student success
   c. Processes that highlight problem solving rather than treatment
5. Availability of referral support. In some isolated communities, there may be very limited mental health services available. The school counselor may represent the only option for help and may need to expand interventions accordingly (Cowie & Quinn, 1997).
6. The location of the problem on the prevention-intervention-treatment continuum. As with our discussion earlier in this chapter about the prevention-intervention-treatment continuum, there are some issues that are best addressed by community mental health treatment professionals. However, issues such as parenting skills or the renegotiation of family relationships to reflect healthy development are very appropriate for school counselor intervention.

What such counseling with our adult partners would look like depends on the situation, but the most common scenario involves defusing or stabilizing the situation, brief counseling toward solutions, and then referral to community mental health professionals if warranted. It is not our intent to suggest that school counselors are responsible for providing long-term treatment to all persons who interact with our students. But a few minutes with a caring listener can make all the difference for an adult partner who is at the end of his or her proverbial rope.

CASE STUDY REVISITED: ◆ Integration

As you return to the Case Studies of this chapter, picture yourself as the counselor.

1. What new insights do you have into possible ways to work with Phillipe?
2. What are the issues you identified for Phillipe and his mother?
3. Where would you place your work with Phillipe in the prevention-intervention-treatment continuum? More importantly, where does each issue fall on that continuum?
4. What are the systemic issues here? Just because the classroom is not an angry place, does that mean the playground isn't either? What can you do to check that out?
5. What are your options with Phillipe's home situation? Would you counsel Phillipe's mother? Why or why not?

APPLICATION (Possible portfolio artifacts are noted)

1. What are some counseling issues around which you need additional training? Use the Internet to research journal articles on these topics.
2. Volunteer to co-lead or facilitate a group for a local school to experience group counseling with young people. Try to get experience in both a structured group and a process group.
3. Revisit the class you took in counseling theories and review the textbook for that class. Find the theory you would like to use with your students and write up a counseling approach for a second-grader, a seventh-grader, and a high school junior, each one with anger as the main issue. Imagine that you will have eight meetings with your student. Make sure you adjust each plan for the developmental level of that age group. (Potential portfolio artifact)
4. Imagine that you are limited to four sessions with each of those students. Design a treatment plan for each in four sessions. Does this cause you to rethink your theory?
5. Imagine you work for a school that limits counseling to a certain number of meetings. Outline a plan to explore community support for your school counseling program. Looking at the National Model, what data about your program would be helpful to take to the community to solicit their support? How will you collect that data?
6. Select a topic with which you are familiar based on a common issue experienced by students at your target educational level. Design a structured group experience for that topic. Now design a process group for the same issue. Which plan seems more comfortable for you? Now design the "perfect" group. Do you blend the two approaches? (Possible portfolio artifact)
7. What is your theory of group counseling? How would you apply that theory in the ideal group you designed in question 6?
8. Outline a plan for the selection and training of peer helpers. What qualities would you look for in a peer helper? (Possible portfolio artifact)
9. Identify at least one formal assessment instrument about which you want more information. Conduct an Internet search to find all the information you can about that instrument. When would you use it and with whom would it be appropriate?
10. Interview a school counselor about the assessment instruments he or she uses. Find out more about the instruments with which you are not familiar.
11. What systems (parents, work, community) have had the greatest impact on your development? How did that system foster your development, and how might it have impeded your development?
12. What issues might you anticipate seeing in the systems of your students? Select one of those issues and conduct a literature or Internet search to learn more. (Possible portfolio artifact)

SUGGESTED READINGS

Bilynsky, N. S., & Vernaglia, E. R. (1999). Identifying and working with dysfunctional families. *Professional School Counseling, 2,* 305–313. This article presents a practical and user-friendly model of problem solving with families that can assist every counselor to feel comfortable with this process.

Dansby, V. S. (1996). Group work within the school system: Survey of implementation and leadership role issues. *The Journal for Specialists in Group Work, 21,* 232–242. This article provides an excellent overview of how counselors view the challenges and benefits of group counseling.

Harrison, T. (2000). Brief counseling in the K–12 developmental counseling program. In J. Wittmer (Ed.), *Managing your school counseling program: K–12 developmental strategies* (2nd ed.; pp. 85–94). Minneapolis, MN: Educational Media. An excellent overview of several models of brief counseling in the schools.

Keys, S. G., Bemak, F., & Lockhart, E. J. (1998). Transforming school counseling to serve the mental health needs of at-risk youth. *Journal of Counseling & Development, 76,* 381–388. This article challenges many traditional assumptions of the school counseling field, a refreshingly holistic view of what school counselors can do to help all students.

Lewis, W. (1996). A proposal for initiating family counseling interventions by school counselors. *The School Counselor, 44,* 93–99. This article provides two practical approaches to conducting brief family problem-solving counseling that, should a referral for long-term family therapy be necessary, would provide the counselor with insight into the family's problems.

McWhirter, J. J., McWhirter, B. T., McWhirter, A. M., & McWhirter, E. H. *At-risk youth: A comprehensive response for counselors, teachers, psychologists, and human service professionals* (most current edition). Pacific Grove, CA: Brooks/Cole. This book is a must-read for anyone working with youth and their families.

Nicoll, W. G. (1992). A family counseling and consultation model for school counselors. *The School Counselor, 39,* 351–361. The model presented in this article provides a strategy that allows the counselor to move between counseling and consultation as needed to address the family's problems.

Ponton, L. E. (1997). *The romance of risk: Why teenagers do the things they do.* New York: Basic. This author's mental health experience provides a frame for understanding why teens often engage in "crazy" risk-taking.

Pryor, D. B., & Tollerud, T. R. (1999). Applications of Adlerian principles in school settings. *Professional School Counseling, 2,* 299–304. For the Adlerian counselor, a wonderful primer of how Adlerian counseling works in the school setting.

Sklare, G. B. (1997). *Brief counseling that works: A solutions-focused approach for school counselors.* Thousand Oaks, CA: Corwin. For the solutions-focused counselor, a wonderful primer of how brief counseling works in a school setting.

REFERENCES

Baker, S. B. (2000). *School counseling for the twenty-first century* (2nd ed.). Upper Saddle River, NJ: Merrill.

Ball, J. D., & Meck, D. S. (1979). Implications of developmental theories for counseling adolescents in groups. *Adolescence, 14,* 528–534.

Bemak, F., & Keys, S. (2000). *Violent and aggressive youth: Intervention and prevention strategies for changing times.* Thousand Oaks, CA: Corwin.

Bilynsky, N. S., & Vernaglia, E. R. (1999). Identifying and working with dysfunctional families. *Professional School Counseling, 2,* 305–314.

Brigman, G., & Goodman, B. E. (2001). *Group counseling for school counselors: A practical guide* (2nd ed.). Portland, ME: J. Weston Walsh.

Carroll, B. (1993). Perceived roles and preparation experiences of elementary counselors: Suggestions for change. *Elementary School Guidance and Counseling, 27,* 217–224.

Corey, G. (2004). *Theory and practice of counseling and psychotherapy* (7th ed.). Pacific Grove, CA: Brooks/Cole.

Cormier, S., & Hackney, H. (1999). *Counseling strategies and interventions* (5th ed.). Boston: Allyn and Bacon.

Cowie, K., & Quinn, K. (1997). Brief family therapy in the schools: A new perspective on the role of the rural school counseling professional. *Family Journal, 5*(1), 57–69.

Craig, G. J. (1996). *Human development* (7th ed.). Upper Saddle River, NJ: Prentice Hall.

Dansby, V. S. (1996). Group work within the school system: Survey of implementation and leadership role issues. *The Journal for Specialists in Group Work, 21*, 232–242.

Dunn, R., Dunn, K., & Price, G. E. (1996). *Learning Styles Inventory.* Lawrence, KS: Price Systems.

Fleming, V. M. (1999). Group counseling in the schools: A case for basic training. *Professional School Counseling, 2*, 409–413.

Fontes, L. A (2000). Children exposed to marital violence: How school counselors can help. *Professional School Counseling, 3*, 231–237.

Foster-Harrison, E. S. (1995). Peer helping in the elementary and middle grades: A developmental perspective. *Elementary School Guidance and Counseling, 30*(2), 94–104.

Geroski, A. M., & Knauss, L. (2000). Addressing the needs of foster children within school counseling programs. *Professional School Counseling, 3*, 152–161.

Goldstein, A P. (1999). *The Prepare curriculum: Teaching prosocial competencies* (rev. ed.). Champaign, IL: Research Press.

Gordon, R. L. (1997). How novice teachers can succeed with adolescents. *Educational Leadership, 54*(7), 56–58.

Gysbers, N. C., & Henderson, P. (2000). *Developing and managing your school guidance program* (3rd ed.). Alexandria, VA: American Counseling Association.

Harrison, T. (2000). Brief counseling in the K–12 developmental counseling program. In J. Wittmer (Ed.), *Managing your school counseling program: K–12 developmental strategies* (2nd ed.; pp. 85–94). Minneapolis, MN: Educational Media.

Hinkle, J. S. (1993). Training school counselors to do family counseling. *Elementary School Guidance and Counseling, 27*, 252–258.

Hutchins, D. E., & Vaught, C. C. (1997). *Helping relationships and strategies* (3rd ed.). Pacific Grove, CA: Brooks/Cole.

Hutchinson, R. L., & Bottorff, R. L. (1986). Selected high school counseling services: Student assessment. *The School Counselor, 33*, 350–354.

Johnson, D. W., & Johnson, F. P. (2000). *Joining together: Group theory and group skills* (7th ed.). Boston: Allyn and Bacon.

Kahn, B. B. (1999). Art therapy with adolescents: Making it work for school counselors. *Professional School Counseling, 2*, 291–298.

Keys, S. G., Bemak., F., & Lockhart, E. J. (1998). Transforming school counseling to serve the mental health needs of at-risk youth. *Journal of Counseling and Development, 76*, 381–388.

Kiselica, M. S., & Pfaller, J. (1993). Helping teenage parents: The independent and collaborative roles of counselor educators and school counselors. *The Journal of Counseling and Development, 72*, 42–49.

Kline, W. B. (2003). *Interactive group counseling and therapy.* Upper Saddle River, NJ: Merrill Prentice Hall.

LaFountain, R. M, & Garner, N. E. (1996). Solution-focused counseling groups: The results are in. *The Journal for Specialists in Group Work, 21*(2), 128–143.

Lazear, D. (1999). *Eight ways of teaching: The artistry of teaching with multiple intelligences.* Arlington Heights, IL: SkyLight Training and Publishing.

Loesch, L. C., & Goodman, W. J. (2000). The K–12 developmental school counselor and appraisal. In J. Wittmer (Ed.), *Managing your school counseling program: K–12 developmental strategies* (2nd ed.; pp. 204–210). Minneapolis, MN: Educational Media.

Magnuson, S., & Norem, K. (1998). A school counselor asks: "Am I prepared to do what I'm asked to do?" *Family Journal, 6*(2), 137–140.

McWhirter, J. J., McWhirter, B. T., McWhirter, A. M., & McWhirter, E. H. (1998). *At-risk youth: A comprehensive response for counselors, teachers, psychologists, and human service professionals* (2nd ed.). Pacific Grove, CA: Brooks/Cole.

Muller, L. E. (2000). A 12-session, European-American-led counseling group for African American females. *Professional School Counseling, 3*, 264–269.

Nassar-McMillan, S. C., & Cashwell, C. S. (1997). Building self-esteem of children and adolescents through adventure-based counseling. *Journal of Humanistic Education and Development, 36*, 59–67.

Noble, J. (2000). Students' educational achievement: What helps or hinders? *The ASCA Counselor, 38*, 14–15.

Parker, L. J. (1998). *Mythopoesis and the crisis of postmodernism: Toward integrating image and story.* New York: Brandon House.

"Peer counselors help kids with problems, study shows." (2000). *The National Certified Counselor, 16*, 16.

Ponton, L. E. (1997). *The romance of risk: Why teenagers do the things they do.* New York: Basic.

Posthuma, B. W. (1999). *Small groups in counseling and therapy: Process and leadership* (3rd ed.). Boston: Allyn and Bacon.

Schmidt, J. J. (1999). *Counseling in schools: Essential services and comprehensive programs* (3rd ed.). Boston: Allyn and Bacon.

Search Institute. (1996). *40 Developmental Assets.* Minneapolis, MN: Author.

Smith, S. L., & Archer, J. (2000). The developmental school counselor and mental health counseling. In J. Wittmer (Ed.), *Managing your school counseling program: K–12 developmental strategies* (2nd ed.; pp. 68–74). Minneapolis, MN: Educational Media.

Stone, G., & Peeks, B. (1986). The use of strategic family therapy in the school setting: A case study. *Journal of Counseling and Development, 65,* 200–203.

Street, S. (1994). Adolescent male sexuality issues. *School Counselor, 41,* 319–325.

Taylor, L., & Adelman, H. S. (2000). Connecting schools, families, and communities. *Professional School Counseling, 3,* 298–307.

Tolan, P., & Guerra, N. (1994). *What works in reducing adolescent violence: An empirical review of the field.* Boulder, CO: Center for the Study and Prevention of Violence.

Wells, M. E., & Hinkle, J. S. (1990). Elimination of childhood encopresis: A family systems approach.

Journal of Mental Health Counseling, 12, 520–526.

Wiggins, J. D., & Moody, A. H. (1987). Student evaluations of counseling programs: An added dimension. *The School Counselor, 34,* 353–361.

Wittmer, J. (2000). Counseling the individual student student. In J. Wittmer (Ed.), *Managing your school counseling program: K–12 developmental strategies* (2nd ed.; pp. 95–110). Minneapolis, MN: Educational Media.

Zinck, K., & Littrell, J. M. (2000). Action research shows group counseling effective with at-risk adolescent girls. *Professional School Counseling, 4,* 50–59.

CHAPTER

8

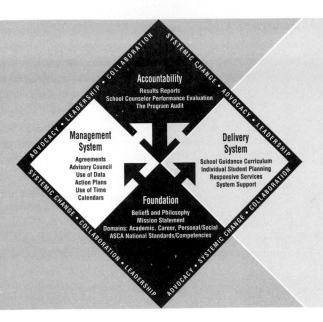

EDUCATING AND ADVOCATING WITH ALL PARTNERS

◆ LEARNING OBJECTIVES

By the time you finish this chapter, you should be able to

1. Define the relationship between educating and advocating
2. Discuss the importance of student competencies in terms of educating and advocating
3. Identify the source of a comprehensive developmental curriculum
4. Describe the process of writing a lesson for the developmental curriculum
5. Write a developmental curriculum lesson that employs multiple intelligence strategies
6. Identify curricular areas within which developmental curriculum could be delivered
7. Outline effective teaching strategies, including how to demonstrate respect for students' personal and intellectual integrity
8. Outline a strategy of classroom management that is respectful and developmentally appropriate, including positive behavior support
9. Identify reasons for educating our adult partners
10. Identify ways that advocacy with adult partners will benefit our students
11. Describe appropriate considerations when educating adults

DOMAINS / ACTIVITIES / PARTNERS MODEL

ACTIVITIES	DOMAINS					
	Academic Development ▼	Career Development ▼	Personal/ Social Development ▼			
Counseling	1a	1b	1c	5	6	7
Educating and Advocacy	2a	2b	2c	8	9	10
Consulting	3a	3b	3c	11	12	13
Leadership and Coordination	4a	4b	4c	14	15	16
	Students			Parents and Caregivers	Colleagues in Schools	Colleagues in Community

PARTNERS IN THE PROCESS

CASE STUDY ◆ Donna's Lunchroom Duty

Donna had been at the high school for several years, and in that time, she found that eating her lunch in the faculty lounge provided her with valuable contact with the teachers. She made it a point to eat there at least twice a week and would use that time to talk to teachers about students, listen to their issues, and consult as needed about student issues. She knew that part of her job was to monitor the emotional climate of the school; time in the teacher's lounge was as important as time in the students' lunchroom for taking the emotional "pulse" of the school.

January was the month for midyear parent conferences, and everyone had been on edge since a car accident in late December in which several students had been injured. The police found marijuana and alcohol in the car. Since the driver and all the passengers were students at Donna's school, she had increased her visibility in classrooms providing developmental curriculum about healthy choices. She had communicated with all the teachers her concerns about the availability of alcohol and drugs in the school, but found that numerous teachers were still reluctant to give up classroom time for her to present her curriculum.

As she entered the lunchroom, several teachers invited her to sit with them, since they were in a debate about something. "We need you to settle this argument."

"Here's the thing, Donna. I say that the parents of the students in that wreck were at fault for not supervising them better. Where did they get the drugs and booze?" one teacher stated.

"No, you're wrong there. I've had a number of conversations with parents during conferences, and they all blame the school and the school counselor. They say the kids got the stuff here, and that it's the school's fault that they are experimenting with this stuff. They say that the school counselor isn't doing her job because no one is keeping the kids from using drugs. They

147

think no one is addressing this. Sorry, Donna, but that's what I hear from the parents," said another.

"What's wrong with these parents anyway?" interjected a third. "Now we have to parent these kids too? Aren't they supposed to monitor their kids' behavior, teach them about right and wrong? I didn't buy the booze those kids had, so why should the school be responsible?"

"Our standards are too slack," posed a fourth teacher. "If we went back to stricter standards, we wouldn't have these problems. They wouldn't have time to mess around with alcohol or drugs—they'd be too busy studying and worrying about exams to get away with partying!"

"So, Donna, what do you think?"

"Yeah, Donna, you're the expert, tell us who's right! Is it our fault, your fault, or the parents' fault?"

"I wish there was an easy answer! The problem is that we all play a part in helping students make good choices. We *all* need to be educated—kids, teachers, and parents—about deadly issues like teenage drinking and drug use," she replied.

"But we already know all that stuff," sniffed one of the teachers. "You need to educate the parents...."

Donna sighed.

CHALLENGE QUESTIONS

1. What do you think about the opinions expressed around the table? Do parents need to be better educated about the realities of alcohol and marijuana? Do teachers need to be educated about parents? Do parents need to be educated about the school and the role of the school counselor? Do teachers need to be educated about the role of academics in the lives of high school students?

2. Who is responsible for educating students, parents, teachers, and the general public about young people, families, schools, and the role of the school counselor? Who is responsible for advocating for students, parents, teachers, and schools when there are misunderstandings?

3. If you were Donna, what would you say next?

◆ DEFINITIONS: EDUCATING AND ADVOCATING

Professional school counselors educate students in new ways of dealing with relationships with self, others, and the world, either by direct instruction or by allowing clients to discover and evaluate their life lessons. In this chapter, we will consider when school counselors are intentional about that instruction, in the second most essential function of school counselors—that of educating others.

The word "educate" has been carefully chosen over "teach." According to the Grolier-Webster International Dictionary (1975), *teach* means "to give instruction to, to guide the studies of" (p. 1007), while *educate* means "to advance the mental, aesthetic, physical or moral development of; to qualify by instruction for the business and duties of life" (p. 313). The difference is subtle, but important. *Teaching* implies the traditional model of instruction, complete with all the connotations of the factory model of schools as described in Chapter 2.

The ASCA School Counselor Performance Standards addressed in this chapter are

Standard 2: The professional school counselor implements the school guidance curriculum through the use of effective instructional skills and careful planning of structured group sessions for all students.

2.1 The professional school counselor teaches school guidance units effectively.
2.2 The professional school counselor develops materials and instructional strategies to meet student needs and school goals.
2.3 The professional school counselor encourages staff involvement to ensure the effective implementation of the school guidance curriculum.

Standard 3: The professional school counselor implements the individual planning component by guiding individuals and groups of students and their parents or guardians through the development of educational and career plans.

3.1 The professional school counselor, in collaboration with parents or guardians, helps students establish goals and develop and use planning skills.
3.2 The professional school counselor demonstrates accurate and appropriate interpretation of assessment data and the presentation of relevant, unbiased information.

The 2001 CACREP Standards for School Counseling Programs addressed in this chapter are

B.1 advocacy for all students and for effective school counseling programs;
B.5 methods of planning for and presenting school counseling-related educational programs to administrators, teachers, parents, and the community;
C.2 (b) individual, group, and classroom guidance approaches systematically designed to assist all students with academic, career and personal/social development;
C.2 (e) developmental approaches to assist all students and parents at points of educational transition (e.g., home to elementary school, elementary to middle to high school, high school to postsecondary education and career options);
C.2 (f) constructive partnerships with parents, guardians, families, and communities in order to promote each student's academic, career, and personal/social success;
C.3 (c) strategies and methods of working with parents, guardians, families, and communities to empower them to act on behalf of their children; and
C.3 (d) knowledge and skills in conducting programs that are designed to enhance students' academic, social, emotional, career, and other developmental needs.

On the other hand, *educating* implies development, discovery, relatedness—all the qualities of developmentally appropriate education that was also discussed in Chapter 2. We believe that school counselors should not view themselves as masters-level teachers, because this implies competition. However, school counselors should view themselves as educators, a role that has been clearly articulated in the National Model and that cements our connection and vitality within the school system (Coy & Sears, 2000; Cuthbert, 2000; Gysbers & Henderson, 2000; Wittmer, 2000).

The connection between educating and advocating is also important (Clark & Stone, 2000). The Grolier-Webster International Dictionary (1975, p. 17) defines to "advocate" as "to plead in favor of, as of a cause, policy, etc.; to recommend publicly; to support." When you plead, recommend, and support, you are trying to persuade others to adopt your point of view; this is best accomplished using both intellect and affect. Intellect and affect are fused when you educate others with passion and conviction. As counselors, you will educate others with passion; this is what elevates education to the level of advocacy. Counselors advocate for healthy choices when they communicate the importance of healthy development and healthy systems (families, schools, and communities). This role, also, is inherent in the National Model; you will recall that Advocacy is one of the Themes describing the context of the work of the school counselor.

As we will see in this chapter, school counselors are a source of information, inspiration, and consolation to many people—our students, the families of our students, our school colleagues, and our community colleagues—educating others about and advocating for healthy development *and* healthy systems.

◆ EDUCATING AND ADVOCATING WITH STUDENTS: HEALTHY DEVELOPMENT

The emphasis on educating and advocating for healthy development has increased with discussions about character education, humanistic education, and values clarification (Kirschenbaum, 2000; Robinson, Jones, & Hayes, 2000; Williams, 2000), violence prevention (Elliott, 1998; Guerra & Williams, 1996; Sherman, Gottfredson, Mackenzie, Eck, Renter, & Bushway, 1998; Tolan & Guerra, 1994), metacognitive skills and academic success (Brigman & Campbell, 2003; Sink, 2005), and helping all youth function more effectively in today's world (Goldstein, 1999; Goleman, 1995; McWhirter, McWhirter, McWhirter, & McWhirter, 1998; Rak & Patterson, 1996). These discussions have emphasized that school counselors must employ strategies to reach every student in the school, and the classroom has been the primary venue for that outreach effort. It is clear that counselors can no longer afford to be reactive, waiting for students to come to them with their concerns (Gysbers & Henderson, 2000; Wittmer, 2000). These perspectives have been clearly articulated in the ASCA National Standards for Student Academic, Career, and Personal/Social Development (Appendix B). The learning objectives derived from these Standards will be referred to as the developmental curriculum (not "classroom guidance").

Furthermore, the discussions of character education, violence prevention, risk reduction, and resiliency enhancement have also sensitized counselors to their crucial role in prevention and early intervention efforts. Recall from Chapter 4 that prevention activities are designed to mitigate the effect of internal and external realities that can cause students problems as they mature, whereas early intervention efforts are designed to help curb current unhealthy risk factors (McWhirter, McWhirter, McWhirter, & McWhirter, 1998). As we encounter young people who struggle with self-esteem, family problems, abuse issues, learning problems, low impulse and emotional control, poor social skills, and a host of other concerns, we must be aware that developmental curriculum delivered in the classroom provides students with critical survival skills that are the essence of prevention and early intervention (Goldstein, 1999; Goleman, 1995; McWhirter, McWhirter, McWhirter, & McWhirter, 1998; Rak & Patterson, 1996). In fact, research suggests that these classroom interventions can be as meaningful, and can provide intervention as powerfully, as small-group counseling (Nassar-McMillan & Cashwell, 1997; Shechtman & Bar-El, 1994; Shechtman, Bar-El, & Hadar, 1997). To ensure that these skills are being addressed, counselors must carefully develop and evaluate the content of their developmental curricula to meet the student competencies defined by the American School Counselor Association (ASCA) and by state or district mandates.

Student Competencies

As indicated on the DAP Model as presented in Chapter 6, educating and advocacy with students is considered one of the primary activities with students. Furthermore, as you will recall from Chapter 5, comprehensive school counseling programs are designed to meet the standards for school counseling programs in terms of the National Standards promoted by ASCA (Appendix B). To accomplish the goal of helping all students to maximize their academic, career, and personal/social development, school counselors structure their comprehensive program around the student competencies articulated in the National Standards. (Recall from the Foundation of the National Model discussed in Chapter 5 that the National Standards are the foundation of the CSCP.)

Moreover, many state departments of education and school districts have used the National Standards to refine their school counseling programs by articulating specific grade-level competencies, as recommended by Gysbers and Henderson (2000). Counselors need to know national, state, district, and local standards to understand which competencies to address in what order.

For the purpose of this chapter, we will continue to use the National Standards as the template of our discussion of the developmental curriculum and the process of educating our student partners. Reviewing Appendix B, you can see that students need specific knowledge, skills, and attitudes to be successful in their academic, career, and personal/social development. To help students to develop these competencies, it is easy to see that a comprehensive developmental curriculum addresses a wide range of developmental topics. The following sections of this chapter are designed to help you understand, develop, and present developmental lessons to students on these areas. (In addition, see Paisley and Hubbard [1994] for examples of lessons.)

◆ DESIGNING LEARNING EXPERIENCES FOR THE DEVELOPMENTAL CURRICULUM

Intent

Where does change begin—with change in thoughts, feelings, or behavior? Think about a significant change you made in your life, such as stopping smoking, starting exercise, or starting graduate school. What process did you go through before you actually made the change in your behavior?

The answers to these questions aren't just mental gymnastics; they are designed to help you think about where to begin when designing learning experiences. This insight is useful for you and your students, because most people know what they need to do to make their lives better. The reason people don't act on this knowledge is that something needs to happen to move that knowledge from their intellect (cognition) into the external world (behavior). What is that something? The answer to that question is the key to help young people move from "Yeah, yeah. I've heard this all before. I can spout all the conflict resolution/drug resistance/delay-of-gratification nonsense. . . ." to "OK. I can do that. I will do that." Here's a clue: That missing link between cognition and behavior is feeling, or affect.

This is where the passion of the counselor will be tapped. To be effective with our students, we have to know, deep in our souls, that what we teach has value, has meaning, and has the ring of human truth to it. Without that conviction from our "bones," we will teach from the intellect only, distancing ourselves from our feelings and knowing of that truth. Palmer (1998) accurately captures what occurs in the classroom when that artificial rift between intellect and intuition is reinforced in the classroom.

> What we teach will never "take" unless it connects with the inward, living core of our students' lives, with our students' inward teachers. . . . We can speak to the teacher within our students only when we are on speaking terms with the teacher within ourselves. . . . Deep speaks to deep, and when we have not sounded our own depths, we cannot sound the depths of our students' lives. (p. 31)

What happens when intellect and intuition are joined, when the teacher's inner core speaks to the students' inner core, is the creation of a community of truth, where students and teacher alike are able to examine the subject as both knowers and learners (Palmer, 1998). The implications for pedagogy, for designing and presenting topics in the developmental curriculum, are consistent with the core concepts of developmentally appropriate classrooms—respect, conversation, discovery, and inclusion (D'Andrea & Daniels, 1996). Within this context, developmental curriculum is carefully planned and thoughtfully executed to establish and enhance the learning community of the classroom.

This does not prevent the counselor from presenting material to students for their consideration, nor does it mean that the class becomes free-for-all, 35-people-all-talking-at-once bedlam. To design developmentally appropriate learning experiences that invite students into the conversation (with you, with each other, with the subject), you begin with the intent to create a developmentally appropriate lesson. This is the first step: Look for ways to engage students in experiences that facilitate discovery and in conversations that allow them to process their existing and emerging truths.

Instructional Purpose

Next, you will articulate your overall purpose within the framework of the student competencies of academic, career, or personal/social development. You will answer two questions: (1) What do you want them to know, to do, and/or to feel by the end of the instructional time? and (2) Is your goal prevention or intervention? The answers to these questions will help you allocate adequate time to delivering the topic.

Instructional time is usually defined in terms of lessons (defined as a single classroom visit, usually one instructional hour or "period") or units (defined as several lessons). Depending on the topic (what you want them to know, do, or feel) and the goal (prevention or intervention), you will extend or shorten the amount of time needed to accomplish your purpose.

For example, if your overall purpose is to help students who fight to learn anger management techniques, you will design a unit consisting of several lessons, each one addressing one topic. In this example, one topic would consist of learning anger triggers; the next would be relaxation techniques; the next would be options to anger; and the last would be role playing and practice. The reason you would want to allot adequate time for each of the four topics is that your goal is early intervention, because these students are already choosing unhealthy behaviors. These behaviors must be unlearned before new behaviors are learned. However, if your students are not already engaged in physical fighting, your goal is prevention, and you might decide that one lesson would enable you to remind students of these anger management skills to prevent future problems. Generally, the less time you spend on a topic, the less "deep" the learning will go.

Learning Objectives

The next step is to create learning objectives for the student, which can be configured for each lesson or for the entire unit. These objectives should be related to outcomes for the student (not the process of presenting the material), specific, and measurable (Mager, 1997). From these objectives, you will have a basis for selecting the materials and instructional strategies for the lesson; you will have structure within which to be flexible and creative; you will have measurable results of your instruction; and you will have a basis for understanding and evaluating your instructional efficiency (Mager, 1997, p. 19). Your goals must also be developmentally appropriate for the age group you are teaching. Examples of learning objectives might include

- ◆ Students will be able to identify at least three healthy responses when someone challenges them to a fight (all age groups).
- ◆ After watching a professional sporting event, students will write down at least ten jobs related to sports, excluding the job of professional athlete (middle or high school).

Instructional Methods and Multiple Intelligences

Once you have identified the overall purpose and objectives of the lesson or unit, you are now free to design the instructional methods that will best meet those objectives within a developmentally appropriate context. It is important to remember that students need to be actively involved, both mentally and physically. Consider how to incorporate the insights gained from the concept of multiple intelligences (see Table 7.1): How can you address students with a variety of different intelligence strengths?

Too often, lessons within the developmental curriculum are targeted to students who think like we do—in other words, for students who are verbal, interpersonally intelligent, and intrapersonally intelligent. This means that those from the other five intelligence orientations are less able to benefit from the insights we hope to offer—left in their confusion, frustration, and perhaps, rejection of the developmental curriculum. There are a variety of instructional strategies that tap each intelligence area, and we should expand our instructional methodology to include all students in the class (Lazear, 1998, pp. 142–145). As you will recall from Chapter 7 (see Table 7.1), these include verbal/linguistic, logical/mathematical, visual/spatial, bodily/kinesthetic, musical/rhythmic, interpersonal, intrapersonal, and naturalist intelligences.

Common developmental curriculum delivery methods include presenting information, discussions, debates, quiet reflection and writing, artwork, journaling, role playing, demonstrations, experiments, and field trips. But don't let this list confine you—be innovative! As you can see from the next section (Integrating the Curriculum Using Multiple Intelligences) and from Tables 8.1, 8.2, and 8.3, the list of ideas is endless. Include discussions about what is important to the students, to their lives and their culture. Consider bringing contemporary music, movies, cultural events, and current events into the classroom. Go where the students are—to the movies they watch, the TV shows they enjoy, the music they listen to, the stores they frequent, the events they attend. Who are their heroes and stars? Pull insights from their lives for the students to consider.

Materials Needed

Based on your instructional methods, identify the materials you will need for each lesson. For example, books, paper, overheads, worksheets, permission slips for the field trip, pre-designed roles for role playing, films, music, and art materials would appear on this list. Again, be creative in selecting your materials, looking for contemporary resources. The importance of timeliness cannot be overemphasized. Imagine you are designing a developmental curriculum lesson on marijuana. You may remember a movie made in the 1950s called *Reefer Madness*, in which the evils of marijuana are presented. If you used that movie today, students would laugh. Of course, if your intent in the lesson is to provide them with a juxtaposition of "old" ideas of drugs with "new" ideas of drugs, this movie would provide a humorous way to accomplish that goal.

Procedure

In this phase of building your lesson or unit, you will identify the specific activities for each lesson. It is helpful to know how each topic will be presented in terms of introduction, activity, processing, and closure (Cuthbert, 2000). Remember that each topic needs to be presented or experienced, processed in terms of how each student will apply the learning or insights gained from the lesson, and closed in terms of what new choices the student will make as a result of the learning. To neglect any of these phases will cause the lesson to be incomplete and fragmented. In the section of this chapter on Delivering the Curriculum, you will see detailed suggestions about how to structure the delivery of each lesson.

Evaluation

Recall that the National Model mandates that counselors collect both perception data (what students think they know, believe, or can do in terms of competencies learned through the developmental curriculum) and results data (how that learning is translated into behaviors

TABLE 8.1 ◆ Curricular Integration, Elementary School, Grades 3–4

Student Competency/ Indicator	Multiple Intelligences	Academic Subject	Lesson Idea
Cooperation/Work and play cooperatively/Describe differences between cooperative and competitive behaviors	Interpersonal using Musical	Music	In groups, students will write and perform music they created from objects in the class
Healthy ways to express needs, wants, feelings/ Learn acceptable ways of dealing with anger/Express feelings with "I" messages in timely, assertive, nonthreatening manner/Communicate with care and respect for self and others	Intrapersonal and Interpersonal	Writing	Students will reflect on the last time they got into a fight and write about what they would say now to that person about the fight.
Describe various occupations/ Understand wide variety of jobs	Visual/Spatial	Art	Students will create a collage of jobs they like cut from magazines
Listening and speaking to obtain information	Verbal/linguistic	PE	Cooperative game
Locate health resources	Naturalistic	Science, History	Students take a field trip to a forest to learn about survival of the early settlers; relate that to how we survive in a modern medical world
Use adult role models to learn more about occupations	Kinesthetic	Social Studies	Dress up as your parents at work
Identify family and cultural background	Interpersonal and intrapersonal	Music History	Students will find out what music represents their family culture
Sense of interconnectedness and co-responsibility/Describe how people work together and depend on each other	Interpersonal	Social Studies	Design a city in the classroom
Identify personal indicators of mental, emotional, social and physical health	Naturalistic and Intrapersonal	Writing	Write a story about a time you were happy (i.e., fun vacation or holiday)
Describe own behaviors, accomplishments and how these influence career choices	Intrapersonal using Bodily/ Kinesthetic	Art, Writing	Students write a play about how someone with their experiences becomes a hero
Anticipate how their lives will be in the future	Verbal/linguistic	Writing	Write about a day in the student's life at the age of 30

TABLE 8.2 ◆ Curricular Integration, Middle School

Developmental Curriculum	Academic Curriculum	Examples of How To Teach Developmental Curriculum in Academic Classroom
Careers	Physical Education	Students will discuss the various careers of the personnel needed to produce a professional football game on TV
Solving problems	Math	Students will take word problems and solve them. In groups, they will then relate those skills to daily problems.
Respecting and appreciating diversity	English	Students will read folk stories and superstitions from various parts of the world and discuss how different experiences lead to unique perspectives. They will write about what they found interesting in each story.
Communication	History	Students will learn about the communication between countries before they went to war with each other and talk about how the communication between them contributed to the choice to go to war. They will relate this to communication that leads to fights.
Cooperation	Science	Students will build a model of a structure from materials given in class, but they will do it without instructions. They will then talk about how they cooperated in the assignment—roles and so on.
Conflict resolution	Biology	Students will study social animals versus solitary animals, and relate what they learn to the "human animal" and human conflicts. What can they learn from the animals that live together?
Setting goals	Science	Students will design their own experiments and will learn how to set up their experiments by establishing goals for each stage of the experiment.
Making decisions	English	Students will watch a popular movie, discussing how the decisions made by the characters resulted in the events of the story. What decisions would they make that differ from those in the movie?
Self-knowledge	Art	Students will be placed in pairs. They will interview each other and create a collage of their partner's best qualities. Students will then discuss how they feel about the collage made about them, exploring discoveries of their good qualities. Were these known or hidden aspects of their persona?

TABLE 8.2 ◆ (Continued)

Developmental Curriculum	Academic Curriculum	Examples of How To Teach Developmental Curriculum in Academic Classroom
Living drug-free	Social Studies	Students will study the social fallout of drug use, focusing on the social problems that addiction creates, such as street people, crime, prostitution, and violence of the drug trade. What conclusions do they come to about drugs?
Making healthy choices about sex	Music	Students will evaluate the lyrics of different types of music in terms of messages about sexual choices. All types of music will be included. They will discuss how they feel about the music and these messages.
Understanding families	History	Students will study a famous family, such as a royal family or a prominent U.S. family for a particular historical period. Various situations within families will be explored, past and present. The student will then research the historical origins of their own family (past three generations) and then will be encouraged to share one interesting thing about their family tree.
Understanding friends	P.E.	Students will be placed in small teams for safe trust-building experiences. Students will then discuss what allowed them to trust their teammates, relating that to qualities of healthy friendships.
Understanding stress	English/Business	Students will study the effect of advertising on their stress. What are the images and/or messages that increase stress? Decrease stress? Why?
Understanding life changes	Science	Students will study geological change in terms of the rise and erosion of mountains. Each phase of the birth to demise of mountains will be related to the life cycle of humans.
Understanding emotions	Music	Students will evaluate the effect of music on their mood and emotional state. They will relate those discoveries to their everyday lives.
Effective study skills	Math	Students will be given a pretest on a math skill, such as adding fractions. Then students will be allowed to review this skill by several different processes—reading, practice, talking to each other in groups, tutoring each other, and so on. They will then be given a posttest. Was their performance what they expected? Why or why not? What method of studying would work better for them?

TABLE 8.3 ◆ Curricular Integration: Secondary School

Intelligence	Academic Curriculum	Developmental Curriculum	Instructional Method
Verbal/Linguistic	English composition	Self-knowledge Self-understanding Self-acceptance Career dreams Job search skills	Journaling Poetry Concept papers Humor Creative writing Resume writing

	Literature	Relationships
		Character flaws:
		  Addiction
		  obsession
		  insanity
			Study of characters
			Storytelling
			Debate of characters

Logical/Mathematical	Mathematics	Decision making
		Problem solving
		Pro-con graphing
		Generation and
		  evaluation of
		  alternatives
		Calculating lifestyles
			Syllogisms
			Outlining
			Logic/pattern games
			Calculating the cost
			  of various lifestyles

Visual/Spatial	Art Drawing Sculpture Photography	Career dreams Future family Lifestyle Self concept Current family Emotional insight Emotion/behavior connections	Painting Drawing Imagery Mind mapping Collage Sculpture

Bodily/Kinesthetic	Physical education	ATODA resistance
		Relaxation training
		Health awareness
		Trust
		Self-protection
		Nonaggressive, self-
		  assertive training
			Exercise
			Physical experiences
			Ropes or challenge
			  experiences
			Martial arts

	Mechanical arts
	Home economics
		Career decision
		  making
		Goal setting
		Planning
			Working through a
			  problem
			Career experience

	Theater	Emotional expression Seeing emotions	Acting Role playing

TABLE 8.3 ◆ (Continued)

Intelligence	Academic Curriculum	Developmental Curriculum	Instructional Method
Musical/Rhythmic	Music Band	Career imagery Stress management Relationships	Evaluating songs for 1. Career messages 2. Emotional messages Relaxation sounds

Interpersonal	Psychology
	Sociology
	Social studies
	History
	Political science
		Social skills
		Cooperation
		Relationships
		Trust
		Self-esteem
		Diversity
		  appreciation
		Social implications of
		  poverty
		Compassion
		Social responsibility
		Emotional communication
			Group experiences
			Conversation
			Empathy
			World court
			Jury duty
			Role playing
			Motivation exercises
			Trust exercises

Intrapersonal	Psychology	Knowing emotions Critical thinking skills Career decisions Personal values Relaxation	Self-reflection Emotional processing Metacognition techniques Personal application Meditation Journaling

Naturalist	Earth science
	Chemistry
	Biology, Botany
	Astronomy
	Health education
		ATODA resistance
		Healthy choices and
		  disease
		Social responsibility
		Family planning
		  choices
			Effects of toxins on
			  the human body
			Diseases (HIV, AIDS)
			Pollution
			Resource depletion

in the school). It is very important that you have a means of evaluating both the effect of the lesson or unit as well as your effectiveness in the presentation of that lesson or unit. To evaluate the effect of the lesson, use the student objectives to assess the extent of their learning. If your lesson involves homework, this provides you with tangible evidence of learning (in theory). (*Remember*: If you ask for homework from your students, always give feedback on those efforts. It isn't respectful to drop the "conversation" without follow-up.) In terms of evaluating your effectiveness in the design and/or presentation of the learning experience, solicit student feedback with an anonymous survey at the end of the class. This process can be informal, such as distributing notecards at the end of the class and asking students to tell you what they liked most and liked least about the lesson they just experienced. This way you will know what to adjust in future lessons.

Reflection Moment ◆

What experiences do you have in designing learning experiences? Are there steps you have found to be important to include in this process? For example, would you feel it necessary to practice the presentation of material before you take it into the classroom with real students? Rewrite the steps listed above, including any steps you feel would be helpful for you in the design and presentation of the developmental curriculum.

◆ ◆

◆ INTEGRATING THE CURRICULUM USING MULTIPLE INTELLIGENCES

One of the biggest challenges to school counselors involves how to schedule the developmental curriculum. School counselors feel they are not able to deliver a developmental curriculum because of increasing pressure on teachers from high-stakes testing, meaning more reluctance to surrender precious classroom time (Dollarhide & Lemberger, 2006). In a study done in 2000, seventy-eight of eighty K–12 counselors were able to deliver group/classroom guidance from once or twice a week, to monthly, to variable scheduling (Burnham & Jackson, 2000). The key to access to the classroom is *curricular integration*, meaning that the developmental curriculum supports the academic standards and benchmarks of learning. To accomplish this integration, counselors need to think about how their lessons dovetail with academic subjects.

Curricular integration involves two levels of effort: practical and conceptual. The practical efforts involve developing and maintaining an advisory cadre of teachers who will assist in the articulation, refinement, and implementation of your comprehensive school counseling program. This ongoing support and advisory cadre should consist of teachers who believe in the CSCP and who are willing to meet regularly to facilitate the holistic development of students through promotion of the program. Through their insights, you can survey other teachers to determine who is already presenting topics that satisfy the developmental curriculum and who is open to your presenting these topics. It is also with the input of this cadre that you can address the conceptual considerations of curricular integration.

The conceptual aspects of integrating the developmental and academic curricula are, once again, facilitated by the concept of multiple intelligences. Many lessons about human nature, relationships, human challenges, and other topics within the developmental curriculum can be explored through experiences associated with other intelligences. As previously mentioned, counseling is a highly verbal, interpersonal, and intrapersonal activity, but five other intelligence strengths are not tapped if all developmental curriculum lessons are focused on the first three. So if you are able to develop a lesson using the naturalist intelligence, it makes sense that you could approach science teachers to see if the developmental curriculum might be integrated there. For example, a science class might be exploring chemicals in the body. What better place to conduct a discussion of the effect of toxic chemicals from drugs, especially contaminated street drugs? The lessons relative to the alcohol, tobacco, and other drugs (ATOD) curriculum would be integrated into the science class, rather than presented as a separate lesson that they have heard over and over again.

Table 8.1 (page 155) presents ideas of curricular integration for elementary school; Table 8.2 (pages 156–157) is for middle schools, and Table 8.3 (pages 158–159) is for high schools. Each one represents a different starting point in the crosswalk process between academic and developmental curricula. Expand this list to consider other teachable moments that exist in extracurricular activities, such as student government, dances, the school newspaper, the yearbook, athletics, and school clubs. What about integration with the school-to-work curriculum? With community service? The possibilities are endless, and you are only bound by the limits of your imagination.

Reflection Moment ◆

What are your intelligence strengths? Think about your favorite classes in high school. Now imagine your least favorite classes. If you could take the excitement of learning through your intelligence strengths into those least favorite classes, what would your learning have been like?

◆ ◆

◆ DELIVERING THE CURRICULUM

Exactly who delivers the developmental curriculum is an important question. In keeping with the concept that colleagues in the schools are our partners in the education of all students, it would be entirely appropriate that teachers would be as involved in the delivery of the developmental curriculum as they would be of the academic curriculum (Myrick, 1993). In many cases, teachers are already presenting topics from the developmental curriculum, but they may not recognize it as such. Meeting with the teacher advisory cadre will help you to determine where students are already learning the developmental curriculum and where additional efforts are needed to reach all students. Whether presented by the teacher alone, a teacher/counselor team, or the counselor alone, the developmental curriculum must be provided to all students.

Teaching Strategies and Lesson Planning

Effective classrooms are founded on respect, both personal and intellectual. Personal respect has been presented in terms of respect for each person and his or her perspective. Let's turn our attention to intellectual respect. What does this mean? You respect someone intellectually when you take the time to understand that person's level of intellectual functioning and then address him or her in terms that effectively match that level. Unfortunately, this is a common problem area for persons who are new to the classroom. Adults often talk down to young people, an error that will cause the adult to lose credibility in the eyes of the student (Valde, 2000).

Furthermore, intellectual respect also involves informing people about what is going to happen and inviting their consent, either tacit or explicit. For example, a physician who does not inform the patient that an injection will be administered, but administers it anyway, is not respecting the patient's right to choose or consent to the treatment. (Imagine how you would feel to be suddenly jabbed with a needle without consenting!) In the same way, a presenter in a classroom who does not inform students what the class entails is not respecting the student's right to choose whether to pay attention and thus, with that assumption, increases the likelihood that the student will choose to "check out." In the classroom, this means informing students the major areas of learning they will experience and asking them to join in the conversation. Getting their agreement up front that what you're presenting is meaningful, interesting, or important will increase their attention and decrease distracting classroom behavior.

There are a variety of models that address effective teaching and classroom management, but they all start from the same premise: When students are engaged in learning because you have structured the learning experience in a developmentally appropriate way, you will have a minimum of interruptions (Travers, Elliott, & Kratochwill, 1993). In general, the qualities that define a well-structured learning experience include

- ◆ Having a meaningful, interesting lesson
- ◆ Getting the lesson started on time
- ◆ Having a clear idea of what you're doing from moment to moment
- ◆ Knowing what you want students to do and how they are to do it
- ◆ Establishing a respectful relationship with students
- ◆ Being aware of what students are doing
- ◆ Keeping the group focused on the topic
- ◆ Being able to design and manage transitions from topic to topic
- ◆ Being able to communicate expectations for appropriate behavior and consequences for inappropriate behavior
- ◆ Classroom rules that are clear, explicit, concrete, basic but global (Example: We will respect all opinions in here. We will communicate that respect by not using any put-downs.)
- ◆ Rules that are enforced fairly
- ◆ Inappropriate behavior is addressed immediately
- ◆ Corrections of behavior are made incrementally: proximity (getting closer to the unfocused student), subtle reminders (looking directly at the student, pointing at the work), verbal reminders (saying the student's name, asking him or her to focus), directions (telling the student to stop what they are doing and return to work), removal for a private conversation (asking the student to step into the hall where you can ask if he or she can work or if he or she needs to go somewhere for

time out), to direct removal (depending on school procedure, sending the student or taking the student to the person or office responsible for discipline) (Eggen & Kauchak, 1994; Geltner & Clark, 2005; Goetz, Alexander, & Ash, 1992; Travers, Elliott, & Kratochwill, 1993).

Since prevention of behavioral distractions is more effective than remediation, useful strategies that are consistent with developmentally appropriate classrooms include those proposed by Cuthbert (2000, pp. 128–129):

◆ Cohesion should be enhanced within the class, reminding everyone that we are all working together toward the same goal.

◆ Cooperation should be explained and modeled by the counselor, including taking turns, listening to others, respecting each other, and working together.

◆ Communication should be emphasized as the key to success for students. Allow students to express their feelings; use active listening, responding, and linking strategies to allow each student to feel heard and respected.

◆ Coaching allows you to help students learn new behavior by direct instruction and practice. Encouragement will help students feel safe taking risks as they practice.

◆ Contribution focus allows each student to feel that he or she has helped the group to reach its goals, either through ideas, respectful quiet listening, or volunteering.

◆ Control issues are important to manage so that you lead the group without dominating it, yet maintain your role as the person responsible for content and delivery.

◆ Configuration refers to how the physical arrangement of the classroom is managed. Varying the layout of the room can add interest to the lesson and can help students break out of more passive learning modes.

◆ Closure, a summary of what is to be learned in the lesson, is important to remember. This allows the group to feel that the topic is finished and that it now "belongs" to them.

◆ Confidentiality, as the hallmark of the counseling profession, is important to address in large groups. Establishing a safe, inviting environment for conversation and learning could inspire students to share more than they intended. You need to remind the group that as listeners, everyone should be respectful of maintaining confidentiality; as speakers, everyone should carefully choose what they share with the group since confidentiality cannot be guaranteed.

Translating these insights into effective instruction involves knowing something about how to deliver instruction to a group of students. Hunter and Russell (1981) describe the seven steps of effective instruction, to which the insights of this chapter have been added. This constitutes what is known as a lesson plan.

1. Review previous learning and focus students' attention on what is to be learned. The example that will be used is from high school: "You already know that some relationships work over years and others do not last. Do you ever wonder why some marriages last and other don't? What are some of the reasons you've seen or heard that describe why relationships fail? What are the effects on people—adults and kids—when a marriage fails?"

2. Inform students about what they should be able to do at the end of the lesson and why it is important that they learn the material. *Example*: "Well, I don't want to see any of you live with those effects (insert class answers to the last question in the previous example: loss of income, loss of home, loss of children, loss of self-esteem). So let's talk today about relationships, what makes them healthy, what helps them last, so that you can think about the relationships that you choose. By the end of today's time, I'd like you to know what makes a healthy relationship and how to evaluate your relationships in terms of whether they are healthy."

3. Provide the lesson, using multiple intelligences and strategies for creative thinking. *Example*: Counselor talks about the qualities of healthy relationships and how to evaluate relationships, showing a clip from a popular movie that depicts a couple in a healthy exchange of ideas, agreement and disagreement, and compromise. The counselor asks "What qualities did these people show that illustrate healthy relationships?"

4. Model what you want the students to know. *Example*: "Here is a description of a relationship. Let's evaluate what is healthy and unhealthy about it. What do you notice about communication style?"

5. Throughout the lesson, check that students understand what you're presenting. *Example*: "How are we doing? Everyone understand?" If there are questions, address them.

6. Provide time for guided practice. *Example*: "Here's another description of a relationship. You can work independently or quietly with one other person" (for insights into providing choices, see Fay and Funk's (1995) *Teaching with Love and Logic*), "and we'll talk about it in ten minutes. Answer each question about the healthy and unhealthy aspects you notice. I'll walk around and answer any questions you have."

7. Review the major concepts of the lesson; then provide independent practice in the form of homework or a paper. *Example*: "OK, today we talked about healthy and unhealthy relationships in terms of. . . We took a look at some examples of each and applied those to evaluations of some relationships. Now I want you to go home and think of a relationship—either one you have been in or one that someone else (a friend, a relative) has been in. Don't tell me whose relationship it is, because that's not what's important. I want you to do two things. I want you to write out a description of that relationship, and then I want you to evaluate that relationship, using the questions on the case studies we talked about here in class today. Any questions? Then I'll see you tomorrow."

Finally, there is one important personal quality that comes from the literature for beginning teachers: the concept of "withitness." According to Gordon (1997), "Beginning teachers need more than knowledge of content and teaching strategies. Insight into [student] culture is critical to success in managing a classroom" (p. 56). Withitness involves social insight, or knowing what is going on with students in the classroom. Effective educators understand how students communicate, both verbally and nonverbally; they know what students value and why; they know how students identify with others, whom they identify with, and why. Gordon proposes five strategies for developing and maintaining this connection with students (p. 58). First, become familiar with student/adolescent culture. Second, affirm the reality of students' concerns. If there is a prom coming up, their attention will be focused on that event. Use the event in your lesson. Third, relate content to students' outside interests: games, music, sports, fashions, trends. Fourth, know your students—their names, their interests, their social connections. And finally, share your humanity with students as appropriate. Let them get to know you as a human being and they will be more open to those times when your humanity shows. This includes some self-disclosure, humor, and your own emotional reality, or "weather."

Classroom Management

"Teaching with love and logic" is derived from a system developed by Foster Cline (Fay & Cline, 1986), in which student misbehavior in the classroom is viewed as ways to avoid the pain of loss of self-esteem and autonomy (Fay & Funk, 1995). An artful blend of Adlerian natural and logical consequences with Control Theory/Reality Therapy's focus on choices (Glasser & Wubbolding, 1997), this approach highlights how young people test the limits of their environment. When this testing is brought into the classroom, an adult's natural reaction is to try to assert control. This sets up a cycle of testing, reacting, punishing, more testing, more extreme reacting, more rigorous punishing, and so on. Rather than perpetuate this system of control and punishment, Fay and Funk believe that people learn best from their own decisions and their own mistakes (p. 26).

The love and logic system consists of six steps. First, you build a relationship with students by noticing the students' likes and dislikes and quietly commenting on them to the students. These comments would not be judgmental or manipulative (not "I like the way you're doing that," but "I see you like skateboards"). Once these positive relationships are built, you set enforceable limits through enforceable statements of what you are willing to do. (Not "I will deduct ten points for each day late," but "I give full credit for papers turned in on time"). Third, you share control with students in terms of "small" decisions (not "I have to have all these papers in today," but "You can turn these in now or after lunch"). Fourth, if there are discipline problems, you implement disciplinary interventions that stop the undesirable behaviors, utilizing empathy and sorrow to connect with the student and to allow them to focus on the consequences ("Janet, I'm sorry that you are unable to work without talking. You can finish your work sitting over here or you can finish your work quietly at your desk. You decide."). Fifth, you would delay consequences to allow the student to think about her or his choices and to decide what he or she can do about the situation, such as in the following scenario:

> **Teacher:** "Tom, seems hard for you to concentrate on your work today. What do you think might happen if you keep talking instead of working?"
> **Student:** "I might get a low grade."
> **Teacher:** "That's a possibility. What else?"
> **Student:** "I might have to stay after school."
> **Teacher:** "That's another possibility. Anything else?"

> **Student:** "You might not let me sit next to my friends."
>
> **Teacher:** "That's another possibility. Tell you what. I'll come back in a couple of minutes. If it seems you're still having trouble concentrating, I'll pick one of those suggestions." (Fay & Funk, 1995, p. 166)

Finally, as you can see in the above example, you give the same assignment the student initially had, underscoring your belief that they will learn from the consequence and make a better decision in the future.

This approach takes practice, since it takes unlearning the test-reaction-punishment cycle and replacing that with the connection-choice-empathic consequence cycle. For counselors who are delivering the developmental curriculum, the principles of this approach are intuitively engaging, since counseling involves the same choices—empathy and working through consequences. The practice and reflection involved in becoming comfortable with this approach are well worth it; becoming comfortable in the classroom determines how successful your teaching will be. And being an educator is an essential part of every counselor's job.

Positive Behavior Support

Positive Behavior Support (Sugai, n.d.) is a strategy from special education for schoolwide behavior management. Taken from strategies that have proven successful for students in special education, there is strong support for using these approaches in all schools. The Office of Special Education Programs in the U.S. Department of Education has a dedicated website at www.pbis.org that disseminates information on this approach.

Positive Behavior Support is a "major advance in schoolwide discipline" that emphasizes "schoolwide systems of support that include proactive strategies for defining, teaching, and supporting appropriate student behaviors to create positive school environments" (www.pbis.org). "Attention is focused on creating and sustaining primary (schoolwide), secondary (classroom), and tertiary (individual) systems of support that improve lifestyle results (personal, health, social, family, work, recreation) for all children and youth by making problem behavior less effective, efficient, and relevant, and desired behavior more functional" (www.pbis.org). This systemwide approach teaches and reinforces positive behavior while concurrently addressing negative behaviors. Insights are applied first in classroom and nonclassroom contexts, as teachers are advised:

1. Classroom positive expectations are taught to students and encouraged.
2. Classroom routines and cues are taught and encouraged.
3. Teachers are to engage in 6–8 positive interactions with students to every 1 negative interaction.
4. Teachers use active supervision and redirection for minor infrequent behavior errors.
5. Teachers use frequent precorrections for chronic errors.
6. Students with behavior challenges will have targeted social skill training and self-management instruction.
7. As needed, individualized instructional and curricular accommodations will be made to help each student learn in the least restrictive environment.

8. In nonclassroom settings, active supervision means scan for behavior, move close to precorrect for problems, interact in positive ways.

Schoolwide, positive behavior support means that there is a common approach to discipline that all personnel endorse, with a clear set of positive expectations for behavior. There is a schoolwide continuum of procedures for both encouraging expected behaviors and for discouraging inappropriate behaviors; there are procedures for monitoring and evaluating both individual student behaviors and schoolwide responses to determine if adjustments are needed. As a research-based and evidence-based approach, Positive Behavior Support combines insights from special education, effective classroom instruction, learning theory, and educational psychology to create an effective strategy for behavior management in schools.

Reflection Moment ✦

Think about your own school years. Can you remember being in trouble? Was that experience handled in a way to allow you to learn, or were you yelled at? Imagine that situation again, recalling as many details as possible. Knowing what you know now, what should have been done to make that a learning experience? Imagine yourself as the person who imposed the punishment; what do you think he or she was feeling as the situation unfolded? If you could go back to that moment and take all these wonderful ideas of classroom management with you, what would you do to enhance the learning of that young person?

✦ ✦

◆ EDUCATING AND ADVOCACY WITH ADULT PARTNERS: HEALTHY SYSTEMS

Educating Adult Partners: Issues

To foster the development of healthy systems, school counselors should also consider themselves educators of, and advocates for, families, schools, and communities. There are many references in the literature to support the need for counselors to educate parents, school colleagues, and community colleagues. And as you can see from Appendix D, Program Goals for Adult Partners in the DAP Model, there is no shortage of ways to help our adult partners develop a greater understanding and appreciation of young people, schools, and the educational process. As the counselor of a CSCP, you are aware of systemic issues that impede our students' potential for success; as an educator, you can see that many of these issues can be addressed through educating our adult partners.

There are calls to provide parent education in almost every issue of professional journals related to school counseling. Educating parents has been called an essential part of every school counselor's training program (Crespi & Howe, 2000; Ritchie & Partin, 1994) to help counselors address parents' rationalization and learned helplessness (Clark, 1995) and to address systemic problems both within the family and between the family and school (Davis & Lambie, 2005; Evans & Carter, 1997). Furthermore, counselors should provide programs to inform parents about the school and to promote parent involvement in the student's education, which can help students feel more connected with the school, address problems with communication, and support at-risk students (Christiansen, 1997; Clark, 1995; Jackson & White, 2000; Peeks, 1993). Finally, it is essential that parents understand the counselor's role in the school so that parental insights can be tapped and parents will support the value of the CSCP (Gibson, 1990; Kaplan, 1997).

The task of educating our adult partners continues with the need to educate our colleagues in the schools. Teachers can benefit from better knowledge about current issues, including family issues such as homelessness, divorce, and custody (Evans & Carter, 1997; Strawser, Markos, Yamaguchi, & Higgins, 2000; Wilcoxon & Magnuson, 1999), and student issues such as ADHD, being an ESL student, being at-risk, sexuality and sexual abuse, and sexual harassment (Christiansen, 1997; Erk, 1999; James & Burch, 1999; McCall-Perez, 2000; Stone, 2000). Teachers can also benefit from training in interpersonal communication skills (Rice & Smith, 1993), dealing with their personal issues (Clark, 1995), and better understanding the role of the school counselor (Gibson, 1990; Jackson & White, 2000). Furthermore, principals can also benefit from a better understanding of the role of the counselor (Burnham & Jackson, 2000; Crespi & Howe, 2000; Gibson, 1990; Kaplan, 1997; Ponec & Brock, 2000) and from better appreciation of school systemic issues (Stone, 2000).

Finally, our colleagues in the community, including school boards, colleges and universities, community mental health providers, employers, and the community at large, could benefit from a better understanding of our students, our schools, and our role in the school (Bemak, 2000; Gibson, 1990; Gysbers, Lapan, & Jones, 2000; Kaplan, 1997; Luongo, 2000; McCall-Perez, 2000; Taylor & Adelman, 2000).

Reflection Moment ◆

Imagine yourself in the role of educating other adults on these subjects. Which of these can you see yourself talking about with parents? With teachers? With administrators? With the public? Which of these topics would you present with the most passion and enthusiasm? Recall that advocacy is educating with passion; for which of these topics, with which partners, would you see yourself as an advocate?

◆ ◆

Educating Adult Partners: Considerations

It is important in this discussion that we briefly touch on the concept of "readiness to learn." This concept is as applicable to adults as it is to young students, and the essence is this: You can lead a horse to water but you can't make it drink. You can, however, make it thirsty in the hopes that it will drink because it *wants* the water. Strong (1968) found that clients evaluated counselors on the basis of their expertness, perceived interpersonal attractiveness (similarities), and trustworthiness; when the counselor was found to be sufficiently expert, similar, and trustworthy, the client felt greater investment in the counseling process. These same variables also influence the investment learners have in the learning process when persuading adults that change (in their opinions of students, families, schools, or the counseling profession) is appropriate.

Translated into concrete suggestions, your expertise in academic, career, and personal/social development should be introduced. Your graduate education in school counseling has provided you with unique training and insights into young people, schools, and the processes of education and growth. You will also want to highlight your similarities to those in your audience, since this tends to increase others' perceptions of you as a role model. Furthermore, your trustworthiness needs to be established; your goal is to foster those conditions that have been proven to be the most conducive to the education, growth, and development of your students. Assuring your audience that you have no ulterior motive, either by example or direct statement of the ethics of the profession, standards of confidentiality, or professional associations, helps them to know that you are not "selling them a bill of goods."

Sometimes, however, in spite of your best efforts, some of your adult partners will refuse to learn anything new. These people are entrenched in their way of viewing the world. They believe that nothing anyone can say is going to change their thinking on a subject. Your approach to these persons would be to assure them that you respect their right to their opinions (as long as those opinions and resulting behaviors fall within the limits of the law) and that, should they ever need to discuss this further, you would be happy to discuss it. At this point, all you can do is hope that they will come to you with questions about students, schools, families, teachers, or the counseling profession, if such questions ever arise.

Putting all these suggestions together for use in educating our adult partners would yield the following suggestions:

1. Know your audience. It is helpful to understand the extent of formal education of the people in the audience so that you can target their vocabulary. For example, when educating teachers, you can use the jargon and terminology of the educational environment, but with parents, avoid the use of jargon.
2. Remember your training in multiple intelligences and present information in multiple formats: words, examples, graphs, exercises, art, music, or examples from sports, science, food, architecture, television, movies, or other venues.
3. Be informed, but do not try to "fake it." If you don't know something, admit it, promise to find out, and arrange to get back to the questioner. Adults are insulted by know-it-alls who are not respectful of the audience's ability to detect false statements. Just one attempt to disguise a guess as a fact will destroy your credibility, trustworthiness, and expertise.
4. Be enthusiastic and passionate. Remember you are an advocate also, and your passion can convince others to consider what you're presenting. Your enthusiasm creates an emotional bond with the audience that enables the learning to have more meaning and long-term impact. Your role as advocate means that you must have a greater sense of social justice and be willing to challenge others in the name of that greater justice.

5. In the presentation, begin with high levels of structure and expertise, then move to an awareness and appreciation of all perspectives on this topic, and then ask them to think of situations in which they found this to be true for themselves. Finish with an affirmation of their right as adults to make their own decisions, but indicate the problems that can arise if they do not apply the insights you are offering (but don't be an alarmist). Remind them that you are happy to consult with them in the future on this topic.

6. Do not lecture *at* your audience. Your audience is comprised of adults, and adults feel insulted when someone scolds them for incorrect behavior and feel patronized when someone talks at them in a lecture-hall format. Parents, teachers, administrators, and community colleagues do the best they can with students, based on what they believe students need. Your job is to help them to better understand what students need and to help them design strategies to best meet those student needs—not to shame or embarrass them.

7. Remember that the audience's perceptions of your expertise, similarity to them, and trustworthiness are important. Establish your expertise by sharing your professional training and experience (as appropriate). Establish your similarity to the audience by sharing relevant personal experiences or personal struggles with this topic (as appropriate). Establish your trustworthiness by assuring them that your sole intention is to help them function better in their lives (as appropriate).

8. Do not be surprised or frustrated with resistance to your topic. In every group, there will be those who will not accept what you have to say. Do not dismiss them, but encounter their resistance with calm equanimity. Find value in their contribution and, if you have time, explore those situational variables that made their experience an exception to your point. In this way, their objection becomes additional support for your topic.

Reflection Moment ◆

What have been your experiences persuading or educating adults? Have those experiences been positive or negative for you? What skills would you like to improve to make those experiences more successful? What can you do now to develop or refine those skills?

◆ ◆

CASE STUDY ◆ Integration

Go back and reread Donna's lunchroom conversation. Now that you have read the chapter, consider the following questions:

1. What messages are embedded in the statements made by the teachers? What insights can you draw about the constraints placed on the CSCP in that school?

2. What ideas do you have for classroom presentations on the subject of alcohol and substance abuse?

3. What ideas do you have for parent programs? For teacher programs?

4. In that conversation, what might Donna have said in her role as advocate for students? Would you advise Donna to be an advocate in that moment, or is there a better time and place for that advocacy? What insights do you now have about timing, a critical aspect of advocacy?

APPLICATION (Possible portfolio artifacts are noted)

1. Inventory your current teaching skills. What are your strengths and what are your challenges? Outline a professional development plan, including strategies for both skill acquisition and practice. (Possible portfolio artifact)

2. Ask a local school counselor for the name of a teacher who is known for being both effective and beloved in the classroom. Interview this person about effective instructional methodology, favorite teaching strategies, and classroom management. Observe this person in the classroom. Write up your insights and compare them to this chapter. How do your insights inform your own presentation style? (Possible portfolio artifact)

3. Examine the list of developmental curriculum topics in the National Standards (Appendix B). Select the most important fifteen topics and rank them in order of importance for students at your target educational level. Time consuming, isn't it? If you only have a limited number of opportunities to make presentations in the classroom, you need to think about which topics you feel are most important.

4. Take one of the top five topics from the list you generated and design a lesson or unit on it that you could present to one or two grades. How will you communicate your passion for this topic? Make sure to include each step from the Designing Learning Experiences part of this chapter. (Possible portfolio artifact)

5. Take one topic from the previous list and design an instructional method for each of the eight intelligence strengths. (Possible portfolio artifact)

6. Take the same topic and write three instructional methods that use current events or persons as the central theme. (Possible portfolio artifact)

7. Write an evaluation instrument for a classroom presentation. What do you want to know from your students? (Possible portfolio artifact)

8. Interview a local school counselor to ascertain a developmental curriculum topic (from the National Standards) that he or she wishes could be integrated into the academic curriculum. Using what you know about multiple intelligences, Tables 8.1, 8.2, or 8.3, and your imagination, design a lesson that infuses that developmental curriculum topic into the academic curriculum. Make sure to address at least four of the multiple intelligences. Now present this plan to the counselor you interviewed.

9. What is the line for you between passionate enthusiasm and overblown emotionalism? With a class colleague, role play an enthusiastic five-minute presentation on your favorite sport, your children, your job, or any other topic about which you feel passionate. Ask the colleague to give you feedback about that presentation. Switch places and listen to a five-minute monologue on a topic about which the colleague is passionate. Note your reactions. Provide feedback to your colleague about your reactions to the presentation. How can you use this experience to better understand your role as an advocate?

10. Interview a school counselor, asking that professional to outline the educational programs he or she provides for adults. Attend a presentation

made to one of the adult partner groups. Critique the presentation to develop insights into how you would present to adults. (Possible portfolio artifact)

11. Adults are bombarded by attempts to persuade them to buy something, believe something, or try something. What are the strategies adults use to resist these attempts? How can you use that insight to help you make better presentations to adults?

12. Conduct an Internet search for information on a topic of interest to families. Select five topics that you feel would be of interest to parents and caregivers and record those addresses. Create a brochure in which you share those addresses with family members and encourage them to visit those sites. (Possible portfolio artifact)

SUGGESTED READINGS

Cline, F., & Fay, J. (1990). *Parenting with love and logic: Teaching children responsibility*. Colorado Springs, CO: Pinon Press. This book is the foundation of the Parenting with Love and Logic program, a very successful and valuable parent program.

Dinkmeyer, D., Sr., McKay, G. D., & Dinkmeyer, D., Jr. (1997). *The parent's handbook: Systematic Training for Effective Parenting (STEP)*. Circle Pines, MN: American Guidance Service. This book is the foundation of the STEP program, also a very successful and valuable parent program.

Fay, J., & Funk, D. (1995). *Teaching with love and logic*. Golden, CO: Love and Logic Press. An extensive look at the effective use of choice in a school and classroom setting, this book provides useful strategies for working with students. The key to these strategies is that students learn to want to act better, reducing the need for adults to force them to behave.

Goldstein, A. P. (1999). *The Prepare curriculum: Teaching prosocial competencies*. Champaign, IL: Research Press. Based on Social Learning Theory, this book is the result of the author's training experiences with youth who needed retraining in aggression reduction, stress reduction, and prejudice reduction. Structured small- and large-group experiences are outlined to enable the reader to use these lessons with prevention and intervention developmental curricula.

King, P. M., & Kitchener, K. S. (1994). *Developing reflective judgment: Understanding and promoting intellectual growth and critical thinking in adolescents and adults*. San Francisco: Jossey-Bass. This book gives the reader a full discussion of learning issues for adults, providing insights for promoting learning.

MacKinnon-Slaney, F. (1994). The adult persistence in learning model: A road map to counseling services for adult learners. *Journal of Counseling and Development, 72*, 268–275. This article is extremely helpful in articulating the relationship between learning and counseling in adults.

Mager, R. F. (1997). *Preparing instructional objectives: A critical tool in the development of effective instruction* (3rd ed.). Atlanta, GA: The Center for Effective Performance. A comprehensive discussion of how to establish the foundation of any well-developed learning experience.

O'Connor, K. (2001). The principal's role in report card grading. *NASSP Bulletin, 85*(621), 37–46. Although intended for a high school principal, this article outlines strategies for grading that could be very useful for counselors who must grade the work of students in the developmental curriculum.

Paisley, P. O., & Hubbard, G. T. (1994). *Developmental school counseling programs: From theory to practice*. Alexandria, VA: American Counseling Association. A compilation of developmental curriculum ideas and modules.

Palmer, P. (1998). *The courage to teach: Exploring the inner landscape of a teacher's life*. San Francisco: Jossey-Bass. A powerful discussion of what constitutes teaching with passion, combining pedagogy and learning into a "community of truth."

Root-Bernstein, R., & Root-Bernstein, M. (1999). *Sparks of genius: The thirteen thinking tools of the world's most creative people*. Boston: Houghton Mifflin. These authors present their ideas on creative thinking and the tools to enhance creativity in very practical terms, with many quotes and examples from science, the arts, and the humanities. Any classroom would be enriched by applying these ideas to modern education.

REFERENCES

Bemak, F. (2000). Transforming the role of the counselor to provide leadership in educational reform through collaboration. *Professional School Counseling, 3*, 323–331.

Brigman, G., & Campbell, C. (2003). Helping students improve academic achievement and school success behavior. *Professional School Counseling, 7*, 91–98.

Burnham, J. J., & Jackson, C. M. (2000). School counselor roles: Discrepancies between actual practice and existing models. *Professional School Counseling, 4*, 41–49.

Christiansen, J. (1997). Helping teachers meet the needs of students at risk for school failure. *Elementary School Guidance & Counseling, 31*, 204–211.

Clark, A. J. (1995). Rationalization and the role of the school counselor. *The School Counselor, 42*, 283–291.

Clark, M. A., & Stone, C. (2000). The developmental school counselor as educational leader. In J. Wittmer (Ed.), *Managing your school counseling program: K–12 developmental strategies* (2nd ed.; pp. 75–82). Minneapolis, MN: Educational Media Corporation.

Coy, D., & Sears, S. (2000). The scope and practice of the high school counselor. In J. Wittmer (Ed.). *Managing your school counseling program: K–12 developmental strategies* (2nd ed.; pp. 56–67). Minneapolis, MN: Educational Media Corporation.

Crespi, T. D., & Howe, E. A. (2000, March). Families in crisis: Considerations and implications for school counselors. *Counseling Today, 42*, 6, 36.

Cuthbert, M. I. (2000). Large group developmental guidance. In J. Wittmer (Ed.), *Managing your school counseling program: K–12 developmental strategies* (2nd ed.; pp. 123–134). Minneapolis, MN: Educational Media Corporation.

D'Andrea, M., & Daniels, J. (1996). Promoting peace in our schools: Developmental, preventive, and multicultural considerations. *School Counselor, 44*, 55–64.

Davis, K. M., & Lambie, G. W. (2005). Family engagement: A collaborative, systemic approach for middle school counselors. *Professional School Counseling, 9*, 144–151.

Dollarhide, C. T., & Lemberger, M. E. (2006). "No Child Left Behind": Implications for school counselors. *Professional School Counseling, 9*, 295–304.

Eggen, P., & Kauchak, D. (1994). *Educational psychology: Classroom connections* (2nd ed.). New York: Merrill.

Elliott, D. S. (1998). *Prevention programs that work for youth: Violence prevention*. Boulder, CO: Center for the Study and Prevention of Violence.

Erk, R. R. (1999). Attention deficit hyperactivity disorders: Counselors, laws, and implications for practice. *Professional School Counseling, 2*, 318–326.

Evans, W. P., & Carter, M. J. (1997). Urban school-based counseling: Role definition, practice applications, and training implications. *Journal of Counseling & Development, 75*, 366–375.

Fay, J., & Cline, F. (1986). *The science of control*. Golden, CO: Cline/Fay Institute.

Fay, J., & Funk, D. (1995). *Teaching with love and logic*. Golden, CO: Love and Logic Press.

Geltner, J. A., & Clark, M. A. (2005). Engaging students in classroom guidance: Management strategies for middle school counselors. *Professional School Counseling, 9*, 164–166.

Gibson, R. L. (1990). Teachers' opinions of high school counseling and guidance programs: Then and now. *The School Counselor, 37*, 248–255.

Glasser, W., & Wubbolding, R. (1997). Beyond blame: A lead management approach. *Reaching Today's Youth, 1*(4), 40–42.

Goetz, E. T., Alexander, P. A., & Ash, M. J. (1992). *Educational psychology: A classroom perspective*. New York: Merrill.

Goldstein, A. P. (1999). *The Prepare curriculum: Teaching prosocial competencies*. Champaign, IL: Research Press.

Goleman, D. (1995). *Emotional intelligence: Why it can matter more than IQ*. New York: Bantam.

Gordon, R. L. (1997). How novice teachers can succeed with adolescents. *Educational Leadership, 54*(7), 56–58.

Grolier-Webster international dictionary of the English language. (1975). New York: Grolier.

Guerra, N. G., & Williams, K. R. (1996). *A program planning guide for youth violence prevention: A risk-focused approach*. Boulder, CO: Center for the Study and Prevention of Violence.

Gysbers, N. C., & Henderson, P. (2000). *Developing and managing your school guidance program* (3rd ed.). Alexandria, VA: American Counseling Association.

Gysbers, N. C., Lapan, R. T., & Jones, B. A. (2000). School board policies for guidance and counseling: A call to action. *Professional School Counseling, 3*, 349–355.

Hunter, M., & Russell, D. (1981). *Planning for effective instruction: Lesson design increasing your teaching effectiveness.* Palo Alto, CA: The Learning Institute.

Jackson, S. A., & White, J. (2000). Referrals to the school counselor: A qualitative study. *Professional School Counseling, 3*, 277–286.

James, S. H., & Burch, K. M. (1999). School counselors' roles in cases of child sexual behavior. *Professional School Counseling, 2*, 211–217.

Kaplan, L. S. (1997). Parents' rights: Are school counselors at risk? *The School Counselor, 44*, 334–343.

Kirschenbaum, H. (2000). From values clarification to character education: A personal journey. *Journal of Humanistic Counseling, Education and Development, 39*, 4–20.

Lazear, D. (1998). *Eight ways of teaching: The artistry of teaching with multiple intelligences* (3rd ed.). Arlington Heights, IL: SkyLight Training and Publishing.

Luongo, P. F. (2000). Partnering child welfare, juvenile justice, and behavioral health with schools. *Professional School Counseling, 3*, 308–314.

Mager, R. F. (1997). *Preparing instructional objectives: A critical tool in the development of effective instruction* (3rd ed.). Atlanta, GA: The Center for Effective Performance.

McCall-Perez, Z. (2000). The counselor as advocate for English Language Learners: An action research approach. *Professional School Counseling, 4*, 13–22.

McWhirter, J. J., McWhirter, B. T., McWhirter, A. M., & McWhirter, E. H. (1998). *At-risk youth: A comprehensive response for counselors, teachers, psychologists, and human service professionals.* Pacific Grove, CA: Brooks/Cole.

Myrick, R. D. (1993). *Developmental guidance and counseling: A practical approach* (2nd ed.). Minneapolis, MN: Educational Media.

Nassar-McMillan, S. C., & Cashwell, C. S. (1997). Building self-esteem of children and adolescents through adventure-based counseling. *Journal of Humanistic Education and Development, 36*, 59–67.

Paisley, P. O., & Hubbard, G. T. (1994*). Developmental school counseling programs: From theory to practice.* Alexandria, VA: American Counseling Association.

Palmer, P. J. (1998). *The courage to teach.* San Francisco, CA: Jossey Bass.

Peeks, B. (1993). Revolutions in counseling and education: A systems perspective in the schools. *Elementary School Guidance & Counseling, 27*, 245–252.

Ponec, D. L., & Brock, B. L. (2000). Relationships among elementary school counselors and principals: A unique bond. *Professional School Counseling, 3*, 208–217.

Rak, C. F., & Patterson, L. E. (1996). Promoting resilience in at-risk children. *Journal of Counseling and Development, 74*, 368–373.

Rice, G. E., & Smith, W. (1993). Linking effective counseling and teaching skills. *The School Counselor, 40*, 201–206.

Ritchie, M. H., & Partin, R. L. (1994). Parent education and consultation: Activities of school counselors. *The School Counselor, 41*, 165–170.

Robinson, E. H., III, Jones, K. D., & Hayes, B. G. (2000). Humanistic education to character education: An ideological journey. *Journal of Humanistic Counseling, Education and Development, 39*, 21–25.

Shechtman, Z., & Bar-El, O. (1994). Group guidance and group counseling to foster social acceptability and self-esteem in adolescence. *The Journal for Specialists in Group Work, 19*, 188–196.

Shechtman, Z., Bar-El, O., & Hadar, E. (1997). Therapeutic factors and psychoeducational groups for adolescents: A comparison. *The Journal for Specialists in Group Work, 22*, 203–213.

Sherman, L. W., Gottfredson, D. C., MacKenzie, D. L., Eck, J., Reuter, P., & Bushway, S. D. (1998). Preventing crime: What works, what doesn't, what's promising. *National Institute of Justice Research in Brief.* Washington, DC: U.S. Department of Justice.

Sink, C. A. (2005). Fostering academic development and learning: Implications and recommendations for middle school counselors. *Professional School Counseling, 9*, 128–135.

Stone, C. B. (2000). Advocacy for sexual harassment victims: Legal support and ethical aspects. *Professional School Counseling, 4*, 23–30.

Strawser, S., Markos, P. A., Yamaguchi, B. J., & Higgins, K. (2000). A new challenge for school counselors: Children who are homeless. *Professional School Counseling, 3*, 162–171.

Strong, S. R. (1968). Counseling: An interpersonal influence process. *Journal of Counseling Psychology, 15*(3), 215–224.

Sugai, G. (n.d.). *School-wide Positive Behavior Support: Overview.* OSEP Center on PBIS, U.S. Department of Education. Retrieved on August 3, 2006, from www.pbis.org/pastconferencepresentations.htm.

Taylor, L., & Adelman, H. S. (2000). Connecting schools, families, and communities. *Professional School Counseling, 3,* 298–307.

Tolan, P., & Guerra, N. (1994). *What works in reducing adolescent violence: An empirical review of the field.* Boulder, CO: Center for the Study and Prevention of Violence.

Travers, J. F., Elliott, S. N., & Kratochwill, T. R. (1993). *Educational psychology: Effective teaching, effective learning.* Madison, WI: Brown & Benchmark.

Valde, G. (2000). [Student reactions to the approach of educators]. Unpublished raw data.

Wilcoxon, S. A., & Magnuson, S. (1999). Considerations for school counselors serving non-custodial parents: Premises and suggestions. *Professional School Counseling, 2,* 275–280.

Williams, M. M. (2000). Models of character education: Perspectives and developmental issues. *Journal of Humanistic Counseling, Education and Development, 39,* 32–40.

Wittmer, J. (2000). Developmental school guidance and counseling: Its history and reconceptualization. In J. Wittmer (Ed.), *Managing your school counseling program: K–12 developmental strategies* (2nd ed.; pp. 1–13). Minneapolis, MN: Educational Media Corporation.

CHAPTER

9

CONSULTATION WITH ALL PARTNERS

Accountability
Results Reports
School Counselor Performance Evaluation
The Program Audit

Management System
Agreements
Advisory Council
Use of Data
Action Plans
Use of Time
Calendars

Delivery System
School Guidance Curriculum
Individual Student Planning
Responsive Services
System Support

Foundation
Beliefs and Philosophy
Mission Statement
Domains: Academic, Career, Personal/Social
ASCA National Standards/Competencies

◆ LEARNING OBJECTIVES

By the end of this chapter, you will

1. Understand what is meant by consultation
2. Be able to enumerate reasons why consultation is an effective way of working in schools
3. Be able to describe differences between consultation and other forms of helping
4. Understand ways in which consultation can be used to help students, parents, teachers, and all other partners
5. Be able to identify a variety of consultation models and processes
6. Be able to discuss a generic process model of consultation
7. Identify which model of consultation will fit best with which situation
8. Understand resistance and ways to address resistance in consultation

DOMAINS / ACTIVITIES / PARTNERS MODEL

ACTIVITIES	Academic Development ▼	Career Development ▼	Personal/ Social Development ▼	Parents and Caregivers	Colleagues in Schools	Colleagues in Community
Counseling	1a	1b	1c	5	6	7
Educating and Advocacy	2a	2b	2c	8	9	10
Consulting	3a	3b	3c	11	12	13
Leadership and Coordination	4a	4b	4c	14	15	16

DOMAINS

Students

PARTNERS IN THE PROCESS

CASE STUDY ◆ An Eye-Opening Lunch for Lupé

Lupé and Caroline met for lunch every Friday. They were both middle school counselors in neighboring districts, and they found much-needed support in their lunch meetings. It was wonderful to be able to talk about school-related and counseling issues freely, without fear of unprofessional disclosure. (Being aware of confidentiality, however, they never used names or details.)

Today it was Lupé's turn to talk, and she needed help with a problem with a teacher. "Caroline, you know me. I'm a patient woman—I'm fairly tolerant. But this one teacher this year is driving me nuts! I can't seem to get her to understand that she's crossing the line with these kids."

"Whoa! Back up. What's she doing?"

"She brings me the names of all these kids she wants me to work with. That's a good thing—at least she cares. The problem is that I think she might care too much. She hounds me with 'Did you see her? Did you work with her?' and it's only been two days since she brought me the name."

"You know, Lupé, that doesn't sound like a problem to me...." Caroline began.

"Let me finish. That's not the half of it. A couple of the kids have told me that she tries to 'counsel' them after class; she pesters them to give them rides home."

"That does seem a little over the line. But just to play the devil's advocate, and I hope you won't be offended if I say so, but are you maybe feeling a little threatened? Maybe she's trying to do your job and you don't like it?" Caroline offered gently.

"No, I have already looked at that. She does nice things, but for the wrong reasons. I just have a feeling there's something more to it. Other teachers have mentioned that she has these favorites, and that they have seen her shower attention on the favored ones to the exclusion of some really needy kids in her classes."

"What's your history like with this teacher? Can you talk with her?"

Lupé paused, lost in thought. "I've known her for eight years. She's never done these kinds of things before. You know, I remember when we met, I thought she was the best teacher I'd ever

177

known. And I was so impressed, because she had just had a family tragedy, and she still kept working. That was really something. I had never seen anyone able to bounce back so quickly from such a heartbreak. Her daughter had just died—poor little thing was only eleven years old, and she was killed by a hit-and-run driver. I'll never forget going to that funeral and seeing her picture on the casket. Such a beautiful little girl, gorgeous blond hair.... Oh my. That's it." Lupé looked at Caroline like she had seen a ghost.

"That's it, Caroline. That's what's wrong. Her favored students—they all look alike. They're all blonde, slim—they look just like her daughter. Wow." Lupé stopped. "I'm going to have to really give this a lot of thought. Maybe I'm wrong. But what if I'm right? She is too good a teacher to let her credibility as a teacher erode like this."

"But what can you do? Tell her she's nuts? That'll help a lot!" Caroline said.

"No, but there has to be something I can do. This one's going to be tough. I'm going to have to find a good way to approach this."

CHALLENGE QUESTIONS

1. Do you agree with Lupé that she can help in this situation, or do you agree with Caroline that there's nothing Lupé can do?
2. If you were Lupé, how would you evaluate your hypothesis? How would you go about exploring if you were right or not?
3. Assuming that Lupé is right, now what? What is the first thing you could do to help? Would you go to the principal? Would you talk to the students? Would you talk to the teacher? What would you say? If you weren't functioning well as a professional, how would you want the situation to be handled?

◆ INTRODUCTION TO CONSULTATION

The premier organization that accredits counseling programs, the Council for the Accreditation of Counseling and Related Educational Programs (CACREP) (2001), requires school counselors to demonstrate knowledge and skill in the consultation process, effectively consulting with teachers, administrators, parents, students, community groups, and agencies as appropriate. In Chapter 1, we discussed the ways that the national professional association, the American School Counselor Association (ASCA), defines the primary interventions provided by school counselors. In that list of interventions, ASCA identifies consultation as "a *collaborative* partnership in which the counselor works with parents, teachers, administrators, school psychologists, social workers, visiting teachers, medical professionals and community health personnel in order to plan and implement strategies to help students be successful in the educational system" (American School Counselor Association, 1999; emphasis added). As a collaborative activity, consultation fits within the Themes of the ASCA National Model. For these reasons, consultation is an important part of the Domains/Activities/Partners model that helps structure this book. It is not only one of the primary activities school counselors engage in with our adult partners, it is a critical way of working with students.

Recent research has established the amount of time that counselors spend in consultation in the schools. Burnham and Jackson (2000) found that counselors from all three

The ASCA School Counselor Performance Standards addressed in this chapter are

Standard 3: The professional school counselor implements the individual planning component by guiding individuals and groups of students and their parents or guardians through the development of educational and career plans.

3.1 The professional school counselor, in collaboration with parents or guardians, helps students establish goals and develop and use planning skills.

3.2 The professional school counselor demonstrates accurate and appropriate interpretation of assessment data and the presentation of relevant, unbiased information.

4.2 The professional school counselor consults effectively with parents or guardians, teachers, administrators and other relevant individuals.

13.5 The professional school counselor collaborates with teachers, parents and the community to promote academic success of students.

The 2001 CACREP Standards for School Counseling Programs addressed in this chapter are

C.2   **(f)** constructive partnerships with parents, guardians, families, and communities in order to promote each student's academic, career, and personal/social success;

C.2   **(g)** systems theories and relationships among and between community systems, family systems, and school systems, and how they interact to influence the students and affect each system;

C.3   **(a)** strategies to promote, develop, and enhance effective teamwork within the school and larger community;

C.3   **(b)** theories, models, and processes of consultation and change with teachers, administrators, other school personnel, parents, community groups, agencies, and students as appropriate; and

C.3   **(c)** strategies and methods of working with parents, guardians, families, and communities to empower them to act on behalf of their children.

levels spend from 1 to 80 percent of their time providing consultation, with a majority spending an average of 18 percent of their time in consultation. Those with whom counselors consulted, in descending rank order, were community agencies (professionals in hospitals, mental health, and social services), teachers, students, and parents (p. 45). The authors of this study expressed concern that "consultation, as an intervention, needs to be more well-defined for counselors. . . . [C]onsultation may be a 'catch-all' for services rendered" (Burnham & Jackson, 2000, p. 47). These authors point out that there is overlap between counseling and consulting skills and that counselors need a better understanding of consulting. More than just a theoretical aspect of school counseling, consulting is a crucial part of the counselor's job.

Most counselor preparation programs will address consultation as part of school counselor training; in fact, many CACREP-accredited programs will offer a course in consultation. This chapter is not meant to suffice as your only exposure to consultation but as a supplement to focus and refine your consultative skills relative to your CSCP.

Definition of Consultation

When we examine consultation, we can see why it is so useful. There are various approaches to consultation, but all define consultation as interaction between the counselor and another person with the primary focus of assisting that other person to function more effectively with a third person or group within a work, school, or interpersonal system. Dougherty (1990) defines consultation as "a process in which a human services professional assists a consultee with a work-related (or caretaking-related) problem with a client system, with the goal of helping both the consultee and the client system in some specified way" (p. 8). Other common characteristics of consultation involve a professional, voluntary, tripartite, and temporary relationship, in which the consultant provides direct service to the consultee in problem solving and indirect service to the client by improving the situation for both (Dougherty, 1990). The relationship is confidential, collaborative, and collegial, without power differential or supervisory implications, where the consultee maintains responsibility for implementing the insights and outcomes of the consulting relationship (Dougherty, 1990; Dustin, 1992; Kahn, 2000; Kurpius & Rozecki, 1992; Mauk & Gibson, 1994).

This definition maintains a focus on the consultee as being another professional or adult (Dougherty, Dougherty, & Purcell, 1991; Erchul & Conoley, 1991; Hall & Lin, 1994; Kahn, 2000; Kurpius & Rozecki, 1992; White & Mullis, 1998) who works with the consultant on behalf of the client system. Inherent in this definition are three parties: the consultant (the school counselor), the consultee (the person who approaches the consultant for assistance), and the client (the third person, usually not present during the consultation, about whom the consultee has concerns). In schools, "client" usually means the student or the student's family; however, to effect systemic change mandated by the ASCA National Model, school counselors must also consider students as consultees.

For our purposes, we will use a broader definition of consultation provided by Brown, Pryzwansski, and Schulte (1998), while maintaining all the characteristics, conditions, and caveats of the relationship and goals of consultation outlined above. "Human service consultation is defined as a voluntary problem-solving process . . . engaged primarily for the purpose of assisting consultees to develop attitudes and skills that will enable them to function more effectively with a client, which can be an individual, group, or organization for which they have responsibility" (p. 6). The way consultants approach the consultee's issues is from a position of respect for the autonomy and independence of the consultee to see problems, generate and evaluate alternatives, and independently select appropriate change strategies.

Consultation provides many benefits to school counselors, the consultees, and the client/system. First, consultation is an efficient use of time, providing an opportunity for the counselor to intervene in a holistic, systemic way with the school, whole classrooms, students, and their families (White & Mullis, 1998). Furthermore, consultation empowers the consultee to address his or her own problems and work them through, providing long-term benefits to both the consultee and those with whom the consultee interacts (Hall & Lin, 1994). These benefits accrue to all parties, whether the counselor is consulting with students, families, teachers, administrators, or community members.

Although it is possible to see many similarities between counseling and consulting, the two processes are distinct and separate. In terms of their similarities, both counseling and consulting are predicated on a helping, genuine, respectful relationship, and both are focused on the goal of an independent, fully functioning helpee/consultee (Brown, Pryzwansky, & Schulte, 1998). Both may employ one-on-one meetings or group education as interventions, and both maintain confidentiality. However, there are substantial distinctions between them. Counseling is dyadic, involving only two parties, and is focused on the intrapsychic, personal problems of the client (Dougherty, 1990), with the goal of altering the behavior, feelings, or beliefs of the client in the deeply interpersonal counseling relationship (Brown, Pryzwansky, & Schulte, 1998). Consultation, on the other hand, is always triadic, involving the consultant, the consultee, and the client (the person or group for whom the consultee *has some responsibility* [Brown, Pryzwansky, & Schulte, 1998; Dougherty, 1990] or *toward whom the consultee feels some responsibility*). Furthermore, consultation focuses on systemic or work issues, not on the personal issues of the consultee (except as they may interfere with work issues) (Brown, Pryzwansky, & Schulte, 1998; Dougherty, 1990; Kurpius & Rozecki, 1992).

Another helping process that is often confused with consulting is advice-giving. Just as there are important distinctions between counseling and advice-giving, so too are there important distinctions between consulting and advice-giving (Brown, Pryzwansky, & Schulte, 1998). Although as popularly used, the term "consulting" is often synonymous with "advice-giving," the process of advice-giving is not consulting. Because the advice-giver assumes the role of an expert, there is no collegial relationship (if, indeed, there is any relationship at all). In addition, there is no assumption of respect or confidentiality. Finally, the goal of giving advice is not to improve the functioning of the helpee; it is on solving problems in the most expedient way possible. Advice-giving is a casual, problem-focused, expert-to-neophyte interaction focused on expediency and convenience. Consultation is an intentional, professional, respectful, collegial, problem- and process-focused interaction to enhance the functioning of both consultee and client/system. When these processes are juxtaposed, it is easy to see the unique qualities of consultation.

Generic Process Model of Consultation

There are a variety of models that outline the process of consultation, each with its own strengths and limitations. Similar to the search for a good match between a counselor's personal theory of change and various counseling theories, school counselors have a variety of consulting approaches that may match their personal styles. Rather than address all these various models, let's examine a generic model of the process of consultation (Hall & Lin, 1994). In this model, Dougherty (1990) identified four major phases of consultation: entry, diagnosis, implementation, and disengagement. Adapted for school counselors, corresponding activities for each stage would include

    I. Stage One: Entry
       A. Establish a professional helping relationship with the consultee.
       B. Explore the needs of the consultee.
       C. Set tentative goal(s) with the consultee.
    II. Stage Two: Diagnosis
       A. Gather information about the situation, the consultee, and the system about which the consultee has concerns.
       B. With the consultee, define the problem.
       C. Confirm goal(s) with the consultee.
       D. Generate possible interventions.

III. Stage Three: Implementation
   A. Facilitate consultee's selection of an intervention.
   B. Facilitate the consultee's creation of a plan of action.
   C. The consultee implements the plan.
   D. Together, the consultant and consultee evaluate the plan.
IV. Stage Four: Disengagement
   A. Formulate a contingency plan with consultee.
   B. Reduce involvement.
   C. Invite consultee back as needed to provide follow-up and support.

This model fits well with both Caplan's and Schien's models that will be discussed later in this chapter.

◆ CONSULTING WITH STUDENTS

The reason for expanding our definition of consultation is that counselors do indeed consult with students as an appropriate part of the job (CACREP, 2001), in spite of what more traditional definitions of consultation might suggest. In fact, Burnham and Jackson (2000) found that counselors consulted with students more than with parents (p. 45).

In terms of the classical definitions of consulting, it is difficult to distinguish when a counselor is *consulting* with students about a third person for whom the student feels responsible, and when the counselor is *problem solving* with the student about a third person. In traditional definitions, problem solving with the student about a third person would not meet the criteria for consultation, because there is no responsibility for the third person; however, this issue does not diminish the counselor's ability to enhance the functioning and interaction of the consultee or the client. You are urged to consider that, as an appropriate extension of the advocate role of the counselor, consulting with students about ways to improve the school environment/system or the family environment/system is an appropriate use of consulting skills. In this view, the student is not responsible *for* the school or family system, but rather, is responsible *to* that system, and student efforts to make change in that system require tremendous courage. Using this perspective, consulting with students about ways to facilitate positive change in family systems or school systems is not an option; it becomes a mandate. One example of this mandate would include sexual harassment (Stone, 2000) where a student may need consultation to understand how to address this serious issue.

Let's examine several situations germane to middle or high schools to understand how consulting works with students.

Scenario 1.   A student comes to the counselor because the student is not getting along well with a group of friends. The counselor provides counseling to help the student articulate his feelings about the rejection by his friends and decide if he wants to continue with the friendship; then the counselor helps the student acquire better communication skills to confront the friends about the problems in the friendship. This is counseling, not consultation. If, however, the counselor and the student work together to strategize ways to improve the interaction and environment within the friendship group, without delving into the intrapsychic dynamics of the student who came for help, this is consultation.

Scenario 2.   A student comes to the counselor because the student is not getting along well with others on the student council. Rather than a friendship, this relationship with the other students is "work" related—addressing the work of the student council. The counselor consults with the student, helps him understand the context of student government, allows him to examine his interaction style relative to the group, and then asks him to let her know how it goes with the council. This is consultation, not counseling. If, however, the counselor and student examine why the student feels he must always have the approval of others, this is counseling.

Scenario 3.   A student comes to the counselor because her family is dysfunctional, with alcohol addiction in both parents. The counselor provides counseling to the student to allow her to process her feelings of despair, grief, and frustration; then they brainstorm ideas for helping her make healthier choices for her own future. This is counseling, not consultation. If, however, the student wants to understand the implications of organizing a family intervention with the goal of helping her parents into treatment, this is consultation. There is no direct or sustained attention paid to the student's feelings about her parents' addiction.

Scenario 4.   A student comes to the counselor because her parents are overly strict. The student asks for help in showing her parents that she is trustworthy. The counselor provides consulting in a systems context (i.e., helping the family "work" more effectively from the student's perspective). The counselor helps the student understand families, and then they brainstorm ideas for proving her trustworthiness to her parents. The goal is that the parents will allow the student to take on more responsibilities and privileges, thereby improving the functioning of the family. This is consultation, not counseling. If, however, the student wants to talk about her feelings of being smothered, and the only goal is to help the student change, then that is counseling.

Scenario 5.   A student comes to the counselor with a problem with a teacher. The counselor provides counseling for the student to help him understand his feelings about the teacher's actions; they talk about perspective-taking to help the student understand the teacher's perspective better. Then they brainstorm ways that the student can adjust his behavior to allow better interaction between teacher and student. This is counseling, not consulting. If, however, the behavior of the teacher becomes one of intimidation, or if the behavior of the teacher suggests serious impairment, the counselor may strategize with the student about how the student could take these concerns to the administration, with the goal of empowering the student to address his concerns directly. Indirectly, the school system may benefit from helping this teacher change his or her behavior. *Important Note*: This situation must be handled very professionally and carefully to avoid serious negative consequences to the student, the teacher, and the counselor.

Scenario 6.   A student comes to the counselor with a problem with the assistant principal. The counselor tells the student to get over it, because the assistant principal is a powerful administrator, and the student only has two years to graduation. The counselor suggests that the student get a hobby to help with stress management. This is disrespectful advice-giving, neither counseling nor consulting.

Reflection Moment ◆

Can you think of a situation in which you have already provided consultation according to the definition of professional consultation outlined above? When consultation is not done appropriately, serious ramifications can result. Can you think of what some of those consequences might be? At what point does poorly done consultation become unhealthy triangulation? (Triangulation occurs when one person becomes involved in a problem between two others, taking sides in the conflict instead of encouraging direct communication between the two with the problem.)

◆ ◆

◆ CONSULTING WITH ADULT PARTNERS

Consultation does appear to be an increasingly important way for counselors to work with adult partners (Dustin, 1992). The advantages of using consultation as an approach to problems with parents, teachers, administrators, other pupil service professionals, and our community partners are numerous. Consultation provides a systemic intervention, allowing counselors to reach into the students' context and mobilize other persons in the students' support network. It is an efficient use of time, providing reinforcement and collaboration among all partners on behalf of the student, and it is proactive and preventive (White & Mullis, 1998). Furthermore, consultation is an important element of the advocate function of school counselors, in which the counselor helps parents, teachers, administrators, and community professionals understand students and their issues (Crespi & Howe, 2000). As a direct result of this enhanced understanding, these adult partners can work more effectively with and for students (Kurpius & Rozecki, 1992)—which is in line with the ASCA National Model's theme of systemic change.

A more detailed look at a model of consultation will help you understand all the forms consultation can take, specific to our adult partners. Caplan's model (1970; Caplan & Caplan, 1993; Erchul & Conoley, 1991) is of particular interest here, because it provides a framework for understanding various dimensions of consultation and strategies for facilitating change both for individuals and for organizations. (*Note.* Caplan's original model was designed for mental health consultation but will be modified here to focus on its application in the school setting.)

It is important to note that Caplan's approaches to consultation depend on accurate assessment of the consultee's and client's contexts in any consultation. Caplan (1970) cautions consultants to be very sensitive to the norms of the consultee's personal and professional context, so that the consultant does not suggest interventions that are contrary to community, professional, or organizational norms and mores. His insights are relevant for school counselors; success of the consultation will depend on the extent to which the consultant accurately understands the culture of the family (consulting with parents), the culture of the school (consulting with school colleagues), the culture of the district (consulting

Focus on Individual versus Organization

	Individual (Case consultation)	*Organization* (Administrative consultation)
Client	I Client-centered Case consultation	III Program-centered Administrative consultation
Consultee	II Consultee-centered Case consultation	IV Consultee-centered Administrative consultation

Focus on Client versus Consultee

FIGURE 9.1 ◆ Caplan's Four Types of Consultation

with student services partners), the culture of the agency (consulting with community professional service providers), and the culture of the community as a whole (consulting with community members). This is an important reminder to school counselors that foundation counseling skills are as essential in consultation as they are in counseling.

Caplan's model (1970) begins with two dimensions: focus on the individual (case consultation) versus the organization (administrative consultation) and focus on the single client (client-centered or program-centered) versus the consultee (consultee-centered). As you can see from Figure 9.1, this results in a 2 × 2 grid with four possible consulting approaches, each with its own focus for intervention. Let's explore these four approaches one at a time.

Client-Centered Case Consultation (I)

According to Caplan (1970), client-centered case consultation is characterized by direct contact between the consultant and the *client* in which the consultant's primary goal is to develop a plan for dealing with the client's difficulties. Secondary to this goal is the goal of helping the consultee improve his or her skills. The consultant is an expert who assesses the environment of the client, the client's level of functioning, and all aspects of the problem in order to arrive at a diagnosis of the problem and a plan that the consultee will then implement. The consultant provides direction to the consultee in the implementation and monitors the progress of the client in this process.

The most common example of this type of consultation is when the school psychologist does assessment for special education referrals, recommending accommodations for teachers to follow. But school counselors also function within this type of consultation when they meet with a student, at the request of a teacher, to determine if a classroom behavior problem is one that should be addressed through counseling or through the disciplinary function of the administration. Similarly, a parent might request that the school counselor meet with a student to determine if counseling or alternative parenting strategies are warranted.

Consultee-Centered Case Consultation (II)

This type of consultation is the most sensitive and intricate of the four types presented by Caplan (1970). In this type of consultation, the consultant is assessing and addressing the functioning of the *consultee*, with the secondary goal of improving the interaction between the consultee and the client(s). The consultant rarely meets with the client(s) in this type of consultation, but deals directly with the consultee in the exploration of the problem and determination of interventions. This exploration of the problem centers around conceptual or affective distortions that the consultee exhibits while interacting with the clients.

Caplan (1970) identifies four sources of difficulties that consultees face, with increasing levels of anxiety and resistance: lack of knowledge, lack of skill, lack of confidence, and lack of objectivity. The first two sources of difficulty, and the easiest to address, are the lack of knowledge and the lack of skill. In these two sources of difficulty, the school counselor can address the challenge faced by the consultee by providing information and/or by providing practice in the missing skill. For example, school counselors may help teachers or parents address the needs of students by providing information relative to developmental issues and may provide role-playing practice with the consultees to improve their communication skills.

The third source of difficulty for the consultee may be lack of confidence. At its least problematic level, the consultant would provide feedback to help the consultee through early professional experiences, such as those experienced by first-year teachers who seek assurance that they are handling classroom management appropriately. Caplan (1970) suggests that consultants (school counselors) support consultees (first-year teachers) in this situation, while also evaluating the extent to which more senior members of the consultee's profession (experienced teachers) would provide long-term support. Another example of this type of situation might include parents who come to the school counselor for assurance that they have handled a rare occurrence, such as the death of their child's friend, appropriately. However, at its most problematic level, serious lack of confidence and resulting anxiety might prevent a consultee from functioning effectively; at this level, the consultant might refer the consultee for more intensive intervention, such as counseling and/or therapy.

The fourth source of difficulty for consultees is the most involved and sensitive. Lack of objectivity involves cognitive and affective distortions that limit the consultee's ability to function professionally. The five distortions described by Caplan (1970) are as follows:

1. *Direct personal involvement.* This occurs when the consultee's professional relationship with the client is transformed into a personal relationship, such as when a teacher becomes romantically involved with a student.
2. *Simple identification.* This occurs when the consultee loses professional perspective because the client represents a struggle in the consultee's personal life. For example, a parent who is ineffective in addressing a student's drinking may be struggling because of her own substance abuse issues.
3. *Transference.* This occurs when the consultee transfers issues from other relationships onto the relationship with the client. An example of this would include a school

social worker who has problems working with gay students because he has not yet worked through his own feelings about his gay son.

4. *Characterological distortions.* If, in the previous example, the consultee has problems working with gay students because he believes all gays are disgusting, this is an example of the distortions coming from prejudicial attitudes and beliefs.

5. *Theme interference.* "A theme represents an unsolved problem or defeat that the consultee has experienced, which influences his or her expectations concerning a client" (Brown, Pryzwansky, & Schulte, 1998, p. 31). In this case, the consultee expresses hopelessness that the situation with the client can be improved. An example of this type of interference would include a teacher who has problems working with attention-deficit students because she perceives them all as threatening and unpredictable, believing the "theme" that all ADD students will disrupt the classroom.

To address all five of these problems, Caplan (1970) believes that consultants should

1. Model professional objectivity and perspective
2. Refocus the consultee onto the issue(s) of the client
3. Unlink the distortions of the consultee from the reality of the client, so that the consultee can perceive the situation more objectively
4. Dispute the predetermined conclusions and themes by
   a. identifying possible outcomes other than those feared by the consultee ("Some ADD students might be disruptive, but let's also look at how much this student could contribute to the class through her humor and creativity")
   b. relaying a "parable" about a situation in which the feared outcome did not manifest ("You have had Carla in your class and you didn't even notice she was diagnosed with ADD")
   c. relaxing the focus on the situation to diffuse the anxiety ("We can talk any time you want about the situation, but I know we won't need to meet that often")

If none of these strategies are successful with the consultee, a referral would be made to allow the consultee to work on these issues with a private counselor or therapist.

Program-Centered Administrative Consultation (III)

A parallel to the client-centered case consultation, program-centered administrative consultation occurs when the consultant is called to provide assistance with a specific need or problem in an organization. In this situation, the focus remains on the need or problem and does not broaden to an examination of the entire organization. For example, a school counselor might be asked to provide a program audit (as discussed in the ASCA National Model) for another school, so that the review of the comprehensive school counseling program is done by an informed but objective professional. When the parent-teacher organization of the school invites the school counselor to present a program on substance abuse issues to the members, it is an example of program-centered administrative consultation. When the local social welfare agency invites the school counselor to work with its social workers to streamline referrals to the student assistance program in the school, this is also an example of this type of consultation.

Consultee-Centered Administrative Consultation (IV)

Caplan's (1970) final type of consultation involves efforts to improve the functioning of the organization as a whole. For example, a school might call in a school counselor from another district to provide consultation for communication problems between the administration and the teachers. (The in-house school counselor would not, in this situation, be the ideal consultant. An outside professional would have the advantage of objectivity, having no history or preconceived ideas about the source of the problem.) In this example, the consultant would enter the system, diagnose the problem, make recommendations to the school administration to resolve the situation, and monitor the success of efforts to facilitate change. Another example of this situation might be a parent-teacher organization that invites the school counselor to provide consultation in the design of an internal structure of officers that can facilitate decision making.

As you can see, Caplan's model and the four types of consultation can be used to conceptualize and plan appropriate strategies for consulting with individuals, groups, or entire organizations of parents, teachers, administrators, pupil/student service professionals, and colleagues in the community. Let's now examine the school counselor's role providing consultation with each of these partners.

Reflection Moment ◆

It's easy to see why many graduate programs in counselor education offer a separate class in consultation. If your program offers such a class, be sure to enroll in it. You are fortunate that you will have more time to absorb these various models. If your program does not offer a class in consultation, consider finding such a class online, from another university, or through independent study.

Can you think of examples in your own experience in which you provided consultation in each of Caplan's four types of consultation?

◆ ◆

Consulting with Parents

In terms of Caplan's (1970) model, most of the work counselors do in providing consultation to parents is done either as client-centered case consultation or as consultee-centered case consultation. In these situations, the consultee is the parent or caregiver, and the client is usually the student. (Occasionally, other persons, such as a teacher, might be the client in the consultation.) The most common situation is client-centered case consultation, in which the parent approaches the school counselor for help with the student's behavior, attitudes, relationships, or other concern. In this type of consultation, the focus remains on the *student*, with the counselor meeting with the student and with the parent to assess the problem, identify possible solutions, and help the parent implement recommendations. In the case of consultee-centered case consultation, the focus is on helping the *parent* function more effectively with the student, addressing the parent's problem that interferes with the relationship with the student.

It is with these personal problems of the parent that we see how counseling and consultation can overlap. In fact, some models describe consultation with the family in the same terms as family counseling, to the point that some authors suggest that if the counselor isn't qualified to provide family counseling, the counselor would apply a model of family consultation and education (Magnuson & Norem, 1998; Nicoll, 1992).

Consulting with School Colleagues

Consultation with colleagues in the schools can be focused on individuals (client-centered or consultee-centered case consultation) or on the school as a whole (program-centered or consultee-centered administrative consultation). One of the most common ways that counselors work with teachers and other student service professionals is as a consultant. If a teacher, school social worker, school psychologist, or school nurse is the consultee, a school counselor would use client-centered consultation to help that professional deal more effectively with students' attitudes or behaviors that are deemed problematic. If the problems seem to reside with the professional, a school counselor would use consultee-centered consultation to help that person deal more effectively with all students by working on that person's attitudes or behaviors. If the principal is the consultee, the tasks involved often require administrative consultation: program-centered consultation to design or deliver a specific program (which may overlap with the activity of educating school colleagues discussed in Chapter 8) or consultee-centered administrative consultation addressing overall school issues such as school climate, communication, or morale among the staff.

If the school counselor is partnering effectively with colleagues in the schools, much of that time will involve consulting with teachers. The importance of contact with teachers was highlighted in a study of teacher perceptions of counselors; the highest level of respect for the skills and dedication of the counselor was found "in those schools where counselors interacted with every teacher on a one-to-one basis at least once per semester" (Gibson, 1990, p. 254).

Consulting with Community Colleagues

School counselors frequently consult with community partners about schools and about the developmental issues of young people, blurring the lines between education, advocacy, and consultation. If we continue to use Caplan's model (1970) of consultation, we can see the many ways that school counselors consult with colleagues in the community. Individual client-centered or consultee-centered case consultation might take place with a colleague who is a professional in health care, mental health, or social services (physician, nurse, psychologist, psychiatrist, counselor, or social worker), who is working with an individual student or family. Program-centered administrative consultation might occur if a community law enforcement, mental health, or social service agency asked the school counselor to present a program on student development or work on ways to coordinate referrals. Consulting with general community members would most often consist of consultee-centered administrative consultation (for example, if the local chamber of commerce or service organization wanted to know how to support school efforts and an educational agenda).

We have seen that the integration of family, community, and school must be accomplished to support young people who have minimal support systems. The most important issues facing education—at risk children and school-community integration, for example—will demand consultation with community colleagues (Dustin, 1992). This requires a very broad focus, the ability to see the big picture of a student's context, and skills in initiating community participation, but the overall benefits are immeasurable (Kurpius & Rozecki, 1992). Improved social and economic conditions can result through voluntary cooperation and self-help efforts (Kurpius & Rozecki, 1992) that can be initiated in the community by mobilizing the community's concern over its young people.

Reflection Moment ◆

Can you see yourself providing consultation to parents, caregivers, teachers, administrators, school psychologists, school nurses, school social workers, community law enforcement, social welfare agency workers, and community health-care and mental health professionals? Which of these groups will present the greatest challenge for you? Which one(s) will present the most comfort for you? Why?

◆ ◆

◆ GENERAL ISSUES: EXPERTISE AND RESISTANCE

In our discussion of the traditional definitions of consultation, we focused on the relationship between the consultant and the consultee as equal and collegial. When working in a school setting, it is likely that counselors might need to be flexible in how their expert status is factored into the relationship, to acknowledge the consultee's expectations of the counselor's expertise. To address these expectations, Schein (as cited in Dougherty, 1990, p. 196) described three templates for consultation in terms of the expectations of the consultee relative to the expert status of the consultant. Schein labeled these approaches as the purchase of expertise model, the doctor-patient model, and the process model of consultation.

In the purchase of expertise model, the consultant is an expert who is expected to provide a solution to a previously determined problem. In the doctor-patient model, the consultant is again an expert, but in this model the consultant is expected to provide both a diagnosis of the situation and the solution. In contrast, the role of the consultant in the process model is not expert as in the other two models, nor is the consultant expected to provide a diagnosis or the solution. Rather, the role of the process consultant is egalitarian, and the consultant's job is to monitor and provide insights into the process of problem solving. In this model, the focus is on helping the consultee formulate his or her own solutions to the problem. Schien's process model has been the primary structure on which other authors (Dougherty, 1990; Dustin, 1992; Kahn, 2000; Kurpius & Rozecki, 1992; Mauk & Gibson, 1994) constructed the traditional definitions.

These templates provide useful perspectives from which to understand consultation in schools, where consultees come with varying levels of insight into the problem, the solutions, and the process to resolve any given dilemma. Many consultees come to the school counselor because they acknowledge the counselor's expertise in certain issues and will engage in consultation with the counselor on the basis of that expert status. Often, students want the counselor to provide some insights into the problem, the solutions, and the best process for problem resolution. Schein's insights allow counselors to accept that status as needed to facilitate the growth of the consultee and improvement of the client system.

In spite of the counselor's best efforts to establish and maintain an egalitarian and respectful posture relative to the consultee and the client, throughout consultation there is always the possibility that the consultee will resist the consulting efforts of the school counselor. As Caplan (1970) pointed out, consultants must understand the reality of the family, culture, and community of which consultees and clients are a part. Even with this sensitivity, there are many sources of resistance to consultation. Understanding these sources may help you design approaches to students, caregivers, teachers, and others in ways that reflect your sensitivity to their concerns.

There are many possible sources of resistance to consultation. Specifically, parents and caregivers might fear being blamed, fear a loss of privacy, or fear that the school will take over their authority (White & Mullis, 1998). These parents may have had negative experiences with schools in general or your school in particular or may resist consultation because they believe everything will work out without intervention (White & Mullis, 1998).

In addition to these issues, school and community colleagues present a variety of fears and concerns in the face of consultation. These include fear of losing status with students, fear of blame, fear of being perceived as incompetent, fear of success (since success may result in more work), fear of change, and fear of the unknown (White & Mullis, 1998). Other possible sources of resistance include rigidity, discouragement, and hopelessness (White & Mullis, 1998).

Intrapsychic sources of resistance include the possibility that consultees may have serious personal problems impeding their efficacy with students, or they may not be able to overcome *your* racial, educational, or economic background (White & Mullis, 1998). Furthermore, all of the adult partners may experience cognitive distortions that can lead to defensiveness, such as overgeneralizing from past experiences to new experiences or from one group of students to another, catastrophizing that prior negative experiences will increase or reoccur, and blaming others for one's shortcomings (Dougherty, Dougherty, & Purcell, 1991).

Fortunately, there are a number of strategies to reduce resistance (Dougherty, Dougherty, & Purcell, 1991). First, counselors should recognize that resistance is normal and not unhealthy (Dougherty, 1990; White & Mullis, 1998). Second, helping the consultee to understand the process of consultation, the role of the consultant, and the appropriate role of consulting within the professional purview of the counselor can increase cooperation. Third, establishing an open, respectful, and confidential relationship that fosters trust will provide comfort to consultees, which, in turn, will help them deal with the stress of change and fears of loss of control or of status. Fourth, counselors can increase cooperation by focusing on the positives of the situation and expressing support for the consultee (White & Mullis, 1998). Furthermore, consultants will find greater success when they remain objective, refrain from engaging in power struggles, use encouragement, and emphasize the control of the consultee in the implementation of the solution (Dougherty, Dougherty, & Purcell, 1991; White & Mullis, 1998).

CASE STUDY REVISTED ◆ Integration

So Lupé's concerns about the teacher in her school were not so far-fetched after all.

1. Should Lupé pursue this issue? With whom? Where would you begin if you were Lupé?
2. Imagine that you have decided to talk to the teacher. This is clearly an example of consultee-centered case consultation. What do you see as the source(s) of the problem with the teacher: lack of knowledge, lack of skill, lack of confidence, or lack of objectivity? Assume that you see some elements from each. What will you do to address each area?

3. Reread the five categories of lack of objectivity. Which of the five categories do you feel explains the situation best? Assume that you see some elements in the problem from each of the five categories. What would you do to address each category?

4. What are all the sources of resistance that you can anticipate? List all of them. What would you do to address each source of resistance, before it becomes a problem?

APPLICATION (Possible portfolio artifacts are noted)

1. Reread Scenario 6 in this chapter, about the problem between the student and the assistant principal. What would you have done if you had been the counselor? Reflect on your solution; is that consultation or counseling? Think of a counseling response to that scenario. Now think of a consulting response. Which response would be more effective? In what ways and for whom? Which response would be more time efficient? In what ways?

2. Identify a recent experience in which you provided some problem-solving assistance for someone about a problem with another person. Was that consultation? Imagine yourself back in that conversation and now imagine you will consciously choose to conduct consultation with that person. Outline a plan for consulting with that person.

3. Talk to a school counselor about the problems students have brought to the counseling office recently. Pick one of those problems and outline a consultation based on that situation. Now do that same assignment with the focus on a problem a parent has brought to the counselor recently. (Possible portfolio artifact)

4. Interview a school counselor about the last time she or he provided consultation. Identify which of Caplan's four types of consultation was used in that situation and explain why you categorized the consultation as you did.

5. Interview a student about positive changes that person wishes were in place in the school. Outline a plan for consulting with that student about how to generate that positive change. (Possible portfolio artifact)

6. Interview a student about positive changes that person wishes were in place in his or her family. Outline a plan for consulting with that student about how to generate that positive change. (Possible portfolio artifact)

7. Reflecting on the needs of your community, outline a plan for consulting with a community agency or organization to address a problem that exists between the community and the school, or outline a way that the community and school can work more effectively with each other. Provide details of that consultation plan, including whom you would approach to propose the consultation. (Possible portfolio artifact)

8. Create a chart of the various sources of resistance for each partner. Then use Schien's models to design some preemptive strategies to prevent that resistance from emerging.

SUGGESTED READINGS

Brown, D., Pryzwansky, W. B., & Schulte, A. C. (1998). *Psychological consultation: Introduction to theory and practice* (4th ed.). Boston: Allyn and Bacon. A seminal text that outlines the variables and implications of the models, styles, skills, ethics, and legalities of consultation.

Caplan, G., & Caplan, R. B. (1993). *Mental health consultation and collaboration.* San Francisco: Jossey-Bass. This book provides a comprehensive and detailed overview of Caplan's model of consultation.

Dougherty, A. M. (1990). *Consultation: Practice and perspectives.* Pacific Grove, CA: Brooks/Cole. This text provides a generic model of consultation as well as an overview of models of consultation.

Kurpius, D. J., & Rozecki, T. (1992). Outreach, advocacy and consultation: A framework for prevention and intervention. *Elementary School Guidance & Counseling, 26,* 176–189. This article outlines a framework for consultation based on the level of intervention needed in schools and communities.

White, J., & Mullis, F. (1998). A systems approach to school counselor consultation. *Education, 119,* 242–253. This article provides an in-depth discussion of consultation with families.

REFERENCES

American School Counselor Association (ASCA). (1999). *The role of the professional school counselor.* Alexandria, VA: Author. Retrieved May 31, 2000, from www.schoolcounselor. org/role.htm.

Brown, D., Pryzwansky, W. B., & Schulte, A. C. (1998). *Psychological consultation: Introduction to theory and practice* (4th ed.). Boston: Allyn and Bacon.

Burnham, J. J., & Jackson, C. M. (2000). School counselor roles: Discrepancies between actual practice and existing models. *Professional School Counseling, 4,* 41–49.

Caplan, G. (1970). *The theory and practice of mental health consultation.* New York: Basic.

Caplan, G., & Caplan, R. B. (1993). *Mental health consultation and collaboration.* San Francisco: Jossey-Bass.

Council for Accreditation of Counseling and Related Educational Programs (CACREP). (2001). *The 2001 standards: CACREP accreditation standards and procedures manual.* Alexandria, VA: Author.

Crespi, T. D., & Howe, E. A. (2000, March). Families in crisis: Considerations and implications for school counselors. *Counseling Today, 42,* 6, 36.

Dougherty, A. M. (1990). *Consultation: Practice and perspectives.* Pacific Grove, CA: Brooks/Cole.

Dougherty, A. M., Dougherty, L. P., & Purcell, D. (1991). The sources and management of resistance to consultation. *The School Counselor, 38,* 178–186.

Dustin, D. (1992). School consultation in the 1990s. *Elementary School Guidance & Counseling, 26,* 65–76. Retrieved November 13, 2000, from http://webnf1.epnet.com (the EBSCO database).

Erchul, W. P., & Conoley, C. W. (1991). Helpful theories to guide counselors' practice of school-based consultation. *Elementary School Guidance & Counseling, 25,* 204–212. Retrieved November 13, 2000, from http://webnf1.epnet.com (the EBSCO database).

Gibson, R. L. (1990). Teachers' opinions of high school counseling and guidance programs: Then and now. *The School Counselor, 37,* 248–255.

Hall, A. S., & Lin, M. J. (1994). An integrative consultation framework: A practical tool for elementary school counselors. *Elementary School Guidance & Counseling, 29,* 16–28. Retrieved November 13, 2000, from http://webnf1.epnet.com (the EBSCO database).

Kahn, B. B. (2000). A model of solution-focused consultation for school counselors. *Professional School Counseling, 3,* 248–254.

Kurpius, D. J., & Rozecki, T. (1992). Outreach, advocacy and consultation: A framework for prevention and intervention. *Elementary School Guidance & Counseling, 26,* 176–189. Retrieved November 13, 2000, from http://webnf1.epnet.com (the EBSCO database).

Magnuson, S., & Norem, K. (1998). A school counselor asks: "Am I prepared to do what I'm asked to do?" *Family Journal, 6*(2), 137–140.

Mauk, G. W., & Gibson, D. G. (1994). Suicide postvention with adolescents: School consultation practices and issues. *Education and Treatment of Children, 17,* 468–484. Retrieved November 13, 2000, from http://webnf1.epnet.com (the EBSCO database).

Nicoll, W. G. (1992). A family counseling and consultation model for school counselors. *The School Counselor, 39,* 351–361.

Stone, C. B. (2000). Advocacy for sexual harassment victims: Legal support and ethical aspects. *Professional School Counseling, 4,* 23–30.

White, J., & Mullis, F. (1998). A systems approach to school counselor consultation. *Education, 119,* 242–253. Retrieved November 13, 2000, from http://webnf1.epnet.com (the EBSCO database).

10

LEADERSHIP AND COORDINATION WITH ALL PARTNERS

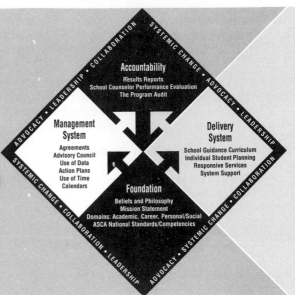

◆ LEARNING OBJECTIVES

By the time you finish this chapter, you will be able to

1. Understand the definition of leadership and its role in effective comprehensive school counseling

2. Challenge common myths about leadership to see that anyone can develop leadership skills

3. Understand and identify the personal qualities of a good leader

4. Understand and identify the professional skills of a good leader

5. Be able to apply a model of leadership to school counseling

6. Understand the definition of coordination and its role in effective comprehensive school counseling

7. Identify opportunities for leadership with students, parents, school colleagues, and community colleagues

8. Be aware of the importance of the activities of the ASCA National Model that include leadership of the advisory council, the management system, and the accountability system

9. Be able to discuss the advantages and disadvantages of various administrative activities that are often assigned to the school counselor

10. Be able to discuss ways that school counselors can challenge some of the administrative tasks that are inappropriately assigned to school counselors

DOMAINS / ACTIVITIES / PARTNERS MODEL

	Academic Development	Career Development	Personal/ Social Development	Parents and Caregivers	Colleagues in Schools	Colleagues in Community
Counseling	1a	1b	1c	5	6	7
Educating and Advocacy	2a	2b	2c	8	9	10
Consulting	3a	3b	3c	11	12	13
Leadership and Coordination	4a	4b	4c	14	15	16

DOMAINS

ACTIVITIES

Students

PARTNERS IN THE PROCESS

CASE STUDY ◆ Harmony's District and the Budget

Harmony threw her notes together at the last minute, even though she knew she would be speaking on behalf of school counseling programs in the district. She grabbed her coat and keys as she headed for her front door. "Don't wait up for me, dear. This may be a long meeting," she yelled. Then she was off to pick up two other district counselors to attend the school board meeting.

The boardroom was packed, full of teachers, parents, and students. No one was in a good frame of mind; the district had announced a large decline in enrollment for the third straight year, and the budget was to be slashed. As the meeting began, the district announced its position. Money was short for the coming year, and cuts were inevitable. The district had to find positions or programs that would be eliminated, period. They had already explored closing schools, cutting salaries, and a host of other options, but those possibilities had been blocked by overwhelming community reaction to school closings and by union reaction to the salary question. Last year's tax referendum was soundly defeated by the community, so there was no new money coming to the district to support the current buildings and teaching staff. Cuts had to be made.

One by one, programs came up for cutting. And one by one, teachers, parents, students, and administrators spoke on behalf of saving their programs. The vocational education program at the high school was in danger, but was then revived; the after-school tutoring program at the middle school was next, but was granted a reprieve. Transportation for after-school activities was discussed, but was spared. With each program and each voice, the level of tension increased. Something would be cut.

Finally, comprehensive school counseling was mentioned as a possible program to cut. Harmony braced herself and then asked for a turn to outline the importance of school counseling programs. She talked about the work counselors do with students, she outlined each school's counseling programs, she described how much the students need the developmental curriculum,

195

and she ended by summarizing the administrative work counselors do. Feeling that she had concisely and objectively argued to keep the counseling program, she ended her comments and waited for the Board's reaction.

"What data do you have that your work helps students?" was the only question.

A lump rose in her throat as she realized that she had no data. She only had her own subjective experience, and that was not going to be enough.

CHALLENGE QUESTIONS

1. It is common for schools to face financial problems. Considering that the funding for schools comes primarily from local taxes, what role do parents play in terms of taxes?

2. What is the connection between parents, willingness to pay for school funding, and data about the comprehensive school counseling program?

3. How does leadership affect the collection of data?

4. In what way(s) is Harmony a leader? In what way(s) did she fail as a leader?

◆ SCHOOL COUNSELOR AS LEADER

Imagine that you're on a plane and there's engine trouble. But in our imaginary world, there is no captain or co-pilot on the plane, no one designated to make decisions about problems or to be responsible for the welfare of the passengers. How safe would you feel? There may be 300 very nice people on board that plane, and you could all talk about how to come to a decision by consensus, but you would likely have 300 different ideas about what to do, each one as uninformed as the next. Without a trained, competent person to focus, coordinate, and lead those 300 nice people, there is likely to be a crash.

Schools are like that plane. The principal is responsible for the academic mission of the school—in a sense, the captain of the plane. But the co-pilot, while responsible to the captain, has responsibilities also—for many technical aspects of the flight, for communication with the ground, for helping the captain remain on course. The co-pilot advises the captain, problem solves with the captain, but is also a leader in the eyes of the passengers and the flight crew. We believe that the school counselor is, in essence, the co-pilot of the school, responsible for the comprehensive school counseling program, the developmental curriculum, and the academic, career, and personal/social development of students. This means that the school counselor must also be aware of and prepared to accept the roles, duties, and responsibilities of being a leader.

Think about the metaphor of school-counselor-as-co-pilot; there are many parallels. First, just as the co-pilot is responsible for advising, problem solving, communication, and direction for the pilot, the school counselor advises the principal, problem solves with that professional, communicates up and down the chain of command and to external constituencies, and helps the school remain "on course" in terms of developmental education, school climate, and the developmental needs of students and families. Second, the co-pilot is perceived by the passengers as part of the flight crew, as a leader in his or her own right, responsible to and for them. Third, the co-pilot acts within his or her own professional duties, ensuring that her or his own unique tasks are accomplished to keep the flight in the air, on time, and on course—in essence, a coordinator of his or her professional activities.

The ASCA School Counselor Performance Standards addressed in this chapter are

5.2   The professional school counselor provides support for other school programs.

Standard 7: The professional school counselor is responsible for establishing and convening an advisory council for the school counseling program.

7.1   The professional school counselor meets with the advisory committee.

7.2   The professional school counselor reviews the school counseling program audit with the council.

7.3   The professional school counselor records meeting information.

Standard 8: The professional school counselor collects and analyzes data to guide program direction and emphasis.

8.1   The professional school counselor uses school data to make decisions regarding student choice of classes and special programs.

8.2   The professional school counselor uses data from the counseling program to make decisions regarding program revisions.

8.3   The professional school counselor analyzes data to ensure every student has equity and access to a rigorous academic curriculum.

8.4   The professional school counselor understands and uses data to establish goals and activities to close the gap.

9.1   The professional school counselor is accountable for monitoring every student's progress.

9.2   The professional school counselor implements monitoring systems appropriate to the individual school.

9.3   The professional school counselors develop appropriate interventions for students as needed and monitors their progress.

10.1   The professional school counselor uses a master calendar to plan activities throughout the year.

10.2   The professional school counselor distributes the master calendar to parents or guardians, staff and students.

10.3   The professional school counselor posts a weekly or monthly calendar.

10.4   The professional school counselor analyzes time spent providing direct service to students.

Standard 11: The professional school counselor develops a results evaluation for the program.

11.1   The professional school counselor measures results attained from school guidance curriculum and closing the gap activities.

11.2   The professional school counselor works with members of the counseling team and with the principal to clarify how programs are evaluated and how results are shared.

11.3   The professional school counselor knows how to collect process, perception and results data.

Standard 12: The professional school counselor conducts a yearly program audit.

12.1   The professional school counselor completes a program audit to determine the degrees to which the school counseling program is being implemented.

(continued)

12.2 The professional school counselor shares the results of the program audit with the advisory council.

12.3 The professional school counselor uses the yearly audit to make changes in the school counseling program and calendar for the following year.

Standard 13: The professional school counselor is a student advocate, leader, collaborator and a systems change agent.

13.1 The professional school counselor promotes academic success of every student.

13.2 The professional school counselor promotes equity and access for every student.

13.3 The professional school counselor takes a leadership role within the counseling department, the school setting and the community.

13.4 The professional school counselor understands reform issues and works to close the achievement gap.

13.5 The professional school counselor collaborates with teachers, parents and the community to promote academic success of students.

13.6 The professional school counselor builds effective teams by encouraging collaboration among all school staff.

13.7 The professional school counselor uses data to recommend systemic change in policy and procedures that limit or inhibit academic achievement.

The CACREP Standards for School Counseling Programs addressed in this chapter are

A.4 strategies of leadership designed to enhance the learning environment of schools;

B.2 coordination, collaboration, referral, and team-building efforts with teachers, parents, support personnel, and community resources to promote program objectives and facilitate successful student development and achievement of all students;

B.6 methods of planning, developing, implementing, monitoring, and evaluating comprehensive developmental counseling programs;

C.1 **(a)** use, management, analysis, and presentation of data from school-based information (e.g., standardized testing, grades, enrollment, attendance, retention, placement), surveys, interviews, focus groups, and needs assessments to improve student outcomes;

C.1 **(b)** design, implementation, monitoring, and evaluation of comprehensive developmental school counseling programs (e.g., the ASCA National Standards for School Counseling Programs) including an awareness of various systems that affect students, school, and home;

C.1 **(c)** implementation and evaluation of specific strategies that meet program goals and objectives; and

C.1 **(e)** preparation of an action plan and school counseling calendar that reflect appropriate time commitments and priorities in a comprehensive developmental school counseling program.

These professional activities for school counselors form the foundation of most graduate programs in counselor education. Typically, counselors are taught in graduate school how to build consensus, how to facilitate others' finding their own answers, how to foster communication within and between groups, and how to empower clients to embrace their own intuitive life direction while simultaneously evaluating their alternatives. With that training, you are now being asked to integrate a new way of viewing yourself as a professional—a leader. This might be a paradigm shift for you. But consider this. If there is no leader for the comprehensive school counseling program of a secondary school, how will you know what your course is, much less whether you're still on it? Who will attend to the communication of constituencies and be responsible for the developmental agenda for students and families? Who will lead the "heart" of the school?

When we return to the ASCA National Model, we see that Leadership is one of the Themes of the Model. In addition, leadership and coordination as defined in this chapter will incorporate both the Management System and the Accountability elements of the Model. Many authors agree that school counselors must accept a leadership role in the school. Clark and Stone (2000a, 2000b) call for school counselors to accept the need for leadership in developing a professional image, accepting certain organizational roles in the school, and providing staff development. Furthermore, they cite the need for counselors to lead the school in advocacy for student success, by leading various committees in terms of external constituencies (i.e., parent groups), multicultural awareness, pupil assistance committees, mentoring programs, student leadership, and political involvement (Clark & Stone, 2000a, 2000b). In a similar vein, Bemak (2000) "focuses on a critical redefinition of the future school counselor as a leader in promoting educational reform and meeting national and state educational objectives inclusive of creating healthy safe school environments. . . . " (p. 324).

Other authors have called for school counselors to become leaders in advocating for specific constituencies (partners in the terms of the DAP model in this book) or for certain issues. For example, Kurpius and Rozecki (1992) suggested that school counselors should take leadership in advocating for students, families, and teachers and in advocating for general school improvement within the building and in the district by collaborating with mental health agencies and the community at large. Smaby and Daugherty (1995) called for school counselors to become leaders in the effort to free schools of drugs and violence. Cole and Ryan (1997) called for school counselors to take leadership in portfolio development and authentic assessment for students. All these authors agree that school counselors cannot be complacent in passively maintaining the status quo. School counselors *must* be leaders in championing students, families, issues of social justice, schools, and most of all, the developmental agendas of students and families.

In fact, The Education Trust (2001) elevates this function to the highest importance for successful school counseling (as defined by The DeWitt Wallace-Reader's Digest Fund, National Initiative for Transforming School Counseling). Founded to promote "educational equity, access, and academic success for all students K–12," the Trust holds that "the trained school counselor must be an assertive advocate creating opportunities for all students to nurture dreams of high aspirations. . . . The school counselor serves as a leader as well as an effective team member working with teachers, administrators, and other school personnel to make sure that each student succeeds" (The Education Trust, 2001). In the transformation from counseling as ancillary to counselor as leader, the Trust advocates that school counselors focus on the whole school and system concerns by performing the role of leader, planner, collaborator, service broker, and program developer as an integral member of the educational team and champion for creating pathways for all students to achieve.

Definition of Leadership

In a synthesis of what other authors have proposed as definitions of leadership, Hersey, Blanchard, and Johnson (1996) defined leadership as "the process of influencing the activities of an individual or a group in efforts toward goal achievement in a given situation" (p. 91). Kouzes and Posner (1995) take the definition one step further, defining leadership as "the art of mobilizing others to *want* to struggle for shared aspirations" (emphasis authors', p. 30). Their point in adding emphasis to the voluntary nature of the struggle is important. Although a person with extrinsic power can motivate someone to do something with the promise of rewards or the threat of retribution, this is not leadership according to their definition. Only when the leader is able to tap intrinsic motivators will there be true leadership. This is important to our discussion of comprehensive school counseling, because most school counselors do not have the power to reward or punish in most school organizations. For school counselors, the issue of choice has important implications for their leadership; there must be attention paid to methods for tapping intrinsic motivators.

The methods for motivating others vary, depending on the context of leadership and the goals that are to be accomplished (Bolman & Deal, 1997; Gardner, 1995; Hersey, Blanchard, & Johnson, 1996). In fact, Bolman and Deal (1997) have identified four leadership "frames" or contexts of leadership: structural leadership, involving the building of viable organizations; human resource leadership, involving the empowerment and inspiration of followers; political leadership, involving the distribution of power; and symbolic leadership, involving the interpretation and reinterpretation of meaning within our society.

Each of these frames has implications for leadership within school counseling. The first frame, structural leadership, involves technical mastery, strategizing for change and growth, and implementation (Bolman & Deal, 1997). The insights from this leadership frame suggest that school counselors must be effective at their jobs and up-to-date with the "science" of counseling and education. For example, school counselors must be informed about innovations in counseling (new theories and strategies, new medications), informed about innovations in school counseling (new programs, new approaches to student issues), aware of the status of student issues (changing families, new drugs on the street, new ways students express their pain), and innovations in schools (new programs and approaches to teaching and learning). School counselors must also be able to plan effectively for changes, both within the comprehensive school counseling program and in the school as a whole. Finally, school counselors must be accountable for implementation; all the good intentions in the world will not make change happen. Change only happens when action is taken in the desired direction.

The second frame, human resource leadership, involves believing in people and communicating that belief, being visible and accessible, and empowering others (Bolman & Deal, 1997). These are the strengths of most school counselors, so leading using these qualities is very comfortable. For school counselors, our belief in our students, families, and colleagues is one of the reasons for being a counselor and a source of passion and joy. Being visible and accessible, being around others, is also a natural part of being a counselor: being in the halls, out at the buses, in the lunchroom with the students. (Incidentally, we call this "counseling by walking around," a play on "management by walking around." The idea is that by being with the students and teachers, the school counselor is available for conversations with those who may not want to make an appointment but who need to talk with the counselor.)

The third frame, that of political leadership, addresses an area in which many counselors report high levels of anxiety and stress. This leadership context involves being realistic about what the leader wants and what she or he can get, being able to assess the distribution of power, building linkages to important stakeholders, and using persuasion and negotiation (Bolman & Deal, 1997). School counselors need to be realists, aware that change is incremental and often comes as a result of negotiation and compromise. School counselors also need to know who is in both formal and informal positions of power in the school and the district, knowing what those in power want and knowing how to overcome opposition by trading on the basis of those interests. School counselors need to know who important stakeholders are and how to connect with them on behalf of the school and the comprehensive school counseling program. Finally, school counselors need to be able to persuade others and to negotiate for benefits to the program, the school, and the students. As we will discuss, the advisory council will provide many benefits in this leadership frame.

The fourth and final leadership frame is symbolic leadership. Within this leadership context, leaders use symbols to capture attention, they frame experience in meaningful ways for the follower, and they discover and communicate a vision (Bolman & Deal, 1997). In addition, leaders have a relationship with and a conversation with the community they represent (the school, families, students) and they embody the story of healthy choices they seek to tell (Gardner, 1995). When a school counselor is an effective leader, the counselor symbolizes many things: mental health, the profession of counseling, the ombudsman for students, to name a few. We can use these symbols to help others understand our position in the school and our comprehensive programs. We can help others frame their experiences in a larger context, perhaps a spiritual context or a historical context. School counselors can lead others by articulating a vision of healthy, resilient students and by maintaining faith in that vision. School counselors must remember that leadership involves a constant conversation with all partners in the process. We must also always remember that we embody the story we tell about our students, our schools, and our profession, and as such, we are role models.

Another way to understand leadership is to examine the roles that are a part of leadership. In a discussion of leadership roles within character education programs, DeRoche (2000) listed the following, which have been adapted to address the roles of leaders of comprehensive school counseling programs:

◆ Visionary for future directions for the program, the school, and the students
◆ Designer and author of the mission statement for the school counseling program
◆ Consensus builder for the importance of the school counseling program, the developmental domains, and the values and content of the developmental curriculum
◆ Information provider about the program, the school, the developmental issues of students and families, and current innovations in the field of education, counseling, and school counseling
◆ Standard bearer for the quality of the comprehensive school counseling program, including methods to "guide and judge the effectiveness of the implementation, maintenance, and evaluation of the program" (p. 43)
◆ Architect of implementation plans for the program
◆ Role model for the values and lessons of the developmental curriculum, comprehensive school counseling, and the counseling and mental health professions
◆ Risk taker and advocate for the development of all students (as stated by DeRoche, "The leader has to take a stand and bear witness to the proposition that there is more to educating children and youth than increasing their test scores" [2000, p. 44])

◆ Communicator, the voice of the program, to inform all partners about the program, the students, the school, and counseling as a profession

◆ Collaborator in efforts to implement the comprehensive school counseling program

◆ Resource provider, which may take the form of materials or ideas for ways to integrate the developmental curriculum into the classroom (see Chapter 8)

Kouzes and Posner (1995) described the outdated myths about leadership that discourage capable people from seeing themselves as leaders. Contrary to popular belief, leaders arise not from maintaining the status quo but from finding new ways to address old problems. They are not renegades who attract a lunatic following but attract followers with their deep faith in the abilities of others. Rather than focus on the short term, they are able to maintain a long-term approach to problem solving, knowing that change is incremental and slow. But their future orientation is not superhuman; it evolves, as all good ideas, from original thinking or the inspiration of someone else.

According to Kouzes and Posner, the "most pernicious myth of all is that leadership is reserved for only a very few of us" (p. 16). Are good leaders born, or are they made? Most authors agree that it is a combination of innate qualities and leadership skills that make an effective leader (Bolman & Deal, 1997; Gardner, 1995; Hersey, Blanchard, & Johnson, 1996; Kouzes & Posner, 1995), but that anyone can become a leader with training and practice. Leadership is an "observable, learnable set of practices" (Kouzes & Posner, 1995, p. 16) that enhances certain qualities. So what are those qualities and those practices?

Personal Qualities of Effective Leaders

In Chapter 1, we talked about personal qualities and professional skills that are needed by effective school counselors. In that discussion, we listed both intuition and training as necessary to this profession, and we defined intuition in terms of creativity and imagination, flexibility, courage and belief/faith, and passion. It is interesting to note that the qualities of effective leaders include those same qualities (Bolman & Deal, 1997; Gardner, 1995; Hersey, Blanchard, & Johnson, 1996; Kouzes & Posner, 1995).

In addition, many other qualities are necessary, including vision, strength, commitment (Bolman & Deal, 1997); adaptability, social awareness, achievement-orientation, assertiveness, cooperation, decisiveness, dependability, energy, persistence, self-confidence, tolerance for stress, responsibility, intelligence, creativity, diplomacy and tact, persuasiveness, ability to be organized (Yukl, as cited in Hersey, Blanchard, & Johnson, 1996, p. 102); charisma, originality (Kirkpatrick and Locke, as cited in Hersey, Blanchard, & Johnson, 1996, p. 104); honesty, forward-looking (visionary), ability to be inspiring, competence, fairness, supportiveness, credibility, and broadmindedness (Kouzes & Posner, 1995).

It is important to note that this list is not exhaustive. It is not a list of qualities that only leaders possess, it is not a list of qualities that someone aspiring to be a leader must have, and it's not a list of qualities all leaders have. These qualities, however, are those that will serve any counselor or any school counselor well; in fact, we believe that we see these qualities in most school counselors in our training programs. The purpose of presenting this list is to challenge you to think about which of those qualities you currently possess and which qualities you might further develop as you move into leadership in your school.

Reflection Moment ◆

What are the qualities you see in yourself? What qualities do others see in you? Which qualities would you like to develop more fully? What can you do now to begin your development in that area (or in those areas)?

◆ ◆

Professional Practices and Skills of Effective Leaders

This list of professional leadership skills will also be familiar in many ways. You will notice a direct overlap with many of the skills you have been challenged to develop in this book. According to Bolman and Deal (1997, pp. 297–298) the following are the most effective leadership skills:

◆ Establishing a vision for the program
◆ Setting standards for performance of tasks or excellence of endeavors
◆ Creating focus and direction for collective efforts
◆ Caring deeply about what the organization or group does
◆ Believing that doing the group's work well is important
◆ Inspiring trust
◆ Building relationships and empowering others
◆ Communicating the vision with passion to others

It is important to note that these skills are among the professional skills of counselors. In establishing a vision, counselors are articulating what they see their school can do for students and how their comprehensive school counseling program moves the school toward that goal. In setting standards, counselors establish an expectation for excellence and identify their accountability. By creating and maintaining focus on students and their development, counselors communicate that they care deeply about how students grow and about all partners in the school and the community. By our belief that the developmental work we do is important, we serve to inspire others to trust in students and in the school. When school counselors build effective and healthy relationships with all constituents, we have the means to communicate our vision with passion. By being sensitive to environmental issues in the school, we are able to remove barriers to learning and foster healthy development. By energizing and aligning the school counseling program within the culture of the school, we connect our students with the school community. By providing the energy and vision to connect, unify, and focus students, families, and colleagues toward the goal of healthy development for students, we reinforce the positive contributions that schools make to students and the community. Finally, by empowering, engaging, and enabling people for their tasks in the education and development of our students, we provide leadership in creating a cycle of healthy and respectful appreciation for all members of the school community and beyond.

Accepting that school counselors are leaders is not so much of a stretch when you think of the professional skills that you have developed and are currently developing. These skills and leadership skills are not so different after all.

Reflection Moment ◆

Have you used any of these skills? If so, where and when? How did that feel? If not, where are there opportunities for you to observe someone model these skills? Can you see yourself as a leader?

◆ ◆

A Process Model of Leadership

Kouzes and Posner (1995) have described their "commitments of leadership" (p. 318) that outline five steps for leaders to follow:

1. Challenge the process
2. Inspire a shared vision
3. Enable others to act
4. Model the way
5. Encourage the heart

These steps are not specific to the business world; according to Kouzes and Posner (1995), they are the means to make a difference in the world.

> Beyond the horizon of time is a changed world, very different from today's world. Some people see beyond that horizon and into the future. They believe that dreams can become reality. They open our eyes and lift our spirits. They build trust and strengthen our relationships. They stand firm against the winds of resistance and give us the courage to continue the quest. We call these people *leaders*. (emphasis authors', p. 317)

◆ SCHOOL COUNSELOR AS COORDINATOR

Definition of Coordination

To understand why this coordination is essential for effective school counseling programs, we must explore what is meant by "coordination." Harrison (2000) summed it up best in his definition: "Coordination is a *counselor initiated leadership process* in which the counselor helps organize and manage the comprehensive guidance program and related services" (emphasis added, p. 190). Within this definition are embedded several important concepts. First, coordination activities are connected to leadership. Second, coordination activities are counselor initiated, and therefore not a passive or second-rate function of the comprehensive school counseling program. Third, coordination is essential for the organization of the program and, finally, coordination is essential for the management of the program. Let's examine each of these observations separately.

The connection of leadership and coordination is important. Good leaders are involved in the day-to-day activities of their work, and so coordination of work, services, and programs is a natural part of effective leadership. This technical mastery increases trust in the professional skills of the leader, and the willingness to actually "get your hands dirty and work" increases everyone's trust in the credibility of the leader. The fact that coordination is not a passive, but an active, part of the school counselor's job is also important. As previously mentioned, good intentions alone do not get the job done; only active, goal-directed movement will lead to progress toward goals.

Counselors utilize coordination in the organization and management of the program. In fact, the Management System of the National Model (Chapter 5) addresses administrative agreements, coordination of the advisory council, action planning, use of time and calendars, and use of data—all of which require the coordination of the school counselor. In addition, the Accountability element of the National Model requires counselors to coordinate the collection, analysis, and dissemination of results reports and program audits to improve the program based on results. (For an excellent comprehensive discussion of accountability, see Stone and Dahir's (2007) *School Counselor Accountability: A MEASURE of Student Success*, 2nd ed.). In all of these activities, counselors coordinate ideas, resources, materials, and personnel to bring about the design and creation of the program, and then coordinate all those ideas, resources, materials, and personnel to make the program happen. In this view, the work counselors must do with personnel involves collaboration and cooperation to coordinate resources for the school counseling program. Recall the Themes of the ASCA National Model. In essence, the National Model emphasizes that a program of effective leadership, collaboration, and advocacy will result in systemic change.

In case this all sounds very conceptual, rest assured, it's not. Much of the work of coordinating the comprehensive school counseling program is very practical. To provide a more concrete view of coordination, see Chapters 11, 12, and 13, in which you will see examples of coordination that include scheduling meetings (with counseling groups, advisory boards, teachers and parents), scheduling appointments (with students, teachers, parents), creating budgets, writing grants, documenting activities and achievements, evaluating the program in the program audit, evaluating events within the program, scheduling facilities for events, securing donations for a program or event, typing flyers and creating brochures, stapling, sealing envelopes, and affixing stamps. Don't assume you will have clerical help in the school; many counselors do their own typing and answer their own phones.

Accountability

Recall from Chapter 5 that the ASCA National Model outlines, in detail, what information is to be compiled to provide accountability. To be accountable for the program, school counselors must present the findings of the results reports, program audit, and other assessment and evaluation processes to the building administrator (or the professional responsible for evaluating the counselor). (Although the School Counselor Performance Standards are presented in Appendix C, you will need to obtain a copy of the National Model from ASCA to view the Program Audit documents.)

Various information will be appropriate to share with various partners. All the information is presented to the administrator, including the results of the assessment process (the report card of the program and the counselor) and the results of the evaluation process (plans for professional development and program improvement determined on the basis of the assessment results that will feed back into the planning process). To the advisory committee, the information presented usually reflects only the outcomes information and evaluation of the program, not the evaluation of the counselor. This means the advisory committee is presented with the overview of how well the program is functioning in terms of needs, outcomes, and quality—and the plan for making changes on the basis of that overview.

Information shared with partners of the CSCP usually consists of how well the program is functioning and plans for improvement. One idea for disseminating the information could be a newsletter sent to students, parents, teachers, colleagues in the schools, and colleagues in the community. Other ideas include columns in the school and community newspapers, a webpage, articles in counselor journals, and reports for the local school board (Schmidt, 2003). A note of caution: it might be advisable to consult with the advisory committee, your administrator, and other counselors in the district to determine how much information to disseminate. In the early years of the program, while you are still building rapport and creating respect for your program and your professionalism, you might want to be selective in how much you share. Too much "negative press," or public discussion of your struggles to launch your program, might damage your attempts to establish your credibility with your partners. Be judicious with the negative information you send out so that you don't end up compromising your program.

Advisory Council: Meetings and Accountability

In addition to the information to be disseminated to the general partners of the CSCP, you will also want to use your advisory council itself as a means of accountability. First, it is important to recognize that your council is a political body, comprising individuals who represent your partners—students, parents, teachers, staff, administration, and community (recall the discussion of the advisory council in Chapter 5). Your leadership of this council will be crucial in your planning, design, evaluation, and growth of the program into an ASCA National Model program, a *comprehensive* school counseling program.

This council will help with the articulation of the foundation of the program in terms of philosophy, mission, and beliefs, so these individuals must be well educated in the six qualities of comprehensive school counseling programs and the ASCA National Model. They must understand schools and young people. You are essential in facilitating their understanding of these issues, and you must educate them and advocate for school counseling and for your students. A chronological view of the lifecycle of the advisory council would include

◆ Introduction of members
◆ Education in school counseling, ASCA National Model, the six qualities of CSCPs, schools, and the developmental issues of young people at your level
◆ Show current functioning of CSCP (outcomes data) and the improvements you desire for the coming year (short term) and subsequent years (long term)
◆ Design strategies for improvement

Topics that you need to present to the advisory council include closing-the-achievement-gap efforts and results, funding issues, innovative directions, program-wide results reports, and the result of the program audit. Meetings twice a year are recommended by ASCA (ASCA, 2003, p. 48), but with efforts to transform your program into a comprehensive program, you may need to meet more often (perhaps up to three times a year). Be sure to develop a clear agenda for each meeting and send minutes after each meeting to keep the members informed of your progress. This group is essential for your leadership efforts; as you move into the muddy political waters of a district, the advisory board will be able to give you insights into the issues of your partner groups and can help you talk to all constituencies in an informed manner.

◆ LEADERSHIP AND COORDINATION: EXAMPLES AND ISSUES

Leadership and Coordination with Students

Leadership and coordination are important activities with each of the partners in the DAP model. In terms of leadership with students, the school counselor is looked to as the professional and personal leader of and advocate for programmatic efforts that focus on effective learning, mental health, respect, and healthy development. As we have discussed, these are important aspects of the learning students must do to become healthy, functional adults in the community, to become healthy parents, significant life partners, contributors to the community in terms of work and/or employment, and community builders. As a visible leader in the school, the school counselor is the role model for students through his or her work in the school and in her or his own personal life and interactions with others.

As the leader of these programmatic efforts, school counselors coordinate programs and events for students in the three domains. Although not intended as an exhaustive list of events all counselors must coordinate, specific examples of possible programs and events in each domain might include the following (Bemak, 2000; Burnham & Jackson, 2000; Clark & Stone, 2000a, 2000b; Cole & Ryan, 1997; Fazio & Ural, 1995; Harrison, 2000; Smaby & Daugherty, 1995):

Academic Development

Academic excellence award programs

Peer tutoring

Academic Olympic games

New student orientation and transition programs

Academic intervention for nonpassing students

Portfolios and authentic assessments

Career Development

Mentoring programs in professions and trades

Career days and events

Career interest testing programs

School-to-work/career programs

Career Cluster programming

Personal/Social Development

Advisor for student groups

Peer mediation programs

Peer mentoring programs

Community service programs

Student recognition for campus/community service

Mental health issues (for example, National Depression Screening Day)

Support groups, crisis and loss groups

Substance abuse prevention, intervention, and referral programs

Referrals for therapeutic intervention and treatment

Leadership and Coordination with Parents

School counselors are directed by professional ethics to involve, as appropriate, the student's family and enlist the family's support when working with students, according to both the American Counseling Association and the American School Counselor Association (Appendix A). Many authors call for school counselors to take the lead in coordinating strong connections between schools and parents/caregivers (Bemak, 2000; Colbert, 1996; Jackson & White, 2000; Kaplan, 1997; Keys & Lockhart, 1999; Peeks, 1993).

These parent/family connections vary from coordination of events such as potluck suppers and community building activities (Jackson & White, 2000), to academic interventions involving parents (Kaplan, 1997), to involving parents as a part of the school's organization and structure, such as in curriculum committees and as trainers of other parents (Colbert, 1996), to providing family services such as family health services, employment services, and lifelong training (Peeks, 1993). Bemak (2000) suggests that schools must develop flexible hours to meet the needs of working parents, develop family advocacy programs and parent inclusion programs within the school, and develop a family space within the school where parents and families can go to feel comfortable and safe. The extent of these parent and family connections with the school will be determined by a variety of factors, just as we have discussed in earlier chapters on counseling with adult partners, educating adult partners, and consulting with adult partners. One thing is clear: School counselors must work extensively with parents/caregivers to be successful (Bemak, 2000).

Leadership and Coordination with School Colleagues

Just as we have seen in our discussion of leadership and coordination with parents and caregivers, school counselors are often called upon to provide leadership with our partners in the school and in the district. An overview of possible ways for accomplishing these coordinated efforts includes

1. Collaborative teams to address the systemic issues of students who are at risk or who are not functioning effectively in the school (Bemak, 2000; Keys, Bemak, & Carpenter, 1998). This team approaches the discussion with a focus on cultural, community,

and school issues that might interfere with the student's functioning, and brings the support of various school professionals to that discussion (Jackson & White, 2000).

2. Collaborating with special educators and other professionals in the schools to
   a. support special education transition services for students who live with disabilities (Sitlington, Clark, & Kolstoe, 2000)
   b. support the holistic development of students with learning disabilities (Koehler & Kravets, 1998) and at-risk and violent youth (Barr & Parrett, 2001)

3. Integrate services of all school-based mental health providers in school-based health clinics, mental health clinics, and "multiple systems" clinics to provide one-stop access to help. Examples cited include integrating violence prevention, parent training, tutoring, daycare, and bereavement with medical services (Porter, Epp, & Bryant, 2000).

4. Better integrate the services of the school counselor with those of the school psychologist to reduce overlap and to draw on each other's professional expertise (Rowley, 2000).

5. Collaborate more with principals to evaluate the school climate for violence, racism, sexual harassment, and gang activity; to help in the selection of new teachers; to deal more effectively with discipline issues that affect the school by adding a counseling component to the school's discipline policy; to address issues raised by athletic programs in the school; and to assist with the development of the school's crisis plan (Niebuhr, Niebuhr, & Cleveland, 1999).

6. Coordinate employee assistance-like services for school employees (Clark, 1995).

When a counselor is thinking holistically about the best way to help students with their development, it would be impossible to ignore the need to coordinate efforts with partners in the school and in the district. Some counselors may be the only counselor in the school, but there are other counselors in other buildings, and there are other professionals who serve in student services (e.g., psychologists, nurses, social workers, and building police or safety officers). Don't let yourself become a "service silo" isolated from other professionals. Students need everyone in the helping professions to be focused on what is best for the students and integrated services for students is clearly more effective and more efficient.

Data Collection for Evaluation and Planning: Monitoring Student Progress. School counselors at all levels must be able to coordinate the collection of data that tell about the health of the school and that signal how well students are learning in all three domains—academic, career, and personal/social. Using the ASCA National Standards for Student Academic, Career, and Personal/Social Development (Appendix B), you must be able to collect information about students' progress. This could include achievement data (grades, test data, promotion and retention rates) and competency-based data (number of students with academic plans, results data from developmental guidance programs). Through understanding how students are progressing, professional school counselors collect and analyze student data to guide program direction, emphasis, and upon evaluation, revisions to the program.

In addition to the use of student progress data for program definition and revision, this data is essential for monitoring student progress. Issues such as choices of classes and equitable access to all educational benefits are also important and are the result of careful and intentional examination of data. Based on documented concerns for the education of all students, school counselors must also help schools design ways to address the achievement gap between students with resources and students without resources (parental, financial). Concerns for student progress do not only occur around grade time; it must be a continual process of monitoring that occurs year-round. This means that school counselors need to be involved in creating *systems* for monitoring student progress—predictable, regular access to data sources and a process by which the data are discussed and analyzed with others in school leadership to design plans for multisystemic (family, classroom, counseling) interventions.

Master Calendar and Time Analysis.   Accountability does not only come from data; it also comes as a part of the Management System that mandates accountability for time spent in the school. The primary vehicle for this accountability is the Management Agreement, in which the counselor and the administrator agree to the emphases of the CSCP and commit this agreement to paper. After the parameters of the program and the position are determined, the counselor must be accountable for his or her work and for the program. To account for time, professional school counselors in CSCPs use a master calendar to plan activities throughout the year, highlighting events and programs with schoolwide themes, as well as reflecting the reality of the ebb-and-flow of the academic year. In addition, this calendar is widely distributed to all partners: students, parents, colleagues in the school, and as needed, to colleagues in the community. In addition to this yearly calendar, counselors should also post a weekly and/or monthly calendar, perhaps posting this in the office to increase access and reduce the likelihood that someone would say "I can never find the counselor. She is never in the office!"

These calendars are designed to reflect the needs of students throughout the year. For example, programs in orientation for new students are more widespread during the fall, whereas programs to help students with testing strategies and the management of test anxiety might be more common around the testing cycle for the school. The use of action plans (to deliver the developmental curriculum and address "closing the gap" activities) serve as important information in the design of the calendar. As part of the evaluation process, it is important to analyze time spent providing direct service to students to determine if future adjustments are needed.

Results Evaluation and Yearly Program Audit.   As mentioned in Chapter 4, every CSCP must be reflective. In the leadership and coordination activities of school counselors, this requirement becomes very clear. Hand-in-hand with collecting student outcomes data, professional school counselors must also develop *systems* for collecting results data on the program. To do this, counselors build data collection into each activity, so that results are evaluated from all activities (counseling, educating, advocacy, consulting, and leadership) designed for each of the Standards for Student Academic, Career, and Personal/Social Development (ASCA, 2003; see Appendix B), and for closing the gap. As discussed in Chapter 5, these results come from process, perception, and results data: what was done, what people report has changed since participating in what was done, and the impact of what was done.

Results reports, with both short-term and long-term results compared over time, are shared with administration, and as appropriate, with other partners determined in consultation with all members of the counseling team and with the principal. In addition, a yearly program audit is conducted to determine the degree to which the school counseling program is being implemented effectively. Finally, each counselor should be evaluated using the School Counselor Performance Standards (ASCA, 2003; see Appendix C). The synthesis of all these data—student data, results reports, yearly program audit, and counselor performance evaluation—comprise the foundation of next year's improvement efforts in the CSCP.

Variety as the Spice of Life: Administrative Tasks. Another important concept in the discussion of coordination is that of using coordinating (administrative) activities as a smoke screen to avoid doing more personal (counseling) work with students (Myrick, 1997). Harrison (2000, p. 191) also noted that some school counselors become involved in "noncounseling, administrator-driven" activities inappropriately. This situation may arise when the school counselor is not the leader of the comprehensive school counseling program, when the counselor's time and energies are defined by noncounselors. Although many counselors also coordinate administrative functions, there are examples of activities that have potential for contributing to out-of-balance conditions (Burnham & Jackson, 2000).

The discussion of coordination and collaboration must also include a discussion of administrative tasks, and this discussion inevitably leads us back to the importance of leadership, the vision of the mission of the comprehensive school counseling program.

Everyone who works in a school will have some administrative tasks to complete. These tasks provide information for the administration, contribute to the well-being and improvement of the school and the district, and enable the building to operate in a safe and orderly fashion. Called system support activities by Gysbers and Henderson (2000, p. 75), these duties include many we have already discussed (research and development to evaluate and improve the program and program management activities), but they also describe duties relevant to this discussion such as service on committees and advisory boards and fair-share responsibilities. When we discuss coordination and leadership within the school and the district, it is essential that we include these activities also.

This is not to imply that all administrative activities must be eschewed by counselors, as there are many activities that on their surface seem to be administrative, but on closer examination, clearly provide substantial holistic benefits to the school, the students, and to the comprehensive school counseling program. To help you understand this issue more clearly, let's take a look at the overall advantages of devoting time to these activities. When evaluating the benefits of academic activities such as writing curriculum guides, assessing transcripts, and designing the master schedule, some counselors believe that their participation cements their connection with the academic mission of the school, giving them greater credibility with teachers. When describing activities such as lunchroom duty, hall monitor, chaperoning dances, scheduling students, and serving as advisor for student groups, some counselors believe that the enhanced contact with students allows for conversation, trust, and greater awareness of student lives and issues. Some counselors simply believe they are "helping out" (Wiggins & Moody, 1987) and may feel more effective as a result.

The disadvantages of these activities are numerous, especially if these activities become out of balance. Counselors might find themselves perceived by teachers and students as being a quasi-administrator, a role that compromises the counselor's credibility and impedes trust (Gibson, 1990). In addition, counselors may believe that they are helping out, but students and teachers may notice the counselor's avoidance of professional tasks (Wiggins & Moody, 1987). But the single biggest problem with out-of-balance clerical and administrative work is time. At all educational levels, administrative activities that do not contribute to the CSCP deplete the counselor's time for working on crucial CSCP activities. This concern is echoed by Gysbers and Henderson (2000, p. 76): "Care must be taken . . . to watch the time given to system support duties because the prime focus for counselors' time is the direct service components of the comprehensive guidance program." The loss of time to devote to the comprehensive school counseling program can leave counselors exhausted and incapable of responding appropriately to student needs (Burnham & Jackson, 2000).

ASCA (2003, p. 56) outlines activities that are, for the most part, outside the purview of a CSCP:

◆ Registration and scheduling of all new students
◆ Coordinating cognitive, aptitude, and achievement tests
◆ Responsibility for signing excuses for tardy or absent students
◆ Performing disciplinary actions
◆ Sending students home who are not appropriately dressed
◆ Teaching classes when teachers are absent
◆ Computing grade point averages
◆ Maintaining student records
◆ Supervising study halls
◆ Clerical record keeping
◆ Assisting with duties in the principal's office
◆ Preparation of individual education plans, student study teams, and school attendance review board
◆ Data entry

Each activity in this category siphons time from the activities of a CSCP; each must be weighed in terms of its unique advantages and disadvantages to the students and the comprehensive school counseling program. Then these must be weighed against the overall effect all these activities have on our ability to meet the goals and objectives of our program. If the activity does not directly contribute to the CSCP, it should be discussed with the principal and noted in the management agreement.

Assessment/Testing.   When the counselor devotes time to serving as the testing coordinator for the building, many hours are lost that could more directly benefit the program's main focus (Burnham & Jackson, 2000; Gysbers & Henderson, 2000). Burnham and Jackson (2000) found that schoolwide testing programs were coordinated by 87.5 percent of their respondents, but in 2005, Dollarhide and Lemberger (2006) found that only 42% of responding counselors coordinated tests and another 11% were involved as proctors and academic remediators. Test interpretation with students and parents, however, would be an appropriate use of the counselor's training and within the scope of the academic, career, and personal/social development of students. In an interesting note, in 1990, Gibson found that teachers ranked test administration and interpretation as the third of the top three responsibilities of the school counselor, behind counseling and career information. This would suggest that there are many persons in schools who believe the school counselor should be the testing coordinator for the building; counselors will need to understand the preponderance of opinion they would encounter when they challenge testing as not congruent with their primary role in the school.

Discipline (Attendance, Hall Monitor, Conflict Resolution, Bus Duty).   There are good reasons that counselors become involved in helping students with attendance problems, observing student behaviors directly in the halls, and helping with conflict resolution between students. These benefits accrue directly to students when counselors are a part of the building discipline process. The key is for counselors to maintain a role in the prevention and intervention of the inappropriate behavior but to not be the primary disciplinarian of the school. That role is better handled by the principal, appropriate vice-principal, school police/safety officer, or dean of students, as the case may be.

Role of Registrar: Scheduling, Transcripts, and Curriculum Guides.   Many counselors are expected to schedule all students, evaluate and maintain transcripts, and prepare curriculum guides. Although we do feel that it is appropriate for counselors to provide academic advice for students and that this role does require an understanding of the curriculum of the school, we do not believe that counselors are responsible for the activities of a registrar. These activities closely relate to the academic mission of the school and should be housed in the offices of academic leadership. Burnham and Jackson (2000) report that, of the nonguidance duties identified by counselors, the most often cited activity was requesting and receiving records, the second most cited activity was scheduling, the third was maintaining permanent records, the fourth was enrolling students, eighth was withdrawing students, and the eleventh was preparing grades and report cards. Clearly, this suggests that many schools are siphoning the time of the counselor away from program duties to perform these inappropriate clerical tasks.

Environmental Assessment.   As was presented in Chapter 2, school counselors can have a tremendous impact on the climate of the school when they are involved in efforts to monitor and improve the emotional environment of the school. In many schools, these conversations take place in committees charged with monitoring the school for "developmental assets," "positive behavior and energy," "inviting elements," or other similar terms. In a nutshell, when school counselors are involved in improving the level of respect, inclusion, and empowerment for all members of the school community, the school as a whole will benefit. We believe that this administrative duty could be an important way the school counselor contributes to the school.

Special Education Case Management and IEPs.   School counselors are an important part of the process of educating all students, including those identified as disabled according to PL 94-142 and the Americans with Disabilities Act (ADA) (Koehler & Kravets, 1998). In the process of educating students with disabilities, school counselors are appropriately involved in the process of referral for evaluation, conversations with parents and caregivers, and meetings to define appropriate accommodations. Counselors are also involved in many Individual Educational Plan (IEP) multidisciplinary meetings that detail the services and programs the student must access to be successful in school. As the professional charged with leadership over the program to secure every student's academic, career, and personal/social development, the counselor must be involved in these meetings. In some cases, however, the school counselor is named the case manager or "lead," and given the responsibility of seeing that the student's IEP is followed and updated yearly. In this situation, the counselor is not the best professional for this role. Those with licensure in special education are specifically trained to understand the needs of students with IEPs, and these professionals are in the best position to handle this responsibility. Burnham and Jackson (2000) report that the fifth most often cited nonguidance activity was special education referrals and placement, which reinforces how quickly a special education agenda can creep into the counselor's domain to the detriment of the comprehensive school counseling program. For a more in-depth discussion of the school counselor's role with special education students, see Koehler and Kravets (1998).

Addressing Out-of-Balance Administrative Tasks. Researchers have consistently found that counselors are too often pulled away from professional programs focused on the academic, career, and personal/social development of students to perform non-CSCP tasks for the school (Burnham & Jackson, 2000; Gibson, 1990; Partin, 1993; Wiggins & Moody, 1987). When Burnham and Jackson (2000) surveyed counselors, they found that the average amount of time spent in nonguidance activities was 25.04 percent—slightly over one quarter of the job. This means that out of every week, approximately ten hours, or more than one day, was spent doing tasks not related to the comprehensive school counseling program. And these figures do not include the activity of testing, which we would argue constitutes another task that does not belong in the school counselor's list of responsibilities (Dollarhide & Lemberger, 2006).

How do you engage in a professional conversation about tasks that are not appropriate for the comprehensive school counseling program? There are a number of suggestions to follow, each specific to the situation.

First, if you are involved in the design of a new program, you would be able to challenge the imposition of those administrative tasks during the discussions about the design of the program. As you will recall from Chapter 5, the Foundation of your program includes philosophy, beliefs, and National Standards for Student Development. These inform the Delivery System and the Management System. As you design these elements in your CSCP, you must be able to discuss why certain administrative or noncounseling tasks would not be appropriate in your program, because the priority for time should be focused on meeting the needs of your student partners first. After student partners, the needs of parents and caregivers would be addressed next. Your stand on how to best meet these competing priorities must be based on the professional literature, your professional judgment, and resources from the profession such as textbooks and expert advice.

If you are employed at a school that has an existing program, Gysbers and Henderson (2000) discuss displacement as the means for finding a better fit between the tasks and the program (p. 202). They describe the displacement process as specifying the nonprogram responsibilities under discussion, broken down into small tasks, and "either eliminating them or shifting the responsibility for doing them to someone else" (p. 203). They believe that discussing smaller tasks, rather than entire functions, will enable others to accept them within their job duties. Also, they believe that it is the responsibility of the counselor to identify the person to whom the tasks should be assigned, determined on the basis of efficiency.

In some cases, the school will struggle to find the best professional to accept the responsibility. In other cases, the district will need to hire someone to perform the displaced activity. An example of this would be the hiring of a middle or high school registrar to handle student records, grades, transcripts, enrollment, withdrawal, registration for classes, and scheduling changes (from one section to another or from one time slot to another) that maintain the student's overall educational plan. (The comprehensive school counseling program would retain responsibility for academic advisement and help students establish the overall educational plan and program of study for each year, but it would no longer include responsibility for transcripts, grades, master schedules, or curriculum guides.)

If it is not possible to completely displace the noncounseling program activity, then Gysbers and Henderson (2000) suggest that counselors streamline these activities. In this process, the goal is to reduce the amount of time the counselors spend in the activity. This is useful for those activities in which counselor's involvement at some level is important, but not to the current extent. "Over time, counselors' involvement has become counselors' overinvolvement" (Gysbers & Henderson, 2000, p. 206). One good example is testing. Counselors "fell into" this responsibility due to their training in the interpretation of assessment instruments; eventually, this became full responsibility for a horrendous and time-consuming task that belongs with the academic leadership of the school. The solution to this overinvolvement would be the hiring of a professional at the district level to coordinate and conduct the district's testing and academic assessment program; counselors' involvement would be streamlined to retain responsibility for the interpretation of the testing results.

In the third situation, the counselor might be approached by someone who thinks it would be a good idea for the counselor to accept another responsibility, one that does not already fall in the comprehensive school counseling program. In response, Partin (1993) recommended that counselors should ask "'In place of what?' Because time is finite, any additional task must be at the expense of something else" (p. 280). He urged counselors to maintain their focus on their program priorities. "If counselors quickly acquiesce to external pressures to take on new projects and duties, others may begin to assume that those counselors must not have had enough to do before or that what they were doing was not important" (p. 280). Clearly, counselors are reminded to focus on their program priorities and to not blindly accept new duties that do not enhance the program.

This is not to imply that new program priorities will never emerge, because new issues and new problems emerge all the time. Remember, though, that you will have an advisory committee and management agreements that can help you in the case of new program priorities or emerging student issues that must be addressed. If new priorities emerge, they should be discussed with your principal and advisory committee, and the discussions must clearly convey that you are asking for their input in the redefinition of the comprehensive school counseling program.

It is not sufficient for schools to argue that school counselors must continue doing non-CSPC activities because they have always done it, or because there is no one else to do it. These are not acceptable reasons. Ultimately, counselors must recognize that they must accept leadership of their comprehensive school counseling programs, and this leadership means setting program priorities to maximize student potential. Counselors are not glorified secretaries, psychometrists, telephone operators, truancy officers, or registrars. They should keep their focus on their program priorities in terms of the developmental domains, the professional activities of school counselors, and their primary partners—students. As a counselor, dare to transform school counseling in your lifetime.

Reflection Moment ◆

What are your reactions to the administrative functions discussed above? Do you believe these functions should be done by counselors? If so, which one(s)?

◆ ◆

Leadership and Coordination with Community Colleagues

Powerful interventions result when community professionals join with school professionals to design comprehensive, wraparound services. Programs that utilize community resources to accomplish the goals of the school counseling program include mentoring programs (Brotherthon & Clarke, 1997), interagency collaboration (Price & Edgar, 1995), school/community collaboration (Ponec, Poggi, & Dickel, 1998), and youth services teams for at-risk youth (Hobbs & Collison, 1995).

The extent of school-community collaboration varies with the needs met by the collaborative. In understanding the needs of the community, motivation to collaborate depends on four variables: the way education is envisioned, the ability to integrate diverse systems of care, the ability to implement prevention/intervention programs, and the ability to meet the needs of adults as well as children and youth (Walsh, Howard, & Buckley, 1999). The needs of the school counselor might determine some linkages; logistics might increase the chance that the school counselor will be compelled to develop strong linkages with community resources. A case in point is the finding that school counselors in isolated rural communities need to collaborate with professionals in the community due to limited resources within the school itself (Morrissette, 2000). In addition, the needs of the students are met with school-community collaboration, as evidenced by Luongo's (2000) argument that partnering child welfare, juvenile justice, substance abuse/mental health diagnostic and treatment services, and schools is essential to meet the needs of our most vulnerable youth.

These variables interact to create various models of collaboration. This wide range of school-community linkages (Bemak, 2000; Walsh, Howard, & Buckley, 1999) varies from school-based coordinated referrals to community professionals, to school-based or neighborhood delivery of community services, to completely integrated "community schools" in which is found "comprehensive delivery of education and related health and human services" (Walsh, Howard, & Buckley, 1999, p. 351). This last concept of fully integrated school-community services closely parallels the systems of prevention, systems of early intervention, and systems of care promoted by Taylor and Adelman (2000). All these authors call for school counselors to assume leadership in conversations about forming these partnerships.

Of particular note, Ponec, Poggi, and Dickel (1998) researched the keys to successful school-community collaboration. They found that communication and personal interaction was crucial to successful collaboration, especially when it allowed each to better understand the roles and responsibilities of the other. This fostered trust and professional relationships, allowing for better referrals and more effective information sharing. Furthermore, the researchers found that developing a sense of professionalism was also important to the collaborators, involving better understanding of each person's area of expertise and the methods of sharing information. Along with this, the researchers found that a shared sense of teamwork improved trust, professionalism, and communication.

It seems logical that school counselors would collaborate with community professionals to meet students' needs, but there are many barriers to such collaboration. Outdated ideas about the role of the counselor and/or the role of schools, site-focused school administrators, turf issues, professional obsolescence, and overloads of "administrivia" are all impediments to moving forward to effect systemic change (Bemak, 2000). But if school counselors are indeed leaders, then it becomes our responsibility to move toward such change.

Reflection Moment ◆

What has your experience been with collaboration across professional lines? Has it been positive or negative? Think about the process you encountered during the collaboration and see if you can outline that process. What are some models presented in this book that parallel the process of collaboration you experienced? Would you see parallels between collaboration and counseling? Collaboration and consultation? Collaboration and leadership?

◆ ◆

CASE STUDY REVISITED ◆ Integration

Now that you have read the chapter, answer the following questions:

1. If you were on that board, what questions would you have for Harmony?
2. How would you feel if you were one of the counselors in the audience listening to her presentation?
3. If you were in Harmony's place, what would you say to the board?
4. Now that you have read the chapter, what do you think the board is looking for?
5. On a more personal level, what questions would you ask a principal or interviewing committee about the school counseling program to help you understand who "leads" the program?
6. How would you establish yourself as the leader of your program? How would you blend the insights from each of the four contexts of leadership to maximize your ability to lead?
7. What functions do you see as appropriate in the coordination of your program? How would you go about establishing your leadership in terms of the programs and services you would coordinate within the structure of your program?

APPLICATION (Possible portfolio artifacts are noted)

1. Watch a contemporary popular movie or TV show about a school. As you watch, see if you can document
   - who the leaders are
   - the leadership frame (structural, human resources, political, or symbolic)
   - the roles they fill in the school
   - the formal and informal power structures
   - the qualities of the leader(s)
   - the skills of the leader(s)

2. Read a book about a leader you admire. What insights into your own leadership style did you glean from your reading?

3. Look at times in your life when you assumed leadership of a group. What was that experience like for you? What can you learn from that experience now in your professional training and development? (Possible portfolio artifact)

4. Interview a school principal to learn about that administrator's expectations for the planning and evaluation process. Find out what the district expects in terms of accountability. In what ways is this similar, and in what ways is it different, from accountability as defined by ASCA?

5. Reflect on the extent to which you believe that school counselors should collaborate with parents. What are some projects you would propose to foster this collaboration? (Possible portfolio artifact)

6. Create a cost-benefit sheet for each of the administrative tasks addressed in this chapter. After designing the sheet, come to your own conclusion about the appropriateness of that activity.

7. Visit the Internet site for the Center for Mental Health in Schools (Adelman and Taylor's organization) at http://smhp.psych.ucla.edu. Outline the insights you gain from the center that are relevant to the discussion of leadership and coordination.

8. Visit the Internet site for The Education Trust at http://www.edtrust.org. Decide for yourself whether this organization's vision of school counseling is congruent with yours. Discuss their position.

9. How do you feel about the conceptual nature of the coordination function of school counseling? How do you feel about the hands-on nature of the coordination function of school counseling? How prepared do you feel for these roles? Outline a plan to increase your abilities to be effective in both these areas. (Possible portfolio artifact)

10. At the end of the chapter, several functions were presented that could belong in academic administration. Assume that you agree with the arguments that the functions belong in academic administration. Outline your arguments to move those functions into the principal or vice-principal's office. Structure a plan that addresses each of the four contexts or frames of leadership: structural, human resource, political, and symbolic. (Possible portfolio artifact)

11. Interview a local school counselor at the level you are targeting. Ask that person to list all the events and programs he or she coordinates. Which ones does that person feel are appropriate and which are inappropriate? Why? Which ones do you feel are appropriate and which ones are inappropriate? Why?

SUGGESTED READINGS

Adelman, H. S., & Taylor, L. (1998). Reframing mental health in schools and expanding school reform. *Educational Psychologist, 33*(4), 135–152. This article lays the groundwork for the foundation of Adelman and Taylor's work in coordination and collaboration from a school perspective.

Barr, R. D., & Parrett, W. H. (2001). *Hope fulfilled for at-risk and violent youth: K–12 programs that work* (2nd ed.). Boston: Allyn and Bacon. This book provides examples of programs that have helped at-risk and violent youth to finish their secondary education. Counselors will find many ideas for collaboration with school and community professionals.

Bemak, F. (2000). Transforming the role of the counselor to provide leadership in educational reform through collaboration. *Professional School Counseling, 3*,

323–331. This article encourages school counselors to address the needs of young people who are most in danger of making unhealthy choices.

Bolman, L. G., & Deal, T. E. (1997). *Reframing organizations: Artistry, choice, and leadership* (2nd ed.). San Francisco: Jossey-Bass. These authors examine the four frames of leadership, applying these typologies to a variety of organizations and institutions. They also provide excellent ideas for developing leadership skills.

Burnham, J. J., & Jackson, C. M. (2000). School counselor roles: Discrepancies between actual practice and existing models. *Professional School Counseling, 4*, 41–49. A current study that describes the work that school counselors do (providing wonderful insights into how counselors actually spend their time) and then compares the findings to two existing models of comprehensive school counseling.

[The] Education Trust. (2001). Working definition of school counseling. Ed Trust: Transforming School Counseling. The DeWitt Wallace-Reader's Digest Fund, National Initiative for Transforming School Counseling. Retrieved March 2, 2001, from www.edtrust.org/main/school_counseling.asp. This organization has challenged school counselors to examine long-held, preconceived ideas of what school counseling should be. There are many important insights into ways that school counselors can improve the quality of the work done in schools.

Keys, S. G., & Lockhart, E. J. (1999). The school counselor's role in facilitating multisystemic change. *Professional School Counseling, 3*, 101–107. In this article, the authors describe the role of the school counselor in collaboration and coordination across the student's subsystems of school, family, and community.

Koehler, M., & Kravets, M. (1998). *Counseling with secondary students with learning disabilities: A ready-to-use guide to help students prepare for college and work*. West Nyack, NY: Center for Applied Research in Education. The title describes this very useful book; a must-have for high school counselors.

Kouzes, J. M., & Posner, B. Z. (1995). *The leadership challenge: How to keep getting extraordinary*

things done in organizations. San Francisco: Jossey-Bass. This book is full of exciting ways of viewing leadership that can help the reader understand the many skills that leaders employ in getting things done in organizations. An inspired and inspiring reading for anyone who hopes to get things done in the world.

Laveman, L. (2000). The Harmonium Project: A macrosystemic approach to empowering adolescents. *Journal of Mental Health Counseling, 22*(1), 17–32. This article describes the collaboration/coordination process from the community perspective, outlining how those in the community conceptualize their work with their school partners.

Scruggs, M. Y., Wasielewski, R. A., & Ash, M. J. (1999). Comprehensive evaluation of a K–12 counseling program. *Professional School Counseling, 2*, 244–247. This article outlines the process of program evaluation, which will help to operationalize the section of this chapter on the leadership/management process.

Sitlington, P. L., Clark, G. M., & Kolstoe, O. P. (2000). *Transition education and services for adolescents with disabilities* (3rd ed.). Boston: Allyn and Bacon. This book provides an excellent overview of the need for transition services for students with disabilities and will generate many ideas for collaborating with special educators to facilitate the career development of these students.

Taylor, L., & Adelman, H. S. (2000). Connecting schools, families, and communities. *Professional School Counseling, 3*, 298–307. In this article, the Adelman and Taylor model of collaboration and coordination is specifically tied to the work of the school counselor.

Walsh, M. E., Howard, K. A., & Buckley, M. A. (1999). School counselors in school-community partnerships: Opportunities and challenges. *Professional School Counseling, 2*, 349–356. This article outlines many aspects of school-community partnerships and discusses variables that will improve the chances for these new models of collaboration to succeed.

REFERENCES

ASCA. (2003). *The ASCA National Model: A framework for school counseling programs*. Alexandria, VA: Author.

Barr, R. D., & Parrett, W. H. (2001). *Hope fulfilled for at-risk and violent youth: K–12 programs that work* (2nd ed.). Boston: Allyn and Bacon.

Bemak, F. (2000). Transforming the role of the counselor to provide leadership in educational reform through

collaboration. *Professional School Counseling, 3*, 323–331.

Bolman, L. G., & Deal, T. E. (1997). *Reframing organizations: Artistry, choice, and leadership* (2nd ed.). San Francisco: Jossey-Bass.

Brotherthon, W. D., & Clarke, K. A. (1997). Special friends: The use of community resources in comprehensive school counseling programs. *Professional School Counseling, 1*, 41–45.

Burnham, J. J., & Jackson, C. M. (2000). School counselor roles: Discrepancies between actual practice and existing models. *Professional School Counseling, 4*, 41–49.

Clark, A. J. (1995). Rationalization and the role of the school counselor. *The School Counselor, 42*, 283–291.

Clark, M. A., & Stone, C. (2000a). The developmental school counselor as educational leader. In J. Wittmer (Ed.), *Managing your school counseling program: K–12 developmental strategies* (2nd ed.; pp. 75–82). Minneapolis, MN: Educational Media Corp.

Clark, M. A., & Stone, C. (2000b, May). Evolving our image: School counselors as educational leaders. *Counseling Today, 42*, 21, 22, 29, 30, 46.

Colbert, R. D. (1996). The counselor's role in advancing school and family partnerships. *The School Counselor, 44*, 100–104.

Cole, D. J., & Ryan, C. W. (1997). Leadership in portfolio development: The school counsellor's role. *Guidance & Counselling, 12*(4), 10–14. Retrieved November 28, 2000, from wysiwyg://bodyframe.9/http://ehostv (the EBSCO database).

DeRoche, E. F. (2000). Leadership for character education programs. *Journal of Humanistic Counseling, Education, and Development, 39*, 41–47.

Dollarhide, C. T., & Lemberger, M. E. (2006). "No Child Left Behind": Implications for school counselors. *Professional School Counseling, 9*, 295–304.

[The] Education Trust. (2001). *Working definition of school counseling. Ed Trust: Transforming School Counseling.* The DeWitt Wallace-Reader's Digest Fund, National Initiative for Transforming School Counseling. Retrieved March 2, 2001, from www.edtrust.org/main/school_counseling.asp.

Fazio, T. J., & Ural, K. K. (1995). The Princeton peer leadership program: Training seniors to help first year students. *NASSP Bulletin, 79*(5), 57–60.

Gardner, H. (1995). *Leading minds: An anatomy of leadership.* New York: Basic.

Gibson, R. L. (1990). Teachers' opinions of high school counseling and guidance programs: Then and now. *The School Counselor, 37*, 248–256.

Gysbers, N. C., & Henderson, P. (2000). *Developing and managing your school guidance program* (3rd ed.). Alexandria, VA: American Counseling Association.

Harrison, T. C. (2000). The school counselor as consultant/coordinator. In J. Wittmer (Ed.), *Managing your school counseling program: K–12 developmental strategies* (2nd ed.; pp. 183–191). Minneapolis, MN: Educational Media Corporation.

Hersey, P., Blanchard, K. H., & Johnson, D. E. (1996). *Management of organizational behavior: Utilizing human resources* (7th ed.). Upper Saddle River, NJ: Prentice-Hall.

Hobbs, B. B., & Collison, B. B. (1995). School-community agency collaboration: Implications for the school counselor. *The School Counselor, 43*, 58–65.

Jackson, S. A., & White, J. (2000). Referrals to the school counselor: A qualitative study. *Professional School Counseling, 3*, 277–286.

Kaplan, L. S. (1997). Parents' rights: Are school counselors at risk? *The School Counselor, 44*, 334–343.

Keys, S. G., Bemak, F., & Carpenter, S. L. (1998). Collaborative consultant: A new role for counselors serving at-risk youths. *Journal of Counseling and Development, 76*, 123–133.

Keys, S. G., & Lockhart, E. J. (1999). The school counselor's role in facilitating multisystemic change. *Professional School Counseling, 3*, 101–107.

Koehler, M., & Kravets, M. (1998). *Counseling with secondary students with learning disabilities: A ready-to-use guide to help students prepare for college and work.* West Nyack, NY: Center for Applied Research in Education.

Kouzes, J. M., & Posner, B. Z. (1995). *The leadership challenge: How to keep getting extraordinary things done in organizations.* San Francisco: Jossey-Bass.

Kurpius, D. J., & Rozecki, T. (1992). Outreach, advocacy, and consultation: A framework for prevention and intervention. *Elementary School Guidance and Counseling, 26*, 176–190. Retrieved November 13, 2000, from http://webnfl.epnet.com (the EBSCO database).

Luongo, P. F. (2000). Partnering child welfare, juvenile justice, and behavioral health with schools. *Professional School Counseling, 3*, 308–314.

Morrissette, P. J. (2000). The experiences of the rural school counselor. *Professional School Counseling, 3*, 197–207.

Myrick, R. D. (1997). *Developmental guidance and counseling: A practical approach* (3rd ed.). Minneapolis, MN: Educational Media Corp.

Niebuhr, K. E., Niebuhr, R. E., & Cleveland, W. T. (1999). Principal and counselor collaboration. *Education, 119*, 674–679. Retrieved November 13, 2000, from http://webnf2.epnet.com (the EBSCO database).

Partin, R. L. (1993). School counselors' time: Where does it go? *The School Counselor, 40*, 274–281.

Peeks, B. (1993). Revolutions in counseling and education: A systems perspective in the schools. *Elementary School Counseling and Guidance, 27*, 245–232.

Ponec, D. L., Poggi, J. A., & Dickel, C. T. (1998). Unity: Developing relationships between school and community counselors. *Professional School Counseling, 1*, 95–103.

Porter, G., Epp, L., & Bryant, S. (2000). Collaboration among school mental health professionals: A necessity, not a luxury. *Professional School Counseling, 3*, 315–322.

Price, L., & Edgar, E. (1995). Developing support systems for youth with and without disabilities. *Journal for Vocational Special Needs Education, 18*(1), 17–21.

Rowley, W. J. (2000). Expanding collaborative partnerships among school counselors and school psychologists. *Professional School Counseling, 3*, 224–228.

Schmidt, J. J. (2003). *Counseling in the schools: Essential services and comprehensive programs* (4th ed.). Boston: Allyn and Bacon.

Sitlington, P. L., Clark, G. M., & Kolstoe, O. P. (2000). *Transition education and services for adolescents with disabilities* (3rd ed.). Boston: Allyn and Bacon.

Smaby, M. H., & Daugherty, R. (1995). The school counselor as leader of efforts to have schools free of drugs and violence. *Education, 115*, 612–622.

Stone, C. B., & Dahir, C. A. (2007). *School counselor accountability: A MEASURE of student success* (2nd ed.). Upper Saddle River, NJ: Pearson.

Taylor, L., & Adelman, H. S. (2000). Connecting schools, families, and communities. *Professional School Counseling, 3*, 298–307.

Walsh, M. E., Howard, K. A., & Buckley, M. A. (1999). School counselors in school-community partnerships: Opportunities and challenges. *Professional School Counseling, 2*, 349–356.

Wiggins, J. D., & Moody, A. H. (1987). Student evaluations of counseling programs: An added dimension. *The School Counselor, 34*, 353–361.

SECTION FIVE

The ASCA National Model in Action: Comprehensive School Counseling Programs

11

THE ASCA NATIONAL MODEL IN THE ELEMENTARY SCHOOL

Charles Lindsey
University of Wisconsin, Oshkosh

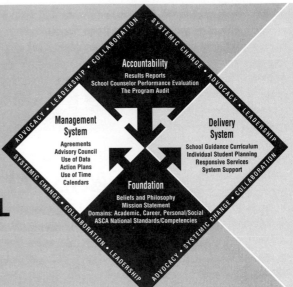

Accountability
Results Reports
School Counselor Performance Evaluation
The Program Audit

Management System
Agreements
Advisory Council
Use of Data
Action Plans
Use of Time
Calendars

Delivery System
School Guidance Curriculum
Individual Student Planning
Responsive Services
System Support

Foundation
Beliefs and Philosophy
Mission Statement
Domains: Academic, Career, Personal/Social
ASCA National Standards/Competencies

◆ **LEARNING OBJECTIVES**

By the end of this chapter, you will

1. Be able to describe what a RAMP program looks like in an elementary school
2. Understand how CSCPs are unique at the elementary level
3. Reflect on whether the elementary level is the ideal level for you

DOMAINS / ACTIVITIES / PARTNERS MODEL

ACTIVITIES	Academic Development	Career Development	Personal/ Social Development			
Counseling	1a	1b	1c	5	6	7
Educating and Advocacy	2a	2b	2c	8	9	10
Consulting	3a	3b	3c	11	12	13
Leadership and Coordination	4a	4b	4c	14	15	16
	Students			Parents and Caregivers	Colleagues in Schools	Colleagues in Community

PARTNERS IN THE PROCESS

CASE STUDY ◆ Mother Goose in the Elementary School

Kanika was taking a moment in her office, tending to paperwork. This morning had already been busy; she had been in one kindergarten class presenting a lesson on saying "please" and "thank you," attended to one fight on the playground at recess, had taken calls from three concerned parents about too much homework in the elementary grades, and needed to compile the perception data from the fifth-grade lessons she presented yesterday. One of the moms who helped out in the first grade popped her head in the door.

"Are you busy?" she asked. Without waiting, she continued, "You don't look busy."

"Well, I can stop what I'm doing right now to talk. If we need to continue for more than fifteen minutes, though, I'll need to schedule a time. I have a meeting with teachers at 11:00," Kanika offered.

"Good! I'm thinking that I'd like to do your job," she said as she sat. When she saw Kanika's surprised expression, she continued. "You seem so calm and so in control. I think I'd like a job where I can work with kids all day, just a laid back job where I can have fun. It will work well with my kids in school, and I just love the idea of working five hours a day and having weekends, holidays, and summers off. How hard can it be? Just reading Mother Goose to the kids all day. See? Just fun all day."

Kanika had to take a deep breath. Where can she begin to explain her job? In her imagination, she saw herself sitting this mother down and beginning to tell the story with "Once upon a time, there was this school. And in this school was a very hard-working woman named Kanika, who taught the kids all about life, and school, and families...."

Kanika smiled and began explaining to this mom what it means to work in a comprehensive school counseling program as defined by the American School Counselor Association.

CHALLENGE QUESTIONS

1. Where would you begin your story with this mom?
2. What is your reaction to the perception that "It can't be that hard—it's elementary school"?
3. Do you have enough information from the first ten chapters of this book to envision what comprehensive school counseling is in the elementary schools?

In the next three chapters, the ASCA National Model is seen at each of the educational levels as it is operationalized in an award-winning program. Each of these chapters has been authored by a counselor educator who interviewed the professional school counselor in a RAMP school—a school in which the comprehensive school counseling program has been recognized as an exemplary ASCA National Model program. For the year in which these schools won this prestigious designation, there were only eight such honorees nationally.

The purpose of these three chapters is to give you an overview of what such exemplary programs involve and to provide an image of what the job, program, and counselor activities might include. After all, the journey to a destination is much smoother when you know where you're going—you need to be able to envision a model program in order to create your own.

In reviewing the American School Counselor Association's (ASCA) website, the following statement introduces the Recognized ASCA Model Program, or RAMP, distinction:

> The RAMP designation, awarded to schools that align with the criteria set in the "ASCA National Model: A Framework for School Counseling," recognizes schools that are committed to delivering a comprehensive, data-driven school counseling program and an exemplary educational environment. (American School Counselor Association, November 22, 2005)

This chapter will focus on Ford Elementary School in Tucson, Arizona, a 2004–2005 RAMP recipient. It will explore the collaborative manner in which this school is connected with the larger mission of the Tucson Unified School District (TUSD) and will examine the inner workings of a RAMP recipient program from interviews with Diana Johnston, the school counselor at Ford Elementary whose program was selected as a RAMP recipient.

◆ A SCHOOL COUNSELING FORCE IN THE DESERT

Anyone who has keept track of the school counseling profession over the past fifteen years is aware that significant contributions to the profession of school counseling have come from Tucson. The Tucson Unified School District's school counseling program, known as the Comprehensive Competency Based Guidance model (CCBG), was first initiated in the district in 1993 (Tucson Unified School District, 2003). When it was adopted, school counselors began to shift their service-based programs to a program-based model that emphasized including all students. The CCBG model has been widely used as an example for school districts across the country, and visitors from numerous states have talked with TUSD counselors to learn about this pioneering guidance and counseling program. In addition, the American School Counselor Association (ASCA) used the TUSD model as a guide

> **The ASCA School Counselor Performance Standards addressed in this chapter are**
>
> **10.1** The professional school counselor uses a master calendar to plan activities throughout the year.
> **10.3** The professional school counselor posts a weekly or monthly calendar.
>
> **The 2001 CACREP Standards for School Counseling Programs addressed in this chapter are**
>
> **C.1** **(e)** preparation of an action plan and school counseling calendar that reflect appropriate time commitments and priorities in a comprehensive developmental school counseling program.

in developing the National Model for school counseling programs released in 2003 (American School Counselor Association, 2003).

Tucson Community

The Tucson metropolitan area supports over 750,000 residents. As metropolitan Tucson continues to grow by nearly 2,000 new residents each month, the challenge of meeting the needs of the community (including adequate schooling) also increases. Tucson celebrates a diversity of cultures, architecture, and peoples, and is rooted in a deep history. The city is considered a premiere health services center for the Southwest, is recognized internationally in the field of astronomy, and is home of the University of Arizona. Tucson's rich cultural heritage centers on a unique blend of Native American, Spanish, Mexican and Anglo-American influences. Set in the picturesque Sonoran Desert and yielding a climate of 360 sunny days a year, Tucson is also a popular year-round tourism destination (City of Tucson, 2006).

In spite of its attributes, Tucson also faces many of the same struggles and disparities of other cities in the United States that are rapidly approaching a population of a million residents. Ford Elementary School, for example, is located in a neighborhood that is largely underprivileged. With approximately 60 percent of the student population receiving free or reduced lunches, the needs within this growing desert community become evident.

The Long Road to Tucson

Diana Johnston was born and raised in Guam and served there as an elementary teacher for six years. In the late 1990s, Diana enrolled in a Master's program that the University of Oklahoma had established on the island of Guam, making school counseling her area of emphasis.

Following the completion of her Master's program, Diana had an opportunity to move to Arizona where she met Judy Bowers, who at that time was serving as President-Elect for ASCA. With some guidance from Judy, Diana began as a substitute counselor in the Tucson Unified School District. Not long afterward, she was interviewed for a position at Ford Elementary School in 2003, where she has worked since. Her position as a school counselor was originally half-time, but thanks to a grant awarded to the district, Diana was hired in a full-time capacity. Five different elementary schools in the district were written into this grant and criteria for receiving the grant funding were that all five part-time school counselors would move to full-time status and would implement the Comprehensive Competency Based Guidance (CCBG) model. In addition, all five counselors agreed that they would apply for RAMP status as part of receiving this grant.

Quite impressively, three of these five elementary schools were recognized as RAMP schools in 2003–2004 following the first year of the grant implementation within the Tucson Unified School District. Diana notes the remarkable support these five school counselors gave each other as they assembled their RAMP applications. Disappointingly, Diana and another first-year school counselor were at the two schools whose programs were not selected for RAMP status in 2003–2004. Diana states that although this was disheartening, she and her colleague were informed by ASCA that they could reapply the following year, after specific program components were more fully addressed in their RAMP applications. The following year (2004–2005), the two programs were honored as RAMP programs. The crucial factor, according to Diana, was the team approach that went into developing her program and subsequently applying for the RAMP designation. As she states, "I wouldn't have been able to do what I did without the input and support of my colleagues. As a team, we were able to discuss our programs openly and pull ideas from each other."

Challenges of Being New

Diana began working as a part-time substitute school counselor in the district in 2002, after the school year had already begun, which proved to be challenging in many regards. After only a couple of weeks in this capacity, Diana was hired for a full-time school counselor position that opened at Ford Elementary School. She recalls that her predecessor at Ford operated from a different philosophy of school counseling, and Diana states that the existing program lacked a comprehensive vision when she stepped into the position. She remembers struggling in her first year to get permission from teachers to enter their classrooms and spent much time in this initial year laying the groundwork for implementing a comprehensive school counseling program. In the Tucson Unified School District (and in accordance with the CCBG model), elementary school counselors are to deliver classroom guidance curriculum at least 45 percent of their time. Diana had much work to do during this first year to connect with teachers and rally support for her vision of her school counseling program.

Diana adds that because her position as a full-time counselor was the result of a grant award, she knew on accepting the position that rather rigorous expectations would need to be fulfilled. Implementing a comprehensive developmental guidance model and completing a RAMP application during an initial year as a school counselor might seem overwhelming, but Diana underscores that she was moving through this process with four other school counselors who had the same objectives to meet. It was from this supportive peer environment that Diana continuously gained encouragement for the program she was developing at Ford Elementary School.

School Demographics

When Diana began her work at Ford Elementary in 2002–2003, the school housed grades K–5. At the onset of the 2005–2006 school year, a pilot program was initiated to include grades K–6. As of spring 2006, there are approximately 350 students in the school.

In looking at the socioeconomic status of the school population in terms of free and reduced lunch, Diana indicates that of the 350 students, approximately 200 receive free lunch, and 60 receive reduced lunch. Demographically, the majority (43.8%) of Ford

Elementary School students are Caucasian. The second largest demographic is Hispanic (approximately 38.3%), with smaller percentages of African American, Native American, and Pacific Islander students comprising the remainder of the school population.

There are fourteen full-time classroom teachers at Ford Elementary School, one counselor, and one administrator. There are approximately 25 total staff when support staff are included. Ford Elementary School is one of seventy-four elementary schools in the Tucson Unified School District. In addition, Ford Elementary has implemented the counseling-related program entitled "Bully-Proofing Your School" and is a leader among elementary schools in the district in using and promoting this program.

◆ COMPREHENSIVE COMPETENCY-BASED GUIDANCE

In conjunction with the Tucson Unified School District, Ford Elementary School follows the Comprehensive Competency-Based Guidance (CCBG) model, which is closely aligned with the ASCA National Model. CCBG shifts the emphasis away from what the counselor does and focuses instead on how students benefit from having counselors in the school. The primary aim of this approach is to provide all students with the competencies they need to be successful in school, career, and relationships. The following summary bullets describe how Diana Johnston has fused the CCBG model in developing a long-term vision of the school counseling program. The School Counseling Program at Ford Elementary

1. Serves all students
2. Is proactive and prevention based
3. Provides developmentally appropriate curriculum
4. Uses the American School Counseling Association National Standards for the elementary level
5. Can be objectively evaluated

The CCBG program is congruent with the school district's mission, philosophy, curriculum, and Arizona Academic Standards (Tucson Unified School District, 2003). In addition, the guidance and counseling program at Ford Elementary School comprises a system of interconnected and interdependent elements, organized into four major areas:

1. *Foundation*. Elements that provide the framework for the counseling program and defines student results
2. *Delivery system*. Ways that the guidance program is delivered to students
3. *Management system*. The process by which the guidance program is managed for results
4. *Accountability*. Measurements of student results, the effectiveness of counselors, and overall program success

Foundation

The foundation provides the counseling program's framework and defines student results. Included in this component are such aspects as mission statement, philosophy, goals, and standards/competencies. Diana approached building the foundation for her program by looking closely at the mission statements and philosophies of both the district and her school, then blended them to create counseling program mission and philosophy statements that fit well with her school specifically.

Diana collaborated with her elementary school counselor colleagues who also were in the process of developing their programs. Through such collaboration with peers, administrators, students, and parents, Diana was able to craft goals for her counseling program that were precisely stated concerning student achievement in learning, working, and relating.

If this last piece rings with a note of familiarity, it is because Diana directly tied her foundational goals to the standards and competencies set forth in the American School Counselor Association National Model (2003). In fact, the TUSD Elementary Standards are adapted from the ASCA National Standards, and these nine standards are organized in academic, career, and personal/social domains. Constantly looking at how various program components relate and interconnect is precisely the technique Diana recommends not only for putting a comprehensive school counseling program together but also in formulating a RAMP application.

Delivery System

The delivery system includes the ways in which the guidance program is delivered to students and is further divided into the subcomponents of guidance curriculum, individual planning, responsive services, and system support. The following table denotes the recommended time allocation for these delivery system components within the Tucson Unified School District.

Delivery System Component	TUSD Elementary Level (% of time)
Guidance curriculum	45–50%
Individual planning	5–15%
Responsive services	20–30%
System support	10–15%

Guidance Curriculum and Individual Planning

Guidance curriculum includes classroom guidance lessons, large-group activities and structured small-group guidance. Diana describes spending a large part of her day in classrooms presenting on an array of CCBG developmentally appropriate topics usually selected with the input of teachers and relating directly to the overarching CCBG model. Diana is consequently able to connect topics directly with competencies outlined in the CCBG model.

Regarding school counseling curriculum lessons, Diana states that the district has a number of counseling-based lessons on line, and that this resource pool is continuously growing.

> As elementary school counselors in the district, we meet once a month. In addition to a variety of topics that are discussed, we take turns presenting to each other as peers the specific lessons we have implemented at our school. In this sense, we are always learning from each other and sharing approaches that we are developing within our schools.

Diana further reports that small-group work has decreased significantly due to the frequency with which she is delivering classroom guidance lessons. She does, however, spend a portion of each day working in smaller groups with children. She typically enters several different classrooms on a daily basis between 8–10 A.M.—what is called a "literacy block" period. During this time she provides individual planning, working individually or in small groups with children who are struggling with an array of issues having a negative impact on their academic performance.

Responsive Services

Responsive services include activities that meet the immediate needs and concerns of students and include consultation, personal counseling, crisis counseling, and referrals to community services. Because Diana is the sole counselor at Ford Elementary School, she plays a significant role as a consultant working with teachers, administrators, parents, and counselor-colleagues within the district in determining how the needs of specific students might best be met. Diana states that although she does not see a large number of students for individual counseling, she will build time into her schedule for personal counseling as needed. In addition, Diana is available if the need for crisis counseling surfaces and will make referrals to community services when warranted, often consulting with other elementary school counselors or the district counseling office to assess appropriate referrals.

System Support

System support comprises management activities that support the guidance program through professional development, research and development, staff and community relations, and consultation activities with staff, parents, and the advisory council. In the Tucson Unified School District, school counselors are required to regularly update their professional knowledge and skills. Diana places much personal importance on professional development and adds that she will take every continuing education opportunity available to her. She is a consistent participant at ASCA National Conferences and Arizona School Counselor Association annual conferences. She also participates in the professional development in-services that occur within the district, in addition to the monthly meeting that is held for all district elementary school counselors.

Consultation is another means by which Diana develops system support for her school counseling program. She regularly consults with teachers, staff members, and parents in order to provide information, to support the school community, and to receive feedback on the emerging needs of students. One specific avenue for consultation that Diana uses, and actually facilitates, is the Ford Elementary Site Council. This is a site-based advisory committee that includes and represents the students, parents, faculty, staff, members of the community, business partners, and the school principal (Inez C. Ford Elementary School, 2006). The goals of the council include providing a framework for site decision making; promoting an improved education process to meet the needs of students; facilitating communication between the site council, the school, community, and TUSD; and reviewing guidance program results and recommending priorities to the appropriate administrative bodies.

Diana emphasizes that through the Ford Elementary Site Council, she is able to build positive relationships and convey vital information to stakeholders. Site Council meetings occur on a monthly basis, and Diana underscores that this team is highly "data-driven"; she typically presents some type of data to the group at each meeting and this requires her to constantly think about research and development within her program. Consequently, she has learned to delve into efforts such as guidance program evaluation, data analysis, follow-up studies, and the continued development and updating of guidance learning activities and resources. Speaking frankly, Diana states that this shift to requiring extensive data has brought its share of challenges:

> I used to think that data wasn't so significant, but I've come to understand how important it is. I think that it is easy for school counselors to tell you what they do, but it's difficult to actually show proof. I see how important data has become in demonstrating that what I do as a school counselor is effective.

Management System

The record keeping, documentation, and process evaluation component that reviews student results are included in the management system.

In the Tucson Unified School District, each counselor takes the initiative in developing a counselor/principal agreement. This agreement is essentially a statement of responsibility by each counselor specifying the results for which he or she will be accountable. The results are delineated in terms of the standards/competencies students will achieve and are related to the program goals. The counselor agreements include a separate section for all of the duties to which the counselor is assigned, and the district administrator responsible for the guidance program is active in the negotiation of these agreements.

The counselor/principal agreement is unique to the Comprehensive Competency-Based Guidance (CCBG) process in that it becomes the single most important document outlining outcomes to be attained with students, staff, parents, community, and the counselor's own professional development. The agreement forms are specific to each level: elementary, middle, and high school. Each counselor completes the agreement, discusses it with their school administrator, and then sends a copy to the district counseling coordinator. Through this process, the expectations for each counselor are clearly communicated among all levels of the management system.

Each TUSD counselor is also responsible for a school plan that addresses how the desired results for the counseling program will be achieved. The plan specifically contains the standards/competencies that will be addressed through the counseling program, in addition to anticipated completion dates. School counselors in the district must also develop a master calendar of guidance events they have planned throughout the school year. These calendars are broken down by month, name of activity, and the grade level being served. Calendars also serve to convey the yearly picture and time frame of the guidance and counseling program. Master calendars may then be used to publicize upcoming events and as a tool to inform the school community of events in the counseling program. While the master calendar is typically distributed at the onset of a new school year, Diana adds that it is helpful to publish a bimonthly or monthly version of the calendar to highlight upcoming events.

In addition to the master calendar, Diana is responsible for documenting the activities of the counseling program by developing a weekly schedule. Weekly schedules, according to Diana, assist in organizing the program and further serve to document the amount of time she spends in each of the areas of the delivery system. Weekly schedules are distributed to all faculty and are also posted on the counseling office door.

Accountability

Accountability serves to measure the overall success of the counseling program. Diana emphasizes that a primary benefit of the assessment system is to examine the needs in her school, as well as assessing the gap between the desired results of the counseling program and results that are actually being achieved. Diana underscores the use of data to determine gaps in the program, and through assessment she is also able to make informed decisions regarding needed changes in the program.

Professional school counselors in the TUSD use a Needs Data Survey to assess what competencies need to be taught, to document the competencies in which students may already be proficient, and to gauge how effective counseling instruction and interventions have been (Tucson Unified School District, 2003). Needs data surveys may be given to students, parents, teachers, administrators, other school personnel, and community members. These surveys are available at all school counseling offices within the district and are also available in a Spanish language version. Other forms of data typically used by TUSD counselors to plan and evaluate their programs include analysis of attendance rates, standardized test scores, performance objectives, mobility information, school quality surveys, and tracking the numbers of students needing additional tutoring. These data are collected, analyzed, and used to drive individual counseling programs.

Diana states that within the district, school counselors have the ability to access the TUSD intranet and therefore have access to a wide array of data. For example, Diana can download attendance records for the entire school and can even focus on a specific classroom if needed. In so doing, she can hone her efforts to look at the school systemically and to boost daily attendance by having specific data at her disposal, as in the following program.

Diana states that she has used the district intranet as a tool in the "closing the gap" effort implemented at Ford Elementary School. By using data, Diana focused on students who were falling below a 90 percent attendance rate and developed interventions to increase attendance for these students. She reports that in a matter of months, the attendance rate for these specific students increased to above 95 percent. More specifically, during the first quarter of the school year, Diana used the database to focus on students below a 90 percent attendance rate. She then informed the parents of these students—in writing—that a goal for the school is to have students attend on a consistent basis and that attendance is directly related to academic performance. Diana adds that she often couples the letter she sends to parents with a "check-in" group in which chronically truant students are required to report to Diana before school begins. As part of this "check-in" process, students simply use a sticker chart to recognize when they are on time for school; when a certain number of on-time arrivals have been consistently achieved, students receive an attendance certificate celebrating their accomplishment. Diana emphasizes that such an approach is quite basic but highly effective. What is most important, according to Diana, is how motivated students become in being on time for school. This approach, when tied to the letter sent home to parents, challenges families to become invested in being on time for school and underscores the importance of consistent attendance.

Additional assessment system measures employed by school counselors in the TUSD include quarterly program audits of guidance activities and specific results of counseling programs; these audits are submitted by counselors to the district guidance office. Counselors are also responsible for annually assessing their programs by using a program evaluation instrument developed by the district. The program evaluation instrument helps counselors assess the level and quality of their programmatic implementation and the general effectiveness of their programs and provides a basis for considering program improvements.

Diana states that TUSD school counselors are also evaluated according to professional counselor performance standards that have been developed for the district. These performance standards serve as both a basis for counselor evaluation by their administrators and as a means for counselor self-evaluation. In the TUSD, counselors are directly evaluated on a support personnel instrument that is completed by the principals of the schools in which they are employed. Although not a requirement, administrators also have the option of completing a supplemental counselor evaluation instrument developed through the Arizona Department of Education.

It is through these accountability components that Diana is charged to continuously reflect on the caliber of her counseling program and the effect it is having on all students at Ford Elementary School, to consider how the program might be improved, and to envision ways to demonstrate the successes of her program to stakeholders.

◆ UNCERTAIN TIMES

When asked to identify how Tucson gets recognized nationally for its school counseling program, Diana readily gives the credit to the school counseling administrators and school counselors within the district who have diligently worked to define the role of the school counselor to stakeholders. She emphasizes that since becoming a school counselor in the TUSD, she has had consistent support from her fellow counselors and counseling coordinators at the district level. Moreover, Diana states that the administrator at Ford Elementary School and the counseling program coordinators at the district level have been instrumental in advocating for full-time counseling positions at every school in the Tucson Unified School District. As a result, counselors in the district are increasingly learning to advocate for themselves and underscore to School Boards how students are different as a result of the comprehensive efforts counselors are making in the schools. However, Diana adds that in recent years district administrators have entertained the idea of abolishing elementary school counselor positions completely and that this has provided additional fuel for elementary school counselors to unite and further demonstrate their effectiveness to stakeholders.

On a personal level, Diana adds that the third year of the grant that has provided her the opportunity to serve in a full-time capacity at Ford Elementary will end with the 2005–2006 school year; beyond that, she is uncertain whether her position will remain full-time or will return to a part-time role split between two different elementary schools.

In light of these uncertain times, Diana emphasizes the solid working alliance she has developed with the staff and administration at Ford Elementary School. The school principal has indicated that she will continue to advocate strongly to retain Diana in the school at a full-time position. When asked about receiving the RAMP award and whether this will bolster her chance to maintain a full-time position, Diana expresses hope that it will. She adds that receiving a national award will hopefully strengthen the argument that a high-caliber comprehensive counseling program is being delivered in the school and that she needs to be present in a full-time capacity to continue the efforts she has initiated.

◆ RAMP: HIGHS AND LOWS

When Diana didn't receive RAMP recognition the first time she applied, she admits being disappointed, but she emphasizes how important putting the RAMP packet together was for her development as a new school counseling professional.

When my program didn't get recognized the first time around, it was really all right because I knew that I was doing a good job at my school. The staff supported me—they saw the material I put together and they saw the hard work that I had done in reaching all of the kids in the school. I felt incredibly appreciated, even though the program didn't initially get the award.

As previously mentioned, Diana and another district colleague reapplied and both received RAMP status the subsequent year. "We supported each other all the way and that was important to me, to have someone who was going through a similar experience that I was." It is this theme of support and collaboration with other school counselors that consistently runs through Diana's story as she highlights the growth and success she has experienced as a school counselor.

On a developmental note, Diana states that receiving the RAMP award has helped her tremendously in a networking capacity. Specifically, she tells about meeting a group of school counselors from her home island of Guam at the 2005 ASCA conference. Subsequently, the group invited Diana and Judy Bowers to Guam in February 2006 to be guest speakers at their annual school counseling conference. Diana expressed great enthusiasm at the opportunity to return home to share her RAMP process and professional school counseling experiences.

◆ CALENDAR YEAR BREAKDOWN

Summer

During the summer, Diana focuses strongly on professional development and attempts to attend as many professional conferences as possible. She will also attend conferences during the regular school year; however, she appreciates the flexibility of summer and the opportunities it brings for attending more professional events. Diana adds that she finds conferences helpful in stimulating her professionally and giving her numerous ideas of new program pieces and modifications that she might implement when the school year begins.

Fall

As the school year begins, Diana has learned to give teachers a couple of weeks to "settle in" with their students. She typically doesn't schedule much during the first two weeks of school and instead uses this time to assist with kindergarten students and to help with other issues that arise as the school year gains momentum. Each year during the first two weeks of school, a districtwide reading test is delivered, and Diana is responsible for overseeing the testing for grades K–3.

After the first couple of weeks of school, Diana then creates a sign-up sheet for teachers to indicate their time preferences for her to enter their classrooms, both to support the teachers during the morning 8–10 A.M. "reading-block period" and for regular CCBG programming. She adds that for school year 2005–2006, her schedule became so full that she had to create "A" and "B" schedules—alternating between them on a weekly basis. She asks teachers for feedback on the types of topics and issues that might be appropriate for their specific classrooms and in so doing attempts to maintain a level of flexibility in her program delivery.

Spring

When school begins again in January, Diana reports that her schedule typically will follow the same rhythm as that developed in the fall. This can change, however, depending on school needs based on an assessment of the fall semester. As an example, Diana notes that when she moved into the spring of 2006, she focused greater attention on kindergarten and first-grade classes, because there seemed to be some significant issues surfacing in these grades. She emphasizes that each spring is unique for the counseling program because it is shaped by what occurred the previous fall. Importantly, each intervention that is implemented is evidenced-based, and data collection is important as Diana provides feedback to the school, district administrators, and the Ford site council.

Diana underscores that by the spring, she usually knows each and every student on a first name basis and has some rapport built with a majority of students. According to Diana, this also provides important insight into programming alterations that might be most appropriate for the latter part of the school year. Diana also serves as the interim principal when the existing principal has to be away from the school. When asked if this proves to be a conflict for her, Diana states, "I have a solid rapport with my students and they know that they can come to me, even though at times I must play an administrative role. I think it comes down to my knowing them on a personal level and relating to them primarily from a counseling perspective."

End of Year

The end of the school year is again marked by a series of reading tests that are delivered schoolwide. Diana, therefore, spends time engaging students in test-taking strategies, developing relaxation skills, and delivering transition lessons with students as they prepare to move to the next grade. The end of the year is also a time for Diana to reflect on the year as a whole and to assess both the strengths and the shortcomings within the program. In so doing, she strives to make continued improvements within the program and to honestly evaluate her role as an evolving professional.

◆ CONTINUED GROWTH

Diana states that while she regularly reports to her school advisory council, she hopes to do more outreach that is directed specifically toward parents. She has been considering the possibility of offering parenting classes but struggles with finding time for such an endeavor in an already full schedule. In addition, she hopes to continue building on the foundation that she has created as a RAMP school. She plans to continue developing an evidenced-based curriculum that can serve to inform and enhance other elementary school counseling programs that are working to strengthen their efforts. Simply put, Diana sees herself becoming more of an advocate for school counselors, not just in her district, but throughout the nation.

> I find it disturbing that in many instances, school counselors divide their time between two schools or may only be employed on a part-time basis. I know that in our district, full-time counselors are needed at each and every school, and I am working hard to demonstrate that

what I do as a school counselor is effective and that my students are enhanced as a result of my being in the school. I'm definitely invested in collaborating with others in an effort to strengthen school counseling as a whole.

Recommendations for School Counselors-in-Training

When asked what recommendations she would give to beginning school counselors, Diana made the following three suggestions:

1. *Develop and nurture relationships.* Diana emphasizes building positive connections with school administration, teachers, the school staff, and the school advisory council. Perhaps most important, according to Diana, is getting to know each of the students in your school, at the very least their names and some piece of information which sends a message that you are interested in them.
2. *Be flexible.* Diana underscores the importance of school counselors being intentional without being overly rigid. Showing flexibility in working with the administration and with teachers will go a long way in building rapport.
3. *Learn to be a proficient data collector and advocate.* As Diana sees it, the future of school counseling will continue to become more data-driven. She strongly recommends learning how to collect, evaluate, and implement data, using data to demonstrate the impact that school counselors have in their schools. "Remember to not overlook data that already exists—what information is already there? Use that data and build upon it. Figure out what it is that you want to focus on in your program and find a way to collect data around that area of focus. The bottom line is being able to show what you do as a school counselor, and data is the proof that demonstrates the role you are playing within that school. Also, present data at every possible opportunity as this is a means of advocating for your role as a school counselor and for the profession."

CASE STUDY REVISITED ◆ Integration

Now that you have read about an award-winning elementary school CSCP, what would you say to the mom who wanted Kanika's job because it was so easy? Based on what you have read in this book, what are this program's strengths? What are its challenges?

REFERENCES

American School Counselor Association. (2003). *The ASCA national model: A framework for school counseling programs.* Alexandria, VA: Author.

American School Counselor Association. (2005, November 22). *ASCA announces fall 2005 RAMP designation honorees.* Retrieved January 9, 2006, from http://www.schoolcounselor.org/files/pr%2011-22-05.doc.

City of Tucson. (2006). *Old pueblo, new Tucson.* Retrieved January 9, 2006, from http://www.tucsonaz. gov.

Inez C. Ford Elementary School. (2006). *Ford Site Council.* Retrieved January 15, 2006, from http://edweb.tusd.k12.az.us/Ford/site_council.htm.

Tucson Unified School District, Comprehensive Competency Based Guidance. (2003). *Program Handbook.* Retrieved January 12, 2006, from http://instech.tusd.k12.az.us/counseling/Documents/program/section1.PDF.

12

THE ASCA NATIONAL MODEL IN THE MIDDLE SCHOOL

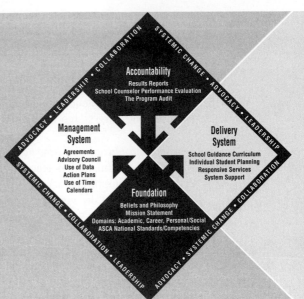

Phyllis K. Robertson
Western Carolina University

◆ LEARNING OBJECTIVES

By the end of this chapter, you will

1. Be able to describe what a RAMP program looks like in a middle school
2. Understand how CSCPs are unique at the middle school level
3. Reflect on whether the middle school level is the ideal level for you.

DOMAINS / ACTIVITIES / PARTNERS MODEL

ACTIVITIES	Academic Development ▼	Career Development ▼	Personal/ Social Development ▼			
Counseling	1a	1b	1c	5	6	7
Educating and Advocacy	2a	2b	2c	8	9	10
Consulting	3a	3b	3c	11	12	13
Leadership and Coordination	4a	4b	4c	14	15	16
	Students			Parents and Caregivers	Colleagues in Schools	Colleagues in Community

PARTNERS IN THE PROCESS

CASE STUDY: ◆ Ask Not for Whom the Bell Tolls; It Tolls for Thee

Pablo Ramirez finished his graduate degree in school counseling in a large university, having loved his time in the city. But his wife's family lived in a small rural community several hours away, and Pablo and his wife decided that they wanted to raise their own family close to relatives. So Pablo conducted his job search in the small towns in the area, and was delighted to accept a job offer at the local middle school. This was his favorite age; he loved the humor, the energy, and the unpredictability of the middle school environment. It was a challenge he looked forward to.

In the August meetings with administration and teachers, Pablo learned what he was facing. First, he learned that he was the only male and the only person of color in the district's counseling staff. There was only one other Hispanic teacher (female), one African American teacher (also female), and the only men in the district were administrators or high school teachers (only two others). In fact, in the middle school, the only other man in the building was the principal.

In addition, Pablo learned that the middle school student population came from four elementary schools, all of which were highly segregated in terms of culture. Two of the schools had predominately Hispanic students, and the other two had primarily European American students. His new students did not have any experiences with other cultural groups, and this was the time of their lives where they were going to be learning about other cultures, peer pressure, cliques, and puberty all at the same time—a steep learning curve indeed.

This morning was the first day of school, and the all-school assembly was about to begin. The kids were in the auditorium, and the noise was deafening. The teachers were all seated on the stage, ready for the meeting, and the principal was at the podium. Pablo thought about how the students were already segregating themselves in the auditorium, and how much they had to learn about each other this year. It was going to be an education for everyone—for the teachers to interact with him as a Hispanic man and a professional, for the kids to accept and learn from him, and for the kids to accept and learn from each other. As the bell rang on the first day of school, Mr. Ramirez adjusted his tie, took a deep breath, and began his new life as a school counselor. It was show time.

CHALLENGE QUESTIONS

1. As you read about Pablo Ramirez, what were your reactions?
2. What are the developmental challenges of middle schoolers that makes this situation especially relevant for this new counselor?
3. What about the middle school interests you?
4. What about that educational level challenges you?

For many practitioners, the middle school is not their favorite level. Those who chose to work at the middle school level are indeed a select breed, as unique as the middle schoolers themselves.

◆ OVERVIEW

The Sequoia Middle School counseling program has adopted the logo of the Eyrie—Where Eaglets Fledge. Like eagles caring for eaglets in a nest, the counseling team wants their students to be nurtured, secure and respected, and given a safe place to spread their wings while learning the skills needed to succeed in life. The counseling program at Sequoia utilizes a comprehensive, developmental approach to delivering services to the entire school community. The concept of the eyrie supports the understanding of the middle school years as times of rapid growth and development in cognitive, emotional, and physical characteristics for students and the necessity for gentle support and guidance by knowledgeable and caring adults. Information about this 2005 ASCA RAMP designated counseling program was provided by Nancy Jarman-Dunn, lead counselor at Sequoia Middle School.

School and Staff Demographics

Before discussing the counseling program in detail, it is necessary to understand community and school demographics of Sequoia Middle School. Sequoia MS is located in southern California in Fontana, a suburban area of Los Angeles. Fontana has grown rapidly as people who work in Los Angeles and Orange counties found the housing more affordable in the former steel mill town. Many of the parents of Sequoia children commute to these two counties for work. The school operates on a trimester schedule and serves seventh- and eighth-graders with an enrollment approaching 1,400. Fifty-three percent of the students receive free or reduced lunch and 11 percent of the students receive special education services. Race/ethnicity percentages for students are Black, 3 percent; Asian, 1 percent; Native American, 0 percent; White, 7 percent; Hispanic, 88 percent; and Other, 1 percent. Of their students, 80 percent speak Spanish with the majority fluent in English as well. Students with limited

The ASCA School Counselor Performance Standards addressed in this chapter are

10.1   The professional school counselor uses a master calendar to plan activities throughout the year.

10.3   The professional school counselor posts a weekly or monthly calendar.

The 2001 CACREP Standards for School Counseling Programs addressed in this chapter are

C.1   **(e)**   preparation of an action plan and school counseling calendar that reflect appropriate time commitments and priorities in a comprehensive developmental school counseling program

English speaking, writing, and reading abilities are identified soon after enrollment and represent approximately 3.3 percent of the students.

Philosophy and Mission Statement

Through counselor leadership and collaboration, school administrators, faculty, parents, and students at Sequoia support the concept of the school counseling program and recognize the value of a comprehensive, developmental counseling program in the school. The school counseling program mission statement currently states:

> A comprehensive, developmental counseling program addressing academic, career and personal/social development is an integral part of the total educational program to prepare ALL students for success in our ever-changing world.

This mission statement is aligned with the school's and district's statements and will be updated as the school board revises its mission statement and goals. The counseling program philosophy is based on the ASCA model, national standards, and ethical guidelines. It states that all students are important, have the ability to be responsible, respectful, and successful, and have the right to participate in a school counseling program with access to a full-time credentialed professional school counselor. It includes a delivery system with guidance curriculum for all students as well as closing-the-gap activities, individual planning, responsive services, and system support.

Pragmatics of the Delivery System

There are 96 faculty and staff at Sequoia, and only two school counselors who serve an average of 700 students each. The lead counselor is Nancy Jarman-Dunn who has been at Sequoia for 19 years, and previously was a middle school special education teacher in the areas of English and history. Students access the school counselors by alphabetical listing or by availability of the counselor. Delivery system domains of career and personal/social are divided by the two counselors and both work in the academic domain. The rationale for division of these duties was based on mutual agreement by the counselors and on the professional development experiences at the district and state level. One counselor is responsible for construction of the master schedule with teacher course assignments and student registration duties, and the other is responsible for coordinating the annual testing program.

The school counselors spend 50 percent of their time in direct service to students with

◆ 35 percent of time delivering guidance curriculum
◆ 15 percent of time with individual student planning
◆ 25 percent of time with responsive services
◆ 25 percent of time with system support

The counselors are employed ten additional days beyond those identified for teachers. Master scheduling takes place before the school session begins in the fall and after regular school hours. Coordination of the annual testing program occurs during and after the regular school schedule.

The school counseling department is open for student/parent/teacher access from 7:00 A.M. to 2:00 P.M. The counselors work together to schedule activities and presentations so that a counselor is always available in the counseling department for responsive services. As the Sequoia counselors strive to meet the needs of all students, group counseling, large-group guidance, closing-the-gap activities, coordination activities, and peer leadership activities are scheduled and posted to allow for optimal interaction with students.

School counselors are also available during evening parent meetings. Programs and services presented and available to parents include guidance advisory committee, counselor websites, school counseling brochure, peer program brochure, consultation with parents, and scheduled parent meetings. Brochures and websites are available in Spanish and English.

The counseling department has a full-time guidance technician who completes data entry for scheduling and assists with the master schedule and schoolwide testing. The clerk also handles student records, grades and progress reports, and student study team paperwork. The school receptionist processes paperwork for new student enrollment.

Needs Assessment Method and Results

Written survey needs assessments are given at the beginning of each school year to students, parents, and teachers, and during the parent orientation program. These surveys are also available throughout the school year in the counseling department and during additional parent meetings for parents to complete. The Support Personnel Accountability Report Card (SPARC) team examines the data and develops a comprehensive program that impacts the overall school climate and safety for all students. This team consists of administrators, counselors, faculty and staff, parents, and community members. In 2005 the top concerns identified from the survey were study skills (50%), decision making (45%), and peer pressure (40%).

The school recently installed a new phone program that will be used to survey parents. Future implementation of this phone program is anticipated for calling each student residence and asking for feedback on programs, needs, and concerns. Recently, the program was used to contact parents about a service project of collecting book bags for student victims of the Gulf Coast hurricanes. The phone service was very helpful in notifying parents of this project and the school exceeded its expectations for donations.

◆ DELIVERY SYSTEM AT WORK

School Guidance Curriculum

Classroom Instruction. With the increased focus on classroom accountability in California, it was initially determined that counselors would provide curriculum through the elective and physical education classes. These classes combined seventh- and eighth-grade students which did not allow for grade-level division of classroom guidance topics. To accommodate this blending of students, the guidance curriculum focuses on seventh-grade competencies and indicators for all students one year, and eighth-grade competencies and indicators for all students the next year. Seventh-grade competencies/indicators focus on study skills and eighth-grade focuses on decision making skills. The same class and topic configuration is maintained so that all students enrolled for two consecutive years will receive all of the lessons.

Initially, the Character Education lessons were delivered by PE teachers who were assigned to provide lessons to all students at the beginning of the school year. The leadership team at Sequoia determined that ongoing lessons were needed throughout the year, which has led to all teachers providing Character Education sessions within their curriculum to promote positive behaviors and relationships on campus. The Sequoia school faculty and staff have "embraced the fact that in order for children to learn with their heads, they have to feel with their heart" (Jarman-Dunn, 2005). This change has led to 90 percent of the school faculty, staff, and students participating in the Character Education program.

Character education lessons are only part of the faculty and staff involvement in implementation of the guidance curriculum. Examples of faculty and staff helping students (beyond their "regular academic responsibilities") include teaching Life Laws lessons, participating in College Day and Red Ribbon Week, club advising, mentoring, Career Plan integration, Mix It Up Day interaction with students, and supporting counselor-led guidance lessons.

Interdisciplinary Curriculum Development. All strong counseling programs must have the support of an educated, active and responsible guidance advisory committee. This committee at Sequoia consists of the two counselors, one administrator, student peer leaders, four to five parents, and teachers. The chairperson is typically a parent, but for 2005, a student led the council. Meetings are held once a trimester in the morning and evening to accommodate member schedules. Meetings have been held later in the evening after parent conferencing nights to eliminate travel time for parents. The committee assists the school counselors in developing goals and objectives, planning and implementing College Day, planning parent trainings and in-services, and discussing and approving the Support Personnel Accountability Report Card. As opportunities arise, the guidance advisory committee is capable of becoming more involved in other areas of the program.

Schoolwide and Small-Group Activities. Make a Friend at Sequoia (MAFAS) day is part of the transition program from the elementary school to the middle school. Each sixth-grade teacher at the feeder schools selects a boy and a girl to spend an entire day with a seventh-grade boy or girl at the middle school. This allows for special attention to be given to students who may be at risk or experience difficulty with change.

Other programs include Kick Butts Day, a national day sponsored by Tobacco Free Kids Organization (2005) for increasing awareness of the dangers of tobacco use, in which peer leaders receive training on prevention activities and then deliver these activities to the rest of the school. On College Day, the faculty and staff wear college shirts and talk about positive college experiences, and the guidance advisory committee passes out college information to students. In addition to these events, Mix It Up Day is an international day sponsored through the Tolerance.org project by the Southern Poverty Law and Study Circles Resource Centers. At Sequoia, 200 students are chosen to go through trainings about diversity, communication skills, social boundaries, and cliques, and experience a variety of group activities. These students promote and participate in the Mix It Up at Lunch Day where students are encouraged to sit and talk with other students they would not normally socialize with at the lunch table. After the event, these students have a discussion and debriefing through the use of a post-survey to determine areas of strength or concern they have for their school population on issues of tolerance and acceptance of differences. Administrators and teachers are actively involved in supporting the event.

Anger management, safety, and conflict resolution services are available for families and students from the school resource officer and campus security officers. These classes are for students who have been involved in a physical altercation at the school.

Parent Workshops and Instruction. Parent workshops have been offered on the topics of bullying, academic improvement, and high school graduation requirements. Work and family demands placed on parents have led to low turnout for some evening workshops, so the counselors have now prepared a series of workshops that are held once a month on multiple topics at different times of day. This strategy allows for flexibility in the parents' work schedule and parents have direct input into topic choice for any of the sessions on the given day.

In addition, the website for the school counseling program provides parenting tips addressing such areas as drug and alcohol prevention, college information, community and national services for adolescents, information on teen health issues, and discipline and communication styles. The website includes a link to a parent conflict survey created by Positive Parenting for Teens on the University of Minnesota's Extension Service website. This survey is straightforward and convenient for parents to use in gaining understanding of their child(ren) and themselves by interpreting responses to communication and discipline conflicts.

As the number of non-English speaking families continues to increase, the school counseling and peer program brochures are published in English and Spanish.

Individual Student Planning

Individual or Small-Group Appraisal. Counselor Catch is a program where the counselors try to "catch" their students being successful and recognize them with rewards. The counselors periodically ask teachers if students (randomly selected) have homework done, or the counselors may go into a classroom to see who has work written in their "planner" or dressed out for PE. In 2004 the school's accountability report card indicated that 66 percent of the students in the school were caught doing their homework.

The counselors have eighth-grade students examine their career aspirations by using the Career Cruising (2005) website in computer lab settings. The counselors monitor students in one-class session for three weeks while they complete surveys on interests and skills while matching these to an extensive list of possible careers. The counselors take an active role in relating the career information to academics through completion of a work-sheet and application of the information discussed in the recorded interviews with people from different career fields. An early development of student career portfolios is supported in these classes. The website program is offered in both English and Spanish.

Individual or Small-Group Advisement.   Each counselor and administrator assumes the role of Administrative Designee for the Exceptional Children's program for involvement in IEP meetings and 504 plan development. Counselors serve the same role as administrators in these meetings and maintain active involvement in securing appropriate services for special needs students.

Prealgebra, algebra, and geometry courses are offered at the middle school with counselors having the chance to advocate for students enrolling in the higher math classes. Through this advocacy, in 2004 the number of eighth-graders has increased in algebra and geometry, and the number of seventh-graders in algebra. The counselors work with the math lead teachers to determine placement based on a set criteria, providing the opportunity for students to enroll in high school classes that will ensure that they meet college entrance requirements.

Responsive Services

Consultation.   Consultation with teachers, administrators, and parents provides many opportunities for counselors to advocate for students. The mentor/mentee program at Sequoia addresses the goals for No Child Left Behind by identifying students who are on the border of passing the state exams. Individual teachers work with 250 students for academic encouragement. Consultation and subsequent counseling referrals from these teachers can often lead to interventions that address attendance issues, basic school supply needs, peer conflicts, and family issues that prevent these students from performing to their greatest potential academically.

As an Administrative Designee to the Exceptional Children's program, the coun-selors stay actively involved in consultation with teachers, parents, and community resources in meeting the needs of students.

Individual and Small-Group Counseling.   While one counselor is delivering classroom guidance activities, the other is available for individual and small-group counseling. During lunch time students can drop by the counseling offices for brief chats and schedule appointments. Scheduled small-group sessions include TEMP (Together Everyone Makes Progress) which are offered each trimester for students who are experiencing some type of turmoil in their life. Such experiences can include divorce or separation, approaching death of a loved one, and domestic violence. The counselors also implement Youth Connections, which is a privately developed program adopted and required by the school district for small-group counseling. The curriculum for the program was created by Rainbow Days Youth Connection and has tested reliability. Seven groups of 8 to 14 students meet for six to ten sessions each year. These students participate in sessions addressing identity development, handling anger, goal setting, decision making, dealing with peer pressure, and drug and alcohol prevention.

Crisis Counseling.   Each counselor participates in crisis intervention training designed and provided by the school district. This allows for uniformity of the delivery of services throughout the district.

Referrals.   For internal school referrals for student services, counselors consult with the school psychologist, resource officer, speech and language specialist, physical and occupational therapist, adaptive physical education specialist, and a district counselor who works with teen parents. An approved list of external referral sources in the county is provided by the school district. Counselors can have input into this list of services but approval for contact remains with the district office.

Peer Facilitation.   Peer mediation is available daily for students. Peer leaders are trained in mediation and communication skills to encourage their peers to make positive choices when dealing with everyday conflict. A peer teacher meets with the students one class period per day to train them as peer helpers using the Peer Assistance Leadership program (PAL) and Schrumpf, Crawford and Usadel's (1997) peer mediation book. In the classes, seventh- and eighth-graders learn listening and attending skills, problem solving strategies, and the mediation process, culminating in peer mediation certification. After one year of class work, students who have excelled are chosen to become peer leaders who are then assigned to the counselor one class period per day for the purpose of providing mediation, personal support, and educational programs for students. These students conduct these programs within the counseling program offices where they receive supervision by a counselor. Peer leaders use power point presentations to work with small groups of eighth-grade students to explain the high school registration process, graduation requirements, and college entrance requirements. These small group meetings are held prior to the high school counselors' involvement in registering the students for high school courses. Another service the peer leaders give is a meet and greet experience for new students by providing a welcome and tour of the campus on their first day.

System Support

Professional Development.   The school counseling team partakes in professional development by participating in the American School Counselor Association conference and list-serv discussions, the California Association of School Counselors conference and Leadership Development Institute, The Education Trust conference, district and regional workshops, and service on district and site committees. The school counselors participate in the California Association for School Counseling Leadership Development Institute each year to become refreshed on innovative and reliable school counseling services. The school counseling department meets monthly among themselves, in faculty meetings, with administrators, and with the leadership team.

In-Service Training.   The lead counselor is actively involved in the school's leadership team monthly meetings where many site school decisions are deliberated. The leadership team members include administrators, the student body director, department chairpersons, and the lead counselor.

Relationship aggression staff in-service was provided for the faculty and staff at Sequoia. Currently, several faculty members have had lunch discussions about the books *Queen Bees and Wanna Bes* (Wiseman, 2002) and *Odd Girl Out* (Simmons, 2002). These discussions have now led to in-service programs after school in which faculty members get together to talk about the readings and their relationship to working with the students at Sequoia. On-site programs and services are presented and available to staff which include adolescent development in-services, participation in leadership team meetings, and dissemination of research and current readings on adolescent development and best practices.

Professional Association Membership.   Ms. Jarman-Dunn maintains active membership in the American School Counselor Association (ASCA) and the California Association of School Counselors (CASC). For eight years she served as a board member for the California Association of Peer Programs.

Postgraduate Education.   All teachers, counselors, and administrators are fluent in Spanish, or are enrolled in Spanish classes, to meet the needs of Sequoia's Limited English Proficient students. Ms. Jarman-Dunn stays actively involved in local and state conferences by attending workshops and events that will keep her abreast of changes in the profession and services to students. She has an interest in pursuing a doctoral degree in counselor education but none are available near her in California.

Consultation, Collaboration, and Teaming.   Consultation about school community and program needs occurs through meetings of the Guidance Advisory Committee (GAC), interaction with counselor websites, dissemination of the school counseling program brochures and peer program brochures, consultations with individual parents, and scheduled parent meetings.

The Guidance Advisory Committee joins the counselors in the development of services for all students through collaboration among parents, students, community members, and staff. As mentioned previously in the Interdisciplinary Curriculum Development section, members of GAC consist of the school counselors, an administrator, parents, teachers, and students. The GAC meets three times a year to discuss student needs and assess the effectiveness of the counseling program. The GAC is divided into subcommittees that address issues and projects such as College Day organization, SPARC (Support Personnel Accountability Report Card) development, parent in-services, and revision of mission, goals, and objectives for the current and coming years.

Sequoia Middle School was recently recognized by the national organization Do Something (www.dosomething.org) for their service learning project of collecting 350 backpacks filled with school supplies and personal items for Hurricane Katrina victims. Each backpack also included a stuffed animal and a personal note from a student.

Sequoia Middle School has many community partnerships/resource services. These partners expose students to community resources, expand their understanding of future occupations, teach tolerance for others, and reward academic success. These services are critically important to students and families as the work is performed by providing academic student incentives, mentoring, tutoring, personal/social counseling services, curriculum training, peer leader training, and College Day information sharing. A special career education program called Lunch with Professionals Day invites members of the community to share their interests and profession with the students. Volunteers are valuable resources at Sequoia and the community is encouraged to continue their involvement through the website, newsletters, and participation in school activities and events. Community members are also encouraged to join the Guidance Advisory Committee, the School Site Council, and the English Language Advisory Committee.

Ms. Jarman-Dunn has served on the School Naming Committee as the district representative for all certificated employees. As new schools are built to meet the growing population in southern California, this committee looks at appropriate names for each new school. Other district committees Ms. Jarman-Dunn has served on include the School Calendar Committee, GATE (Gifted and Talented) Steering Committee, Peer Advisor Training Committee, Parent Education Committee, and the School Counselor Committee.

As an active mother, Ms. Jarman-Dunn's committee service to the community includes being a Girl Scout Leader for 13 years, a Cub Scout Leader/Boy Scout Troop Committee member for 12 years, a Boy Scout Merit Badge Advisor for 6 years and a member of the California Turtle and Tortoise Association, which works for the preservation of endangered desert tortoises, for 9 years.

Program Management and Operations.   Funding resources supporting the school counseling program include school site funds, Safe and Drug-Free School funds, and tobacco use prevention funds. Successful provision of counseling services is supported by the procurement of computers and supporting software, peer program training materials, office supplies, career plans, and guidance lesson and closing-the-gap instructional materials and supplies. The Peer Program Club for which Ms. Jarman-Dunn is a sponsor holds fund raisers for the peer leaders to attend regional and district peer program conferences.

Data analysis for the counseling program consists of record keeping of individual and small-group contacts, where pre- and post-surveys are completed for all activities. The program uses an internal data collection system for obtaining information on attendance, GPA, and the number of discipline referrals. Achievements in the three domains of academic, career and personal/social development are noted in the school's SPARC report card. In the academic domain:

- Study skills guidance lessons developed by the Guidance Advisory Committee (GAC) were provided for all students to reinforce academic skills. District test scores indicate an 8.5 percent increase of students scoring basic, advanced, and proficient after completing the lessons combined with classroom instruction from their language arts teachers.
- Counselor Catch caught and rewarded students who did their homework, and demonstrated responsible behavior.
- Classes developed by the GAC familiarize students with testing locations and test-taking strategies.
- The Academic Performance Indicator target for Sequoia was 614. The school showed significant improvement in overall annual test scores with all the subgroups meeting their targets.

In the career domain:

- Career plans were integrated into guidance lessons and language arts classes, where students explored skills and education needed for future success.
- Peer education for all eighth-graders helped them prepare for the requirements of high school and college.
- The perception data indicated that 61 percent of the students successfully identified the relationship between education and career plans. College Day activity evaluations showed an increase in awareness of local colleges by 26 percent.

In the personal/social domain:

◆ Peer mediation services were available to all students.
◆ Youth Connection group counseling was available to all students. Group participants had an 18 percent overall decrease in the number of discipline infractions at school. Fighting has decreased as students use responsibility, diligence, and respect on campus and in the community.
◆ After completion of anger management classes, participants had an 88 percent reduction in repeated fights.
◆ The school results data indicated that fighting at school had decreased by 5.1 percent as students exhibited positive behavior.

Other Duties and Responsibilities. The counselors at Sequoia have their fair share of responsibilities in the operations of the school and extracurricular activities. Currently, Ms. Jarman-Dunn is the Peer Program Club advisor. In the past she has served as an advisor of student government, the drill team, cheerleaders, and a member of the middle school and high school Band Boosters, and Parent Boosters. Table 12.1 summarizes the responsive and support services and activities employed at Sequoia each trimester.

TABLE 12.1 ◆ Sequoia Middle School Program Calendar 2004/2005

First Trimester	Second Trimester	Third Trimester
Seventh-grade orientation	Youth Connection group work	Personal/social guidance lessons
Career Plan Development	TEMP group counseling	Kick Butts Day
Character education lessons	Leadership meeting (3)	Leadership meetings (3)
Leadership meetings (3)	Mentor/mentee program starts	CAT testing
Guidance advisory committee management	Mix It Up Day	Staff meetings (3)
Academic development guidance lessons	Personal/social development guidance lessons	Career development guidance lessons
College Day	Second Youth Connection group	Staff in-service
Relationship aggression staff development	Second TEMP group	Make a Friend at Sequoia Day
Red Ribbon Week	Peer program training	Career plan development
Staff meetings (3)	College Day	Counselor Catch
Counselor Catch	Peer education of graduation and college entrance requirements	Guidance advisory committee management
Honor roll evening program	Staff meetings (3)	
	Guidance advisory committee management	
	High school registration	
	Counselor Catch	
	Honor Roll evening program	

◆ CONCLUSION

The ASCA RAMP designation is just one award the counseling program at Sequoia Middle School has received in 2005. The counseling program also received the Academy Award for their Support Personnel Accountability Report Card through the State of California. Later in the year, the program received the Golden Bell Award which promotes excellence in education by recognizing outstanding programs in school districts and county offices of education throughout California. Sequoia's program was recognized by meeting the following criteria for the award: (a) innovative, exemplary and sustainable program that has been developed and successfully implemented by California teachers and administrators; (b) indicates an investment of extra energy and time to make a demonstrated difference for students; (c) the model can be replicated by districts and county offices throughout the state; and (d) it focuses on the commitment to ensure the needs of all students are met.

This review has described many components of Sequoia Middle School's comprehensive counseling program. Strong support from the administration and teachers, counselor determination to provide services to all of the students, and dedication to an annual review process using the ASCA audit program have all contributed to the strengths of the counseling program. Challenges to the program include time for delivery of services, including integration of guidance lessons into the schedule, counselor caseloads, and the priority of academic accountability placed on the schools.

Ms. Jarman-Dunn believes there are several additional components to add to their program so that it continues to be an integral part of the school. "School counseling can and should be a part of each school—the same as math and English." Advocacy for the counseling program will require the counselors to continue recruiting support for activities that work, investing personal and professional energy for maintaining leadership roles, and using collaboration skills to encourage the staff to integrate the affective domain into the established curriculum. As the *eaglets fledge the nest* at Sequoia, the faculty and staff will have significantly contributed to the growth in knowledge, skills, and awareness in students for them to be successful in their future academic, career and personal/social endeavors. The counseling program at Sequoia will continue to evolve in the twenty-first century as one that seeks practical, creative, and responsible activities to meet the educational and counseling needs of its students.

CASE STUDY REVISITED ◆ Integration

It is now the end of Pablo Ramirez's first year as a middle school counselor. What would you want to ask him? What do you think was his greatest challenge? Helping the kids deal with their own physical/emotional changes? Helping the kids overcome their preconceptions about each other? Their preconceptions about him? Working with the teachers, as they react to his gender or his culture? Perhaps working with the principal, who is used to working with women? What do you hope were his greatest triumphs?

WEBSITES AND OTHER RESOURCES

School Websites

Nancy Jarman-Dunn's counseling website at http://fusd.tv/sites/middle/jarman/IndexMain.html.

Sequoia Middle School's website at www.fusd.net/schools/MiddleSchool/Sequoia/index.stm.

SPARC (Support Personnel Accountability Report Card) for Sequoia Middle School at www.lacoe.edu/orgs/1077/index.cfm.

Activity Links

Backpack collection for Hurricane Katrina Victims at http://dosomething.org.

Career Cruising website at http://careercruising.com/default.asp.

Kick Butts Day activities at http://TobaccoFreeKids.org.

Mix It Up Day activities at www.tolerance.org/teach/mix_it_up/about.jsp.

Rainbow Days Youth Connection has the Youth Connection small-group curriculum at www.rdikids.org/yc_c.shtml.

Publications

Peer Assistance Leadership Program is designed by the Orange County Department of Public Instruction at www.ocdek12.ca.us/PAL.

Schrumpf, F., Crawford, D., & Usadel, H. C. (1997). *Program guide peer mediation: Conflict resolution in the schools.* Champaign, IL: Research Press.

Simmons, R. (2002). *Odd girl out.* Orlando, FL: Harcourt.

Wiseman, R. (2002). *Queen bees and wanna bes.* Norwalk, CT: Crown Publishing.

13

THE ASCA NATIONAL MODEL IN THE HIGH SCHOOL

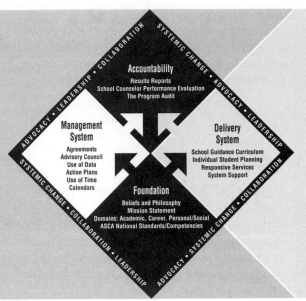

Robert I. Urofsky
Clemson University

◆ LEARNING OBJECTIVES

By the end of this chapter, you will

1. Be able to describe what a RAMP program looks like in a secondary school

2. Understand how CSCPs are unique at the secondary level

3. Reflect on whether the secondary level is the ideal level for you

DOMAINS / ACTIVITIES / PARTNERS MODEL

	DOMAINS					
	Academic Development ▼	Career Development ▼	Personal/ Social Development ▼			
Counseling	1a	1b	1c	5	6	7
Educating and Advocacy	2a	2b	2c	8	9	10
Consulting	3a	3b	3c	11	12	13
Leadership and Coordination	4a	4b	4c	14	15	16
	Students			Parents and Caregivers	Colleagues in Schools	Colleagues in Community

ACTIVITIES (vertical label)

PARTNERS IN THE PROCESS

CASE STUDY ◆ Misha Fears Being Mashed in the High School

Misha came to the United States as a college student, working hard to finish her bachelor's degree in psychology and learn about this culture and language. Then she did some counseling in the university counseling center as a peer counselor as she worked on her graduate degree. She was now an experienced counselor, having worked for eight years in an elementary school, a job she adored. She loved working with kids and they loved her. She especially loved the hugs that she got from the kids all day long—it made her feel connected, meaningful, and valued. In addition, her program was very successful and was considered a model program in the district.

Then the funding problem arose. Even though her program was flourishing and won accolades from her colleagues, the district was having budget problems, and the parents of this affluent community did not think that their children needed counseling in the elementary schools. The district's entire elementary program, in all five of the elementary schools, was cut. This meant that counselors would have to move to another level, go back to the classroom, or find other employment.

Misha did not have a teaching credential, but she was certified to work K–12 as a counselor. A retirement at the high school level created an open position, for which Misha applied. Fortunately, she was hired.

Now here she is, in the third week of class, having another panic attack. Every time she goes in the hallway between classes, she has another attack. She feels so small and vulnerable in the human sea of towering students—being only five feet tall, she could easily be crushed by the students who loomed over her. Besides, why was she in the hallway in the first place? No one could hear her over the loud voices

253

and banging locker doors, and she knew she couldn't physically make anyone do anything if a problem arose or a fight broke out. She had hoped this transition to a new school would go smoothly, but her anxiety was only increasing with each passing day and each new image of disaster in the hallway. How she yearned for her elementary students, where she felt loved and safe, and where she was perceived as an adult. Here, kids kept asking her what grade she was in! She was going to have to talk to the principal about this.

CHALLENGE QUESTIONS

1. What would you suggest to help Misha with the mismatch between her and her environment?
2. How do you think she could create more of a connection between herself and her student population, or do you think she was overattached to her elementary students?
3. In what way(s) do you see the connection between personality/personal attributes and preferences for different educational levels?
4. What are the personal attributes that you possess that would naturally draw you to connect better with your preferred educational level?

High schools, more than the other two levels, struggle with outdated definitions of school *guidance*. Many high schools still expect counselors to maintain many of the administrative tasks of career guidance, college admissions, registration, and scholarships, often to the detriment of other duties that come with a comprehensive school counseling program. In this chapter, you will read about a RAMP designee at a high school to explore what a model program looks like at that level.

◆ OVERVIEW

This chapter describes the comprehensive school counseling program at Wakefield High School in Raleigh, North Carolina, a Recognized ASCA Model Program. As a RAMP designee, this program represents the best that school counselors aspire to—the ability to serve students in a professional manner. The majority of information in this report was obtained through discussions with and materials provided by Deirdra Williams, Dean of Student Services, Wakefield High School.

◆ COMMUNITY CONTEXT

Wakefield High School is located in Wake County in north central North Carolina, an area of the state referred to as the Triangle, a metropolitan area centered in Wake, Durham, and Orange counties. The county seat of Wake County is the city of Raleigh, which is also the state capital. Wake County is roughly 860 square miles in size (About Wake County—Geographic Facts, n.d.).

The ASCA School Counselor Performance Standards addressed in this chapter are

10.1 The professional school counselor uses a master calendar to plan activities throughout the year.

10.3 The professional school counselor posts a weekly or monthly calendar.

The 2001 CACREP Standards for School Counseling Programs addressed in this chapter are

C.1 **(e)** preparation of an action plan and school counseling calendar that reflect appropriate time commitments and priorities in a comprehensive developmental school counseling program

Wake County has seen significant population growth in recent years, likely attributed to job growth in the Triangle area, with the number of county residents doubling in the twenty-year period from 1980 to 2000. The forecasted population of Wake County for 2005 was around 750,000 people. The population is projected to surpass one million people by the year 2016 (Wake County Planning, Land Use and Zoning—Population, n.d.). With the solid job market, there has been relatively linear growth in per capita and median household incomes, although there has been a slight slowing in growth from 1989 to 1999. The overall job market has seen significant structural changes in the period between 1990 and 2000. Total employment numbers in agricultural, retail trade, and wholesale trade declined, with the biggest growth in the total employment numbers in professional services, health care, and construction jobs. In 2003, the county unemployment rate was 4.7 percent, with 9.6 percent of the population (64,489 people) living below the poverty line (Wake County Planning, Land Use and Zoning—Economy, n.d.).

The racial makeup of the population is predominately White (72.4%). The next largest racial group is Black or African American (19.7 percent). Hispanics or Latinos comprise 5.4 percent of the population, Asians 3.4 percent, and Native Americans 0.3 percent. A total of 2.5 percent of the population identify as being from other races, and 1.6 percent identify as being from two or more races (U.S. Census Bureau—State and County Quick Facts, n.d.).

In Wake County, 91 percent of the adult population possess at least a high school diploma, and 46 percent possess a B. A./B. S. or higher. Reflecting the growing population in the area, the Wake County Public School System has seen significant growth in recent years. In 2004–2005, the system had an enrollment of 114,068 students. Between 1990 and 2003, the system's enrollment grew more than four times the growth in the previous fifteen years. In 2004–2005, the system had 135 schools and fourteen charter schools (Wake County Planning, Land Use & Zoning—Education, n.d.).

◆ SCHOOL CONTEXT

Wakefield High School is a comprehensive public secondary school located in the northern suburbs of Raleigh. The school is located in a fairly new community that saw a large growth in new homes beginning around 2000. The school opened in 1999 in response to growing population in the area. That year the building housed students from another school while their building was built and housed another high school as well while their school was remodeled. Since 1999, two more high schools have opened in the area, and two more high schools will open in fall of 2006.

Wakefield High School is accredited by the Southern Association of Colleges and Schools and is a 4-A high school as denoted by the North Carolina Athletic Association. It had a total enrollment of 1920 students in 2004–2005 and 2156 students in 2005–2006. The 2005 senior class enrollment was 469 students. There are 516 Wakefield High School students identified as special education students and 239 students with Individualized Education Plans, as well as 277 considered academically gifted. The 2003–2004 school year saw the start of a Ninth-Grade Academy at Wakefield as part of a countywide Ninth-Grade Academy initiative. The Wake County Student Services Department has been involved in a lot of data gathering surrounding this initiative.

The school's administration consists of a principal, an assistant principal for instruction, three assistant principals, and an assistant principal intern. In 2004–2005, the school had 175 full staff with 128 teachers and a support staff of 12 administrative and clerical assistants. The school's Counseling and Student Services Department consists of a Dean of Student Services, four school counselors, a Student Assistance Program counselor, a career development counselor, and an intervention coordinator.

The ethnic makeup of the school closely mirrors that of the county as a whole. Approximately 64 percent of the students are White, 23 percent African American, 6 percent Hispanic, and 4 percent Asian. Wake County employs districting or zoning to maximize the mix of socioeconomic status of students in the schools. Some students come from 15 to 20 miles away to attend Wakefield High School. Eighteen percent of students at Wakefield receive a free/reduced lunch. Wakefield has an English-as-a-second-language student population of approximately 100 students from the northeast portion of the county. Not all schools in Wake County have these ESL programs.

The mission statement for Wakefield High School states, "The Wakefield High School educational community will work together to guide and encourage students to become lifelong learners and productive citizens of a global society." The school offers three courses of study: career prep, college tech prep, and college/university prep. Approximately 66 percent of students indicate plans to attend a four-year college, 23 percent plan to attend a two-year college, and 11 percent indicate plans for military/other. The 2005 average SAT score for Wakefield High School was 1057 (Verbal 518, Math 539) which was slightly lower than the Wake County total of 1075 and above the North Carolina total of 1010. The 2005 AP test averages data showed average scores above four in the areas of calculus AB, calculus BC, economics-macro, German language, and human geography; above three in art/drawing, biology, chemistry, English literature, European history, French language, government/politics US; psychology, Spanish language, and statistics. In 2004, Wakefield met 100 percent of the target goals for Adequate Yearly Progress (AYP) standards for No Child Left Behind (NCLB), as well as ABC standards used with the North Carolina Department of Public Instruction.

Wakefield High School offers courses on a 4 × 4 block schedule. In line with its mission statement, Wakefield High School offers advanced placement and honors courses, as well as a vocational and business program designed to prepare students for the world of work. Coursework in this program includes drafting, carpentry, business education, and family and consumer science. The school has award-winning programs in instrumental music, chorus, theater, visual arts, and dance. Wakefield High School provides dual enrollment opportunities for selected elective courses not offered at Wakefield through cooperative arrangements with local universities and technical community colleges.

◆ PROGRAM CONTEXT

Wakefield High School's Counseling and Student Services Department consists of a Dean of Student Services, four school counselors, and a Student Assistance Program (SAP) counselor. One counselor is assigned to the ninth grade and the remaining grades are split alphabetically among the other three counselors. The Dean of Student Services functions as a liaison between the counselors and the school administration, coordinates departmental activities and course registration, works with the assistant principal of instruction on curriculum and instruction matters, serves as the scholarship coordinator for Wakefield High School, and serves as the counselor for midyear graduates. The average number of students served by each counselor is approximately 450 students. The school is allotted counselors according to the number of students enrolled at the school. The school started in 1999 with two counselors. After two years, two more counselors were added and then another was added a year later. There is the possibility that another counselor will be added soon. In addition to the counseling staff, there are two full-time clerical assistants. The clerical assistants free up the counselors' time by taking care of many noncounseling tasks such as scheduling appointments, maintaining up-to-date information resources, and helping students locate information.

In addition to the school counselors, there are a number of other student service personnel providing support to students at Wakefield High School. There is a career development counselor included in the Counseling and Student Services Department, whose position is different from the other counselors. This counselor handles students who are participating in internships, coordinates a career fair, conducts career education with each grade, and works with a Business Alliance. There is also an intervention coordinator who works closely with ninth-graders who scored low on the eighth-grade end-of-year tests to develop personal education plans. This individual also works with the school's credit recovery program. A transition counselor is spread out over several schools in the district, working specifically with students who are suspended long-term. There are school-based mental-health personnel working with students with mental health needs who do not have insurance to cover a private therapist. Qualifying students with Medicaid or Health Choice coverage may meet with a school-based mental health professional once per week. Depending on the needs of the student, the school-based mental health counselors may get releases so that the school counselor can work with the student as well. In addition, Wakefield High School shares the services of a school psychologist, a school nurse, a speech pathologist, a physical therapist, and an academically gifted coordinator with other schools in the district. There are financial aid counselors who come in once per week to work with students and their families on completing FAFSA applications.

The Wakefield High School Counseling and Student Services Department began its implementation of the American School Counselor Association's National Model for School Counseling Programs in the 2002–2003 school year following a Wake County

School System's Counseling and Student Services Department initiative for implementation of this model throughout the system. The Wake County School System's Counseling and Student Services Department served as an important resource aiding in the transition to the model through facilitating work sessions for each department and helping the departments to establish realistic goals. The work sessions were useful to the departments as they were able to see and compare each others' goals.

◆WAKEFIELD HIGH SCHOOL RAMP COUNSELING PROGRAM

Foundation

As stated, Wakefield High School's mission statement reads: "The Wakefield High School educational community will work together to guide and encourage students to become lifelong learners and productive citizens of a global society." Wakefield High School's vision statement reads: "Wakefield High School will provide opportunities and the best possible environment in which students can achieve individual excellence." In addition, Wakefield High School has clarified the following value statements:

- ◆ All students are capable of learning and should be given the opportunity to do so.
- ◆ The school community has the right to a safe, healthy, and orderly environment.
- ◆ Learning requires the active participation, mutual respect, and individual accountability of students, teachers, staff, parents, and community members.
- ◆ Education extends beyond the classroom environment, lays the foundation for lifelong learning, and encourages ethical behavior.
- ◆ All students should be given equal opportunity and resources to learn.
- ◆ The Wakefield High School community values the unique contributions of each student and appreciates individual worth.

The school counselors in the Counseling and Student Services Department at Wakefield High School connected to and built on these statements in developing their own philosophy/vision, belief, and mission statements. The following philosophy/vision, belief, and mission statements guide the school counselors' actions and activities at Wakefield High School:

Wakefield High School Counseling and Student Services Department Philosophy and Vision Statement

The Counseling and Student Services Department of Wakefield High School will foster a learning environment and opportunities in which all students can achieve academically, socially, and prepare for postsecondary career options. This statement is consistent with the No Child Left Behind reform movement of the United States Government, the NC Accountability Plan (ABC Plan) and Wake County Public Schools' Goals 2008. The Wake County Schools Goal 2008 states: "By 2008, 95 percent of students in grades 3 through 12 will be at or above grade level as measured by the State of North Carolina End-of-Grade or Course tests, and all student groups will demonstrate high growth."

**Wakefield High School Counseling and Student Services Department
Belief Statements**

The counselors in Wakefield High School believe

- All students can learn and should be given the opportunity to do so.
- All students have dignity and worth.
- All students have the right to participate in the school counseling program.
- All students' ethnic, cultural, racial, sexual differences and special needs are considered in planning and implementing the school counseling program.
- All students have access to a full-time, state-certified, master's degree level school counselor to deliver the counseling program.

The school counseling program should

- Be based on specified goals and developmental student competencies for all students
- Be based on the fact that learning requires the active participation, mutual respect, and individual accountability of students, teachers, staff, parents, and community members
- Include education that extends beyond the classroom environment allowing students to develop lifelong learning skills and encourage ethical and moral behavior
- Be based upon data, which will be used in assessing the needs of the school counseling program and will drive program development and evaluation

All counselors at Wakefield High School

- Will abide by the professional school counseling ethics as advocated by the American School Counselor Association
- Will participate in professional development activities essential to maintain a quality school counseling program

**Wakefield High School Counseling and Student Services
Department Mission Statement**

The Counseling and Student Services Department of Wakefield High School will provide a comprehensive developmental counseling program addressing the academic, career, and personal/social development of all students. School counselors are professional school advocates who provide support to maximize student potential and academic achievement. In partnership with the local educational community including other educators, parents or guardians, and students, school counselors will facilitate the support system to assure that students of the Wake County Public School System have access to and are prepared to become lifelong learners and productive citizens of a global society.

The school's principal, all of the school counselors, a school board member, and an advisory council member all signed off in agreement to these philosophy/vision, belief, and mission statements.

Delivery System

Guidance Curriculum.   The Wakefield High School Counseling and Student Services Department uses the Wakefield High School Curriculum Crosswalking Tool once per year as an assessment tool to determine where they are meeting their curriculum goals. The standards used are from the ASCA National Model.

The school counselors do classroom guidance by grade level, generally beginning in November of the school year. By this time the counselors have already met individually with all seniors for senior interviews. As the school utilizes 4×4 block scheduling, the counselors meet for classroom guidance with half of all freshmen, sophomores, and juniors during the first semester and half during the second semester. Academic-related guidance is done through the English classes. Half of the students in the class are taken to the media center while the other half remain in the classroom focusing on their academic studies. During classroom guidance, the counselors focus on high school graduation requirements and the importance of academic success. These sessions are done in conjunction with the career development coordinator to make the idea of success more meaningful for the students. During the classroom guidance sessions, the students complete graduation plans and select their course of study. The counselors also provide copies and explain student transcripts in terms of college admissions. The counselors may also do some need-based lessons depending on teacher requests in certain classes. Examples include lessons on study skills, time management, PSAT interpretations, and college admissions.

Part of the classroom guidance includes career development activities. All students complete career interest inventories. The freshmen participate in a program called Futures for Kids. The juniors go to the College Foundation website where, in addition to completing interest inventories, they establish accounts at no charge with the College Foundation. This gives them access to information on careers, links to colleges and universities, and a universal college application. The counselors have the students take interest inventories online to infuse technology with the lessons.

Individual Student Planning.   Because Wakefield High School is so large and the caseload per counselor is approximately 450 students, individual planning is an area of challenge for the counselors. The counselors work to ensure that they see each student one to two times per year, but it is a challenge to personalize these meetings. The counselors meet with each senior for senior interviews during the first part of their senior year to begin to finalize postsecondary plans, and there is a freshman camp held at the beginning of the year to assist freshmen with the transition to high school. A significant portion of individual planning occurs during classroom guidance. The counselors hold a number of workshops throughout the year to provide information to students and parents on academic and postsecondary planning issues.

Responsive Services.   There is one counselor at Wakefield High School who is assigned to work with ninth-grade students in the Ninth-Grade Academy. The other counselors split up the remaining grades alphabetically. The counselors provide individual counseling to students on an as-needed basis. In addition, there are school-based mental health professionals who can provide services to qualifying students with Medicaid or Health Choice if the students do not have insurance coverage for private therapists. At times depending on a student's individual needs, the school-based mental health professional may obtain a release so that the school counselor can work with the student as well. The Student Assistance Program (SAP) counselor administers a needs assessment to students at Wakefield High School and then runs small groups to help meet identified needs. Target groups have included students who were newcomers to the area, children of divorce, substance abusers and their families, students interested in increased racial and ethnic understanding, gay and lesbian supporters, and retained ninth graders.

Another responsive service area in which the Counseling and Student Services Department is involved is that of truancy. Every two to three weeks a list of truant students is generated. The SAP counselor attempts to call the student's family if it has been more than ten days. Prior to the Central Office setting truancy charges in motion, the school will work with the students and parents to try attendance contracts and other interventions. Wakefield High School also makes use of NovaNet, a countywide credit recovery program for students who completed but failed a class. This is also used with homebound students.

System Support. The Dean of Student Services acts as a liaison between the school counselors and the school's administration and helps coordinate many of the Counseling and Student Services Department's programmatic activities. There are a number of Management System activities (discussed later in the chapter) which act to support the counseling program in place at Wakefield High School.

The Counseling and Student Services Department also engages in a number of public relations activities to help make various constituent groups aware of programs and services and to build support for and involvement in their programs:

◆ placing recordings on the phone master system
◆ publishing a "Counselors Corner" in the PTSA newsletter which is mailed to every household
◆ putting scholarship information on the Student Services website
◆ sending emails to parents of seniors
◆ putting notices in the local weekly newspaper
◆ placing announcements on the in-house student-run television station
◆ putting information in the Teachers Daily Memo.

Management System

Agreements. The school counselors at Wakefield High School work with the principal each year to create a Wakefield High School Counselor/Administrator Agreement. The 2004–05 agreement established the following goals and specifications:

Programmatic Delivery. The school counseling teams will spend approximately the following time in each component area to ensure the delivery of the school counseling program.

15 percent	Delivering guidance curriculum
35–40 percent	Individual student planning
25 percent	Responsive services
15–20 percent	System support

School Improvement/Closing-the-Gap Goals

Goal I Increase minority enrollment in AP English III by 5 percent

Implementation

1. Conferences with students, parents, and current Honors English II teachers
2. Quarterly meetings with minority parents to increase awareness of relationship between rigorous course selection and postsecondary opportunities

Goal II   Increase parent involvement of LEP/ESL students by 20 percent

Implementation

1. Conduct parent/student conferences once per semester to increase participation in their child's educational process

Goal III   Increase promotion rate of ninth-graders to 85 percentage.

Implementation

1. Freshman orientation for ninth-graders and parents
2. Parent nights to increase parent involvement
3. Conduct small-group counseling sessions for repeating ninth-graders
4. Appropriate course selection to increase academic rigor and success

Programs, Information, Assistance, Outreach

Teachers. Closing-the-gap strategies for minority students at faculty meetings

Parents. Parent open houses, topic-focused and grade-level parent nights

Community. Business Alliance–Friday Career Fairs; PTSA Family Day

Professional Development for School Counseling Staff.   The school counseling team will participate in the following professional development:

1. National Model for School Counseling Level II training
2. Addressing transition issues of ninth-graders

Budget Materials and Supplies.   Needed materials, supplies, and expenses:

1. Group counseling supplies
2. Postsecondary opportunity books for counseling students
3. Career fairs
4. Parent nights

Counselor Availability/Office Organization.   The school counseling department will be open for students, parents, and teachers from 7:00 A.M. to 3:30 P.M. (with staggered hours during registration in March). The career center will be open from 10:30 A.M. to 3:00 P.M.

Roles and Responsibilities of Other Staff and Volunteers.   Volunteers will assist with career fairs and in the student services office during lunch two days per week.

Advisory Council.   Wakefield High School's Leadership Team functions as an advisory board for the Counseling and Student Services Department. The Leadership Team meets twice a month to focus on schoolwide issues and needs. It is composed of the school's administration, department chairs, the Dean of Student Services, and representative teachers and parents. The Leadership Team has been able to provide feedback to the Counseling and Student Services Department about organizational and operational aspects of issues such as working with newly enrolled students. An advisory council member signed off on the department's philosophy/vision, beliefs, and mission statements as well as the statement of program goals.

Use of Data. In determining their program goals, the Counseling and Student Services Department looks at school data. The Wake County School System is effective in gathering and presenting data on particular schools, and Wakefield High School has access to a statewide program called NCY through which they can obtain student information specific to Wakefield, including data on different groups of students. One purpose of this program is to ease a student's entry into a school if they transfer because the student's information can be transferred school-to-school quickly. In addition, the school system generates at-risk data on particular students identified on the basis of certain risk factors including suspensions, failed courses, and achievement on state exams. The school counselors get together at the beginning of every year and look at this collection of data to help determine their goals and objectives. In addition, they are able to review their results reports (discussed later) at the end of each year to help determine the effectiveness of activities and which activities to continue, discontinue, and/or modify.

Action Plans. The Wakefield High School Counseling and Student Services Department generates action plans and results reports related to their program goals for each year. The Principal and the Dean of Student Services sign the action plan and results forms following submission and review. The following is an example from the Wakefield High School Guidance Curriculum Small Group Counseling Action Plan 2004–2005.

1. *Grade level*: 9th grade

   Lesson Content: Newcomers small group

   ASCA Domain and Standard: Academic A1.1, A2.3, A3.2, B1.4, C1.2; Personal/Social A1.4, A2.8, C1.6

   Curriculum and Materials: Orientation to building, staff and procedures of WHS

   Start and End Dates: August 27th thru Sept 17th, 2004

   Number of Students Affected: 19

   Location: Freshman Center

   Evaluation and Assessment: Student survey

   Process and Challenges: Establishing rapport and trust between new students from different areas

   Results and Data: 100 percent responded "strongly agreed" to Question 1 regarding enjoying the group; 50 percent responded with "agree" to Question 5 regarding still needing help; 88 percent responded with "strongly agree" or "agree" to Questions 3, 4, 6, 7

Use of Time. The 2004–2005 Wakefield High School Counselor/Administrator Agreement specified the following time allocations: 15 percent of time delivering guidance curriculum, 35 to 40 percent of time with individual student planning, 25 percent of time with responsive services, 15 to 20 percent of time with system support. In addition to the counseling staff, there are two full-time clerical assistants who take care of many noncounseling clerical tasks.

Use of Calendars. The Wakefield High School Counseling and Student Services Department uses and publishes a master calendar specifying important dates and deadlines, as well as counselor and program activities. (See the Student Services Activity Timeline on pages 268–271.) The October 2005 calendar included the following representative examples:

◆ Teen pregnancy group
◆ Grief/loss group
◆ Anger management group
◆ Post-hurricane support group
◆ Morehead scholarship applications due
◆ Faculty meeting
◆ Senior workshop: resumes/essays
◆ Senior workshop: choosing a college
◆ Closing-the-Gap parent meeting

Accountability System

The school counselors at Wakefield High School generate different types of data throughout the year including process data, perception data, and information on number of students affected by different programs. This information is put into results reports throughout the year. At the end of the year, the school counselors are able to review the results reports to determine how successful they were in achieving their goals and which programs they want to continue, discontinue, and/or modify.

Results Reports. The Wakefield High School Counseling and Student Services Department generates action plans and results reports related to their program goals for each year. The following are examples of action plans and results related to two of the 2004–2005 goals:

1. *Target group*: LEP/ESL Students

    Target group selection is based on the following criteria: To improve opportunity for academic success for this high-risk group

    Data that drove this decision: Parent involvement in academic conferences was at 22 percent during the 2002–03 and 2003–04 school years.

    Counselor: Dean of Student Services, ESL staff

    Intended Effects on Academics, Behaviors or Attendance: Parent involvement of LEP/ESL students will increase by 20 percent

    ASCA Student Competency: A:A1.1, A:A1.2, A:A.1.3, A:A1.4, A:A1.5, A:A2.2, A:A2.3, A:A3.1, A:A3.2, A:A3.3, A:A3.4, A:A3.5, A:B1.1, A:B1.2, A:B1.3, A:B1.4, A:B1.5, A:B2.1, A:B2.2, A:B2.3, A:B2.5, A:B2.6, A:B2.7, A:C1.1, A:C1.3, A:C1.5, A:C1.6, PS-A1.1, PS-A1.3, PS-A1.4, PS-A1.10, PS-A2.2., PS-A2.6, PS-A2.7, PS-B1.1, PS-B1.3, PS-B1.5, PS-B1.9, PS-B1.10, PS-B1.11, PS-B1.12

    ASCA Domain Standard: Academic, personal/social

Type of Activity to be Delivered in What Manner: half-hour meeting with each ninth-grade LEP/ESL student and parents or guardians once per semester to discuss educational performance and planning

Resources Needed: 4-year plans, LEP plans

Projected Number of Students Impacted: 94

Evaluation Method: percent of parent/student attendance for conferences

Project Start/End: 10/2004–3/2005

Results Data: 88 percent of ESL parents attended their child's individual conference— 83/94 attended

2. *Target group*: Minority students in rigorous courses

   Target group selection is based upon the following criteria: percent in honors and AP

   Data that drove this decision: low enrollment of minority students in AP English III

   Counselor: Dean of Student Services

   Target group: Members of student group with one or more Fs during high school who agreed to spend time after school to get help for academics and to prepare for college

   Standards, competencies and indicators addressed: A:A1, A:A2, A:A3, A:B1, A:B2, A:C1, C:C1.1, PS:A1, PS:A2, PS:B1

   Type of service delivered: facilitate monthly workshops with guest speakers on self-esteem, leadership, cultural code switching for survival, college visits to WSSU, NCSU, NCCU, UNCW, facilitate development and performance of Black History program, facilitate parent meetings that focus on course registration, graduation requirements

   Start/end dates: 9/04–05/05

   Number of students affected: 52

   Perception data: 15 members participated in the WSSU trip, 8 participated in the NCSU trip, and 22 participated in the UNC-CH trip, 98 percent of members participate in the monthly workshops. Other data in progress.

   Results data: 45 parents attended parent meeting; 22 responded to survey; 45 percent were not aware of credits their son/daughter already earned or courses and number of credits needed for graduation prior to the meeting, 40 percent knew nothing or little about the student information database and how to access it prior to the meeting; after the meeting 100 percent reported they knew how to access the database and knew the number of credits already earned and courses still needed for their son/daughter; other data in progress

   Implications: Parent involvement, knowledge and participation in academic planning will be vital to student success. Monthly workshops are better attended than college tours. What other motivational strategies can be used for the students?

Leadership, Advocacy, Systemic Change, and Collaboration

Leadership.   The Counseling and Student Services Department's involvement in leadership activities at Wakefield High School has positive effects for Wakefield's students. The counselors serve in many leadership roles throughout the infrastructure of the high school.

The school counselors currently are involved with the Student Support Team, the Graduation Requirements Committee, the At-Risk Committee, the National Honor Society and Honors Committees, the School Improvement Team, the Scholarship Committee, the Ninth-Grade Academy, the Leadership Team, and the Administrative Team. Through their involvement in these committees and groups, the school counselors are able to contribute to schoolwide decisions and to consistently advocate for students.

The school counselors are assuming a leadership role with the 2005–2006 registration process. Each counselor is meeting with her assigned students in small groups to review graduation requirements, explain the registration process, review transcripts, and ensure that each student registers for the necessary courses to keep him or her on track for graduation. It is hoped that by meeting in small groups with the students, the counselor will be able to prevent many of the mistakes that students tend to make when registering without guidance.

The school counselors have also taken a leadership role in increasing minority student enrollment in AP courses. Beyond encouraging students who have performed well to move up to the higher AP course level, the counselors are working with the teachers to encourage them to identify students with the potential to succeed. The counselors noted that teachers had been hesitant to do so in fear that they would be held responsible if a student did not succeed. The counselors are advocating for the stance that until the students have a chance to participate in an AP class, they will not understand the amount of work and time necessary to succeed, and that this unknown may prevent the students from enrolling in the courses in the first place. The counselors and teachers are spending time with minority students sharing information about the courses and encouraging good work habits in the hopes of instilling the confidence needed to be successful in AP classes.

Advocacy. Advocacy efforts are infused throughout the work of the Counseling and Student Services Department at Wakefield High School. The SAP counselor conducts a needs assessment to help target small group efforts toward the specific needs identified by the students. The school counselors have conducted outreach efforts to inform and update parents on the student assistance activities of the SAP program. Recently, the school counselors held an off-campus parent meeting for parents of retained ninth graders, in the hopes that this would make it easier for parents to attend. Unfortunately, attendance was very low and the school counselors are now seeking ways to allow the parents to communicate more directly how they would like to maintain involvement in their children's educational and social development, while concurrently persisting in the message of how important this involvement is for the students.

Advocacy is also evident in the Counseling and Student Services Department efforts to increase minority enrollment in AP courses and to increase the involvement of ESL students' parents. Beyond their own targeted programs, the school counselors are also encouraging faculty and administration to promote advanced courses to eligible students. The school counselors are now holding quarterly meetings with the parents of minority students to increase minority parent involvement in the life of the school and to keep them informed of pertinent information.

Systemic Change. The push for greater minority student enrollment in AP courses is a prime example of the Counseling and Student Services Department's efforts to enact systemic change that makes a positive difference in student achievement. Because this as an approved goal with a written action plan, the school counselors are devoting their energies to making a change in the way teachers, students, and parents think about AP courses. Promoting systemic change can also be seen in the Counseling and Student Services Department's implementation of the ASCA National Model that is included as a part of Wakefield High School's school improvement plan. This has resulted in a high level of support from faculty for the Counseling and Student Services Department to be more student-centered and to follow national guidelines for comprehensive school counseling programs.

Collaboration.   The counselors in the Counseling and Student Services Department engage in many collaborative activities to facilitate positive change in students. The SAP counselor often has representatives from community agencies share information or facilitate group meetings. School Business Alliance members help with the retained ninth-grader group on career development and work readiness topics. Some universities and colleges have held onsite admissions meetings with students in addition to the regular attendance of college representatives to share information with potential applicants. College and military representatives participated in a Junior Parent Post-Secondary Opportunities Night organized through Student Services. The career development counselor also works to pull in representatives from community businesses and training programs for the Friday Fairs available for students to see the kinds of careers that exist in different occupational cluster areas.

◆ CONCLUSION

The counselors at Wakefield High School feel that planning their Counseling and Student Services program around the ASCA National Model has resulted in increased accountability for the counselors and the program. The counselors spend time critically reviewing their roles as school counselors and how they make a difference. In their opinion, it has positively changed how others in the school community understand who they are and what they do. In many ways, they feel that they are busier now than they were before the change to the National Model but that their work is part of a larger program and that they are doing fewer "Random Acts of Counseling and Guidance." In their National Model implementation efforts, the counselors at Wakefield High School put an increased focus on accountability and communication with others about what they are doing. They feel this has resulted in their services being requested more often by all members of their school community.

While the counselors are currently planning on a year-to-year basis, with current planning focusing primarily on the needs of the Ninth-Grade Academy at Wakefield High School, the counselors are moving through their implementation of the National Model toward an evolving and dynamic preventative and responsive program. Toward this end and in recognition that faculty perception of the Counseling and Student Services Department is critical to their ability to be effective in sparking systemic change, the counselors implemented a faculty survey to gauge the faculty's attitudes and impressions of the department. The initial results, while primarily positive, did indicate a desire among faculty for greater involvement of the department in the registration process and in addressing the needs of minority students at the school. The counselors were able to incorporate these messages into their goals and efforts.

The following statement from the Counseling and Student Services Department's RAMP application reflection statement effectively summarizes who they are and where they are headed:

> The Wakefield High School Student Services Department effectively uses advocacy, leadership, systemic change, and collaboration to promote positive differences in the student body. Though there is always room for improvement, and the department constantly self-evaluates and looks for ways to more effectively assist students, the existing program is highly functional and student-centered. Each counselor in this department brings her unique talents to the aid of Wakefield students, and together this team provides a school counseling program that addresses the whole child—personally, academically, and career-based.

CASE STUDY REVISITED ◆ Integration

High school counselors need to be able to work with students who bring more adult-like qualities to the table (the operative term is adult-LIKE). Often, adult physical size belies youthful vulnerability. What would you say to Misha about her situation? Would you advise her to work it out, or to find something at the elementary level that she loves? After reading this chapter and thinking about what a model CSCP in the high school involves, what about this level appeals to you? What concerns you about this level?

Student Services Activity Timeline (dates are approximate)

Month	Dates	Activities/Programs
August	3	Dean's meeting
	4	Department meeting
	9	Parent Orientation
	10–12	Freshman Camp/New Student Orientation
	11	SAM drop/add training
	20	PTSA Newsletter deadline
	22	High Five—High School Convocation
	22	Start historical data
	24	Department meeting
	31	Teaching Fellows meeting
September	1	Senior Night
	2–29	Senior interviews
	6	PSAT info to juniors
	7–19	PSAT registration
	9	Morehead nominations due
	12	Department meeting
	13	College board meeting
	16	Park Scholarship nominations due
	18	College Fair
	19	Faculty meeting
	20	Morehead interviews
	22	Official rank for seniors due

Student Services Activity Timeline (Continued)

Month	Dates	Activities/Programs
	23	National Model Level III training
	26	Teachers submit names for conferencing
	26	Governor's School process begins
	27	Teaching Fellows interest meeting
	30	Phonemaster to parents for conference
October	1–31	Groups (grief/loss, anger management, newcomers, post-hurricane support groups)
	1	Park nominations due
	3–8	Schedule evening conferences
	3	Morehead applications due
	3–4	Professional Learning Communities (PLC) conference
	5	Dean's meeting
	5	Homebuilder's Scholarship luncheon
	10	Faculty meeting
	10	Parent/student/teacher conferences
	11	Senior workshop—resume and essays
	12	Senior workshop—choosing a college
	12	PSAT
	17–21	Extended hours for senior assistance
	17	Department meeting
	20	Closing-the-gap parent meeting
	24	Department meeting
	26	Teaching Fellows writing sample
	26–28	NCSCA Fall Conference
November	1–30	Small groups: anger management, newcomers, post-hurricane support, grief and loss
	2	ASVAB/Teaching Fellows interviews/deans' meeting
	7–18	Junior English class small groups
	7	Northern Regional High School meeting
	8	Potential senior failures inquiry
	8–9	ECU onsite admissions
	9	Deadline to submit National Model plan
	10	Failure letters to parents
	15	Campbell University onsite admissions
	15	Early graduate financial aid interviews
	21–30	Signs of suicide awareness via health/PE classes
	28	Department meeting
	28–30	Freshman English class small groups
	29	Early graduate meeting

(*continued*)

Student Services Activity Timeline (Continued)

Month	Dates	Activities/Programs
December	1	Signs of suicide program
	1–9	Freshman English class small groups
	7	Deans' meeting
	8	Closing-the-gap parent meeting/Business Alliance
	12–22	Sophomore English class small groups
	19	Advisory council meeting
January	4	Deans' meeting
	9	Department meeting
	11	High school registration meeting/Career Club
	12	Business Alliance
	1–31	Restart classes/midyear promotions
	1–31	Schedule adjustments for second semester
	17	PSAT Interpretation Night/Heritage Middle School visit
	23	Early graduate rehearsal
	24	Early graduation ceremony
	30	Financial aid night
	31	Last day for student schedule change request/report cards
February	1	Deans' meeting/failure letters
	2	Middle school counselor registration breakfast
	2	Job shadowing/Meet the Teacher Night
	3	Friday Fair
	6–28	Preregistration small group meetings
	6	WCPSS counselor celebration
	6–17	AP exam registration
	8	Getting Off to a Fresh Start Program/Career Club
	9	Business Alliance
	10	Friday Fair
	16	Closing-the-gap parent meeting
	17	Friday Fair
	24	Friday Fair
March	1–10	Preregistration small groups
	1	Dean's meeting
	3	Interim reports/Friday Fair
	6–14	AP exam registration
	8	Career Club
	9	Business Alliance
	10	Friday Fair

Student Services Activity Timeline (Continued)

Month	Dates	Activities/Programs
	14	Open House/Curriculum Fair
	15	Visit to Heritage Middle
	16	Wakefield Middle drop-in for parents
	17	Department meeting/Friday Fair
	21	Junior/Sophomore Night
	22	Department meeting
	23	Wake Forest Middle drop-in for parents
	24	Friday Fair/end of quarter
April	5	Pyramid of intervention workshop
	6–12	Course registration
	11	Final senior GPA and rank for honors/report cards
	12	Career Club/failure letters to parents
	13	Business Alliance
	17–28	Junior English small groups
	27	Closing-the-gap parent meeting
	28	Son/daughter to work day
May	3	Dean's meeting
	4	Department meeting
	1–18	AP exams
	12	Interims
	1–11	Sophomore English class small groups
	15	Advisory Council meeting
	15–26	Freshman English class small groups
June	7–9	Final exams
	12	Promotions/retentions
	10	Graduation
	20	Final transcripts sent to colleges

REFERENCES

About Wake County—Geographic facts. (n.d.). Retrieved January 18, 2006, from http://www.wakegov.com/about/geography.htm.

US Census Bureau—State and County Quickfacts. (n.d.). Retrieved January 18, 2006, from http://quickfacts.census.gov/qfd/states/37/37183.html.

Wake County planning, land use and zoning—economy. (n.d.). Retrieved January 18, 2006, from http://www.wakegov.com/planning/demographic/dd_Economy.htm.

Wake County planning, land use and zoning—education. (n.d.). Retrieved January 18, 2006, from http://www.wakegov.com/planning/demographic/dd_Education.htm.

Wake County planning, land use and zoning—population. (n.d.). Retrieved January 18, 2006, from http://www.wakegov.com/planning/demographic/dd_Population.htm.

SECTION SIX

Developing a K–12 Perspective on Professional Issues

CHAPTER

14

MORAL, ETHICAL, AND LEGAL ISSUES IN SCHOOL COUNSELING

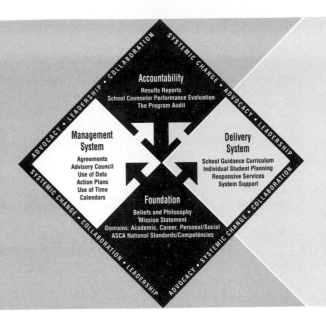

◆ LEARNING OBJECTIVES

By the end of this chapter, you will

1. understand the source of our moral standards for counseling
2. understand the relationship between those moral standards and the ethical statements of counseling
3. understand the importance of knowing the Code of Ethics and Standards of Practice of the American Counseling Association
4. be able to identify the major components in the Ethical Standards for School Counselors of the American School Counselor Association (Appendix A)
5. understand the laws that pertain to school counseling
6. understand and apply a model of ethical decision making
7. be familiar with several common ethical dilemmas in school counseling
8. understand the importance of professional insurance and certification
9. be familiar with and able to implement a plan of action for responding to legal action
10. be familiar with several resources from which to obtain information in the event of future ethical dilemmas
11. know several strategies for practicing in the most ethical manner possible

DOMAINS / ACTIVITIES / PARTNERS MODEL

	Academic Development ▼	Career Development ▼	Personal/ Social Development ▼			
Counseling	1a	1b	1c	5	6	7
Educating and Advocacy	2a	2b	2c	8	9	10
Consulting	3a	3b	3c	11	12	13
Leadership and Coordination	4a	4b	4c	14	15	16
	Students			Parents and Caregivers	Colleagues in Schools	Colleagues in Community

ACTIVITIES (vertical label on left)

DOMAINS (bracket over first three columns)

PARTNERS IN THE PROCESS

CASE STUDY ◆ Jason's Casual Comment

Jason was flying through his advising appointments, proud that he had been on schedule all day. His 305-student roster was almost done; the principal would be happy that the counselors had been able to schedule all 1,213 high school students in the three weeks they were given. The computer hadn't crashed once so far this year, and with luck, he was keeping to his 10-minute scheduling appointments like clockwork. He knew that the director of their counseling program was trying to move the scheduling part of this process to the secretaries in the office, but until then, he was content to do as he was asked. At least it gave him time every year to talk with every one of his assigned students.

Two o'clock, and he was almost done for the day. He'd been on a roll all day, his energy high. "OK, Kim, right? How are you? It's been a long time since we last talked. Do you have your schedule ready?"

Kim was a quiet, withdrawn girl, very petite for her age. She was a sophomore this year, making average grades. She was one of those students who faded into the background in class, in the hallways, in the lunchroom. Jason never saw her in the halls talking to anyone; she was always alone. He wondered why she worked so hard at being invisible. He looked at her file while she came in and sat down.

"I've got a problem, Mr. Whitney," she mumbled, "but I'm not sure who to talk to. I don't want this getting around school."

Jason was thinking about her schedule, and offhandedly said, "Well, you can tell me. You know I won't tell your friends."

"Ok, then. I've been doing some things with my boyfriend that I'm not really proud of, but I don't know how to make it stop without losing him."

Jason's head snapped out of the file when he realized what she had said. "Oh, Kim, I don't know that I can keep that a secret. There are laws about reporting the sexual activity of minors, and your parents should...."

"No way! Forget it then! You said you wouldn't tell, just now, you said you wouldn't tell! You lied! I'm out of here."

"Don't go, we need to talk about this!"

"No, there's nothing to say. Nothing. I'll deny I said anything. I'll make another appointment to work on my schedule. I'm feeling sick and want to go home. Don't make me puke on your rug to prove it." She looked at him with contempt, grabbed her bookbag, and left.

All he could do was watch her leave. It was going to take him hours to straighten out this mess, and he didn't know if he could ever make it right with Kim. If he reported as he was supposed to do, she would deny everything, she would never trust another counselor, and things could get much more difficult for her all around. If he honored her wishes and didn't report, he could get into legal trouble involving the school, her parents, and heaven knows what else. So much for being on time.

CHALLENGE QUESTIONS

There are a variety of internal and external factors that contributed to Jason's problem. Based on your best estimate, what were the internal factors—things about Jason's personality—that affected his actions? What were the external factors?

What is the ethical dilemma? What are Jason's competing concerns?

Reread the scenario. Did Jason jump to a conclusion about what is happening with the boyfriend? Are there other interpretations of her words? What if he reports she is sexually active, only to find out that she wasn't talking about sex at all?

Does Jason have options in ways to proceed? What are those options? Are there ways to address all his concerns? What are they?

What would you do?

◆ SCHOOL COUNSELING AND ETHICS

Counseling graduate students often ask, "How will I know what to do in an ethical dilemma?" And the only answer is, "It depends on what's important to you." A dilemma only exists when there are two or more equally compelling priorities confronting you. You have to know your professional ethics, relevant federal, state, and local laws, and the policies of your district and building, but this is only part of the whole picture. The missing pieces of the puzzle involve obtaining current information, knowing your professional priorities, and knowing how to think through the dilemma. The puzzle, when assembled, reveals a holistic picture of ethical counseling:

1. You have to know ethics, laws, policies and procedures that pertain to your students very well.
2. You have to know how to get more information about current issues, laws, and expert advice.
3. You have to know your own professional priorities.
4. You have to know a process by which you can factor these elements together.

The ASCA School Counselor Performance Standards are silent on this issue, but many standards addressing "positive relationships" may indirectly be considered to address ethical behavior as a professional school counselor.

The CACREP Standards for School Counseling Programs addressed in this chapter are

A.6 current issues, policies, laws, and legislation relevant to school counseling;

A.10 ethical and legal considerations related specifically to the practice of school counseling (e.g., the ACA Code of Ethics and the ASCA Ethical Standards for School Counselors).

In this chapter, we will address all these topics.

In terms of ethics, the school setting is unique in many ways. Because school counselors work with minors, they must have an awareness of the rights of parents and legal guardians. Furthermore, because schools are highly regulated and legislated, counselors must have a sharp awareness of federal, state, and local laws; court decisions; state regulations; and school board policies. (For a detailed discussion of the sources of laws relative to school counselors, see Schmidt, 2003, Chapter 11.) In addition, school counselors must continually update their knowledge about each of these topics, because ignorance of the law is no excuse. This is not to suggest that counselors must become lawyers in order to practice counseling. The point is to know where to go when you have questions about your practice.

This chapter could easily be a course by itself. It is important to note that the discussion in this chapter is not intended to be your only exposure to ethics; you should take additional course(s) in ethics, read in the professional literature about ethics, and be open to professional development opportunities (workshops, conferences) that address contemporary issues and changes in ethics, because ethical statements are regularly revised by professional associations. In this chapter, we will focus on ethical issues that are most relevant to school counselors. Let's begin with a discussion of the source of our ethics: morals and values.

◆ THE MORAL VISION OF COUNSELING: OUR VALUES

Counseling as a profession has evolved a set of moral guidelines that shape our ethics and in some cases, has resulted in the passage of laws to protect clients and the public (Christopher, 1996). The moral guidelines come from a shared set of assumptions about the therapeutic conditions that facilitate human development—those underlying assumptions of human nature as articulated in theories of counseling.

Everything we do is predicated on the satisfaction of needs, as filtered through our values. These values are interlocking systems of meaning and of significance, providing us with the foundation of our choices; we value one thing more than another, so we choose actions that provide us with what we value. These values are interwoven with our views of the world and provide the structure for defining good, bad, healthy, and unhealthy.

Christopher (1996) argued that, in Western culture, "good" is defined as authenticity, autonomy, and individualism. Counseling as a whole emphasizes self-actualization, self-esteem, autonomy, assertiveness, internal locus of evaluation and control, self-acceptance, and individuation. From this tradition, it is possible to ascertain the source of the counseling values of beneficence (doing good), nonmaleficence (doing no harm), justice (fairness), autonomy (independent decision making), and fidelity (being true to one's word) (Hall & Lin, 1995; Herlihy & Corey, 1996).

It is important to note, however, that not everyone subcribes to this Western values system. In many multicultural traditions, "good" is defined in terms of collectivism, in which the self is viewed in terms of the referent group (family, neighborhood, and culture). In this tradition, emotional maturity is defined in terms of one's ability to uphold one's duty to family, maintain harmony, and demonstrate sensitivity to others' feelings. A person's self-worth comes from the ability to excel in social roles (Christopher, 1996). From this tradition, counseling has now added a sixth value: context and systems awareness.

Since our values shape our choices, we must think about how our values shape our therapeutic choices. As counselors, we promote what we believe helps the client make healthy choices and we discourage what we believe to be unhealthy choices. If we believe that individuation helps clients to make healthy, independent choices, we will encourage clients to individuate, to make choices independent from the undue influence of others. However, if we are not sensitive to non-Western values systems, it would be easy to push a client to make independent choices that could ultimately alienate the client from his or her social and cultural support system, which may not be in the client's best interest overall.

It is important to see that our personal value system and our professional value system will affect our choices as counselors. Students have said, "Then this means that I must not have any values when I'm counseling," as if they could become values-neutral, somehow negating all their values as they counsel. This is not possible, and if it were possible, it is not beneficial. Our values are the essence of our humanity, and we can't, nor would we ever want to, negate that which makes us most human. To do so would negate the very thing that makes us effective counselors. Consider this metaphor. Our values are like a hearing aid that we wear. We attend to the world better as a result of the hearing aid, because it gives us access to the messages that are important to us. But for many, this hearing aid is tuned to only amplify certain frequencies, allowing us to hear only some messages and not others. We don't want to take off the hearing aid altogether—we want to broaden the frequency setting so that we can hear all messages. Rather than strive to become values-neutral (taking off the hearing aid), counselors should examine their values and attempt to make them as broad as possible (tune it to hear as many frequencies as possible), to acknowledge the wide range of various value systems that exist in the world.

According to Christopher (1996), awareness of our personal and professional values and morals leads us to examine our assumptions. Because different moral visions and values exist, we must be able to see the greater common moral strands that bind us together, such as truth, honesty, and the Golden Rule ("Do unto others as you would have done unto you"). Counselors must acknowledge cultural embeddedness and must seek to clarify and question their moral vision. Furthermore, we must ascertain how our moral vision affects our work as counselors and engage in critical dialogue about moral visions and values.

When we examine our values, we become aware of how these values shape our work as counselors. It is only with this continual examination that we are able to truly help our clients to find their own life-path, because we can see how our values might interfere with the values of the client. For example, rather than simply assume that individuation is the best way for clients to grow and develop, we must question that assumption and jointly explore the client's view of individuation and potential isolation from cultural supports. As we mature in our ability to see our value system and explore the value system of the client, we become more effective counselors. It is easy to see why we need a deep understanding of our professional ethics; this is the instrument by which we protect the client from harm.

Reflection Moment ✦

How would you prioritize the six professional values just presented? Rank order them: beneficence, nonmaleficence, justice, fidelity, autonomy, and context and systems awareness. Now justify the rankings. Hard, isn't it?

✦ ✦

◆ THE ETHICS OF THE PROFESSION

In general, ethics statements are the codification of our shared professional values. They function like curbs on the road; they define the limits of our practice, but within these limits, there is room to express individual preferences in how we practice the art and science of counseling. Some ethical statements mandate those activities that the profession deems essential for every counseling relationship (respecting the dignity of the client, fostering the client's positive growth and development, involving the family when appropriate, etc.). Other ethical statements define those activities that the profession deems inappropriate for every counseling relationship (engaging in dual relationships, seeking to meet personal needs, sexual intimacies, etc.). Between the "right" and the "wrong" are immeasurable shades of ambiguous gray. There is no such thing as perfectly ethical practice, and school counselors will be challenged to deal with this ambiguity as will every other counselor.

You will see that the values of the counseling profession are made operational in the codes of ethics (the Code of Ethics of the American Counseling Association [ACA, 2005] are available at www.counseling.org/Resources/CodeOfEthics/TP/Home/CT2.aspx). Several examples will help to illustrate this point. For example, the value of beneficence (do good) is found in the directive to foster the client's positive growth and development, and the value of nonmaleficence (do no harm) is seen in the directives prohibiting discrimination, meeting personal needs at the expense of the client, dual relationships, and sexual intimacies. Justice is addressed in the ethical provisions involving appropriate fees and advertising for clients. The value of autonomy is addressed in the ACA Code's provisions addressing freedom of choice, informed consent, respecting differences, personal values, and confidentiality. The profession's value of fidelity is manifest in the Code's provisions for disclosure to clients, clear communication with other therapists serving clients, and responsibilities to multiple clients. Finally, the newest value, that of context and systems-awareness, is visible in the directive to involve the family as appropriate, the responsibility to provide socially beneficial pro-bono services, and the responsibility to inform a third person about a contagious, fatal disease.

In general, clients have three rights: the right to information, the right to choose, and the right to privacy (Herlihy & Corey, 1996). Under the right to information, clients have the right to have information about what the counselor is going to do, how it will work, any limitations to the counseling approach, any risks inherent in counseling, and the limits of confidentiality. The second right is the right to choose (e.g., the right to engage in or terminate counseling and the right to make personal choices). The counselor will respect the dignity and autonomy of the client to choose what is in the client's best interest, free from the values of the counselor. The third right is the right to privacy, which involves two issues: privileged communication and confidentiality.

Privileged communication is a legal concept protecting the content of therapy sessions from compelled testimony in court that must be spelled out in state statute (Herlihy & Corey, 1996). Most states do *not* name counselors as under the protection of privileged communication. On the other hand, confidentiality is both an ethical and legal concept, addressing the commitment of the counselor to keep confidential what is shared in counseling within the prescribed limits. These limitations to confidentiality must be disclosed as part of informed consent and will be discussed in detail later in this chapter. It is important to note at this point that in all states school counselors are mandated reporters in cases of suspected child abuse and/or neglect. This mandate is a higher professional priority than confidentiality (Remley & Herman, 2000).

Codes of Ethics

Both the American Counseling Association (ACA) and the American School Counselor Association (ASCA) have codified standards of ethical practice. The American Counseling Association (ACA) (2005) has defined a Code of Ethics document that outlines the guidelines of the counseling profession as a whole. This document spells out prescribed and prohibited behavior in terms of the general counseling profession. All counselors, regardless of the setting in which they work, must be familiar with the Code of Ethics. As noted, this is available online. The Ethical Standards for School Counselors authored by the American School Counselor Association (Appendix A) is not an optional set of standards; it is required of all school counselors. In addition, when you provide group counseling you must know and abide by the ethics of the Association for Specialists in Group Work (ASGW); you can find their Best Practices document (1998) at www.asgw.org/best.htm. And because you will be working with students in terms of their career development, you must also follow the code of ethics for the National Career Development Association (NCDA); you can obtain their Ethical Standards (2003) from their webpage at www.ncda.org/pdf/Ethical-Standards.pdf. You must follow the ACA, ASCA, ASGW, and NCDA ethical codes; a process for working through dilemmas that arise due to conflicting directives in these documents will be addressed later in this chapter. However, for the purpose of this book we will focus on the ACA and ASCA codes.

The ASCA Ethical Standards for School Counselors (2004) is presented in its entirety in Appendix A. As you can see, the Ethical Standards document begins with an important preamble that outlines fundamental beliefs and values of the American School Counselor Association (ASCA, 2004). In the first section, it addresses responsibilities to students in terms of priorities, confidentiality, counseling plans, dual relationships, referrals, group work, danger to self or others as a limitation of confidentiality, student records (counseling notes), issues of assessment, technology, and peer helper programs. The next section addresses responsibilities to parents/guardians, described in terms of parents' rights and confidentiality. The third section outlines the counselor's responsibilities to colleagues and professional associates, specifically addressing professional relationships and the appropriate sharing of information.

Next, the Ethical Standards address the counselor's responsibilities to the school and the community in terms of protecting the welfare of the school and the comprehensive school counseling program, addressing conditions that infringe on the effectiveness of the counselor, as well as providing a mandate to collaborate with agencies, organizations, and individuals to deliver a comprehensive school counseling program. In the section addressing responsibilities to self, the Standards discuss professional competence and mandatory multicultural skills. In the section addressing responsibilities to the profession, the Standards outline appropriate behavior in terms of adhering to the ASCA Ethical Standards and Position Statements, professionalism, and research. Furthermore, professional school counselors are expected to contribute to the profession through membership in professional associations, sharing expertise with others, and mentoring new counselors. Finally, procedures for addressing the unethical conduct of colleagues is outlined.

As mentioned, you need to know the ethical expectations of both ACA and ASCA, as well as for ASGW and NCDA. As these documents are continually updated and revised, you would be wise to download and print all these ethical codes, keeping them close at hand for your personal review and reflection. It is easy to lose sight of the nuances of ethics in the busy crush of the day. For easy reference, you can obtain the Ethics from the following websites:

American Counseling Association: www.counseling.org/Resources/CodeOfEthics/TP/Home/CT2.aspx

American School Counseling Association

Ethical Standards: www.schoolcounselor.org/content.asp?contentid=173

Position Statements: www.schoolcounselor.org/content.asp?pl=127&sl=178&contentid=178

Association for Specialists in Group Work: www.asgw.org/best.htm

National Career Development Association: www.ncda.org/pdf/EthicalStandards.pdf

◆ LEGAL ISSUES

Legal issues of school counselors become more involved as the student matures toward the age of majority. With attainment of the age of 18 years, the student becomes autonomous in the eyes of the law and is vested with adult status (Remley & Herman, 2000). This is an important milestone in terms of the legal relationships in general and in terms of relationships with the school in particular.

One of the most important laws is the Family Educational Rights and Privacy Act (FERPA) of 1974, also known as the Buckley Amendment (Remley & Herman, 2000) and its recent modifications in the Grassley Amendment (Sealander, Schwiebert, Oren, & Weekley, 1999). In this legislation, schools receiving federal funds must provide access to all school records to parents of minor students and to the students themselves after they reach the age of 18. Parents and adult students have the right to challenge information in the records (Schmidt, 1999). Schools are prohibited from releasing records to any third party without the parents' written consent (for a minor) or the adult student's written consent.

Confidentiality of the records and protection of the identity of any persons receiving drug or alcohol abuse treatment are guaranteed by the Drug Abuse Office and Treatment Act of 1976 (Sealander, Schwiebert, Oren, & Weekley, 1999). In middle and high schools, this act is important to know because it applies to "all records relating to the identity, diagnosis, prognosis, or treatment of any student involved in any federally assisted substance abuse program" (Sealander, Schwiebert, Oren, & Weekley, 1999, p. 124). This would suggest that the counseling records of any students participating in substance use programs maintained by *any* organization receiving federal funds would need to be given greater protection than other counseling records; the information is protected even from the student's parents (under applicable state law). According to Sealander and colleagues (1999), the Drug Abuse Office and Treatment Act

> protects any information about a youth if the youth has received alcohol and/or drug related services of any kind including school-based identification. . . . When a teacher, counselor, or other school professional identifies student behaviors that could indicate a drug and/or alcohol problem, they can discuss this with the student or other school personnel. However, from the time an evaluation is conducted and/or a student assistance program begins alcohol or drug related counseling, the federal regulations are in effect. (pp. 126–127)

Awareness of this law is essential because it raises issues related to the appropriate and legal release of records and information about whether the student is receiving services.

Another legal area with which you must be familiar is legislation pertaining to the reporting of suspected child abuse or neglect (Remley & Herman, 2000; Schmidt, 2003). The definition of abuse or neglect generally includes physical and sexual abuse, psychological and emotional torment, abandonment, and inadequate supervision. School counselors are mandated reporters of suspected abuse, meaning that counselors are not responsible for investigating the allegations, but must report when there is reason to suspect abuse or neglect (Schmidt, 2003; Sealander, Schwiebert, Oren, & Weekley, 1999). You must obtain a copy of your state legislation and become familiar with its provisions, because these will vary widely from state to state. Procedures for reporting, who must report, and when the report must be made are important variables you must know. In addition, there may be school or district procedures for reporting; for example, the district may require all reports to be made by one designated individual. Reporting to this individual, however, does not absolve you of your legal responsibility to act to protect a child (Tompkins & Mehring, 1993). You must follow up to ensure that the report has been made.

Special education legislation has been increasingly important as instances of lawsuits increase. The Americans with Disabilities Act, the Individuals with Disabilities Act (Public Law 101-476), the Education for All Handicapped Children Act (Public Law 94-142), and Section 504 of the Rehabilitation Act of 1973 all address the rights of children to free and appropriate education and services (Erk, 1999; Schmidt, 2003). Counselors must be informed about these laws, because educational services for students are often coordinated with counseling services. Furthermore, as advocates for all students, counselors can educate others (students, parents, colleagues) about rights and responsibilities under the law (Erk, 1999; Schmidt, 2003).

Finally, Title IX of the Education Amendments of 1972 protects students against discrimination on the basis of sex, marital status, or pregnancy (Schmidt, 2003). This legislation guarantees equal access to educational programs, extracurricular activities (such as sports), and occupational opportunities. This law is also the foundation of the sexual harassment guidelines making student-on-student cross-sex and same-sex harassment a violation of the victim's civil rights, and as such, mandates that harassment be reported to school officials who have the responsibility to take appropriate action (Stone, 2000). As advocates for students and monitors of school policies and programs, counselors are in a unique position to address conditions or situations in the school that are discriminatory.

◆ MORAL/ETHICAL DECISION-MAKING PROCESS

Most ethical decisions are easy. You perform your job duties in a manner that is consistent with the ethics of ACA and ASCA, with the laws of your state, and with the policies of your school and your district. But what if those directives conflict with each other? How do you choose which of those to follow?

Ethical dilemmas are never easy; that's why they are called dilemmas. However, with a decision-making model, you can structure this decision-making process in a way that is professionally accepted. This means that if you are ever required to explain your decision to parents, school administrators, or legal representatives, you have followed a procedure that is supported by others in your profession.

One model is adapted from Herlihy and Corey (1996). In this model, there are seven steps:

1. Identify the problem, obtaining as much information as possible. Do not look for a simplistic solution. If it concerns a legal issue, obtain legal advice.
2. Apply the ACA Code of Ethics as well as the ASCA Ethical Standards for School Counselors.
3. Determine the nature and dimensions of the dilemma, considering the moral principles, reviewing the professional literature, consulting with professional colleagues and supervisors, and contacting state and national professional associations to obtain other perspectives.
4. Generate potential courses of action.
5. Consider the potential consequences of all actions and determine a course of action. In this step, you are looking for a solution or combinations of actions that best fit the situation and accomplish the priorities you have established.
6. Evaluate the selected course of action to determine if it is fair, if it would be an action you would want reported in the press, and if you would recommend the same actions to another counselor.
7. Implement the course of action.

An alternative model is that adapted from Stadler (1985). Before applying this model, Stadler suggests that you think through the following questions:

◆ What is legal? Do laws address this situation? If so, what are they?
◆ What is the policy of my employer?
◆ What is balanced for everyone involved that will promote a win/win for everyone's needs?
◆ How will I feel about myself if this becomes public knowledge? How will I feel if my family finds out about my choice?

If at the answer does not become clear in that analysis, you implement the following four-step process.

Step 1: Identify competing moral principles that apply to the dilemma. This grounds you in the values of the profession. For review, these values are
1. Nonmaleficence—do no harm
2. Beneficence—promote good
3. Autonomy—promote self-determination
4. Justice—be fair; promote fairness
5. Fidelity—be faithful; keep promises
6. Context and systems awareness

Step 2: Implement moral reasoning strategy. This step consists of several substeps and directives.
1. Secure additional information about the situation, your professional standards related to the situation, any laws that pertain to this situation, and any special circumstances surrounding this situation.
2. Secure additional information about the situation. Determine who has the information and what the procedures and processes would be for obtaining that information. Is informed consent required? Is a court order required? Obtain all needed information.
3. Rank the moral principles you identified from Step 1. This involves the application of your own individual professional judgment. Expect that all ethical dilemmas involve all of these values to some extent, so do not be alarmed when you discover that others would rank the principles differently.
4. Consult with colleagues to find out what they would do in your situation. Be sure to maintain confidentiality in this process.

Step 3: Prepare for action. This step also consists of several substeps.
1. Once you have ranked the moral principles and consulted with others, you have a direction from which you will further examine your decision. You will now identify hoped-for outcomes. What is the ideal situation for all parties involved?
2. Brainstorm actions that you believe will lead to these ideal outcomes. List all possibilities, no matter how remote.
3. Evaluate effects of all these possible actions on everyone involved. This means you must consider the student, other students, the student's family, the staff with whom you work, the profession of counseling in general and school

counseling in particular, the school, the community as a whole, yourself, and your family.

4. Much as we would like to believe that these decisions are grounded in the noble ideals of the profession, often these decisions are influenced by other emotions and concerns, such as power, prestige, reputation, fear of being sued, time constraints, poor time management, revenge, need for love, sexual attraction, and so on. At this stage, identify these competing issues and concerns that will influence your decision. Be honest with yourself. Discard optional actions that are primarily grounded in these issues and concerns.

5. With your prioritized values, consultation, self-awareness, and evaluation of actions, you will now choose a course of action that allows you to maximize benefits and reduce risks to everyone involved.

6. Before you act, you must test the action by considering all possible outcomes (intended or not) and all the possible problems that might occur as a result of your choice. Obtain more consultation if needed.

Step 4: At this stage, you are ready to act. To do this, you will

1. Strengthen your willpower, knowing that taking the action you have chosen may not be easy. Not everyone will agree with your decision. Stadler (1985) suggests
   a. maintain your focus on your higher purpose
   b. maintain pride in yourself and in your integrity
   c. have patience with the process and with the outcomes
   d. be persistent with your goals, confident that you are following the best course for all concerned
   e. maintain a balanced perspective in hearing feedback

2. Identify concrete steps necessary to take action.

3. Act.

4. Evaluate the effects of your actions and adjust as needed.

5. Attend to the moral traces that come as a result of your actions. This refers to the residual feelings of regret or pride that you feel as the effects of your actions become manifest. Would you do the same thing again in the future or would you make a different choice? Sometimes the best we can do is resolve to make a better choice in future situations. (Butler, 1993)

You will undoubtedly notice many consistencies between the two models just presented. Both models emphasize consultation, fairness, and careful consideration of all consequences. However, while the Herlihy and Corey (1996) model provides a reminder to consult with state and national professional associations, the Stadler (1985) model makes self-examination and self-awareness an explicit part of the process. Both of these actions are vital to appropriate ethical decision making. Consulting with state and national associations provides you with a broad view of what other professionals would do in your situation, reducing skewed perspectives as a result of local biases. Conducting a thorough and honest self-evaluation highlights your professional priorities and prevents selfish or selfserving motives from influencing your decision. Both the macro and micro levels of examination will help you maintain balance within your choices. We now turn to an examination of the nature of many of these choices.

Reflection Moment ◆

Think back to the last time you confronted an ethical choice. (Can't think of one? Think of a time when you had to resolve a conflict between two people you cared about: two children, two siblings, your parents, two friends in college. That is a similar situation.) What, specifically, did you do about it? How did you resolve it? How similar or dissimilar was your process from those outlined above?

◆ ◆

◆ COMMON LEGAL/ETHICAL PROBLEMS

Before you read this section of the chapter, reread the ACA Code of Ethics (available online as noted on p. 279) and the ASCA Ethical Standards for School Counselors (Appendix A). This section addresses some problematic issues for school counselors, but you will note that no definitive conclusions can be drawn about any of them. What is most appropriate to do in the face of any of these dilemmas depends on the context and your own professional priorities.

Confidentiality

It would be safe to say that the majority of dilemmas faced by school counselors involve confidentiality (Herlihy & Corey, 1996; Isaacs & Stone, 1999; Ledyard, 1998; Tompkins & Mehring, 1993). When confidentiality should be maintained, when confidentiality must be limited, how to communicate the concept of confidentiality, and how to secure the student's permission to disclose information are all highly legalized and problematic concerns.

In general, it is most helpful to think of confidentiality as the need to keep private the details of a counseling session, unless a compelling reason exists to reveal those details. In balance, however, both the ACA and ASCA urge counselors to involve parents and families in the counseling of minor children when appropriate. In addition, the ASCA Ethical Standards has an entire section of the ethics (Section B) titled Responsibilities to Parents/Guardians. This provides an excellent reminder to involve parents as appropriate while concurrently respecting the rights of the counselee. Remley and Herman (2000) issue a reminder that until a student reaches the age of 18, he or she is legally a minor and that, although your professional responsibilities are to minor clients, legal obligations exist to the parents' rights (p. 314). A parent invoking his or her parental rights does not compel revealing the details of counseling conversations, but in the role as advocate and consultant, counselors cannot be adamant in the refusal to share any information. The general advice is to empower students to find ways to share their struggles with their parents and to inform and consult with students before giving information to parents (ASCA Ethical Standards). It may also be possible to negotiate the request for information with the parent, so that the trust between the counselor and the student is preserved and the concerns of the parent are assuaged (Kaplan, 1996; Remley & Herman, 2000). Again, the general rule of thumb would be to share general information with parents rather than the details of your work with students. Only in the case of the Drug Abuse Office and Treatment Act of 1976 is information about the student not to be released, even to the parent (Sealander, Schwiebert, Oren, & Weekley, 1999). This may be modified, however, by state statute.

As cautious as you must be with confidentiality, there are still various legally mandated situations that require breach of confidentiality and should be revealed as a part of informed consent. These situations involve

1. Danger to self or others (disclosure is "required to protect clients or identified others from serious and foreseeable harm") (ACA, 2005, B.2.a)
2. Suspicions of child abuse or neglect (in other words, crimes against a child) (Remley & Herman, 2000; Sealander, Schwiebert, Oren, & Weekley, 1999)
3. When there is an emergency that requires information to protect the safety of the student and others (Sealander, Schwiebert, Oren, & Weekley, 1999)
4. When court ordered (Remley & Herman, 2000)
5. In cases of sexual harassment (Stone, 2000)
6. In some states, when there is sexual activity, discussions of abortion, or criminal activity on the part of the minor

State variations in these mandates provide another reminder that school counselors must know the laws of the state in which they are employed.

There are differences in the ways that school counselors perceive confidentiality, depending on the issue, the age of the student, and the amount of contact with concerned others in the school setting. In a study examining the differences among counselors in terms of confidentiality, Isaacs and Stone (1999) found that high school counselors would breach confidentiality less often than counselors at other levels, depending on the danger level of the student's activity and the age of the student. "Counselors tend to see serious drug use, abortion, use of crack cocaine, suicide intent, robbery, and sex with multiple partners as areas which are serious enough to warrant a breach of confidentiality, though less so at the high school level" (p. 265). The authors believe that high school counselors breach confidentiality less often from the view that as students mature, they develop the ability to make independent decisions and become "mature minors" (p. 265).

Furthermore, the issue of confidentiality becomes more diffuse the more contact the counselor has with concerned others. Specifically, school counselors work closely with teachers and administrators, many of whom are interested and concerned about the progress of students. Counselors are often tempted to share too much information in their desire to help students be successful; care must be taken to obtain the student's permission before revealing detailed information to school colleagues (Davis & Ritchie, 1993; Watson, 1990). In addition, school counselors need to function as a part of the school's multidisciplinary treatment team, often involving both in-district and nonschool personnel and specialists. In this setting also, confidentiality can be addressed by informing students in advance that information may be shared with the team on their behalf (Strein & Hershenson, 1991). To maintain the student's trust, however, it would be wise to secure the student's permission, and then to only share general information.

Rights of Parents and Informed Consent

Informed consent involves consent for counseling itself, as well as consent for services within the limits and conditions of counseling. Here again we see how parental rights influence the work counselors do with students. Even though parental permission for counseling is not required by law in most states, the legal ability of the student to consent for counseling itself might be an issue (Remley & Herman, 2000). While the law holds that the age of majority is 18, there have been indications that younger persons might be "capable of assuming responsibility for their rights" (Ledyard, 1998). This means that a *mature* minor might be able to give informed consent for counseling (Isaacs & Stone, 1999; Ledyard, 1998), but counselors should be aware that if parents insist that counseling be discontinued, they "*probably* have a legal right to have their wishes followed" (emphasis authors'; Remley & Herman, 2000, p. 315). Counselors are advised to follow their district's policy about obtaining parental consent for counseling; generally, the younger the client, the more careful schools are to obtain parental permission.

The second issue of informed consent involves the information that is shared with students about the limits of confidentiality. This issue involved two topics: the timing of the information about informed consent, and the ability of the student to understand these limitations due to developmental maturity. In terms of timing, Isaacs and Stone (1999) found that 98 percent of the high school counselors they studied responded that they inform students about the limits of confidentiality. What is troubling, however, is that they also found that 50 percent of these same counselors indicated they inform students of the limits of confidentiality *only at a time when the discussion turns to the topics that might have to be reported.* Both the ASCA Ethical Standards and the ACA Code of Ethics requires that information relative to the limits of confidentiality be discussed as the counseling relationship is initiated and throughout the counseling process as needed.

This is a challenge for elementary counselors, who may, by light of being present in hallways and playgrounds, be informed of confidential and private information about the student or the family in rather public places. To prevent such public family and self-disclosures, elementary counselors often share the role of the counselor, limits to confidentiality, and the meaning of counseling during classroom developmental curriculum presentations. These classroom presentations also provide counselors with the ability to find developmentally appropriate language to help young students understand these mature concepts.

For counselors at all levels, being respectful of the student's right to informed consent means that the limits of confidentiality are clearly explained to the student early in the counseling relationship, in developmentally appropriate terms.

Defining the "Client": Conflict of Interest between Student and School

Is the counselor foremost a *counselor* or an *employee*? There may be situations in which responsibility to students will conflict with responsibility to the school. While the ASCA Ethical Standards states that the counselor must inform officials of conditions that may be disruptive or damaging, this is couched in terms of concurrently honoring the confidentiality between the counselee and counselor. ACA directs counselors to establish clear agreements with employers about the conditions of the work but then also indicates that accepting employment implies that counselors agree with the employer's general policies and principles. If a school policy requires disclosure of confidential information, such as mandating that all employees report all suspicions of intoxicated students, the counselor could be caught in a dilemma. Issues of trust (How will students get help if they are afraid of getting into trouble?) as well as credibility (What if all the counselor has is an unsubstantiated rumor?) arise in such situations. What if the person spreading the rumor later recants the story, claiming that the report of an intoxicated student was revenge after a quarrel? Does the counselor still have to report? What if all attempts to change the policy are unsuccessful?

Kaplan and Allison (1994) would suggest that confidentiality with the student should be maintained, especially if the limits of confidentiality were not disclosed before the student shared the confidential information with the counselor. However, Remley and Herman (2000) indicate that school counselors must follow the rules, regulations, or policies of the school and the district, even while they work to get them changed. These authors argue that dismissal for insubordination could give you a forum to confront the employer's policy, but the burden of proof would be on you to show that the employer's policy was in violation of the standards of the profession and therefore unreasonable. They propose that educating the employer through information and persuasion would be a more collegial way to approach the situation. Notice in this discussion that even the authors in the field may disagree about the appropriate action to take, reinforcing the need for you to have a process by which you think through professional dilemmas as they arise.

Counselor Competence

Competence refers to skill areas in which you must be competent and skill areas in which you are not considered competent without additional, specialized training. Skills areas in which you must be competent include the foundation counseling skills, the ability to encourage client growth and development in ways that foster the client's interest and welfare, the ability to design collaborative counseling plans, and others. These are competencies implied in the Code of Ethics (ACA) and in the Ethical Standards (ASCA) in which the profession defines those minimum performance standards required of all counselors and all school counselors. In addition to these skills, there are specialized issues—such as gender and cultural identity development, psychosocial development, and family development—that are foundation competencies for counselors working with young people (Lawrence & Kurpius, 2000). Counselors not performing in a manner consistent with these minimum performance standards are considered impaired, are required to seek assistance, and, if necessary, limit, suspend, or terminate their professional responsibilities.

Conversely, there will also be skill areas in which you will need additional training to be competent. In this book, we have defined school counseling within the parameters of counseling, educating and advocacy, consultation, and leadership and coordination. In each of these activities, there will be areas beyond which you might be in danger of practicing outside the scope of your skills. For example, if you do not have a teaching certificate in your state, you cannot call yourself a teacher; if you do not have the professional qualifications, even though some of your work involves social work–like activities, you cannot call yourself a social worker. This is logical. However, can school counselors work with students with mental health issues such as depression and eating disorders? If you have attended a one-hour workshop on the interpretation of the Myers-Briggs, are you "competent" in its administration and interpretation? These are gray areas in the concept of competence.

In general, there are established standards of proficiency within the counseling profession to help you answer these questions. For example, most graduate programs in counselor education require a class in appraisal procedures and techniques, assessment, tests and measurement, or some other term referring to training in the evaluation, selection, administration, and interpretation of formal and informal instruments used in counseling. Successful completion of this course in your graduate program qualifies you to administer and interpret master's level assessment instruments. Instruments that are required to be administered by a master's-plus-training or doctoral-level professionals would be beyond the scope of your competence without such training.

Procedures from other specialty areas, such as marriage and family therapy, may also be beyond the scope of the practice of most school counselors, unless they have additional training in that area (Davis, 2001; Magnuson & Norem, 1998). Family systems therapy is more in-depth than doing counseling with a parent and student to help them communicate more effectively, and family systems therapy does require additional training. But, if a student in your school is diagnosed as having Asperger's Syndrome, you could work with that student to facilitate his or her academic, career, and personal/social development, as long as you obtain additional education through coursework, the professional literature, and/or conferences, and as long as you obtain consultation from expert others while you deepen your own understanding of all issues involved with that diagnosis.

As you develop professionally, you would want to remain aware of the lifelong need for professional development, renewal, and training. What you are learning in your graduate program is not all you will ever need to know to be an effective professional counselor. Remaining competent means you must attend conferences, workshops, and classes; you must be up to date in the professional literature; and you must monitor your effectiveness at all times to ensure that you are providing the best possible service for all your partners in the comprehensive school counseling program.

Clinical Notes

Clinical records in the form of private notes kept in the sole possession of the counselor are not subject to the Family Educational Rights and Privacy Act (FERPA), even though administrative records are. According to Remley and Herman (2000), as long as the counselor does not show them to anyone else, these are considered the counselor's private notes. The only access anyone would have to them is through court order, subpoena, or other legal process. Remley and Herman further suggest that counselors document enough information to jog their memory, "to document events that . . . demonstrate [they] have performed [their] responsibilities in an appropriate and professional manner based on 'standards of practice,'" written in a manner that would be appropriate to read in front of the student and his or her family (p. 317). These authors suggest that all public and private clinical notes be put on a record destruction calendar consistent with the destruction schedule for all records held by the district; ASCA (2004) recommends that "sole possession records [be shredded] when the student transitions to the next level, transfers to another school, or graduates." However, ASCA recommends "discretion and deliberation" before destroying records pertaining to notes on child abuse, suicide, sexual harassment, or violence.

Online Counseling and the Use of Technology

Technology and its effect on the world cannot be denied, and counseling is not immune to these changes in the world. It is entirely possible that school counselors might be contacted by students, parents, and colleagues who need professional services, but their only or best access to their counselor is from the privacy of their homes. In the event that this occurs, you should be aware that there are specific ethical issues involved in online counseling. ACA addresses these issues in the Code of Ethics (2005) in Section A.12, Technology Applications. In addition, the National Board of Certified Counselors (NBCC, 2001) has defined Standards for the Ethical Practice of Internet Counseling (available from www.nbcc.org/webethics2, updated February 2005). In this document, the NBCC details various modalities and forms of technology-assisted counseling, and details important ethics of using these modalities; you will want to download and print the NBCC standards for your own reference.

While this is not a complete list of all of the standards, NBCC highlights the following issues:

1. Counselors should take steps to address impostor concerns by using code words, numbers, or graphics.
2. Counselors should verify the identity of the consenting adult when counseling minors.
3. Counselors should provide instructions for contacting the counselor when he or she is offline by explaining how often email messages are to be checked by the counselor.
4. Counselors should explain to clients the possibility of technology failure and direct them to call if problems arise in sending and receiving email messages.
5. Counselors explain to clients how to cope with potential misunderstandings arising from the lack of visual or auditory cues from the counselor or the client by asking for clarification.
6. Counselors should provide information about local crisis on-call and emergency services to clients.
7. Counselors should be respectful of clients' values and be sensitive to the local conditions and customs that affect clients' values.
8. Counselors should inform clients about encryption methods being used to ensure the security of communications.
9. Counselors should inform clients if, how, and how long session data are being preserved.
10. Counselors should follow appropriate procedures regarding the release of information and should work to ensure the confidentiality of the Internet counseling relationship.
11. Counselors should facilitate consumer protection regarding certification and licensing by providing links on their webpages to the websites of all certification bodies and licensure boards.

While the technology exists to provide counseling online, there is no reason to believe that counseling must be delivered using the Internet. It may be an option for various students, parents, and counselors, but there is no mandate to make online counseling available to your students. Certainly, the younger the student/client, the more concerns arise about the appropriateness of contact via technology. If you choose to use this medium, be aware of the issues and questions surrounding its use and potential misuse by being aware of relevant ethics.

In addition, many school counselors will establish and maintain a webpage for the CSCP. These are wonderful ways to inform all our partners about what we do and why we do it. Consider how invaluable that resource can be for students, parents, and teachers to access important information about student issues (anger management, bullying, friendship, cutting, eating disorders, etc.), learning styles and study skills, and career information. The caveat with providing this information is that most counselors will find it easiest to provide a link to the source but be very careful to check the link regularly. Official sites for organizations such as ACA, the Department of Labor, or the Department of Education will remain relatively consistent, but organization websites owned by private web providers may change without notice. We know of a counselor who lost her job because the address of a private website that was linked to a link on her counseling webpage was sold to another organization—and this new organization changed the content of the site to pornography. In addition, any computer connected to the Internet must have firewalls to protect against hacker access to confidential school and counseling records.

Diversity and Values

Although it is ethically mandated that counselors are competent in counseling persons of diversity, not all counselors are equally competent in this area. In terms of cultural diversity, recent studies suggest that school counselors still need additional understanding of racial identity development and multicultural within-group differences (Holcomb-McCoy, 2001), as well as a sense of competence to address cross-cultural issues (Constantine & Yeh, 2001). Many counselors do not attend to multiculturalism as an important part of their work, believing that "Students of color would rather work with someone from their own culture, so why should I pursue training in their culture?" It is clear from recent research that ethnicity is not what helps to establish a strong therapeutic alliance; rather, it is the perceived similarity between the counselor's and student's attitudes, values, background, and socioeconomic status (Esters & Ledoux, 2001). "After all, a school counselor who shares a student's attitudes and values and a similar background and socioeconomic status will, by most definitions of culture, share more of the culture and will thus be more similar than a school counselor who is simply a member of the same race. This finding should be encouraging to school counselors who find themselves attempting to build a counseling relationship with a student or a group of students with whom they differ in either race, sex, or both" (p. 169).

However, as humans, our identity does provide greater comfort in dealing with some students and greater challenge when dealing with others. Understanding racial identity development and multicultural dynamics will help counselors understand more clearly those areas of congruence between their values and attitudes and those of their students. In a recent qualitative study exploring the comfort level of middle school counselors in terms of same-sex or cross-sex working relationships with students, all of the respondents indicated that they found same-sex working relationships "more comfortable and natural" (Rayle, 2005, p. 155). As Rayle stated, "It is possible that cross-gender relationships are a substantive cultural issue for middle school counselors due to young adolescents' emerging sexuality, relationship, and gender identity issues" (p. 155). Similarly, Thorn and Contreras (2005) describe one district's decision to hire a Latina counselor to address the needs of their growing Latino population, as students' and families' needs for support, free of a translator, became crucial to address.

The establishment of a nurturing counseling relationship is the counselor's responsibility under the moral imperative of beneficence, but there is also a moral imperative to protect from harm (nonmaleficence). Issues of diversity also extend to the rights of students to have a safe, harassment-free educational environment. Not only does this pertain to students of cultural diversity, it also extends to students of economic diversity, sexual diversity (gay, lesbian, bisexual, and questioning youth), and values diversity (religious choice, moral choice).

The first source of diversity we will discuss is economic diversity. One of the most critical source of values is socioeconomic status. As the gap widens between the richest and the poorest, and as more and more families fall below the poverty line, the gulf between the "haves" and the "have nots" also gets wider (Payne, 1996). School counselors at every level, as stewards of the climate of the school, must be alert to the school experience of those who are most impoverished, those who may well become the target of teasing or bullying because they don't have the latest clothes or shoes. It is easy to become complacent in our own affluence and not notice those who exclude and diminish others on the basis of income, or worse yet, join in when students victimize each other on that basis.

In terms of sexual diversity, schools have a legal obligation to address student-on-student sexual harassment, and schools that do not can be held liable for violating the federal civil rights law under Title IX of the Education Amendments of 1972 (McFarland & Dupuis, 2001). By extension, students who are harassed by virtue of their sexual orientation must be protected and nurtured (McFarland & Dupuis, 2001), and their educational experience must not be marred by sexual violence and harassment (Stone, 2000). Recall that school counselors must report instances of sexual harassment to administration under Title IX, but the identity of the victim may be protected by the student's request for confidentiality, even if it hampers the school's ability to respond to the report (Stone, 2000).

Finally, in the widest context, diversity really refers to differences in value systems. Counselors are enjoined from imposing their values on their clients, no matter what the age of the client. Both ACA and ASCA address this specifically in their respective ethical documents, mandating that counselors actively respect the dignity of the client and promote the welfare of the client. It is only through careful self-analysis and self-awareness that counselors can come to articulate their own value system and avoid imposing that value system on clients. (Recall the hearing aid metaphor earlier in the chapter?) To examine how challenging this can be for school counselors, consider the following questions:

1. Do you believe in abortion, the right to life, or does it depend on the situation?
2. Do you believe in corporal punishment? When does a spanking become a beating? When does striking a young person become child abuse?
3. Do you believe that a 16-year-old is old enough to consent to sexual relationships? How old is old enough to give consent for sex? How old is old enough to give consent for marriage? What is the difference between those concepts?
4. What are your attitudes regarding same-sex relationships? Do same-sex parents provide the same home environment that traditional parents provide?
5. What are your attitudes regarding mixed-race relationships?
6. What are your attitudes concerning nontraditional families? Is divorce acceptable? Is single parenting as good as having both parents in the home (even if the relationship between the parents is hateful and destructive)?

7. What are your assumptions about people who live in poverty? What about people who live in the wealthiest neighborhoods?

8. Hard work is a value also. How would you react to a student or parent who wants to go on welfare rather than work? How would you react to a student or parent who wants to contemplate nature rather than work? Who wants to write a great novel, a great play, a symphony, rather than work? Do your answers differ depending on the situation? Why?

9. Your student and the student's parent defines "fun" as drinking to inebriation. Your spouse "relaxes" the same way—sometimes, you do too. Is it OK for the adults and not for the student? Or is it OK for the student? If marijuana were not illegal, would that be OK?

These questions just scratch the surface of the values questions faced every day by school counselors. If you aren't careful, your values and your attitudes will be communicated in your work, and then you're in violation of the ethics. You have to begin to think of these issues now.

It is important to note that the intent is to advocate for respectful, inclusive, and safe schools because everyone has the right to be free from harassment and the inappropriate imposition of another's values, not just because the counselor or school wants to avoid being sued. The intent is to reinforce our belief that respect, inclusiveness, and safety are the right conditions under which to educate young people, no matter who they are. Our laws and ethics make it our moral imperative to protect all young people and to promote their healthy development.

◆ PROFESSIONAL LIABILITY, INSURANCE, AND CERTIFICATION

Many school counseling students are surprised and alarmed when they learn that they may be sued in the course of their work as a school counselor. With the rise in student risk behaviors, suicides, and school violence, the duty to warn and protect takes on a much heavier burden than in previous years (Remley & Herman, 2000; Simpson, 1999). School counselors may be held liable for breach of confidentiality, negligence, or malpractice, for providing inadequate services, and for not protecting the student from suicide and/or threats of harm from others.

But aren't school counselors covered by the insurance of the school? Not if the interest of the school and the interest of the counselor are different (Remley & Herman, 2000). If the charges suggest that the counselor acted in contradiction to school policy, the counselor's interests and the district's interests may be very different. To distance itself from fiscal liability, the district may suspend or dismiss the counselor, claiming that the counselor was not acting on behalf of the district when the problem behavior occurred. For example, a counselor is charged with sexual harassment of students. The school has a policy against sexual harassment and will dismiss or suspend the counselor when the complaint is filed. In this way, the school minimizes its liability, and the defense used by the school's attorney will be to locate the blame on the accused, thereby distancing the school from responsibility and reducing the monetary judgment. The counselor must now obtain legal services, paying out-of-pocket for attorney's fees and any judgments against him or her.

It is for this reason that school counselors are urged to obtain their own professional liability insurance ("Personal Liability Insurance," 2000; Remley & Herman, 2000). Such insurance is available through membership in the national counseling professional associations: the American Counseling Association and the American School Counselor Association. (Contact these organizations via the Internet to learn more about professional liability insurance.)

Factors that may mitigate the cost of such liability insurance are professional licenses and certifications. In addition to state certification and/or licensure for school counselors, school counselors may want to consider national certification as a counselor and/or school counselor through the National Board of Certified Counselors (NBCC), as discussed in Chapter 1. This additional level of professional recognition is obtained through successful completion of the National Counselor Exam (NCE), a comprehensive exam offered around the country, and documented postgraduate experience and supervision. This qualifies counselors to become Nationally Certified Counselors, or NCCs. With additional documented hours of school counseling education and experience, counselors can qualify to become Nationally Certified School Counselors, or NCSCs. Continued credentialing with these certifications require additional professional development and education. To obtain more information about these certifications at the national level, you can contact the NBCC through its website: www.nbcc.org.

In addition, school counselors in some states are eligible for status as a Licensed Professional Counselor, or LPC (different states refer to this status by different names; consult your state for the appropriate designation). Since standards vary from state to state, you will want to obtain information from your state to explore this possibility. Furthermore, the National Board for Professional Teaching Standards (NBPTS) offers counselor certification, and many states will increase the salary of counselors who obtain this level of credentialing. (See their website for their requirements at www.nbpts.org.) The point is that school counselors who are willing to go the extra mile to document their professional expertise and commitment will benefit in terms of professional recognition, and possibly, remuneration.

◆ RESPONDING TO LEGAL ACTION

The first thing most counselors do when they are served with legal papers is become very anxious. But it is not necessary to panic. If you are served with a subpoena for records, information, and/or testimony, the following steps are recommended *before you comply with the court order*:

1. Consult with professional colleagues about the situation.
2. Consult with your administration about the situation.
3. Consult with the school's or the school district's attorney.
4. Consult with your state and/or national professional school counseling association.
5. Review your documents about the situation.
6. Be prepared to protest the subpoena in court, arguing that the information in your possession is not relevant or appropriate. This protects the confidential nature of the counseling relationship.

7. If necessary, obtain legal advice on your own.

8. If the subpoena is for testimony at a custody hearing, Remley and Herman recommend that you do not become voluntarily involved. If you are forced to testify, limit your testimony to only factual information, not your opinions on the competence of one parent over the other. (Remley & Herman, 2000)

◆RESOURCES AND RECOMMENDATIONS FOR SCHOOL COUNSELORS

There are a variety of resources pertaining to ethics, laws, policies, and other issues. As has been mentioned several times, you will want to invest the time and energy in obtaining information about the professional standards and expectations of the American Counseling Association (ACA), the American School Counselor Association (ASCA), the Association for Specialists in Group Work, the National Career Development Association, the National Board for Certified Counselors, as well as the references for articles and books about ethics from leaders in the profession. In addition, membership in your national and state counseling and school counseling associations entitles you to professional consultation with peers, most often through an ethics committee. Listservs may also be a way of communicating with professional peers to obtain feedback about ethical issues, but due to the public nature of the list discussions, caution would be necessary to protect confidentiality. Strategies for establishing and maintaining your work as an ethical school counselor include the following:

1. Obtain professional supervision periodically from a peer. This involves inviting feedback from a colleague about your counseling, educating and advocacy, consultation, and leadership skills. Most supervision focuses on counseling skills, however. This could be done in a conversational format but is most effective when done with a video or audiotape of your counseling with a student client. Due to confidentiality issues, you would need to ensure that you have permission from the student and the student's parents or guardians to tape counseling for supervision purposes.

2. Read about ethics in the professional literature. For example, take the ethics quiz (Huey, Salo, & Fox, 1995). Check your answers for accuracy in both the current ACA Code and the ASCA Ethical Standards because they have been revised since the quiz was written.

3. Take additional workshops, courses, and/or conference sessions on current issues in ethics.

4. Keep current on contemporary issues in counseling, such as counseling strategies, new theories and techniques, and client issues. All of these areas are constantly evolving, and you must remain informed about each of them.

5. Obtain professional consultation as needed with peers about national, state, and local issues in schools and in school counseling (Ledyard, 1998). Networking with colleagues is essential.

6. Do not limit yourself to contact with school counselors alone. You need a broader perspective, so become networked with community, college, rehabilitation, and other counselors in your area.

7. You must have an effective referral network in place, so you must know the resources in your community. Learn about these professionals in terms of who they help, how they help, where they are located, how much they cost, and other details.

8. To avoid working in a setting with whose leadership you have an ethical difference of opinion, inquire into administrative policy during the interview to determine if you can live with its administrative philosophy (Tompkins & Mehring, 1993). For example, you can ask the interviewer about his or her experiences, positive and negative, with school counseling. Listen for areas in the response that indicate a lack of awareness or appreciation for important counseling issues such as confidentiality, parental consent, and mandated reporting.

9. You must know the laws for your state (Tompkins & Mehring, 1993). This involves some digging on your part, but you have to know what your state requires you to know before you step into a school.

10. You must be able to work with persons who hold different values than you do. Research continues to show that the best way to understand diversity is to know diverse persons; get to know people from many walks of life on a personal level. It is only through being open to diversity that you can truly know and become comfortable with various value systems. It is then that you can see, underneath the diversity, those common threads that bind us all.

CASE STUDY REVISITED ◆ Integration

Now that you've read the chapter, go back and reread Jason's Casual Comment.

1. What was the comment he made that created the situation?
2. If Kim's comment was related to sexual activity, what do you think Jason should do? What are the questions you would like to ask her? What else do you need to know before you can act?
3. Assume that Kim's comment was not related to sexual activity. Now what are the questions you would like to ask her?
4. What do you believe is the appropriate level of parental involvement in this situation? What is the appropriate level of school involvement? Under what conditions, specifically, would you be mandated to report? List all of them.
5. How have your values shaped the answers you gave to these questions?

APPLICATION (Possible portfolio artifacts are noted)

1. Return to the section on values and respond in writing to the questions posed.
2. Go to the Internet and obtain the addresses for organizations that provide information on ethical issues that would be of interest in a school setting. Be sure to include academic issues, career issues, and personal/social issues. At a minimum, record these for your files. Establish a web page for your ideal school counseling program, complete with links to important sources of information. (Possible portfolio artifact)
3. If your state's statutes are accessible on the Internet, access child protection legislation and record the address for your files. Summarize these into a usable document that you can use on the job. (Possible portfolio artifact)

4. Search the Internet for more information on each of the laws named in this chapter. Print or download what you believe pertains to school counseling. Record those addresses for your files, and summarize each piece of legislation into a usable document that you can use on the job. (Possible portfolio artifact)

5. Interview a school counselor about her or his experience with ethical dilemmas. Take one of those scenarios and work through the ethical decision-making model proposed by Stadler. Did you arrive at the same ethical decision that counselor did? Why or why not?

6. Outline all the situations you can imagine in which you would violate a student's confidentiality. Take that list and organize it into a plan for informed consent that you would use with potential students for early elementary (grades K–3), intermediate (grades 4–6), middle school (grades 7–8) and high school students. Include in that informed consent document everything

that ACA indicates must be included in informed consent. (Possible portfolio artifact)

7. Design a letter that you could send to parents explaining everything needed to meet the ACA criteria of informed consent, asking for their permission to counsel their student. In addition, draft a letter to parents in which you request permission to tape your counseling for supervision purposes. (Possible portfolio artifact)

8. Go to the NBCC website and find out everything you need to be certified at the national level. List all the reasons for and against such certification in a pro/con format. Would you pursue this certification? Why or why not?

9. Go to the website for the National Board for Professional Teaching Standards and find out everything you need to be credentialed at the national level by that organization. List all the reasons for and against such credentialing in a pro/con format. Would you pursue this certification? Why or why not?

SUGGESTED READINGS

American Counseling Association. (2005). *ACA code of ethics*. Alexandria, VA: Author. It is imperative that all counselors understand the Code of Ethics for the profession. This document is also available at www.counseling.org.

Herlihy, B., & Corey, G. (1996). *ACA ethical standards casebook* (5th ed.). Alexandria, VA: American Counseling Association. This book presents the ethics of the ACA with illustrative vignettes and discussion chapters written by experts in the field.

Isaacs, M. L., & Stone, C. (1999). School counselors and confidentiality: Factors affecting professional choices. *Professional School Counseling, 2*, 258–266. This article presents a study in which school counselors at various levels respond to hypothetical situations, involving age- and situation-specific

concerns, in which they would break confidentiality. The findings highlight the unique perspectives of high school counselors juxtaposed with those of middle and elementary schools.

Payne, R. K. (1996). *A framework for understanding poverty* (3rd ed.). Highlands, TX: aha! Process. This is an excellent book written for educators working with economically diverse students. It is well advised for school counselors to understand the issues of generational poverty as discussed in this book.

Sealander, K. A., Schwiebert, V. L., Oren, T. A., & Weekley, J. L. (1999). Confidentiality and the law. *Professional School Counseling, 3*, 122–127. This article presents current information relative to the laws affecting confidentiality in schools.

REFERENCES

American Counseling Association. (2005). *ACA code of ethics*. Alexandria, VA: Author.

American School Counselor Association. (2004). *Ethical standards for school counselors*. Alexandria, VA: Author.

Association for Specialists in Group Work. (1998). *Best practices*. Retrieved August 4, 2006, from www.asgw.org/best.htm.

Butler, E. R. (1993, March). *Basic principles for ethical decision making*. A paper presented at the meeting of the National Association for Student Personnel Administrators, Boston.

Christopher, J. C. (1996). Counseling's inescapable moral visions. *Journal of Counseling and Development, 75*, 17–25.

Constantine, M. G., & Yeh, C. J. (2001). Multicultural training, self-construals, and multicultural competence of school counselors. *Professional School Counseling, 4*, 202–207.

Davis, K. M. (2001). Structural-strategic family counseling: A case study in elementary school counseling. *Professional School Counseling, 4*, 180–186.

Davis, T., & Ritchie, M. (1993). Confidentiality and the school counselor: A challenge for the 1990s. *The School Counselor, 41*, 23–30.

Erk, R. R. (1999). Attention deficit hyperactivity disorders: Counselors, laws, and implications for practice. *Professional School Counseling, 2*, 318–326.

Esters, I., & Ledoux, C. (2001). At risk high school students' preference for counselor characteristics. *Professional School Counseling, 4*, 165–170.

Hall, A. S., & Lin, M. (1995). Theory and practice of children's rights: Implications for mental health counselors. *Journal of Mental Health Counseling, 17*, 63–80.

Herlihy, B., & Corey, G. (1996). *ACA ethical standards casebook* (5th ed.). Alexandria, VA: American Counseling Association.

Holcomb-McCoy, C. C. (2001). Exploring the self-perceived multicultural counseling competencies of elementary school counselors. *Professional School Counseling, 4*, 195–201.

Huey, W. C., Salo, M. M., & Fox, R. W. (1995). An ethics quiz for school counselors. *The School Counselor, 42*, 393–398.

Isaacs, M. L., & Stone, C. (1999). School counselors and confidentiality: Factors affecting professional choices. *Professional School Counseling, 2*, 258–266.

Kaplan, D., & Allison, M. C. (1994). Family ethics. *Family Journal, 2*(1), 54–57.

Kaplan, L. S. (1996). Outrageous or legitimate concerns: What some parents are saying about school counseling. *The School Counselor, 43*, 165–170.

Lawrence, G., & Kurpius, S. E. R. (2000). Legal and ethical issues involved when counseling minors in nonschool settings. *Journal of Counseling and Development, 78*, 130–136.

Ledyard, P. (1998). Counseling minors: Ethical and legal issues. *Counseling and Values, 42*(3), 171–198.

Magnuson, S., & Norem, K. (1998). A school counselor asks: "Am I prepared to do what I'm asked to do?" *Family Journal, 6*(2), 137–140.

McFarland, W. P., & Dupuis, M. (2001). The legal duty to protect gay and lesbian students from violence in school. *Professional School Counseling, 4*, 171–179.

National Board for Professional Teaching Standards. (2006). *Home page.* Retrieved August 4, 2006, from www.nbpts.org.

National Board of Certified Counselors (NBCC). (2001). *Standards for the ethical practice of WebCounseling.* Retrieved November 16, 2004, from www.nbcc.org/ethics/webethics.htm.

National Career Development Association (2003). *Ethical standards.* Retrieved August 4, 2006, from www.ncda.org/pdf/EthicalStandards.pdf.

Payne, R. K. (1996). *A framework for understanding poverty* (3rd ed.). Highlands, TX: aha! Process.

Personal liability insurance: Do you need your own policy? (2000, March/April). *The ASCA Counselor, 37*, 24.

Rayle, A. D. (2005). Cross-gender interactions in middle school counselor-student working alliances: Challenges and recommendations. *Professional School Counseling, 9*, 152–155.

Remley, T. P., & Herman, M. (2000). Legal and ethical issues in school counseling. In J. Wittmer (Ed.), *Managing your school counseling program: K–12 developmental strategies* (2nd ed.; pp. 314–329). Minneapolis, MN: Educational Media Corp.

Schmidt, J. J. (2003). *Counseling in schools: Essential services and comprehensive programs* (4th ed.). Boston: Allyn and Bacon.

Sealander, K. A., Schwiebert, V. L., Oren, T. A., & Weekley, J. L. (1999). Confidentiality and the law. *Professional School Counseling, 3*, 122–127.

Simpson, M. D. (1999, February). Student suicide: Who's liable? *NEA Today, 17*, 25–26.

Stadler, H. A. (1985). *Confidentiality: The professional's dilemma: Participant's manual.* Alexandria, VA: American Counseling Association.

Stone, C. B. (2000). Advocacy for sexual harassment victims: Legal support and ethical aspects. *Professional School Counseling, 4*, 23–30.

Strein, W., & Hershenson, D. B. (1991). Confidentiality in nondyadic counseling situations. *Journal of Counseling and Development, 69*, 312–316.

Thorn, A. R., & Contreras, S. (2005). Counseling Latino immigrants in middle school. *Professional School Counseling, 9*, 167–170.

Tompkins, L., & Mehring, T. (1993). Client privacy and the school counselor: Privilege, ethics, and employer policies. *The School Counselor, 40*, 335–342.

Watson, C. H. (1990). Gossip and the guidance counselor: An ethical dilemma. *The School Counselor, 38*, 35–39.

CHAPTER

15

EMERGING ISSUES FOR SCHOOLS AND STUDENTS

With Robert I. Urofsky
Clemson University

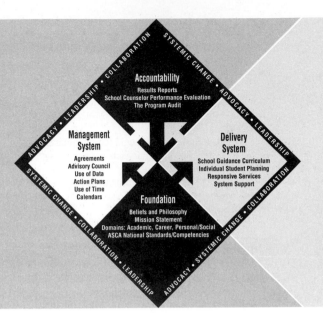

◆ LEARNING OBJECTIVES

By the end of the chapter, you will

1. understand the mental health concerns faced by school counselors in the field
2. appreciate the diversity in the schools and feel a renewed commitment to learn more about different persons
3. understand the effect of poverty on our students and feel a renewed commitment to help every child succeed in school and life
4. consider new forms and structures of schools relative to educational reform
5. understand the connection between spirituality and mental health and the appropriate role school counselors can play in the development of students
6. consider new ways of looking at educational structures
7. understand the importance of technology in school counseling and the need to remain current with technological developments
8. consider the process of collecting data through action research
9. understand the various ways to secure alternative funding for programs

DOMAINS / ACTIVITIES / PARTNERS MODEL

ACTIVITIES	Academic Development	Career Development	Personal/ Social Development			
Counseling	1a	1b	1c	5	6	7
Educating and Advocacy	2a	2b	2c	8	9	10
Consulting	3a	3b	3c	11	12	13
Leadership and Coordination	4a	4b	4c	14	15	16
	Students			Parents and Caregivers	Colleagues in Schools	Colleagues in Community

PARTNERS IN THE PROCESS

CASE STUDY ◆ Samuel's Mother

Erin always participated in the events of her school, so that parents and teachers would see her as integral to the school community. So on Parent's Night at Gila Vista Elementary School, she walked from room to room as she always did, introducing herself and inviting parents to visit her counseling office before they left. Entering the second-grade classroom, she was surprised to hear a woman's voice screaming at the second-grade teacher about the progress of Samuel, a new student in the school. She was accusing the teacher of treating her son unfairly, holding him to higher behavioral and academic expectations than others. It was clear that the teacher was trying to escape the mother's tirade, as she nervously looked around the room at the embarrassed parents who were unwilling witnesses to this exchange. After a few minutes, Erin decided to intervene, to see if the parent might be interested in processing her concerns in private, but the mother yelled "You're all a bunch of trained monkeys!" and left, slamming the door.

The next day, Erin approached the teacher to offer consultation. "Is there anything I can do to help you with her?"

The teacher shrugged. "I've worked with lots of parents like her. I'm not sure what I can do to help her or her son. They come from such a different world; I'm not even sure how to reach out to them. I don't think the mother had a good experience at school when she was young. I can't even begin to imagine why she's so angry." Erin felt a surge of pity for both Samuel and the second-grade teacher. She made a mental note to get him from class at the first opportunity.

CHALLENGE QUESTIONS

What was your reaction as you read this case study? What might be going on with this parent? What do you do to remind yourself to listen with compassion to someone who is so angry?

Most people will generate a mental image of the scene as they read. Being completely honest, attend to the image of the mother you "saw" as you read the case study. How did you imagine the mother looked? What was her culture, her age, her dress, her mental condition? What are all the things you would want to know about her?

◆ EMERGING ISSUES IN SCHOOL COUNSELING

We wish we had a crystal ball to see into the future for our profession of school counseling; we would use it to help future counselors prepare for everything that the world will throw at them. We must be aware of what is happening in our communities and our schools to foresee answers to future needs. This is how we will survive as a profession—through being proactive, not reactive.

There are many issues emerging in the field that will affect school counseling but we will attend to those that are most critical for school counseling. If our programs are indeed comprehensive—holistic, systemic, balanced, proactive, integrated, and reflective—we will be well-situated to address these emerging issues.

◆ MENTAL HEALTH NEEDS OF STUDENTS

School counselors report that the frequency with which they encounter students with mental health issues is increasing at an alarming rate, and it has been posited that about "one in five children or adolescents in the U.S. manifest a diagnosable mental health or addictive disorder" (Cauce & Srebnik, 2003). In one study, only about 25 percent of those students who recognized they had a mental health problem sought out professional help (Saunders, 1994, as cited in Cauce & Srebnik, 2003). Of those seeking help, one study found that the most frequently used formal sources for mental health help were medical doctors (78%), school personnel (57%), school principals (36%), and sports team coaches (35%) (Dubow et al., 1990, as cited in Cauce & Srebnik, 2003). Think about what these statistics mean. Extrapolating from these studies, we can calculate that approximately 20 percent of young people need mental health assistance, indicating how prevalent the need is for mental health services for young people. But only a quarter of those students (meaning 25% of 20%, or 5% of all students) seek help from mental health providers, suggesting how important it is for mental health to be destigmatized. Of the 5 percent who come for help, only about half of them (2% to 3%) will come to school personnel (counselors or teachers) for that help. What does this say about this issue for professional school counselors?

Add to your consideration of these issues some information about psychotropic medication. In a national survey of school counselors, Bauer, Ingersoll, and Burns (2004) examined the experiences of school counselors with psychotropic medication in the schools. They found that of the 138 respondents, 42 percent estimated between 1 and 10 percent of their students were taking these medications and 17 percent estimated that from 11 to 20 percent were taking medications. When asked to identify all the diagnoses for which the medications were prescribed, 94 percent listed ADHD, 80 percent listed ADD and depression, 69 percent listed hyperactivity, and 57 percent listed bipolar. Other diagnoses mentioned include

The ASCA School Counselor Performance Standards addressed in this chapter are

13.1 The professional school counselor promotes academic success of every student.

13.2 The professional school counselor promotes equity and access for every student.

13.4 The professional school counselor understands reform issues and works to close the achievement gap.

13.7 The professional school counselor uses data to recommend systemic change in policy and procedures that limit or inhibit academic achievement.

The 2001 CACREP Standards for School Counseling Programs addressed in this chapter are

A.6 current issues, policies, laws, and legislation relevant to school counseling;

A.9 knowledge and application of current and emerging technology in education and school counseling to assist students, families, and educators in using resources that promote informed academic, career, and personal/social choices;

C.1 **(f)** strategies for seeking and securing alternative funding for program expansion; and

C.1 **(g)** use of technology in the design, implementation, monitoring and evaluation of a comprehensive school counseling program.

anxiety, obsessive-compulsive disorder, mood disorder, oppositional defiance disorder, and posttraumatic stress disorder, among others. While the school nurse was most often identified as the professional responsible for the dispensation of medications in the school, other persons included school counselors, teachers, and office staff. Over half of the school counselors responded that they had received no formal training in psychopharmacology, yet 91 percent agreed or strongly agreed that it was important for school counselors to understand medication issues and 96 percent agreed that such training would be helpful in their work. The authors conclude that "School counselors need access to this information [diagnosis and treatment of childhood psychiatric disorders] to function effectively as child advocates and consultants in the school system" (p. 209).

These realities—the prevalence of mental health issues, the lack of help seeking, and the increasing reliance on psychotropic medication for youth—make mental health one of the most critical issues for school counselors. Counselors report that students with emotional disabilities, such as problems with depression, autism spectrum disorders, anger management, posttraumatic stress, reactive attachment disorder, and oppositional defiance disorder are being increasingly diagnosed at all educational levels. It is crucial that counselors become knowledgeable about these issues to assist in the early assessment, identification, and referral of these students to school and community resources. Furthermore, school counselors must be able to provide counseling and support services for these students to facilitate their academic, social and emotional, and career development. A student's DSM IV diagnosis doesn't eliminate the counselor's vital role in promoting school success. School counselors must understand diagnostic, treatment, and special education terminology, legislation, and issues, since counselors must understand educational responses to a student's mental health status.

Counselors must also work to help students and families understand mental health issues and encourage them to access school and community resources as needed. They need to normalize both developmental struggles and mental health concerns so that students and families are more comfortable talking about their needs (with the reminder that there are often culturally determined preferences for sources of mental health assistance).

For those who come to school counselors for help, responses to these needs are shaped by the ASCA National Model and insights into comprehensive school counseling. In a comprehensive school counseling program, you would attend to the student's holistic development while working to support the learning process. You would demonstrate awareness of contextual implications with the student's diagnosis, evaluating the student's classroom context and family context to facilitate support for the student. You would balance your responses to the student to meet his or her needs, ranging from counseling, educating, and consultation, with an emphasis on proactive activities that will mitigate the damaging effects of the diagnosis on all aspects of development. Finally, you would design feedback and documentation of your work with the student for reflection and accountability.

It is important to note that if counselors eschew their role in the mental health issues of students and walk away from the counseling foundation of our profession, we leave a void that others will fill. In many districts, school psychologists and school social workers also provide mental health support, and in a recent development, school nurses have been promoted as "well positioned to bridge school and community health activities" and to "facilitate medical/psychiatric intervention and alter the trajectories for students vulnerable to mental health problems and violence" (Hootman & DeSocio, 2004, p. 27). Our student support colleagues can be essential partners in providing help for all students. In a world of ever-growing mental health needs, ignoring the work we do as *counselors* in a comprehensive school counseling program will result in the loss of our roots and our identity. To create the best possible scenario for students, school counselors must continue to provide counseling for students, while concurrently emphasizing the importance of educating, advocating, consulting, leading, and coordinating for all our partners.

Crisis Counseling

As a part of the discussion of mental health, it is important to mention the need for counselors to provide crisis counseling. Counselors must be able to work effectively with students who are in crisis and must be able to act decisively in cases of suicide risk. In a recent study of 186 secondary school counselors, researchers found that 87 percent of them felt that suicide work was part of the job, but only 38 percent of them felt they had the skills to be effective with suicidal students (King, Price, Telljohann, & Wahl, 1999, 2000). Yet according to the National Mental Health Association, "Each year, almost 5,000 young people between the ages 15 to 24 take their own lives. The rate of suicide for this group has nearly tripled since 1960, making it the third leading cause of death in adolescents and the second leading cause of death among college-age youth" (National Mental Health Association, n.d.). School counselors must have skills in the assessment of suicide potentiality. Furthermore, it is crucial that counselors know the answers to the following questions:

1. What are the expectations of the district and the school administrators in terms of notification of caregivers and school administration?
2. What are the processes and roles of social services, law enforcement agencies, school professionals, and counselors in terms of getting the student to a safe location?

3. How do you access local mental health emergency services? What is the location, address, phone, and placement procedures of the local mental health facility if a commitment becomes necessary?
4. What are the implications of transportation, information sharing, and notification of all parties (caregivers, administrators, law enforcement, and mental health professionals)?

In a comprehensive school counseling program at any educational level, counselors must anticipate the need for addressing students in crisis. In a proactive and preventive effort, counselors would educate all partners in the warning signs of crisis (as developmentally appropriate). Thinking systemically (because people in crisis often indicate their suicidal thoughts to friends) students would be trained to be aware of warning signs in their friends and the need to inform an adult of their concerns (Nelson & Galas, 1994). Parents, teachers, and administrators, also, would benefit from education in this area. Furthermore, prevention/intervention efforts would involve leadership activities in the school that would yield (1) the development of a plan for the eventuality of dealing with a student who is suicidal, (2) the documentation of a process that answers all the preceding questions, and (3) the provision of in-service training for the adult partners in the school to outline the plan.

Self-Destructive Behaviors

Along with mental health issues, school counselors are reporting increasing instances of unhealthy and self-destructive behaviors. According to McWhirter, McWhirter, McWhirter, and McWhirter (2004), young people are engaging in high-risk behaviors, such as intake of alcohol and other drugs, in alarming numbers. Along with these unhealthy and high-risk behaviors, some students express their pain in self-destructive behaviors such as self-mutilation, cutting, pinching, scratching, biting, self-hitting, burning, and interfering with wound healing (Kress, Gibson, & Reynolds, 2004). As an example of the need for reflection in a CSCP, counselors need to understand their own reactions to some nontraditional ways of self-decoration, such as tattooing, piercing, branding, and carving, to be able to understand when self-marking is self-destructive and when it is self-decoration. In addition, reflection and self-supervision is important when working with clients who self-injure, as clinical work with self-injurious students is identified as the most traumatizing to the professional (Kress, Gibson, & Reynolds, 2004).

One theory describing the etiology of cutting suggests that the intent of the behavior is not to die; rather, it is in response to a numbing dissociative state associated with psychological trauma. Sources of the trauma that often result in self-injury are identified as sexual and physical abuse, anxiety and depression, family violence, eating disorders, peer conflict, low impulse control, and traumatic loss (Kress, Gibson, & Reynolds, 2004; Levenkron, 1998). However, self-injurious behaviors are also known to be contagious; other adolescents, in what might be considered a "rite of togetherness" (Taiminen et al., as cited in Kress, Gibson, & Reynolds, 2004, p. 199), may engage in social self-mutilation as an outgrowth of psychological and social factors (Kress, Gibson, & Reynolds, 2004).

In a CSCP, counselors would attend to all self-destructive behavior in holistic, systemic, balanced, proactive, integrated, and reflective ways. It is important to note that this issue, due to its severity and safety issues, requires notification of parents and possible hospitalization; as such, the event must be handled with attention paid to informing students of confidentiality issues (Froeschle & Moyer, 2004). School counselors responding to these behaviors would examine the effect of the behavior on academic, career, and personal/ social development, and would provide counseling, referrals, advocacy, and consulting as appropriate. Furthermore, counselors should take into account the student's family, school, and community contexts to examine prevention and intervention strategies that would provide the most support for the student's recovery and aftercare. Appropriate intent on the prevention/intervention/treatment continuum would suggest that activities would be balanced in terms of education of all partners (prevention efforts), counseling and advocacy for the student as well as consulting and leadership with all adult partners (intervention efforts), and referrals to the community (treatment efforts). Integrated efforts to inform students (as developmentally appropriate) of the dangers of self-mutilation might include presentations in health classes, for example. Finally, all efforts would be documented to provide data for accountability and reflection.

Reflection Moment ◆

What is your level of knowledge about mental health diagnoses, medications, and the ways that counselors can support students with mental health issues in the schools? What do you know about crisis and crisis counseling? What do you know about self-destructive behaviors?

In addition, think about your feelings on these topics, as they generate reactions from us based on our values, our faith traditions, and our sociocultural background. How do you feel about these issues, and how do you react to young people who manifest these issues?

What are the resources in your community to assist you with these questions? What do you need to do to become more proficient in these topics?

◆ ◆

◆ MULTICULTURALISM AND DIVERSITY

Many excellent books have been written that explore this topic in detail, and this short discussion is not intended to convey all the subtleties and nuances of effective multicultural and multivalues interactions. The intent is to highlight the most salient issues relative to school counseling, especially as it relates to the ASCA National Model and the DAP model as discussed in this book. It is hoped that, as you come to better appreciate the need for advocacy, social justice, and systemic functioning in school counseling, you will cement your commitment to your education and experiences to foster healthy development for all students.

The importance of this topic cannot be understated; students of color and linguistic diversity are expected to comprise the majority of all students by the year 2020 (Holcomb-McCoy, 2004; Sue & Sue, 1999), and already constitute a numerical majority in many locations and communities in the country (Sue & Sue, 1999). Furthermore, there are many diversity constructs, including culture, ethnicity, gender, sexual orientation, ability and disability levels, religious/faith traditions, and age, among others. Each of these diversity constructs is interwoven into our values systems and merged with our unique personalities to yield our personal phenomenology and epistemology. As the world becomes more diverse, the assumptions that we hold as products of our own diversity constructs and values orientations must be amended to become more inclusive, more empowering, and more just.

Without exception, the need for *all* counselors—of all ethnic, cultural, and values statuses—to improve their skills in this area is paramount. As stated by Sue and Sue (1999), "If counselors and therapists are to provide meaningful help to a culturally diverse population, we must not only reach out and acquire new understandings, but develop new culturally effective helping approaches" (p. 10). But all counselors must also be aware that diversity comes from a variety of sources—linguistic, cultural, ethnic, gender, religious, sexual orientation, national origin, ability level, among others—and make the commitment to value, learn about, and empower all others who might be different from ourselves. Awareness of one source of values orientations and resulting oppression (such as ethnicity or gender) cannot be substituted for the others (such as sexual orientation or ability level) (Helms, 1994). And we cannot forget that oppression comes in many forms, some of which are hidden, but nonetheless insidious and destructive. Examples of subtle oppression include silencing of females (Reinharz, 1994), denial of positive attributes in male identity development (McCarthy & Holliday, 2004), differential encouragement of postsecondary options based on learning disabilities (Durodoye, Combes, & Bryant, 2004), and lack of understanding of the needs of Muslim students (Carter & El Hindi, 1999).

This learning about others is also grounded in the need to learn about ourselves. The need to understand one's own diversity constructs is evident when you consider the implications of Embedded Intergroup Relations (Alderfer, 1994), which posits that interaction between people depends on (1) the unique personalities of the individuals, (2) the messages the individuals receive and internalize from their own group (defined as any diversity construct with which the person identifies), and (3) the present and historical relationships between the groups that the individuals represent (p. 221). Consider what this implies for communication, but most especially for counseling: If counselors are to truly counsel others (developing empathy, trust, unconditional positive regard, etc.), then counselors must reflect on and remain aware of the following:

1. The counselor's personality as shaped and defined by identity development processes and values development
2. The client's personality, as shaped by the same forces
3. The counselor's messages internalized from her or his own group
4. The client's messages from his or her group
5. The present relationship between the group of the counselor and the group of the client
6. The historical relationship(s) between the group of the counselor and the group of the client

Effective multicultural counseling begins with understanding ourselves and our identity development. Next, we must develop a visceral, personally derived understanding of others, which means understanding at the "gut" level, not just the intellectual level; it involves personal interaction with diverse others. Finally, we must recognize that the present *and* the past will affect how others perceive us and the groups to which we appear to belong. This has a direct impact on whether students of diversity and their families perceive the school counselor as someone to whom they can turn in times of need.

These insights provide a backdrop from which to better understand Holcomb-McCoy's (2004) list of multicultural counseling competencies for school counselors. These competencies include

◆ Competence in multicultural counseling. This means becoming aware of strategies and approaches that are relevant and appropriate for diverse students, rather than assuming that traditional strategies (which have been developed for nondiverse students) will suffice for all.

◆ Competence in multicultural consultation. As observed in the development of the DAP model, consultation is a crucial skill, and diverse students, families, and colleagues need consultation strategies that are appropriate. Furthermore, negative racial and/or cultural attitudes can and should be confronted using consultation.

◆ Competence in understanding racism and student resistance. In working toward a diverse and multiculturally appreciative and respectful school climate, school counselors must be aware of all forms of resistance to tolerance and inclusion. From rabid, overt racism to denial of the oppression of all forms of diversity, the spectrum of racism must be challenged when found in schools, colleagues, students, and families.

◆ Competence in understanding racial identity development. Most difficult for counselors from traditional White, middle-class backgrounds is understanding the anger (Sue & Sue, 1999) that is a natural part of being a member of a disenfranchised and oppressed group (person of color, female, gay/lesbian, for example). Added to this, of course, is the reminder that this includes the identity development process for all persons of diversity (Helms, 1994). The understanding of diversity identity development must then be applied to the issues and concerns of students and their families, as well as to colleagues.

◆ Competence in multicultural assessment. As high-stakes testing becomes more widespread and assessment becomes more ubiquitous, the adaptations needed by diverse students, in terms of language, testing environment (for students with attention issues), and content, become critical.

◆ Competence in multicultural family counseling. Awareness of contextual issues, including families of diversity, is imperative. As stated by Holcomb-McCoy (2004), "counseling interventions with families must take into account its [sic] cultural kinship networks, socialization experiences, typical interactive patterns, and culturally linked attitudinal and behavioral arrangements" (p. 180).

◆ Competence in social advocacy. Social action and social advocacy are necessary for systemic change, and it is through these activities that schools can become inclusive, respectful places for learning that are safe for diverse students, families, and staff.

◆ Competence in developing school-family-community partnerships. Holcomb-McCoy (2004) suggests that counselors should take a leadership role in developing partnerships that empower families to access services in the school and community that can provide support for families in need.

◆ Competence in understanding interpersonal interactions. Issues of inclusion, respect, and valuing are communicated through words, voice, subject, and nonverbals. Counselors must be aware of their own attitudes and how those are communicated to diverse students, ensuring that the context of counseling is affirming, safe, and welcoming.

As you can see from the above competencies, leadership is a basic requirement for any meaningful change to take place. It is critical that counselors empower themselves to transform the climate of the school on behalf of students, to create a welcoming environment in which everyone can learn, free from harassment and hatred.

Reflection Moment ◆

Where are you in the evolution of your sense of social justice? What can you do to expand your awareness of persons from other diversity constructs?

◆ ◆

◆POVERTY

Although the issues of diversity and poverty are often interconnected, they are not synonymous. In many cases, economic realities transcend cultural ones; in other words, economic class can have a more defining impact on values development than culture or ethnicity. One study (Weis, as cited in Holcomb-McCoy, 2004) found that "teachers initiate more frequent and more varied interactions with students from middle and upper class backgrounds than they do with those from the poor and working classes" (p. 181). Payne (2003) discusses the "hidden rules" of economic classes (p. 59), and suggests that the rules of the middle class dominate our educational institutions. Because most educational professionals come from the middle class, educators presume that everyone knows the "rules": the value of education; an emphasis on future planning; the use of formal, written, sequential narrative structure; a belief in choice ("Good choices now can provide a better future"); and the certainty that hard work and achievement are the keys to success. In contrast, students from generational poverty live with the hidden rules of poverty: the value of entertainment; an emphasis on the present; the use of informal, spoken, circular narrative structure; a belief in fate ("That's the way life is; what can you do?"); and the certainty that survival depends on relationships which can change without notice. In the world of poverty, school is a source of entertainment, a time to be with friends; it is not a way out of poverty (p. 79).

Payne discusses specific student behaviors that result from the hidden rules of poverty, such as laughing when disciplined, arguing loudly with the teacher, physical fighting, not following directions, being disorganized, and incessant talking (pp. 103–104). She goes on to outline educational strategies that can help mitigate the effects of poverty's rules and help teach students the rules of the middle class, which will help with educational and career efforts. Recognition that these behaviors are not the result of flaunting of rules, but rather are manifestations of a unique value system, can reframe educators' frustrations with children from poverty. Mentoring, explicitly teaching alternatives to habituated behaviors, and recognition of underlying messages and needs can help further students' educational, career, and personal/social efforts.

In terms of a holistic, systemic, balanced, proactive, integrated, and reflective comprehensive school counseling program, recognition of the challenges of students of poverty come from systemic awareness of students' lives. Balanced, proactive activities with all partners would involve the following:

◆ Counseling and educating students experiencing poverty to help them learn new behaviors and expand career options
◆ Educating parents about parenting skills and community resources and consulting with parents about the school system (since suspicion of authority in general, and schools in particular, is a legacy of generational poverty [Payne, 2003])
◆ Educating school and community colleagues on the effects of poverty, advocating for the families and children of poverty, and consulting with school colleagues to facilitate understanding in how to educate these students
◆ Leading the effort to transform the climate of the school toward respectful inclusion on the basis of income

In a CSCP, reflection is necessary to improve the program and the counselor's function within that program. In the case of families and students experiencing poverty, it is important that counselors examine their own assumptions and class-bound hidden prejudices to determine if such persons are treated with respect and to ensure that these students and families feel welcome and valued in the school counseling office.

Reflection Moment ✦

What are the "rules" of the socioeconomic culture in which you were raised? How do those rules affect your perceptions today? What do you need to do to expand your awareness and understanding of those from other socioeconomic strata?

✦ ✦

◆ SPIRITUALITY

Meaningful learning cannot take place if the child does not feel safe emotionally in the learning environment, and emotional safety cannot happen without a sense of community in the school (Bluestein, 2001; National Research Council, 2000; Starkman, Scales, & Roberts, 1999). Research consistently shows that a sense of community—a climate of caring support, of sharing, of mutual respect—provides the setting in which a child can ask questions, take risks, and modify his or her cognitive constructs to allow for change and growth. These descriptors have deepened the awareness of many education and counseling professionals that the conditions that foster a sense of community in a school also foster spirituality, because programs that nurture a sense of community in a school (hope, compassion, respect, honesty, integrity, service to others, purpose in life or career) also develop persons who are spiritually well (Ingersoll & Bauer, 2004, p. 304).

In this book, "spirituality" is defined as "humans' expressions of and attempts at meaning-making that are uniquely personal as well as communal or sociocultural" (Sink & Richmond, 2004, p. 291). Religion is an organized, communal or cultural expression of spiritual beliefs, but the two terms are not synonymous. As cited in MacDonald (2004), one survey found that 50 percent of those sampled in the United States said that religion was very important in their lives, whereas other surveys have found that 80 to 90 percent of U.S. respondents believe in a "spirituality that included a god or gods" (p. 293). It can be concluded that, for many persons, spiritual realities are not expressed in organized religions; yet, as Sink and Richmond (2004) point out, these realities may be expressed in simple activities such as career exploration, reflection on a poem, painting a powerful image, or taking a walk and reflecting on nature. As such, the topic of spirituality, once taboo due to the separation of church and state, is becoming an acceptable topic for school counselors to explore, as long as it is given careful consideration.

There are many reasons that counselors need an expanded awareness of the role of spirituality in the lives of students. First, spiritual development is a crucial developmental issue, connected to cognitive development and moral reasoning skills (Ingersoll & Bauer, 2004; Sink, 2004); second, spiritual exploration and discussion are natural in the counseling process, as students need to examine the meaning of their lives and the events therein (Koch, 2003; Myers, Sweeney, & Witmer, 2000); third, as a diversity construct, it can be considered unethical if issues of oppression and exclusion on the basis of religion and spirituality are ignored (Carter & El Hindi, 1999; Hanna & Green, 2004; Ingersoll & Bauer, 2004; Koch, 2003; Lonborg & Bowen, 2004); fourth, knowledge of the student's spiritual traditions can enhance the counseling relationship and engender trust with the student and his or her family (Hanna & Green, 2004). This would suggest that school counselors must prepare to counsel students in the spiritual context (1) through a deeper understanding of the role of spirituality in terms of development, (2) by exploring our own spirituality and resolving to live a more meaningful spiritual life, (3) by understanding our misconceptions and biases about other religions and spiritual traditions, and (4) by making the commitment to expand our understanding of other religious and spiritual traditions.

Once that "inner" work is done, counselors are ready to engage students on this topic. As outlined in the discussions of multiculturalism and poverty, comprehensive school counseling programs promote activities that enhance spirituality to facilitate academic, career, and personal/social development, and maintain a broad systemic view of the student to interface effectively with peers, family, and friends. Balanced, proactive activities would include the following:

◆ Counseling students with a focus on understanding the student's meaning-making (spiritual) structures and faith traditions, educating students in skills that enhance their own spiritual development (Koch, 2003; Sink, 2004), and educating students about other faith traditions

◆ Consulting with parents about the values or faith traditions of the family

◆ Educating school and community colleagues on various faith traditions or spiritual orientations, advocating for the families and children of "minority" faith traditions, and consulting with school colleagues to facilitate understanding in how these faith traditions may manifest in academic, career, or personal/social development

◆ Leading the effort to transform the climate of the school toward respectful inclusion on the basis of religion, faith tradition, and/or spirituality

And, as always, the need for self-examination is clear when evaluating one's own faith traditions and spiritual realities. As counselors, we cannot be unhealthy in our own lives and hope to have credibility as we try to help others become more healthy.

Reflection Moment ✦

Where are you in the journey within your own spirituality, and what is your reaction when considering talking about these issues with others? What can you do to make yourself more at ease when talking about this topic?

✦ ✦

◆EDUCATIONAL REFORM

In 1983, the National Commission on Educational Excellence published *A Nation at Risk*, a scathing report on the state of the educational system in the United States. The report warned that the United States was losing ground to foreign competition in commerce, industry, science, and technological innovation. Although the authors of the report recognized that there were many contributing factors, a great deal of responsibility was attributed to the failings of the educational system and society's handling of it:

> Our society and its educational institutions seem to have lost sight of the basic purposes of schooling, and of the high expectations and disciplined effort needed to attain them. . . . That we have compromised this commitment, is, upon reflection, hardly surprising, given the multitude of often conflicting demands we have placed on our Nation's schools and colleges. They are routinely called on to provide solutions to personal, social, and political problems that the home and other institutions either will not or cannot resolve. (National Commission on Educational Excellence, 1983)

The report warned of dire consequences for the health and prosperity of the United States if it did not enact significant educational reform.

The publication of *A Nation at Risk* sparked the current school reform movement in the United States (Estes, 2004). Although changes have occurred in the way that the U.S. educational system is organized and has operated since 1983, many reformers feel that not much has improved and that the current educational system requires significant overhaul. The depth of the feelings that underlie the educational reform debate can be seen in the Pacific Research Institute's (Riley, 2000) (a strong proponent of such an overhaul) assessment of the public school system:

> Despite tinkering with methodology, standards, class size, and other measures, the system remains a public utility with captive customers and guaranteed funding—a monopoly producing bad products at high prices—and has shown such resistance to change, some have argued for a different approach. (p. 1)

In 2001, the United States Congress enacted, at the urging of President George W. Bush, the No Child Left Behind Act of 2001, a broadbased reform of the Elementary and Secondary Education Act governing kindergarten through twelfth-grade public education. This reform plan calls for "stronger accountability for results, expanded flexibility and local control, expanded options for parents, and an emphasis on teaching methods that have been proven to work" (U.S. Department of Education, Fact Sheet on No Child Left Behind, n.d.).

The No Child Left Behind Act (NCLB) is representative of several significant strands within the educational reform movement. NCLB requires all states to establish state-guided accountability programs that require yearly testing of students in grades 3-8 on progress in reading and math, and the dissemination of the results by school in yearly report cards. Individual states must also report on a yearly basis disaggregated data on student performance so they may demonstrate progress toward closing the achievement gap between disadvantaged students and other students in the public schools (U.S. Department of Education, Fact Sheet on No Child Left Behind, n.d.).

A second and related aspect of educational reform included in the No Child Left Behind Act is the call for comprehensive school reform efforts based on scientifically based research and effective practices. The Comprehensive School Reform (CSR) Program provides grants to schools, particularly Title I schools serving disadvantaged students, throughout the United States that enable them to enact "coherent school-wide improvements that cover virtually all aspects of a school's operations, rather than piecemeal, fragmented approaches to reform" (U.S. Department of Education, About CSR, n.d.). Whether the schools choose a nationally recognized comprehensive school reform program or choose to develop their own, the schools must integrate the following eleven components of reform. Each school must do the following:

◆ Employ proven methods and strategies based on scientifically based research
◆ Integrate a comprehensive design with aligned components
◆ Provide ongoing, high-quality professional development for teachers and staff
◆ Include measurable goals and benchmarks for student achievement
◆ Be supported within the school by teachers, administrators and staff
◆ Provide support for teachers, administrators and staff
◆ Provide for meaningful parent and community involvement in planning, implementing, and evaluating school improvement activities
◆ Use high-quality external technical support and assistance from an external partner with experience and expertise in schoolwide reform and improvement
◆ Plan for the annual evaluation of strategies for the implementation of school reforms and for student results achieved
◆ Identify resources to support and sustain the school's comprehensive reform effort
◆ Be found to significantly improve the academic achievement of students or demonstrate strong evidence that it will improve the academic achievement of students (U.S. Department of Education, About CSR, n.d.).

The Northwest Regional Educational Laboratory (NWREL) offers a catalog of such reform models which currently contains 29 models that are either schoolwide or single-subject models implemented schoolwide (NWREL, n.d.).

Another important educational reform strand included in the No Child Left Behind Act is school choice. Fuller, Burr, Huerta, Puryear, and Wexler (1999) characterized the basic underlying concepts of the school choice movement as follows:

Choice is founded upon a human-scale theory of accountability. Give parents the option to exit their neighborhood school and shop from a wider variety of alternatives. Or, bypass the school system entirely and give public dollars directly to parents via vouchers, boosting their purchasing power. Thus, school principals and teachers—if the theory's underlying assumptions are met—become directly accountable to parents, not to school boards or state education agencies. This market competition for parents, enacted by a more diverse set of schools, will raise the quality of public education. (p. 5)

There are a number of different types of school choice options for which reformers have advocated over the years, including charter schools, private voucher programs, site-based management, tax credits, home schooling choice, and public school choice, including magnet schools and open-enrollment options. Charter schools are public schools that agree "to meet certain performance standards in exchange for exemptions from public school regulations other than those governing health, safety, and civil rights; accepts accountability for results in exchange for autonomy in the choice of methods for achieving those results." While there is great variation in voucher programs, they are generally "supported by individuals, businesses, and other groups that give vouchers directly to low-income children to enable them to attend private school." Under site-based management, decision-making authority rests with committees consisting of principals and teachers at a school rather than with school boards or central administrations (Rees, 2000). Magnet schools are public schools with a specific curricular focus, and open enrollment allows parents to enroll their child in a public school outside their immediate neighborhood (Fuller et al., 1999). School choice is evident in the No Child Left Behind Act in that parents whose children are in schools identified as failing may choose to transfer their child to another school or a charter school, and the act expands support for the creation of new charter schools (U.S. Department of Education, Fact Sheet on No Child Left Behind, n.d.).

While the No Child Left Behind Act has had its critics, related, among other things, to the adequacy of its funding or its inadequate attention to social issues impacting achievement of students in the schools, it is clear that the act represents a number of components of the educational reform movement. Furthermore, the act and these components are having a significant effect on the current look and feel of public education in the United States, including school counseling (Dollarhide & Lemberger, 2006). A growing number of public educational options, new forms of accountability demands and approaches, increased opportunities for parental input and participation, an increased emphasis on standards and testing of progress toward meeting standards, and the enactment of research-supported comprehensive school reform programs are all part of the changing educational landscape in the early twenty-first century.

◆ GENDER AND SCHOOLS

The No Child Left Behind Act of 2001 (NCLB), a broadbased reform of the Elementary and Secondary Education Act governing kindergarten through twelfth-grade public education in the United States, calls for "stronger accountability for results, expanded flexibility and local control, expanded options for parents, and an emphasis on teaching methods that have been proven to work" (U.S. Department of Education, Fact Sheet on No Child Left Behind, n.d.). NCLB puts increased pressure on schools to be accountable for their student achievement outcomes. However, the law also contains provisions to assist schools in developing innovative ways to boost student achievement outcomes.

One provision within Title V of the Act, which addresses parental choice and innovative programs, allows local education agencies (LEAs) to use federal funds for developing innovative assistance programs including programs to provide same-gender schools and classrooms (V.A.3.5131[a][23]). As the U.S. Department of Education sought to provide additional information to the states regarding this provision, it acknowledged that single-sex classes or activities were generally prohibited under Title IX of the Education Amendments of 1972 prohibiting sex-based discrimination. However, it maintained that there were allowable instances and that an LEA could offer single-sex schools if the action constituted remedial or affirmative action. LEAs pursuing this option, it maintained, would need to be aware of the constitutional requirements in this area and that they could be challenged in court litigation.

Since that time, the Department of Education has worked to address some of the limitations on schools offering same-sex classes and schools, proposing Title IX amendments under which "single-sex classes would be permitted if they are part of an evenhanded effort to provide a range of diverse educational options for male and female students, or if they are designed to meet particular, identified educational needs of students (U.S. Department of Education, 2004). Rod Paige, U.S. Secretary of Education, maintained that while the research in this area was "incomplete," there was evidence to suggest that single-sex education can help some students in some settings.

This component of NCLB is, in part, representative of a growing concern about a gender achievement gap in public education. Clark, Oakley, and Adams (2006) write

> In the United States, boys are achieving at lower levels than girls as shown by test scores, grades, and drop-out rates. They have a higher incidence of ADHD, discipline referrals, and special education referrals and placements. Reports show that boys represent more than two-thirds of high school students with disabilities, including physical, learning, and emotional. Women have surpassed men not only in high school graduation rates but in university enrollment and degree completion. In this country, girls capture more academic honors, outscore boys in reading and writing and score about as well on math at the three grade levels (fourth, eighth and 12th) tested by the National Assessment for Educational Progress exam. (¶ 1)

It is important to recognize that this gender achievement gap is not without its controversy and critics. Rivers and Barnett (2006) state that the crisis is a "manufactured" one, "the product of both a backlash against the women's movement" and the media's tendency to report on the next big crisis for the nation (¶ 6). These authors assert that when the data is disaggregated by race and class, the problem emerges as one for inner-city and rural boys.

Educator and therapist Michael Gurian (2001) maintains that there are important reasons to attend to differences between boys and girls in their education, because they have significantly different needs in certain areas. A one-size-fits-all approach to education, he maintains, is not appropriate as there are certain developmental and structural differences between male and female brains that may lead them to process emotional and cognitive input differently. In addition, he indicates there are a number of chemical differences, hormonal differences, and functional differences that may influence how males and females process information. These differences have significant implications for a learning environment and for the work of school counselors. Consider the following example provided by Gurian:

> The female brain processes more emotive stimulants, through more senses, and more completely than does the male. It also verbalizes emotive information quickly. Boys can sometimes take hours to process emotively (and manage the same information as girls). This lesser emotive ability makes males more emotionally fragile than we tend to think. A boy who has had a crisis at home this morning may come to school with a higher cortisone (stress-hormone) level than, say, his sister because he has held in, or not processed, the emotional stress of the crisis at home. He may be unable to learn for much of the morning, whereas his sister may quickly process and even talk out the hard edges of the stress so that she can learn efficiently the very same morning. The male is often, thus, intrinsically fragile because he cannot guide his own emotions to processing and to words as quickly as a female does, and his fragility may extend to his ability to learn that day. (pp. 31–32)

Gurian goes on to point out other brain differences affecting this type of processing, including evidence indicating female brains tend to move sensory information with emotive content up in the brain toward areas where thinking occurs whereas male brains tend to move such information down, to areas more likely to invoke a fight or flight response. Through understanding these and other differences, Gurian maintains, schools and teachers can develop organization and teaching strategies more likely to assist both males and females in achieving academic and personal/social success.

A number of other authors have begun to emphasize developmental issues unique to either males or females. Clinical psychologist Mary Pipher, in her best-selling book *Reviving Ophelia* (1994), presented numerous case studies chronicling the significant negative psychological changes occurring in girls as they transitioned from childhood to adolescence. Pipher attributed these changes to a "girl-poisoning culture" in which young girls were bombarded by negative media messages and images about females (p. 12). Brown and Gilligan (1992), likewise, chronicled the difficult transition females experience from childhood to adolescence. This passage, they assert, is a passage into silence, disconnection, and a loss of a sense of self. Wiseman (2002) and Simmons (2002) have brought attention to the relational nature of female interaction and assert that female adolescents may use this emphasis on relationships to wield power over one another and, potentially, to inflict psychological harm. Simmons encourages schools to view this relational aggression as a form of bullying. Similar to the work he has done with male development, Gurian (2003) details the impact biological factors and brain development have on female social and other forms of development.

Pollack (1999) and Gurian (1997) have chronicled the difficult developmental transitions boys experience as they progress from childhood into adolescence and on to adulthood. Similar to Brown and Gilligan's (1992) descriptions of female developmental challenges, Pollack (1999) asserts that the journey for boys is often one into sadness and disconnection as they are shamed from a very early age into conforming to an unwritten Boy Code. This code mandates that they must be tough, dominant, and unemotional, and leads them to hide their fears and feelings. Both Horne and Kiselica (1999) and Beymer (1995) have sought to offer strategies for counselors to use to meet the counseling and guidance needs of boys and adolescent males.

Whether or not there is a formal gender achievement gap, these and other authors make a compelling case for attending to differences between males and females that may help us to differentiate instructional and counseling strategies to maximize achievement and success for both genders.

Reflection Moment ◆

What is your reaction to the concept of single-sex educational environments? Can separate be equal? What do you consider the advantages and disadvantages of both mixed-gender and single-gender classrooms? As a new school counselor, what are the implications you see for each?

◆ ◆

◆TECHNOLOGY

As new technologies become more affordable, students will need help understanding the power and the dangers of computers: how to use them as effective and efficient tools for learning and how to avoid the problems that new technologies might bring. Counselors are often the best resource for teachers and students to help humanize the school environment and to facilitate conversations among all persons in the school setting.

In a recent survey of 92 school counselors from elementary, middle, secondary, and vocational schools, Owen and Weikel (1999) found that 88 percent of the counselors reported that a computer had been assigned to them to support the counseling program. They also found that middle and secondary counselors used computers more in their work than elementary counselors (an average of 12.5 and 14.5 hours per week, respectively). In terms of confidence in their computer skills, elementary counselors reported the lowest confidence, middle school counselors somewhat higher, and secondary school counselors reported the highest level of confidence. This same pattern described the reported level of agreement that their productivity had been enhanced by computers. When examining computer use for counselors at all levels, the results revealed computer use for routine word processing by 95 percent of respondents, grade/record keeping by 65 percent, class scheduling by 64 percent, statistical analysis by 33 percent, educational programs by 30 percent, email by 28 percent, Internet research by 13 percent, and teaching by 5 percent. The authors lamented the fact that counselors still were not using computers for activities directly related to student counseling functions.

Numerous authors call for counselors to become more computer-friendly. Sabella and Booker (2003) have identified numerous benefits of using computers: increasing administrative understanding of the work of the counselor, fostering greater respect for how counseling enhances student development, informing parents and teachers about the referral process, networking with other counseling professionals, interfacing with the local business community, informing student counselors about the field, and assisting student service personnel to learn how they can work more effectively with the school community. Some of the ideas to increase computer use include supervision with university, peer, and district professionals, as well as consultation among counselors (Myrick & Sabella, 1995); listserv discussions (Logan, 2001); instruction (Sampson & Krumboltz, 1991); promotion of the comprehensive school counseling program through multimedia presentations (Sabella &

Booker, 2003); and student advocacy (through an examination of student data and the advocacy for the elimination of barriers to student success) (Hohenshil, 2000).

In addition, counselors could use computers to establish connections with students and families through a web page or could use email with students and families. It is possible that a listserv could be used to conduct discussions with students after a developmental curriculum session or to foster communication with students who are in groups, especially with the advent of live video communication. While there are numerous arguments against relying on computers for communication (confidentiality, security of communication, uncertain identity of communicator), computers are not going to go away. In fact, ACES, the Association for Counselor Education and Supervision, has identified twelve technical competencies that should be expected of counselor education students at the completion of their graduate program (Hohenshil, 2000). Counselors should be able to

1. Develop web pages, presentations, letters, and reports
2. Use audiovisual equipment
3. Use computerized statistical packages
4. Use computerized testing, diagnostic, and career decision-making programs
5. Use email
6. Conduct Internet searches
7. Subscribe to, participate in, and sign off counseling-related listservs
8. Access and use counseling-related CD-ROM databases
9. Know of legal and ethical codes related to counseling services via the Internet
10. Know strengths and weaknesses of counseling on the Internet
11. Use the Internet for finding and using continuing education opportunities in counseling
12. Evaluate the quality of Internet information

It is easy to see how useful computers would be in a CSCP, especially with the emphasis of the National Model on leadership, advocacy, collaboration, and systemic change. With the many uses of computers in today's world, the counselor who is not computer-savvy ignores a valuable resource. Computers can supplement all the counselor's activities in the DAP model (counseling, educating and advocacy, consultation, and leadership and coordination) to accomplish the systemic and proactive work of the counselor and can facilitate contact with all partners.

Reflection Moment ◆

How comfortable are you with technology? What do you need to do to become more comfortable with technology as a school counselor?

◆ ◆

◆ ACCOUNTABILITY AND DATA

Accountability means that school counselors can document the work that is done for the partners in the educational process—students, parents and caregivers, colleagues in the schools, and colleagues in the community. According to Stone and Dahir (2007) and

Loesch and Ritchie (2005), school counselors are not being singled out in this call for data-driven self-reporting; rather, it is an opportunity for school counselors to provide concrete evidence of their work. As discussed in Chapter 5, the importance of accountability even merits its own Element of the ASCA National Model (ASCA, 2003).

There is no need to become stressed over the need to collect data. First, there are excellent resources that will provide both the why and the how of this data collection (see, for example, Stone & Dahir, 2007, and Loesch & Ritchie, 2005). According to Stone and Dahir, the data you collect should be meaningful (guided by the mission of the school and your program); broken down into the essential elements of data that are important to know; analyzed to identify problem areas, organized to establish a baseline from which to measure change and then to set goals for change; shared with select partners (students, parents, colleagues) to design strategies for change; collected again to examine what change has occurred after implementing the strategy; and finally, shared with all partners to highlight the contribution of the CSCP. These authors suggest using a document they call the SPARC or "School Counseling Program Accountability Report Card" (p. 35), in which these steps are summarized for dissemination.

Methods of data collection include existing information on grades, test scores, attendance rates, free and reduced lunch rates; electronic and hard-copy questionnaires, surveys, and scales; interviews; and counselor-designed instruments (Loesch & Ritchie, 2005). The type of data collected is determined by the questions you are asking about your school, your students, and your program. As you will recall from Chapter 11, one program at Ford Elementary School targeted attendance rates and truancy, so attendance data was collected to establish a baseline, an intervention was designed, and then the attendance data was collected again to measure change. If discipline for fighting is a problem in your middle school, you would first collect baseline data on referrals for fighting and suspension rates, then design programs for anger management and other factors, such as gang affiliation, that you believe contribute to fighting, and finally, after delivering your program(s), you would again collect data on referrals and suspension rates for fighting. The key is to (1) make data collection meaningful (related to the important results you hope to obtain); (2) make it fun, both for you and for the person whose skills, knowledge, and/or dispositions you are targeting; and (3) make it a standard part of everything you do, so that you are not faced with collecting data once a year.

Reflection Moment ◆

Can you think of problems in schools that might be targeted for programs? What data would you collect to measure your effectiveness?

◆ ◆

◆ ALTERNATIVE SOURCES OF FUNDING

Funding for schools will become more of an issue for taxpayers as the cost of living goes up. The answer for many educators, including counselors, is to seek outside funding from private and public granting sources. It is valuable to know about possible funding sources and the process for applying for grant funding.

There are distinct strategies for grant writing (Education World, 2004). Before you begin the search for external funds, you need three things: (1) permission to secure external funding from your administrator (building and/or district), (2) a project that is unique or innovative, and (3) a detailed plan to implement your project. Specific to your project, you need (a) to document the need for the project (demographics, test results, evidence of current gaps in service); (b) a mission statement that clearly spells out the project's desired outcome; (c) measurable and specific goals and objectives; (d) a detailed project timeline; (e) assessment tools to document and evaluate the attainment of your goals and objectives; (f) a list of all needed materials, personnel, and supplies; and (g) the total cost of your project.

In terms of process, you would want to do the following:

1. Assemble a team (of teachers, fellow counselors, parents, students) to work on the grant application with you so that you can assign tasks (researching, writing, proofing, etc) to share the burden of time devoted to this process
2. Research various funding sources to find one that best fits the project you have in mind
3. Collaborate with everyone involved in your project on the grant itself so that all parties are informed and supportive
4. Carefully read the call for proposals from your target funding source(s), following their directions exactly
5. Have someone who is not directly involved with the project read the proposal before submission to ensure accuracy, clarity, and consistency within the application.

When writing a grant, successful grant writers (Education World, 2004) encourage new writers to provide balanced attention to each of the three parts of the grant: the application form or forms, the narrative, and the budget. The application forms must be completed carefully, double-checking for accuracy. The narrative must be clearly written, based on evidence (research-based), detailed, concise, and interesting to read. Finally, the budget should be reasonable, detailed, accurate, realistic, and flexible.

In addition to these insights, SchoolGrants (2006) emphasize that a "well documented needs statement is critical to your proposal" (p. 5). They recommend that you examine previous funded programs to gain a better understanding of your potential funding source, and if you are not funded, they recommend that you request reviewer comments so that you can improve your next grant application.

The Internet is a rich source of information on educational grants that would be of particular interest for school counselors. Consider corporate or private philanthropic organizations in addition to federal, state, or local funds.

Reflection Moment ✦

What has been your experience with grants? Is there a way to gain grant experience while you are still in graduate school? People in charge of hiring, such as principals, are always impressed with a candidate who is able to demonstrate grant experience.

✦ ✦

CASE STUDY ◆ Integration

Now that you have read the chapter, go back and reread the Case Study. What guesses do you have about this child and his mother? What would you want to know about Samuel? What would you want to know about his mother and/or any other relatives? His support system? His school experiences thus far?

Based on what you want to know, what would you do with the information? Using the DAP model as a template for planning your response, identify actions you could take in each block, based on your best guesses about the situation. Remember to be holistic, systemic, balanced, proactive, integrated, and reflective.

For each action you suggest in the previous question, what data will you collect and how will you collect it?

How might technology be useful in your work with this family? What grant ideas might be generated from knowing Sam and his mother attend your school?

Topics I would Explore: **Source(s) of Information:**

_____   _____

_____   _____

_____   _____

_____   _____

_____   _____

_____   _____

APPLICATION (Possible portfolio artifacts are noted)

1. What do you know about mental health issues? New information and new insights into mental health diagnoses emerge almost daily.
   a. You must be able to access accurate, up-to-date information quickly. Identify at least four Internet sites on which you can locate relevant, accurate information. Record those Internet addresses (URLs) for future reference. (Possible portfolio artifact)
   b. Identify at least three community mental health resources for future referrals. Contact those organizations to ascertain and record clientele population, costs, exact services, and a contact professional for possible consultation in the future. (Possible portfolio artifact)
   c. Find out if there is a support group in the community for specific mental health issues and explore volunteering with that group to gain group experience and to deepen your understanding and compassion for persons living with mental health challenges.

2. There are a number of different models in the literature that outline identity development for unique diversity constructs, such as ethnicity, gender, and sexual orientation. Locate one or two of these models that describe your own diversity construct(s) and outline your life process of identity development, using those models as a template for your reflection. For example, an African American female lesbian adoptee who was raised in a Caucasian family could research African American identity, female identity, sexual orientation identity, and cross-cultural adoption identity issues.

3. The section on Multiculturalism and Diversity contains several competencies that are recommended for school counselors. Where are you in the development of each competency? What do you need to do to improve in each competency? Create a portfolio in which you document your proficiency, or work toward proficiency, in each competency. (Possible portfolio artifact)

4. It has been said that one of the easiest prejudices to acquire, and one of the hardest to confront, is classism, the assumption that those of different socioeconomic strata are "more than" or "less than." Journal your reactions to persons of poverty, persons of the working poor, of the middle class, and of wealth, being as honest as you can. Then explore the following questions:

   a. Where did those images and biases come from?

   b. What current messages reinforce those biases? (*Hint.* Explore movies, music, news, sports, books, other media)

   c. What can you do to challenge those biases in your own life?

5. It won't be appropriate for you to discuss spirituality until you have "sounded the depths" of your own spiritual life. In a journal, reflect on the faith traditions or spiritual teaching of your family of origin and then explore your own thinking and conclusions that result in the spiritual beliefs you hold today.

6. Identify two faith traditions about which you know little. Research those traditions, outlining the beliefs about the higher power or powers, ways the faithful express their beliefs, and the values held by the faithful. How similar or dissimilar are those beliefs, expressions of faith, and values to your own? (Possible portfolio artifact)

7. What are your reactions to charter schools, private voucher programs, home schooling, and public school choice, including magnet schools and open-enrollment options? Select two of these concepts and research them in depth to create a list of advantages and disadvantages. If you have one or more of these programs in your community, visit the site to interview the principal or counselor to juxtapose with your research. (Possible portfolio artifact)

8. What are your reactions to single-gender learning environments? Create a list of advantages and disadvantages for each environment. Locate a single-sex learning environment in your community and interview the principal, teacher, and/or counselor about it. Record their experiences and juxtapose that with your own advantage/disadvantage list. (Possible portfolio artifact)

9. Review the list of competencies in the section on Technology. Where are you in the development of each competency? What do you need to do to improve in each competency? Develop a portfolio artifact in which you provide evidence for your proficiency, or work toward proficiency, in each competency.

10. The most common concern about accountability involves how to collect data on the outcomes of counseling. Outline a plan for documenting the efficacy of both individual and group counseling, using variables to which school counselors have access. (Possible portfolio artifact)

11. What are some ideas you have for grant funding? Outline a plan for a project that you would see as grant-worthy, including the details of the project (goals, activities, ideal timelines, and funding needs), at least two possible funding sources, and documented funding priorities of each source. Use the Internet as your primary source of information and document the sites you visit in your search. (Possible portfolio artifact)

SUGGESTED READINGS

Bauer, A. L., Ingersoll, E., & Burns, L. (2004). School counselors and psychotropic medication: Assessing training, experience, and school policy issues. *Professional School Counseling, 7*, 202–211. This article presents important research into the prevalence and issues of the administration of psychotropic medications in the schools.

Hohenshil, T. H. (2000). High tech counseling. *Journal of Counseling and Development, 78*, 365–369. This article outlines some important information about computers and counselors, including suggestions about ways that counselors could infuse computers into their work. It also contains an appendix in which the Technical Competencies for Counselor Education Students are presented.

Holcomb-McCoy, C. (2004). Assessing the multicultural competence of school counselors: A checklist. *Professional School Counselor, 7*, 178–186. This article is a comprehensive overview of the literature discussing multicultural skills in the schools. Furthermore, it includes a checklist of multicultural competencies that will enable the reader to reflect on current skill levels and plan for professional development.

Kress, V. E. W., Gibson, D. M., & Reynolds, C. A. (2004). Adolescents who self-injure: Implications and strategies for school counselors. *Professional School Counselor, 7,* 195–201. This article provides an excellent overview of the current literature and thinking about etiology and interventions for self-injurious behaviors and then extrapolates from these insights various intervention strategies appropriate for school counselors.

Payne, R. K. (2003). *A framework for understanding poverty* (3rd ed.). Highlands, TX: aha! Process. This book provides much-needed insights into the issues facing students of poverty and uses compassion and empathy in outlining school-appropriate interventions.

Spirituality and School Counseling [Special issue] (2004, June). *Professional School Counseling, 7*(5). This entire issue is devoted to the topic of spirituality in comprehensive school counseling programs and

represents an important discussion on the issues of addressing spirituality in the schools.

Stone, C. B., & Dahir, C. A. (2007). *School counselor accountability: A MEASURE of student success* (2nd ed.). Upper Saddle River, NJ: Pearson/Merrill/Prentice-Hall. This book presents the rationale, strategies, and examples of documents that comprise school counselor accountability.

Additional readings in gender issues would include the following:

Gurian, M. (1997). *The wonder of boys: What parents, mentors, and educators can do to shape boys into exceptional men.* New York: Penguin.

Gurian, M. (2001). *Boys and girls learn differently! A guide for teachers and parents.* San Francisco: Jossey-Bass.

Gurian, M. (2003). *Wonder of girls: Understanding the hidden nature of our daughters.* New York: Simon and Schuster.

Pollack, W. S. (1999). *Real boys: Rescuing our sons from the myths of boyhood.* New York: Owl Books.

Simmons, R. (2002). *Odd girl out.* Orlando, FL: Harcourt.

Wiseman, R. (2002). *Queen bees and wanna bes.* Norwalk, CT: Crown.

REFERENCES

Alderfer, C. P. (1994). A white man's perspective on the unconscious processes within Black-White relations in the United States. In E. J. Trickett, R. J. Watts, and D. Birman (Eds.), *Human diversity: Perspectives on people in context* (pp. 201–229). San Francisco: Jossey-Bass.

ASCA. (2003). *The ASCA National Model: A framework for school counseling programs.* Alexandria, VA: Author.

Bauer, A. L., Ingersoll, E., & Burns, L. (2004). School counselors and psychotropic medication: Assessing training, experience, and school policy issues. *Professional School Counseling, 7,* 202–211.

Beymer, L. (1995). *Meeting the guidance and counseling needs of boys.* Alexandria, VA: American Counseling Association.

Bluestein, J. (2001). *Creating emotionally safe schools: A guide for educators and parents.* Deerfield Beach, FL: Health Communications.

Brown, L. M., & Gilligan, C. (1992). *Meeting at the crossroads: Women's psychology and girls' development.* Boston: Harvard University Press.

Carter, R. B., & El Hindi, A. E. (1999). Counseling Muslim children in school settings. *Professional School Counseling, 2,* 183–188.

Cauce, A. M., & Srebnik, D. (2003). Before treatment: Adolescent mental health help-seeking. *The Prevention Researcher, 10*(4), 6–9.

Clark, M. A., Oakley, E., & Adams, H. (2006, January 1). The gender achievement gap challenge. *ASCA School Counselor* [Electronic version]. Retrieved April 5, 2006, from www.schoolcounselor.org/printarticle.asp?article=822.

Dollarhide, C. T., & Lemberger, M. E. (2006). "No Child Left Behind": Implications for school counselors. *Professional School Counseling, 9,* 295–304.

Durdoye, B. A., Combes, B. H., & Bryant, R. M. (2004). Counselor intervention in the post-secondary planning of African American students with learning disabilities. *Professional School Counseling, 7,* 133–140.

Education World. (2004). Show me the money: Tips and resources for successful grant writing. Retrieved February 14, 2006, from www.educationworld.com/a_curr/profdev/profdev.039.shtml.

Estes, M. B. (2004). Choice for all?: Charter schools and students with special needs. *The Journal of Special Education, 37*(4), 257–267.

Froeschle, J., & Moyer, M. (2004). Just cut it out: Legal and ethical challenges in counseling students who self-mutilate. *Professional School Counseling, 7,* 231–235.

Fuller, B., Burr, E., Huerta, L., Puryear, S., & Wexler, E. (1999). *School choice: Abundant hopes, scarce evidence of results.* Policy Analysis for California Education (ERIC Document Reproduction Service No. ED 476 193).

Gurian, M. (1997). *The wonder of boys: What parents, mentors and educators can do to shape boys into exceptional men.* New York: Penguin.

Gurian, M. (2001). *Boys and girls learn differently! A guide for teachers and parents.* San Francisco: Jossey-Bass.

Gurian, M. (2003). *Wonder of girls: Understanding the hidden nature of our daughters.* New York: Simon and Schuster.

Hanna, F. J., & Green, A. (2004). Asian shades of spirituality: Implications for multicultural school counseling. *Professional School Counseling, 7,* 326–333.

Helms, J. E. (1994). The conceptualization of racial identity and other "racial" constructs. In E. J. Trickett, R. J. Watts, and D. Birman (Eds.), *Human diversity: Perspectives on people in context* (pp. 285–311). San Francisco: Jossey-Bass.

Hohenshil, T. H. (2000). High tech counseling. *Journal of Counseling and Development, 78,* 365–369.

Holcomb-McCoy, C. (2004). Assessing the multicultural competence of school counselors: A checklist. *Professional School Counselor, 7,* 178–186.

Hootman, J., & DeSocio, J. (2004, July/August). School nurses' important mental health role. *Behavioral Health Management, 24*(4), 25–29.

Horne, A., & Kiselica, M. S. (Eds.). (1999). *Handbook of counseling boys and adolescent males: A practitioner's guide.* Thousand Oaks, CA: Sage Publications.

Ingersoll, R. E., & Bauer, A. L. (2004). An integral approach to spiritual wellness in school counseling settings. *Professional School Counselor, 7,* 301–308.

King, K. A., Price, J. H., Telljohann, S. K., & Wahl, J. (1999). How confident do high school counselors feel in recognizing students at risk for suicide? *American Journal of Health Behavior, 23,* 457–467.

King, K. A., Price, J. H., Telljohann, S. K., & Wahl, J. (2000). Preventing adolescent suicide: Do high school counselors know the risk factors? *Professional School Counseling, 3,* 255–263.

Koch, G. (2003). Adolescent spirituality: An oxymoron? In C. Dollarhide and K. Saginak (Eds.), *School counseling in the secondary school: A comprehensive process and program* (pp. 361–372). Boston: Allyn and Bacon.

Kress, V. E. W., Gibson, D. M., & Reynolds, C. A. (2004). Adolescents who self-injure: Implications and strategies for school counselors. *Professional School Counselor, 7,* 195–201.

Levenkron, S. (1998). *Cutting: Understanding and overcoming self-mutilation.* New York: W. W. Norton.

Loesch, L. C., & Ritchie, M. H. (2005). *The accountable school counselor.* Austin, TX: CAPS Press.

Logan, R. (2001, March/April). Creating a listserv—A key to communication. *The ASCA Counselor, 38,* 12.

Lonborg, S. D., & Bowen, N. (2004). Counselors, communities, and spirituality: Ethical and multicultural considerations. *Professional School Counseling, 7,* 318–325.

MacDonald, D. (2004). Collaborating with students' spirituality. *Professional School Counseling, 7,* 293–300.

McCarthy, J., & Holliday, E. L. (2004). Help-seeking and counseling within a traditional male gender role: An examination from a multicultural perspective. *Journal of Counseling and Development, 82,* 25–30.

McWhirter, J. J., McWhirter, B. T., McWhirter, E. H., & McWhirter, R. J. (2004). *At risk youth: A comprehensive response* (3rd ed.). Pacific Grove, CA: Brooks/Cole.

Myers, J. E., Sweeney, T. J., & Witmer, J. M. (2000). The Wheel of Wellness counseling for wellness: A holistic model for treatment planning. *Journal of Counseling and Development, 78,* 251–266.

Myrick, R. D., & Sabella, R. A. (1995). Cyberspace: New place for counselor supervision. *Elementary School Guidance and Counseling, 30,* 35–45.

National Commission on Educational Excellence. (1983). *A nation at risk.* Retrieved April 22, 2006, from www.ed.gov/pubs/NatAtRisk/risk.html.

National Mental Health Association. (n.d.). Facts about teen suicide. Retrieved November 3, 2006 from www.nmha.org/suicide/youngPeople.cfm.

National Research Council. (2000). *How people learn: Brain, mind, experience, and school* (expanded ed.). Washington, DC: National Academy Press.

Nelson, R. E., & Galas, J. C. (1994). *The power to prevent suicide: A guide for teens helping teens.* Minneapolis, MN: Free Spirit.

Northwest Regional Educational Laboratory (n.d.). The catalog of school reform models. Retrieved April 22, 2006, from www.nwrel.org/scpd/catalog/index.shtml.

Owen, D. W., & Weikel, W. J. (1999). Computer utilization by school counselors. *Professional School Counseling, 2,* 179–182.

Payne, R. K. (2003). *A framework for understanding poverty* (3rd ed.). Highlands, TX: aha! Process.

Pipher, M. (1994). *Reviving Ophelia: Saving the selves of adolescent girls.* New York: Ballantine.

Pollack, W. S. (1999). *Real boys: Rescuing our sons from the myths of boyhood.* New York: Owl Books.

Rees, N. S. (2000). *School choice 2000: What's happening in the states.* Heritage Foundation Report (ERIC Document Reproduction Service No. ED 440 176).

Reinharz, S. (1994). Toward an ethnography of "voice" and "silence". In E. J. Trickett, R. J. Watts, and D. Birman (Eds.), *Human diversity: Perspectives on people in context.* (pp.178–200). San Francisco: Jossey-Bass.

Riley, P. A. (2000). A charter school survey: Parents, teachers, and principals speak out. Retrieved February 16, 2005, from www.pacificresearch.org/pub/sab/educat/chartersurvey.pdf.

Rivers, C., & Barnett, R. C. (2006, Apr. 9). The myth of 'The Boy Crisis.' *Washington Post.* Retrieved April 9, 2006, from www.washingtonpost.com/wp-dyn/content/article/2006/04/07.

Sabella, R. A., & Booker, B. L. (2003). Using technology to promote your guidance and counseling program among stake holders. *Professional School Counseling, 6,* 206–213.

Sampson, J. P., Jr., & Krumboltz, J. D. (1991). Computer-assisted instruction: A missing link in counseling. *Journal of Counseling and Development, 69,* 395–397.

SchoolGrants (2006). 10 grant writing hints. Retrieved February 14, 2006, from www.schoolgrants.org/tips/10_tips.htm.

Simmons, R. (2002). *Odd girl out.* Orlando, FL: Harcourt.

Sink, C. A. (2004). Spirituality and comprehensive school counseling programs. *Professional School Counseling, 7,* 309–317.

Sink, C. A., & Richmond, L. J. (2004). Introducing spirituality to *Professional School Counseling. Professional School Counseling, 7,* 291–292.

Starkman, N., Scales, P. C., & Roberts, C. (1999). *Great places to learn: How asset-building schools help students succeed.* Minneapolis, MN: Search Institute.

Stone, C. B., & Dahir, C. A. (2007). *School counselor accountability: A MEASURE of student success* (2nd ed.). Upper Saddle River, NJ: Pearson/Merrill/Prentice-Hall.

Sue, D. W., & Sue, D. (1999). *Counseling the culturally different: Theory and practice* (3rd ed.). New York: John Wiley & Sons.

U.S. Department of Education. (n.d.) About CSR. Retrieved April 22, 2006, from www.ed.gov/programs/compreform/2pages.html.

U.S. Department of Education. (n.d.). Fact sheet on No Child Left Behind. Retrieved April 22, 2006, from www.ed.gov/print/nclb/overview/intro/factsheet.html.

U.S. Department of Education. (March 3, 2004). Department to provide more educational options for parents. Retrieved April 22, 2006, from www.ed.gov/print/news/pressreleases/2004/03/03032004.html.

Wiseman, R. (2002). *Queen bees and wanna bes.* Norwalk, CT: Crown.

CHAPTER

16

PERSONAL AND PROFESSIONAL ISSUES

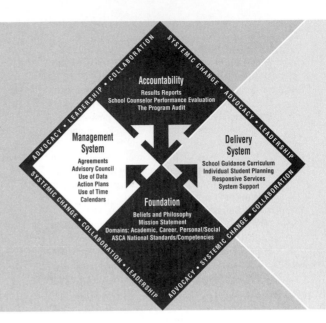

◆ LEARNING OBJECTIVES

By the end of this chapter, you will

1. understand the challenges of comprehensive school counseling in terms of holistic life management
2. understand the relationship between personal balance and professional health
3. understand the limitations of school counselors and how to deal with those limitations
4. have some concrete strategies for addressing the stress of professional school counseling
5. discuss the development of professional identity
6. identify the need for professional supervision
7. understand how consultation and networking can alleviate feelings of isolation
8. discuss the need for continued education as a professional school counselor

9. understand the role of involvement with professional associations in terms of membership, leadership, conference attendance, and contributing to the profession through conference presentations
10. identify the benefits of involvement with action research for district information as well as professional publications
11. understand the strategies for locating and engaging a mentor to enhance your professional development as well as understanding the benefits of serving as a mentor to other professionals

DOMAINS / ACTIVITIES / PARTNERS MODEL

ACTIVITIES	Academic Development ▼	Career Development ▼	Personal/ Social Development ▼			
Counseling	1a	1b	1c	5	6	7
Educating and Advocacy	2a	2b	2c	8	9	10
Consulting	3a	3b	3c	11	12	13
Leadership and Coordination	4a	4b	4c	14	15	16
	Students			Parents and Caregivers	Colleagues in Schools	Colleagues in Community

PARTNERS IN THE PROCESS

CASE STUDY ◆ Emily's Turn to Learn

Emily's week was not turning out as she had hoped. Here it was, only Wednesday, and she was already looking forward to the weekend; spring break was a distant memory, and the year seemed like it would never end. She came out of the building to go home, only to find she had a flat tire on her car. She waited in her car for the repair truck and thought about her week so far.

On Monday, she had gotten the first bit of bad news; the district was not going to replace Jose's position, so they were going from four counselors down to three. And student needs were higher than ever—with rezoning this year, several high-needs elementary schools were now part of the middle school's attendance district. Then, with the homeless shelter opening up down the street from the middle school, they had several students in and out within weeks—a lot of time spent there with scheduling and transition services, only to have them leave within a couple of days. Every year, the counselors worked with more students with greater needs but weren't going to have one-fourth of their staff next year.

Then, yesterday, Emily had gotten her annual professional performance review. She was not pleased with her review. She was supposed to learn email and the new school registration and student record package, but she had not had enough time last year to learn those things. The final report on the grant funds from last year still wasn't done. She was also supposed to conduct an in-service for the staff on the workshop she attended on reactive attachment disorder, but she never got around to that either. And even though she was elected to serve on the state's advisory council for professional school counseling, she had not attended any meetings. Emily thought she worked hard enough; she deserved the time she took off to relax. Besides, she was trying to spend more time with students, but there were so many other things that got in the way. The director of pupil services for the district had judged her too harshly for these other minor failings. Didn't central office care about the professional counselors at all?

Now this flat. Sighing, she checked her watch. Another twenty minutes before the tow truck would come. She decided to go back into the building to go to the restroom. Inside, she ducked into the closest girls' bathroom. Within seconds, several girls entered, and Emily became an unwilling witness to the conversation.

One voice said, "Yeah, she said the counselor didn't really understand anything she was telling her. Ms. Dorado just kept pushing her to tell her mother, tell her mother, you know? She said it really made her mad that Ms. Dorado wasn't listening to her. I thought counselors were supposed to listen to you!"

The second voice laughed. "Maybe it's just a problem with time. I know every time I go to talk to Ms. Dorado, she has about five minutes for me, then she has to go to another meeting, or whatever it is that counselors do. No one can ever find her. No one seems to know what the heck she does. I see her in the faculty lounge all the time."

" 'Look at me—I'm so overworked I need a break!' " Both voices giggled. "No one I know has ever gotten any help from her. They should fire her. Everyone always goes to the other counselors. She's a big joke. She never does what she says she's going to do. That new kid said she was supposed to get back to him with changes in his schedule, but she never did." The voices moved toward the door, then faded as the conversation moved out into the hallway.

Emily wanted to cry. She waited until the voices were out in the hall, then she went back out to wait in her car. Deep in thought, she didn't even see the repair truck arrive. She jumped a mile when the driver came to her window and asked, "Are you Emily Dorado? You called for a tire repair?"

CHALLENGE QUESTIONS

What was your reaction as you read the scenario? What conclusions did you come to about the counselor's job performance? What were some areas for potential improvement that you could see?

If you were this counselor, you could choose to ignore the feedback or you could choose to learn from it. What would your choice be?

◆ PERSONAL MENTAL HEALTH: THE SEARCH FOR BALANCE

Life is a series of choices, and we are all responsible for our choices. We can choose to live life out of balance, either self-focused and self-absorbed (me-first) or other-focused ("I'll give you my soul if you will just approve of me"). Both of these lifestyles are out of balance and unhealthy, causing problems in both work and personal life. One is no better than the other.

In Chapter 4, we discussed the need for balance in a CSCP in terms of balanced activities based on the need of the partner. In this current chapter, we are shifting the concept of balance to focus on the life of the counselor. In this context, "balance" can be conceptualized as the means by which the needs of the internal reality (the counselor's personal needs) and the external reality (the needs of all partners of the CSCP) are brought into alignment. We will use the metaphor of a *boundary*, where the needs of the self and the needs of others meet. It is often here that creativity emerges and we bring out the best in ourselves. In research describing creative thinking, this boundary causes contact between imaginary and visceral, between logical and intuitive, between body and mind, between science and art (DeBono, 1992; Gruber, 1993; Morris, 1992; Root-Bernstein & Root-Bernstein, 1999). For the purposes of

The ASCA School Counselor Performance Standards are silent in terms of this topic, but the importance of professional health and viability are embedded within standards that address effective programs and relationships.

The CACREP Standards for School Counseling Programs addressed in this chapter are

A.3 role, function, and professional identity of the school counselor in relation to the roles of other professional and support personnel in the school; and

A.6 current issues, policies, laws, and legislation relevant to school counseling.

this book, we will view balance as the need to nurture both the personal needs and the professional needs of the counselor, to the benefit of both aspects of existence. To function well as a counselor, you need to understand how to take care of your personal issues and needs while simultaneously taking care of the needs of your partners in the DAP model. Without balance, your personal needs will drive your professional choices, or your professional needs will compromise your personal self mentally, physically, and/or emotionally. Counselors are the models for mental health in the schools; counselors living with these out-of-balance conditions compromise their own and other counselors' credibility and ability to function.

In general, there are many sources of stress for a school counselor. Stress comes from working with others who don't understand the work that counselors do, from struggles of the students, and from budgets that do not keep up with needs. Other stressors include a lack of privacy and anonymity due to heightened visibility as a mental health professional and feelings of isolation resulting from a lack of professional peers within the school setting (Morrissette, 2000). We cannot change the context or realities of the job; what we can do is understand and prepare for ways to counteract these stressors.

In Chapter 1, we discussed the professional competencies for school counselors as outlined by the American School Counselor Association (ASCA) and the Council for the Accreditation of Counseling and Related Educational Programs (CACREP), and the rest of this book has been designed to help you to develop those competencies. In Chapter 1, we also outlined the personal qualities that professional school counselors need: creativity and imagination, flexibility, courage and belief, and passion. These are the antidotes for the stressors of working as a school counselor. This chapter is devoted to helping you to evaluate and refine those personal qualities that typify the best school counselors.

Where do these qualities come from? They are partly the result of temperament and they are partly the result of personal and professional health. We can't change temperament, but we can maximize our personal and professional health.

Finding Your Center

The term *center* is used in this context to refer to various aspects of our existence. It is used to refer to a spiritual center, involving our relationship with a higher power or higher purpose, and to a moral center, involving our relationship with our own values and morals.

Our awareness of our own values and morals is a crucial piece of being able to understand ourselves and, by extension, our students and partners. Since many concepts within our traditional definitions of "mental health" resonate with Western values of individualism, autonomy, environmental mastery, self-acceptance, happiness, and purpose in life, we must understand our own moral center and openly dialogue with clients about the "ongoing interpretive process" between our moral center and theirs (Christopher, 1999, p. 150). This inner work has implications both for helping our students and for helping us work on our own issues. It is necessary for our connection with our students; it is also necessary for our connection with our inner resources. In this context, finding our moral center involves reflection and insight, which requires quiet reflection, compassion, patience, and a commitment to deepening our self-understanding.

Palmer refers to this as "sounding our own depths" (1998, p. 31). Deep self-knowledge facilitates the creation of a learning community. Palmer reinforces the connection between our inner reality and our outer work (counseling or educating), and challenges us to develop an ongoing dialogue with our own inner teachers. These inner teachers are the source of our professionalism, our desire to help others grow, and ultimately, our wisdom.

Other authors use the terms *spirit* and *wisdom* to describe this sense of connection between self, others, and higher purpose. Fox (1994) suggests that education of the whole person—heart, body, mind, and spirit; books and life; intellect and imagination—should be a part of our curriculum, where students learn awe, wisdom, compassion, and inner growth. This new vision of education would transform the role of counselors, giving additional support to the idea that counselors must know their own center to help students locate and nurture theirs.

In another context, Young-Eisendrath and Miller (2000) examine the connection between spiritual development and health. "[W]e regard spiritual development to be a necessary component of a healthy, effective life as a human being. . . . Mature spirituality is the honing of integrity, wisdom, and transcendence in the service of the question of what it means to be human. . . ." (p. 5). As counselors, educators, and human beings, there is support for the idea that being centered fosters the elements needed to maintain balance in life. It is from our "center," or core, that we find the spring from which creativity, imagination, flexibility, courage, belief, faith, and passion flow. If we drain this spring dry, we have nothing left to give others. If we dam the flow to save all these precious qualities, we are no longer of service to our CSCP partners. We must be able to dip from the spring as needed to replenish ourselves, while monitoring the flow to ensure enough reserves for the future.

Reflection Moment ◆

Where do you go to get centered? How often do you go there? Do you need to go there more often?

◆ ◆

Doing Your Best, Then Letting Go

One of the most difficult lessons for new counselors is learning when to let go. When do you know you've done all you can to help a student, parent, co-worker? When is enough *enough*? In general, as with any counseling situation, the first step comes with the recognition that each of us is responsible for our own choices in life. As counselors, it is our job to make sure the door to change is open and that the client's movement toward healthy choices is applauded and commended. We can open the door, we can make the "healthy" side of the door attractive and appealing, we can point out the costs of remaining on the other side of the door, but we cannot force anyone to walk through the door. We are only human, with all the limitations that implies. But we are obligated by profession and training to give 100 percent in these efforts to persuade someone to make healthy choices.

With adults, most counselors feel comfortable leaving the choice with the client. However, with young people, give extra effort to helping them. In keeping with the metaphor, consider giving 110 percent. School counselors should open the door, encourage students to walk through the door, make the other side of the door very unappealing, and invite them again to walk over that threshold. When does enough constitute enough? Only you can answer that for yourself. What can you live with, without compromising your own personal and professional health?

"Letting go" involves an additional concept inherent in counseling in general—that of time. Change takes place when the client is ready, and not a moment before. The student needs time to evaluate the risks and benefits of walking through the door to change. If a student, in spite of the counselor's best efforts in giving 110 percent, chooses not to walk over the threshold, "letting go" involves the recognition that the student, for his or her own reasons, is not ready to change yet. Many of the most meaningful conversations counselors have with students are those that take place years after students have left school, in which students share with counselors how meaningful the counselors' interventions were all those years ago.

In this way, there is a strong similarity between counseling and parenting. Often, it's not until we reach our twenties that we realize what our parents were trying to tell us in our teens, that the lessons they were trying to teach us really did have value after all. Just as good parents must let go of their children to allow them to learn their lessons, so too must good counselors. Sometimes the best lessons come from bruised knees or bruised egos, and we can't save them from the lessons life has to teach them.

Reflection Moment ✦

Have you had experience with finding the limit of your professional endurance? Have you had to make the difficult choice to let go? What was that experience like for you?

✦ ✦

Stress Management Strategies

As school counselors, you will have many opportunities to talk with your DAP partners about stress. Children, adolescents, and adults can benefit tremendously from understanding how stress affects decision making; physical, emotional, and spiritual health; and relationships. Stress compromises performance, erodes stamina, and disables the natural resilience of both body and spirit. But stress cannot be avoided; it is a natural part of our everyday existence and keeps us striving to improve ourselves and our lives (Seaward, 1994). The best we can do is understand and manage stress, because it cannot be eradicated.

First, it is important to understand that stress comes from the way we interpret and internalize events in our lives. Any given event does not cause stress; the emotions we experience as a result of our beliefs about these events are the sources of stress. Our beliefs about the "fairness" of life, our "right" to happiness, the way we "deserve" to be treated by life and others often result in anger, frustration, fear, and indignation. Of these, the strongest stress triggers are the emotions of anger and fear (Seaward, 1994). These emotional states, in turn, trigger physiological responses that involve the nervous system and the immune system, which in turn telegraph our internal emotional states into physical reality (Seaward, 1994).

The ultimate anti-stress weapon, according to Seaward (1994), is self-esteem. It is strong self-esteem that allows us to keep fear from hijacking our nervous and immune systems. With strong self-esteem, we are less likely to catastrophize events in our lives, and we are better able to bounce back from life's inevitable disappointments and frustrations. You will undoubtedly notice that many of the strategies for managing stress are designed to enhance this fragile and elusive quality.

Managing stress can be accomplished in a variety of ways. The following stress management strategies are adapted from Seaward (1994).

1. Enhance your spiritual connection with your internal reality. Be centered within all elements of your identity. Get to know yourself well and explore your inner reality with compassion.
2. Enhance your spiritual connections with however you perceive and define the divine. Seaward provides an excellent reading list, including various perspectives on spirituality—Carl Jung, M. Scott Peck, Black Elk, Matthew Fox, Joan Borysenko, Jesus Christ, Lao Tzu, and Albert Einstein—that are then woven into some common themes of spirituality.
3. Enhance your spiritual connections with loving others, to increase healthy bonding, acceptance, peace, compassion, and respect in your daily life.
4. Explore and define your personal value system, so that you live with greater congruence and authenticity within that value system.
5. Explore and define a meaningful purpose for your life. Have goals to achieve, serve to promote love and respect in the world, or have some purpose to fill. This helps you keep your life in perspective and allows you to better handle disappointments and pain.
6. Explore the connection between your thoughts, expectations, and experiences to determine if you could restructure your cognitions to reduce your experience of stress.
7. Learn and practice assertiveness skills to help you maintain healthy boundaries.
8. Consider journaling as a means of exploring your feelings and experiences.
9. Use art therapy to tap, explore, and/or release your feelings about your experiences.
10. Use humor therapy to cope with disappointments and frustrations. It is important to recognize that there are healthy and unhealthy applications of humor. Those that enhance connection, compassion, and relief are healthy; those that ridicule or demean others are not healthy. To foster stress relief, humor used in a healthy way can build connections with others, reframe experiences, and allow us to view ourselves, others, and our world with more hope and compassion.
11. Use creative problem-solving strategies, such as brainstorming, clustering, and metaphors. Effective problem solving fosters self-efficacy and self-esteem.
12. Enhance your communication skills. Much of the stress of life comes from difficult relationships with others; communicating more effectively can substantially improve our relationships.
13. Improve your time-management skills. Having an efficient means of allocating and accounting for time can help you manage the busy schedule of a school counselor. Recall that the establishment and maintenance of a calendar is a part of the ASCA National Model.
14. Consider a support group to help you cope with your own unique life situation.
15. Having a hobby can increase your social connections and creativity.

16. Consider the practice of forgiveness to manage your stress.
17. Taking care of your body is also essential. The primary strategies for taking care of yourself involve a three-pronged approach:
    ◆ Exercise with a physician's approval
    ◆ Proper nutrition that supports a healthy lifestyle
    ◆ Relaxation, including diaphragmatic breathing, meditation, Hatha yoga (meditation, breathing, and various body postures), mental imagery (taking a mental vacation), music, massage, T'ai Chi Ch'uan (movement, breathing, and concentration), progressive muscular relaxation, autogenic training, and biofeedback

These ideas are offered as a means of promoting your holistic well-being and health. After all, if you're not healthy, you will not be of much use to your students or adult partners.

Reflection Moment ◆

How do you know when you're having problems with your stress level? How do you deal with stress? Are there stress management strategies that you can put into place now to help you deal with the stress of graduate school?

◆ ◆

◆PROFESSIONAL HEALTH

A counselor's professional health is also an issue of this chapter. Although there is substantial overlap between your personal and professional health, the strategies of this section are designed to help you address the work-related challenges of school counselors. Many of the challenges faced by school counselors have already been discussed, but an overview here might help you understand the context of this discussion.

1. Counselors often feel isolated since there is a limited number of counselors in any given district or building.
2. The role of the counselor is not well understood by parents, students, teachers, or administrators.
3. Counselors are often defined as ancillary services, not central to the functioning of the school.
4. Counselors' time often is eroded by activities that are not essential for the effective functioning of the comprehensive school counseling program.
5. There is little recognition for the hard work counselors do.
6. There may be little privacy for school counselors and their families in communities where school professionals are well known.
7. There are tremendous needs among all the partners, and students, families, co-workers, and entire communities look to the school counselor to address a variety of problems.
8. Information about ways of helping, perspectives on new or emerging problems, and technology are always evolving.
9. Burnout is high in the helping professions, and opportunities to "re-charge one's batteries" are few.

Following are some ideas to help you mitigate the effects of these challenges.

Professional Identity

In Chapter 5, we talked about the professionalization of school counseling and the development of professional identity for school counselors, which resulted in the development of the ASCA National Model. Similarly, school counselors undergo a personal process in the development of a professional identity. It is helpful to have an overview of this process to understand how unique and diverse school counseling programs evolve. According to Brott and Myers (1999), this process involves the slow internalization of external standards and priorities. At first, the school counselor defines his or her role solely in external terms, derived first from graduate training and secondarily from the school and/or district administrators, other counselors, and existing programs. In the middle of this developmental process, school counselors interact with a variety of perspectives that provide feedback about the school counseling program and the role and skills of the school counselor. In other words, the counselor confronts a wide variety of evaluative voices (p. 344). In the final stage of professional development, the school counselor uses personal judgments in the definition of the role of the school counselor and in the design and definition of the comprehensive school counseling program. These personal judgments are now defensible as coming from professional experience and perspective, as professional and personal identities merge, unify, and solidify.

This process explains why it is difficult for new counselors to engage in strong advocacy for the professional identity of all school counselors. For the most part, the development of this professional "voice" does not manifest until the third stage of the process as outlined by Brott and Myers (1999). In spite of how difficult advocacy may be, one of the most important ways school counselors can work to mitigate the problems of the profession is through enhancing the identity and professionalism of the counseling profession in general, and the school counseling profession in particular. Johnson (2000) argues that school counselors must "refine their professional identity as highly trained practitioners, whose goal is to facilitate all students to become effective learners through the provision of a contemporary, integrated school counseling program that promotes the achievement of developmentally based competencies across academic, career, and personal/social domains. . . . [T]heir operational identity needs to be shifted from focusing on the individual services they provide to focusing on the integrated school counseling program as a whole. Similarly, their . . . target of services needs to move from being the individual student to the school system as a whole. . . ." (p. 32). To accomplish this, school counselors must align their mission as congruent with the academic mission of the school and document ways in which their work helps students to become effective learners (Johnson, 2000). Education of the DAP partners, advocacy for the role of the school counselor, and leadership of the program in terms of leadership teams of the school and district will help provide a common ground from which school counselors can establish their contribution to students and the school.

Portfolios

Documentation of your contributions is essential, and there are a variety of ways to do this. In addition to the Results Report and the Program Audit of the National Model (see Chapter 5 for these topics), the professional portfolio provides a venue for that documentation (Boes, VanZile-Tamsen, & Jackson, 2001; James & Greenwalt, 2001; Johnson, 2000) which would be appropriate for the School Counselor Performance evaluation (ASCA National Model). Portfolios are the compilation and maintenance of various "artifacts" (documents, photographs, letters, disks, audio- and videotapes, computer disks—any work-related product) that describe and validate one's work history. James and Greenwalt (2001) refine this definition even further, describing the elements of a "working portfolio" as the documentation of one's entire professional development, and the "presentation portfolio" as a select portion of the working portfolio that is used for a specific purpose (a job interview or a consulting presentation, for example).

As you have noticed from the Application section of each chapter of this book, these portfolio artifacts are selected and/or designed to illustrate what you can do as a professional school counselor. Elements of the working portfolio could include the following (adapted from Boes, VanZile-Tamsen, & Jackson, 2001; James & Greenwalt, 2001; Johnson, 2000):

1. Your philosophy of education
2. Your philosophy of comprehensive school counseling
3. Curriculum vitae (a comprehensive overview of all work locations, dates, and duties, and all educational experiences, courses, workshops, and conferences)
4. Resume (a summary of those work and educational experiences)
5. Practicum and internship experiences
6. Results of work projects (such as new programs, surveys, grant proposals, needs assessments, outcomes assessments, reports)
7. Professional credentials, such as licenses, certifications, or endorsements
8. Continuing education courses, workshops, or presentations you have attended, with dates, locations, and presenters noted
9. Presentations you've made (including developmental curriculum lessons, workshops, in-services, and/or groups you have conducted)
10. Publications you have authored (including in-house publications such as brochures, flyers, or handbooks for students, parents, faculty, etc.)
11. Professional memberships, including dates and offices held
12. Service to school, district, and/or community in terms of committee membership, volunteer positions, and so on

Presentation portfolios, as mentioned, are selected artifacts from the work portfolio that serve to document a selection of your professional history. For example, if your state has specific competencies that must be documented for licensure, you might use a presentation portfolio for that purpose. Boes, VanZile-Tamsen, and Jackson (2001) suggest that you organize this special portfolio using the ASCA National Standards for Student Academic, Career, and Personal/Social Development (Appendix B), and include a reflective self-evaluation. Alternatively, it could make more sense to structure your portfolio around the School Counselor Performance Standards (Appendix C) as articulated in the National Model and as encouraged in the Application section of each chapter of this book. A more common example of a presentation portfolio is one that is used for purposes of a job search, in which the applicant takes the presentation portfolio to the interview to share with the search committee. *Note:* Electronic portfolios, those stored to a disk, CD, or available on a web page, are increasingly viewed as "cutting edge" for counselors who must be able to function in this age of technology.

Supervision

It is clear from the literature that there are problems in the field in terms of supervision of counselors (Dollarhide & Miller, 2006). Supervision can be conceptualized in terms of three functions:

1. Administrative supervision, involving accounting for time, daily attendance, communication skills, adherence to school policies; may be provided by building or district administrator (these are articulated in the management agreements described in the National Model)
2. Program supervision, involving feedback relative to the progress of the comprehensive school counseling program; may be provided by district pupil services administrator or a counselor supervisor within the building
3. Technical, clinical, or counseling supervision, involving feedback on counseling, intervention, and developmental curriculum delivery skills; best if provided by a more experienced counselor (Roberts & Borders, 1994; Schmidt, 1990)

It is important that you understand that each of the three supervision venues listed above is designed to accomplish a unique purpose. The first is to help you function in the school setting; the second, to help you function in an effective comprehensive school counseling program; and the third, to help you function effectively with students, families, and colleagues.

As a counselor trainee, you will receive supervision from a supervising counselor. As a professional, you will be supervised by a number of supervisors, depending on the way the district designates personnel for the three supervision functions listed above. The most common scenario is supervision by a senior counselor for clinical and program supervision, and supervision by the principal for the administrative supervision. Depending on the district, the district pupil services director may also provide program supervision (which is good if this person has a counseling background). It is a challenge when a noncounselor is designated for any other type of supervision than administrative supervision, for good reason. Noncounselors usually do not have adequate understanding of the counseling profession, and it will be up to you to educate that person about counseling.

Although there is no shortage of people in the schools who will give you feedback about how you are doing your job, there is a general hands-off philosophy among counselors in terms of clinical supervision. But this kind of supervision, especially for new professionals in the field, can be extremely helpful in your development of a sense of professional efficacy (Crespi, Fischetti, & Butler, 2001). In spite of a lack of supervisors in the field who have received training in supervision (Kahn, 1999; Roberts & Morotti, 2001), you are urged to voluntarily solicit clinical feedback. The ideal situation would involve obtaining this supervision from an experienced counselor (Dollarhide & Miller, 2006), but a study of peer group supervision suggested substantial professional advantages accrued to the participants (Agnew, Vaught, Getz, & Fortune, 2000). Specifically, 97 percent of the 29 participants cited positive growth in clinical skills, increased sense of professionalism, increased consultation and referral skills, increased confidence, increased comfort with the job, decreased feelings of burnout, and increased professional validation. In addition, supervision is an important strategy to improve ethical counseling (Herlihy & Corey, 1996).

As you progress through your graduate training to become a school counselor, you will receive supervision in your field experiences (termed "practicum" and/or "internship" in most programs). According to Miller and Dollarhide (2006), you can begin your own professional development as a supervisee, by attending to and learning about supervision *while you are experiencing it.* Although formal training in supervision is usually reserved for doctoral-level students, you can explore the possibility of taking the class and/or read the professional literature in supervision, because it will enhance your ability to gain the maximum benefit from the supervision you receive. In addition, it will increase your ability, once you have been a professional for a couple of years (two years of experience is mandated by the Council for Accreditation of Counseling and Related Programs [CACREP, 2000]), to serve as a supervisor for upcoming counselor trainees.

Colleague Consultation and Networking

There is very little in this world that can help us feel better about our situation than consulting and networking with others. Although there may be few formal opportunities to network with your school counseling colleagues, nothing prevents you from initiating a "counselors' lunch" once a month or once a semester. Some counselors take advantage of in-service time provided by the district to call a meeting of the counselors and/or pupil services professionals to discuss issues of importance in the district and community. In this situation, the director of pupil services is usually involved to design the official agenda.

In addition, one-on-one consultation with your peers can establish resources and expertise that can help you do your job more effectively. This consultation is not limited to counselors; other pupil services professionals provide a rich source of perspectives and expertise. Access the expertise you will find in the teachers, school social worker, school psychologist, and others. In addition, there are many resources in the community with whom you could consult to enhance your functioning in your CSCP.

Both formal and informal networks are essential to your professional survival. It is important that you have opportunities to understand the challenges facing the school, the district, and the entire community. After all, how can you design systemic interventions and build community in your school if you can't build it among your colleagues and peers?

Lifelong Continuing Education

All counselors are in need of lifelong professional training and education, a position supported in the professional ethics of both ACA and ASCA. School counselors in the field sometimes lament that their districts won't pay for their ongoing educational needs. But note that you should not wait for your district to pay for your continued education. That is not the district's responsibility—it is your professional responsibility to remain up-to-date with the innovations in the field. In addition, new perspectives on important topics, such as multicultural counseling strategies (Constantine & Yeh, 2001) keep skills fresh and enhance self-efficacy.

There are many opportunities for continuing education. These include

1. In-service topics offered by the district
2. University classes
3. Continuing education programs offered by universities
4. Presentations by local mental health organizations and hospitals
5. Online programs for continuing education
6. Conferences offered by national and state professional associations (American Counseling Association, American School Counselor Association, and their state affiliates)

In addition, you will want to remain up-to-date with the professional literature from your professional associations. You must read new books that address the issues your students, families, and community are facing. Remain aware of new music, movies, TV shows, and images pervading our culture that send messages to students about how they should be—how they should act, feel, think, and look—and that send messages about how their families, schools, and community should be. You must commit to your own lifelong learning.

Professional Associations

Membership and active involvement in your national, state, and local professional associations will provide you with a number of substantial benefits that will directly enhance the work you do in the schools. Networking with colleagues, professional journals with current perspectives on the field, professional liability insurance, and opportunities for continuing education through conferences are the benefits of membership in professional associations. In addition, your contribution to those associations in terms of your time and involvement provides you with a greater connection to other dedicated professionals. Service in a leadership capacity in an association can range from being a member of a committee to running for office; a wide range of talents and perspectives is necessary for these associations to function effectively. And this does not supplant the need for counselors to be involved in terms of legislative and social activism, supporting legislation that enhances the professionalization of counseling or that provides support for schools. In addition, professional associations rely on their members to share their expertise in the form of conference presentations. Consider membership, service, involvement, activism, leadership, and presentations when you join the professional ranks of school counselors in the field.

Action Research

If your program is comprehensive, you will be structuring your program to conform to the ASCA National Model, and as such, you will use data for management and accountability. It is important to note that this information could also be invaluable to your colleagues in other schools, districts, and locations. Action research refers to insights gained by professionals in the field—data collected from students, schools, teachers, programs, activities—any source of information in your job or school. Such information is vital for understanding individual schools in context, providing a basis for locating your situation relative to another's situation. Are your students experiencing something different from those at another school, community, or state? Is there a program that works better than this one to address these issues? How might your students react to this new program? Are the needs of your students and families different from those elsewhere? If so, how are they different? What have others learned about this resource, this counseling strategy, this approach to parents? These questions can only be answered by practicing professionals who are in the field, working directly with students, resources, and parents.

When you initiate a new program and compile your data for your outcomes assessments and results reports, consider how your data might help others in the field. Don't hide behind "No one would want to read anything written by little ol' me." Consider sharing with others through a district newsletter, state association newsletter or journal, or national association newsletter or professional journal.

Just as geese flying in a V-shape benefit from the uplift of the wings of the goose in front, as professionals, we benefit from the wisdom of those who have come before us.

Being Mentored and Mentoring Others

Mentoring provides numerous benefits to both the person being mentored and the mentor. For the mentor, the benefits include opportunities for self-reflection and the positive feelings about making a contribution (VanZandt & Perry, 1992). Overall, mentoring provides an orientation for new professionals that helps them grow in their sense of intellectual competence, sense of purpose, feelings of autonomy, and personal integrity (Bova & Phillips, 1984). It is a forum in which mentees learn

1. risk-taking behaviors: dealing with failure, dealing with risk
2. communication skills
3. political skills: how/where to get jobs, inside information about people in power, and the organization's values (a socialization function)
4. specific professional skills: putting theory into practice, getting the big picture, professional skills, and learning how to put problems into context (Bova & Phillips, 1984)

If mentoring is such a wonderful thing, why doesn't everyone do it? There are a number of reasons that mentoring is not a universal experience. These reasons usually include lack of time, lack of a direct payoff with so many professional priorities, lack of interest in that kind of relationship with co-workers, and lack of knowledge or expertise in mentoring another person. It is important to recognize that locating a mentor is often a challenge, but it must be voluntary. Too much structure can kill the instinctive and voluntary commitment of mentors and the interest of mentees (Bennetts, 1995; Blunt, 1995).

Mentoring is a new way of thinking about a professional relationship. It is a connection between learner and teacher, centering around the teaching of meaning within the context of a professional setting. In this relationship, the goal is to help the new professional develop a professional identity in an environment of support and challenge. To help you understand what makes mentoring unique, consider the following illustrations. In Figure 16.1, various roles are described in terms of support and challenge. In Figure 16.2, the three roles of mentor, consultant, and counselor are located on a continuum describing the focus of the relationship.

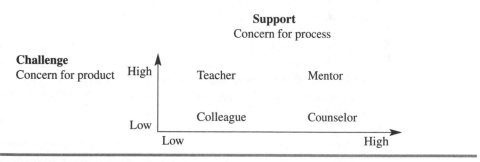

FIGURE 16.1 ◆ Roles of Mentors

Role:	**Consulting**	**Mentoring**	**Counseling**
Focus:	Answers to problems	Balance between solutions and exploration	Personal issues

FIGURE 16.2 ◆ Focus of the Relationship

Tentoni (1995) outlined a number of activities of mentors. These include sponsoring the mentee's involvement in the environment, supporting the mentee, encouraging and affirming the mentee's independence and professionalism, and inspiring the new professional to work hard. In addition, mentors provide problem solving, listening, clarifying, and advising, similar to an effective counselor. The mentor also befriends the new professional, accepting new ideas and relating to the new professional. Finally, the mentor is also a teacher, modeling professional behavior and informing the mentee about the job. It is also important to recognize that there are four phases of the mentoring relationship: initiation, cultivation, separation, and ending, in which the relationship is redefined as that of colleagues (Daloz, 1988; Parks, 1990).

To help you determine if you want to seek out a mentor and to help you decide if you would like to mentor others, the following are traditional strategies for mentoring (Borman & Colson, 1984). It is important to note that these strategies about mentoring must be balanced with information about the mentoring needs of women and persons of color (Christopher, 1996; Hawks & Muha, 1991; Heinrich, 1995; Smith & Davidson, 1992). Some of these traditional strategies for mentoring are premised on a male, Eurocentric value system, which may pose certain challenges for women and persons of color who are not necessarily socialized to be comfortable with these behaviors. These potentially challenging strategies are italicized.

1. Encourage a positive attitude.
2. Encourage the mentee to establish personal values and goals.
3. Encourage the mentee to maintain an open mind to new ideas.
4. Interactions should be that of sharing, caring, and empathizing.
5. Encourage the mentee to use creative problem-solving processes.
6. Encourage the mentee to be an attentive listener and *an assertive questioner*. (Being too assertive might be contrary to cultural norms to be passive in relationships.)
7. Encourage the mentee to be an *independent thinker*. (Some people are socialized to consider the needs of others before self.)
8. Encourage the mentee to *recognize individual strengths and uniquenesses* and build on them. (Independent thinking and focus on individual strengths presumes an individualistic worldview versus a collectivistic worldview.)
9. Assist the mentee in developing *confidence*. (For those from a more collective worldview, this process involves more support and less challenge.)
10. Stress that the mentee should be aware of the environment, *intuitive* (intuition could be culturally or gender-influenced), problem-sensitive, and ready to make the most of *opportunities*. (There are implications in terms of competitive versus cooperative cultural norms).
11. Encourage the mentee to be an *active participant*, not a spectator. (This may depend on the action orientation of the mentee's culture in a new setting; for example, many Native American cultures stress patient observation of a new environment before becoming actively involved.)
12. Encourage the mentee to be a risk-taker.
13. Encourage the mentee to be flexible and adaptable in attitudes and actions, looking for alternatives, and seeing situations/persons from different perspectives.

In addition to these traditional strategies, the following are suggestions for mentoring based on recent research.

14. Encourage your mentee to be flexible in the expectations of the mentoring relationship. Not all mentoring needs can or should be met through one mentoring relationship.
15. Strive to minimize dependence. Encourage the mentee to try it on his or her own, just as a good parent's goal is to help a child live his or her own life.
16. Monitor your own attachment to the relationship. Recognize that all mentoring relationships must eventually end to be healthy.

If you decide that you are interested in locating a mentor, you will want to look for a seasoned counselor who is not your direct supervisor. This will reduce dual relationship issues with a supervisor and will enable you to more freely share your concerns and lack of confidence. Trust is an important part of the mentoring relationship (Heinrich, 1995), so you will want to get to know the potential mentor well to determine if you would have a good match between personality, trustworthiness, and personal style. Often you do not need a formal request of the mentor to determine if that person is interested in mentoring you; usually the best mentoring relationships evolve naturally between a novice and a seasoned professional.

As you mature in your own professional identity, remember that new, incoming professionals could also benefit from your support in their professional journey. Just as you are being encouraged to consider involvement in research and association leadership, you are also urged to consider mentoring new professionals.

Reflection Moment ◆

Each of these topics for your professional health is important to your professional future. Which ones can you make a commitment to at this point in your training?

◆ ◆

CASE STUDY REVISITED ◆ Integration

Now that you have read the chapter, consider again Emily's situation.

1. As you review the topics of this chapter, what activities would help Emily do her job better?
2. Apply each of these topics to her situation, one at a time. In what ways would her situation have been different had she followed all the suggestions in this chapter?
3. Do you believe that she can turn this around and salvage her career? To do that, what does she need to do differently with students? With the district administration? With her colleagues in the school?
4. If you were Emily, what would you do first?

APPLICATION (Possible portfolio artifacts are noted)

1. In each chapter of this book, you have been encouraged to do Application activities to deepen and broaden your understanding of the book's contents. Many of these activities are directly relevant for your presentation portfolio in which you document what you can bring to a CSCP. Create this portfolio, selecting at least one possible portfolio artifact from each chapter.
2. Select two or three of the most interesting topics from this chapter and conduct an Internet search on those topics. Compile those sites for sharing with your classmates.

3. Think about the activities or places that make you feel most at peace. How do those relate to your profession? (Or do they?)

4. Interview a local school counselor in terms of the opportunities for networking and supervision. How does that professional attend to these issues? Are the structures for these contacts built into the job, or will you need to create these opportunities for yourself? Based on your interview, create a plan for obtaining networking and supervision as a professional. (Possible portfolio artifact)

5. What are your plans for involvement with professional associations? Interview a school counselor about his or her membership in professional organizations. Would you ever be interested in service, leadership, or presentations? Outline a plan for that involvement. (Possible portfolio artifact)

6. What are the current issues facing schools, counselors, and school counselors in your state or city? Contact the local professional associations (state ACA or state ASCA) to learn about their legislative agendas for these issues. Outline a strategy to help them generate counselor support and public support for the identified legislation. (Possible portfolio artifact)

7. Outline a plan for your continuing education for the next five years. Determine the financial resources you would need to commit to follow your plan. (Possible portfolio artifact)

8. Outline a plan for action research in a practicum or internship site. Consider a needs assessment of students, parents, teachers, administrators, or other pupil service professionals. What specific information do you think would be of interest to the readers of a state journal of school counseling? (Possible portfolio artifact)

9. Have you ever been mentored? Have you ever been a mentor? Journal those experiences.

SUGGESTED READINGS

Boes, S. R., VanZile-Tamsen, C., & Jackson, C. M. (2001). Portfolio development for the 21st century school counselor. *Professional School Counseling, 4,* 229–231. This article outlines a very comprehensive approach to the creation of a professional portfolio for school counselors.

Brockman, J. (Ed.). (1992). *Creativity.* New York: Simon & Schuster. This book presents perspectives on creativity written by authors from many different fields, including science, art, medicine, and psychology. These perspectives help the reader consider ways to increase creativity in one's own life.

Brott, P. E., & Myers, J. E. (1999). Development of professional school counselor identity: A grounded theory. *Professional School Counseling, 2,* 339–348. This article outlines the process and stages of development of a professional identity for school counselors. This perspective can help new counselors understand their feelings of confusion and being overwhelmed by the role ambiguity of school counselors.

Seaward, B. L. (1994). *Managing stress: Principles and strategies for health and wellbeing.* Boston: Jones & Bartlett. This book outlines the sources and mechanisms of stress and then takes a broad and holistic look at the strategies for managing stress. It is an excellent tool for counselors who are providing developmental curriculum programs and/or group counseling experiences on stress management, as well as a wonderful tool for counselors to manage their own stress.

REFERENCES

Agnew, T., Vaught, C. C., Getz, H. G., & Fortune, J. (2000). Peer group clinical supervision program fosters confidence and professionalism. *Professional School Counseling, 4,* 6–12.

Bennetts, C. (1995). The secrets of a good relationship. *People Management, 1*(13), 38–40.

Blunt, N. (1995). Learning from the wisdom of others. *People Management, 1*(11), 38–40.

Boes, S. R., VanZile-Tamsen, C., & Jackson, C. M. (2001). Portfolio development for the 21st century school counselor. *Professional School Counseling, 4,* 229–231.

Borman, C., & Colson, S. (1984). Mentoring—An effective career guidance technique. The *Vocational Guidance Quarterly, 32*(3), 192–197.

Bova, R. M., & Phillips, R. R. (1984). Mentoring as a learning experience for adults. *Journal of Teacher Education, 35*(3), 16–20.

Brott, P. E., & Myers, J. E. (1999). Development of professional school counselor identity: A grounded theory. *Professional School Counseling, 2,* 339–348.

Christopher, J. C. (1996). Counseling's inescapable moral visions. *Journal of Counseling & Development, 75,* 17–25.

Christopher, J. C. (1999). Situating psychological well-being: Exploring the cultural roots of its theory and research. *Journal of Counseling and Development, 77,* 141–152.

Constantine, M. G., & Yeh, C. J. (2001). Multicultural training, self-construals, and multicultural competence of school counselors. *Professional School Counseling, 4,* 202–207.

Council for Accreditation of Counseling and Related Educational Programs (2000). *The 2001 standards: CACREP accreditation standards and procedures manual.* Alexandria, VA: Author.

Crespi, T. D., Fischetti, B. A., & Butler, S. K. (2001, January). Clinical supervision in the schools. *Counseling Today, 43,* 7, 28, 34.

Daloz, L. (1988). Into the trenches: A case study in mentorship. *Management of Lifelong Education Alumni Bulletin, 1*(2), 1–3.

DeBono, E. (1992). *Serious creativity: Using the power of lateral thinking to create new ideas.* New York: HarperCollins.

Dollarhide, C. T., & Miller, G. M. (2006). Supervision for preparation and practice of school counselors: Pathways to excellence. *Counselor Education and Supervision, 45,* 242–252.

Fox, M. (1994). *The reinvention of work: A new vision of livelihood for our time.* San Francisco: Harper.

Gruber, H. E. (1993). Aspects of scientific discovery: Aesthetics and cognition. In J. Brockman (Ed.), *Creativity* (pp. 48–74). New York: Simon & Schuster.

Hawks, B. K., & Muha, D. (1991). Facilitating the career development of minorities: Doing it differently this time. *The Career Development Quarterly, 39*(3), 251–260.

Heinrich, K. T. (1995). Doctoral advisement relationships between women: On friendship and betrayal. *Journal of Higher Education, 66*(4), 447–469.

Herlihy, B., & Corey, G. (1996). *ACA ethical standards casebook* (5th ed.). Alexandria, VA: ACA.

James, S. H., & Greenwalt, B. C. (2001). Documenting success and achievement: Presentation and working portfolios for counselors. *Journal of Counseling & Development, 79,* 161–165.

Johnson, L. S. (2000). Promoting professional identity in an era of educational reform. *Professional School Counseling, 4,* 31–40.

Kahn, B. B. (1999). Priorities and practices in field supervision of school counseling students. *Professional School Counseling, 3,* 128–136.

Miller, G. M., & Dollarhide, C. T. (2006). Supervision in schools: Building pathways to excellence. *Counselor Education and Supervision, 45,* 296–303.

Morris, J. (1992). *Creative breakthroughs: Tap the power of your unconscious mind.* New York: Warner.

Morrissette, P. J. (2000). The experiences of the rural school counselor. *Professional School Counseling, 3,* 197–208.

Palmer, P. J. (1998). *The courage to teach: Exploring the inner landscape of a teacher's life.* San Francisco: Jossey-Bass.

Parks, S. D. (1990, Fall). Social vision and moral courage: Mentoring a new generation. *Cross Currents,* 350–367.

Roberts, E. B., & Borders, L. D. (1994). Supervision of school counselors: Administrative, program, and counseling. *The School Counselor, 41,* 149–157.

Roberts, W. B., Jr., & Morotti, A. A. (2001). Site supervisors of professional school counseling interns: Suggested guidelines. *Professional School Counseling, 4,* 208–215.

Root-Bernstein, R., & Root-Bernstein, M. (1999). *Sparks of genius: The thirteen thinking tools of the world's most creative people.* Boston: Houghton Mifflin.

Schmidt, J. J. (1990). Critical issues for school counselor performance appraisal and supervision. *The School Counselor, 38,* 86–94.

Seaward, B. L. (1994). *Managing stress: Principles and strategies for health and wellbeing.* Boston: Jones & Bartlett.

Smith, E. P., & Davidson, II, W. S. (1992). Mentoring and the development of African-American graduate students. *Journal of College Student Development, 33,* 531–539.

Tentoni, S. C. (1995). The mentoring of counseling students: A concept in search of a paradigm. *Counselor Education and Supervision, 35,* 32–42.

VanZandt, C. E., & Perry, N. S. (1992). Helping the rookie school counselor: A mentoring project. *The School Counselor, 39,* 158–163.

Young-Eisendrath, P., & Miller, M. E. (2000). Beyond enlightened self-interest: The psychology of mature spirituality in the twenty-first century. In P. Young-Eisendrath & M. E. Miller (Eds.), *The psychology of mature spirituality: Integrity, wisdom, transcendence* (pp. 1–7). Philadelphia, PA: Routledge.

APPENDIX A

ETHICAL STANDARDS FOR SCHOOL COUNSELORS

ASCA's Ethical Standards for School Counselors were adopted by the ASCA Delegate Assembly, March 19,1984, revised March 27, 1992, June 25, 1998 and June 26, 2004.

◆ PREAMBLE

The American School Counselor Association (ASCA) is a professional organization whose members are certified/licensed in school counseling with unique qualifications and skills to address the academic, personal/social and career development needs of all students. Professional school counselors are advocates, leaders, collaborators and consultants who create opportunities for equity in access and success in educational opportunities by connecting their programs to the mission of schools and subscribing to the following tenets of professional responsibility:

- ◆ Each person has the right to be respected, be treated with dignity and have access to a comprehensive school counseling program that advocates for and affirms all students from diverse populations regardless of ethnic/racial status, age, economic status, special needs, English as a second language or other language group, immigration status, sexual orientation, gender, gender identity/expression, family type, religious/spiritual identity and appearance.
- ◆ Each person has the right to receive the information and support needed to move toward self-direction and self-development and affirmation within one's group identities, with special care being given to students who have historically not received adequate educational services: students of color, low socio-economic students, students with disabilities and students with nondominant language backgrounds.
- ◆ Each person has the right to understand the full magnitude and meaning of his/her educational choices and how those choices will affect future opportunities.
- ◆ Each person has the right to privacy and thereby the right to expect the counselor-student relationship to comply with all laws, policies and ethical standards pertaining to confidentiality in the school setting.

In this document, ASCA specifies the principles of ethical behavior necessary to maintain the high standards of integrity, leadership and professionalism among its members. The Ethical Standards for School Counselors were developed to clarify the nature of ethical responsibilities held in common by school counseling professionals. The purposes of this document are to:

◆ Serve as a guide for the ethical practices of all professional school counselors regardless of level, area, population served or membership in this professional association;
◆ Provide self-appraisal and peer evaluations regarding counselor responsibilities to students, parents/guardians, colleagues and professional associates, schools, communities and the counseling profession; and
◆ Inform those served by the school counselor of acceptable counselor practices and expected professional behavior.

◆A.1 RESPONSIBILITIES TO STUDENTS

The professional school counselor:

a. Has a primary obligation to the student, who is to be treated with respect as a unique individual.
b. Is concerned with the educational, academic, career, personal and social needs and encourages the maximum development of every student.
c. Respects the student's values and beliefs and does not impose the counselor's personal values.
d. Is knowledgeable of laws, regulations and policies relating to students and strives to protect and inform students regarding their rights.

◆A.2 CONFIDENTIALITY

The professional school counselor:

a. Informs students of the purposes, goals, techniques and rules of procedure under which they may receive counseling at or before the time when the counseling relationship is entered. Disclosure notice includes the limits of confidentiality such as the possible necessity for consulting with other professionals, privileged communication, and legal or authoritative restraints. The meaning and limits of confidentiality are defined in developmentally appropriate terms to students.
b. Keeps information confidential unless disclosure is required to prevent clear and imminent danger to the student or others or when legal requirements demand that confidential information be revealed. Counselors will consult with appropriate professionals when in doubt as to the validity of an exception.
c. In absence of state legislation expressly forbidding disclosure, considers the ethical responsibility to provide information to an identified third party who, by his/her relationship with the student, is at a high risk of contracting a disease that is commonly known to be communicable and fatal. Disclosure requires satisfaction of all of the following conditions:
   ◆ Student identifies partner or the partner is highly identifiable
   ◆ Counselor recommends the student notify partner and refrain from further high-risk behavior

◆ Student refuses

◆ Counselor informs the student of the intent to notify the partner

◆ Counselor seeks legal consultation as to the legalities of informing the partner

d. Requests of the court that disclosure not be required when the release of confidential information may potentially harm a student or the counseling relationship.

e. Protects the confidentiality of students' records and releases personal data in accordance with prescribed laws and school policies. Student information stored and transmitted electronically is treated with the same care as traditional student records.

f. Protects the confidentiality of information received in the counseling relationship as specified by federal and state laws, written policies and applicable ethical standards. Such information is only to be revealed to others with the informed consent of the student, consistent with the counselor's ethical obligation.

g. Recognizes his/her primary obligation for confidentiality is to the student but balances that obligation with an understanding of the legal and inherent rights of parents/guardians to be the guiding voice in their children's lives.

◆A.3 COUNSELING PLANS

The professional school counselor:

a. Provides students with a comprehensive school counseling program that includes a strong emphasis on working jointly with all students to develop academic and career goals.

b. Advocates for counseling plans supporting students right to choose from the wide array of options when they leave secondary education. Such plans will be regularly reviewed to update students regarding critical information they need to make informed decisions.

◆A.4 DUAL RELATIONSHIPS

The professional school counselor:

a. Avoids dual relationships that might impair his/her objectivity and increase the risk of harm to the student (e.g., counseling one's family members, close friends or associates). If a dual relationship is unavoidable, the counselor is responsible for taking action to eliminate or reduce the potential for harm. Such safeguards might include informed consent, consultation, supervision and documentation.

b. Avoids dual relationships with school personnel that might infringe on the integrity of the counselor/student relationship

◆A.5 APPROPRIATE REFERRALS

The professional school counselor:

a. Makes referrals when necessary or appropriate to outside resources. Appropriate referrals may necessitate informing both parents/guardians and students of applicable resources and making proper plans for transitions with minimal interruption of services. Students retain the right to discontinue the counseling relationship at any time.

◆A.6 GROUP WORK

The professional school counselor:

a. Screens prospective group members and maintains an awareness of participants' needs and goals in relation to the goals of the group. The counselor takes reasonable precautions to protect members from physical and psychological harm resulting from interaction within the group.

b. Notifies parents/guardians and staff of group participation if the counselor deems it appropriate and if consistent with school board policy or practice.

c. Establishes clear expectations in the group setting and clearly states that confidentiality in group counseling cannot be guaranteed. Given the developmental and chronological ages of minors in schools, the counselor recognizes the tenuous nature of confidentiality for minors renders some topics inappropriate for group work in a school setting.

d. Follows up with group members and documents proceedings as appropriate.

◆A.7 DANGER TO SELF OR OTHERS

The professional school counselor:

a. Informs parents/guardians or appropriate authorities when the student's condition indicates a clear and imminent danger to the student or others. This is to be done after careful deliberation and, where possible, after consultation with other counseling professionals.

b. Will attempt to minimize threat to a student and may choose to (1) inform the student of actions to be taken, (2) involve the student in a three-way communication with parents/guardians when breaching confidentiality or (3) allow the student to have input as to how and to whom the breach will be made.

◆A.8 STUDENT RECORDS

The professional school counselor:

a. Maintains and secures records necessary for rendering professional services to the student as required by laws, regulations, institutional procedures and confidentiality guidelines.

b. Keeps sole-possession records separate from students' educational records in keeping with state laws.

c. Recognizes the limits of sole-possession records and understands these records are a memory aid for the creator and in absence of privilege communication may be subpoenaed and may become educational records when they (1) are shared with others in verbal or written form, (2) include information other than professional opinion or personal observations and/or (3) are made accessible to others.

d. Establishes a reasonable timeline for purging sole-possession records or case notes. Suggested guidelines include shredding sole possession records when the student transitions to the next level, transfers to another school or graduates. Careful discretion and deliberation should be applied before destroying sole-possession records that may be needed by a court of law such as notes on child abuse, suicide, sexual harassment or violence.

◆A.9   EVALUATION, ASSESSMENT AND INTERPRETATION

The professional school counselor:

a. Adheres to all professional standards regarding selecting, administering and interpreting assessment measures and only utilizes assessment measures that are within the scope of practice for school counselors.

b. Seeks specialized training regarding the use of electronically based testing programs in administering, scoring and interpreting that may differ from that required in more traditional assessments.

c. Considers confidentiality issues when utilizing evaluative or assessment instruments and electronically based programs.

d. Provides interpretation of the nature, purposes, results and potential impact of assessment/evaluation measures in language the student(s) can understand.

e. Monitors the use of assessment results and interpretations, and takes reasonable steps to prevent others from misusing the information.

f. Uses caution when utilizing assessment techniques, making evaluations and interpreting the performance of populations not represented in the norm group on which an instrument is standardized.

g. Assesses the effectiveness of his/her program in having an impact on students' academic, career and personal/social development through accountability measures especially examining efforts to close achievement, opportunity and attainment gaps.

◆A.10   TECHNOLOGY

The professional school counselor:

a. Promotes the benefits of and clarifies the limitations of various appropriate technological applications. The counselor promotes technological applications (1) that are appropriate for the student's individual needs, (2) that the student understands how to use and (3) for which follow-up counseling assistance is provided.

b. Advocates for equal access to technology for all students, especially those historically underserved.

c. Takes appropriate and reasonable measures for maintaining confidentiality of student information and educational records stored or transmitted over electronic media including although not limited to fax, electronic mail and instant messaging.

d. While working with students on a computer or similar technology, takes reasonable and appropriate measures to protect students from objectionable and/or harmful online material.

e. Who is engaged in the delivery of services involving technologies such as the telephone, videoconferencing and the Internet takes responsible steps to protect students and others from harm.

◆ A.11   STUDENT PEER SUPPORT PROGRAM

The professional school counselor:

> Has unique responsibilities when working with student-assistance programs. The school counselor is responsible for the welfare of students participating in peer-to-peer programs under his/her direction.

◆ B.   RESPONSIBILITIES TO PARENTS/GUARDIANS

B.1   Parent Rights and Responsibilities

The professional school counselor:

a. Respects the rights and responsibilities of parents/guardians for their children and endeavors to establish, as appropriate, a collaborative relationship with parents/guardians to facilitate the student's maximum development.

b. Adheres to laws, local guidelines and ethical standards of practice when assisting parents/guardians experiencing family difficulties that interfere with the student's effectiveness and welfare.

c. Respects the confidentiality of parents/guardians.

d. Is sensitive to diversity among families and recognizes that all parents/guardians, custodial and noncustodial, are vested with certain rights and responsibilities for the welfare of their children by virtue of their role and according to law.

B.2   Parents/Guardians and Confidentiality

The professional school counselor:

a. Informs parents/guardians of the counselor's role with emphasis on the confidential nature of the counseling relationship between the counselor and student.

b. Recognizes that working with minors in a school setting may require counselors to collaborate with students' parents/guardians.

c. Provides parents/guardians with accurate, comprehensive and relevant information in an objective and caring manner, as is appropriate and consistent with ethical responsibilities to the student.

    d. Makes reasonable efforts to honor the wishes of parents/guardians concerning information regarding the student, and in cases of divorce or separation exercises a good-faith effort to keep both parents informed with regard to critical information with the exception of a court order.

◆ C. RESPONSIBILITIES TO COLLEAGUES AND PROFESSIONAL ASSOCIATES

C.1   Professional Relationships

The professional school counselor:

    a. Establishes and maintains professional relationships with faculty, staff and administration to facilitate an optimum counseling program.

    b. Treats colleagues with professional respect, courtesy and fairness. The qualifications, views and findings of colleagues are represented to accurately reflect the image of competent professionals.

    c. Is aware of and utilizes related professionals, organizations and other resources to whom the student may be referred.

C.2   Sharing Information with Other Professionals

The professional school counselor:

    a. Promotes awareness and adherence to appropriate guidelines regarding confidentiality, the distinction between public and private information and staff consultation.

    b. Provides professional personnel with accurate, objective, concise and meaningful data necessary to adequately evaluate, counsel and assist the student.

    c. If a student is receiving services from another counselor or other mental health professional, the counselor, with student and/or parent/guardian consent, will inform the other professional and develop clear agreements to avoid confusion and conflict for the student.

    d. Is knowledgeable about release of information and parental rights in sharing information.

◆D. RESPONSIBILITIES TO THE SCHOOL AND COMMUNITY

D.1   Responsibilities to the School

The professional school counselor:

    a. Supports and protects the educational program against any infringement not in students' best interest.

    b. Informs appropriate officials in accordance with school policy of conditions that may be potentially disruptive or damaging to the school's mission, personnel and property while honoring the confidentiality between the student and counselor.

c. Is knowledgeable and supportive of the school's mission and connects his/her program to the school's mission.

d. Delineates and promotes the counselor's role and function in meeting the needs of those served. Counselors will notify appropriate officials of conditions that may limit or curtail their effectiveness in providing programs and services.

e. Accepts employment only for positions for which he/she is qualified by education, training, supervised experience, state and national professional credentials and appropriate professional experience.

f. Advocates that administrators hire only qualified and competent individuals for professional counseling positions.

g. Assists in developing: (1) curricular and environmental conditions appropriate for the school and community, (2) educational procedures and programs to meet students' developmental needs and (3) a systematic evaluation process for comprehensive, developmental, standards-based school counseling programs, services and personnel. The counselor is guided by the findings of the evaluation data in planning programs and services.

D.2   Responsibility to the Community

The professional school counselor:

a. Collaborates with agencies, organizations and individuals in the community in the best interest of students and without regard to personal reward or remuneration.

b. Extends his/her influence and opportunity to deliver a comprehensive school counseling program to all students by collaborating with community resources for student success.

◆ E. RESPONSIBILITIES TO SELF

E.1   Professional Competence

The professional school counselor:

a. Functions within the boundaries of individual professional competence and accepts responsibility for the consequences of his/her actions.

b. Monitors personal well-being and effectiveness and does not participate in any activity that may lead to inadequate professional services or harm to a student.

c. Strives through personal initiative to maintain professional competence including technological literacy and to keep abreast of professional information. Professional and personal growth are ongoing throughout the counselor's career.

E.2   Diversity

The professional school counselor:

a. Affirms the diversity of students, staff and families.

b. Expands and develops awareness of his/her own attitudes and beliefs affecting cultural values and biases and strives to attain cultural competence.

   c. Possesses knowledge and understanding about how oppression, racism, discrimination and stereotyping affects her/him personally and professionally.

   d. Acquires educational, consultation and training experiences to improve awareness, knowledge, skills and effectiveness in working with diverse populations: ethnic/racial status, age, economic status, special needs, ESL or ELL, immigration status, sexual orientation, gender, gender identity/expression, family type, religious/spiritual identity and appearance.

◆ F. RESPONSIBILITIES TO THE PROFESSION

F.1   Professionalism

The professional school counselor:

   a. Accepts the policies and procedures for handling ethical violations as a result of maintaining membership in the American School Counselor Association.

   b. Conducts herself/himself in such a manner as to advance individual ethical practice and the profession.

   c. Conducts appropriate research and report findings in a manner consistent with acceptable educational and psychological research practices. The counselor advocates for the protection of the individual student's identity when using data for research or program planning.

   d. Adheres to ethical standards of the profession, other official policy statements, such as ASCA's position statements, role statement and the ASCA National Model, and relevant statutes established by federal, state and local governments, and when these are in conflict works responsibly for change.

   e. Clearly distinguishes between statements and actions made as a private individual and those made as a representative of the school counseling profession.

   f. Does not use his/her professional position to recruit or gain clients, consultees for his/her private practice or to seek and receive unjustified personal gains, unfair advantage, inappropriate relationships or unearned goods or services.

F.2   Contribution to the Profession

The professional school counselor:

   a. Actively participates in local, state and national associations fostering the development and improvement of school counseling.

   b. Contributes to the development of the profession through the sharing of skills, ideas and expertise with colleagues.

   c. Provides support and mentoring to novice professionals.

◆G. MAINTENANCE OF STANDARDS

Ethical behavior among professional school counselors, association members and nonmembers, is expected at all times. When there exists serious doubt as to the ethical behavior of colleagues or if counselors are forced to work in situations or abide by policies that do not reflect the standards as outlined in these Ethical Standards for School Counselors, the counselor is obligated to take appropriate action to rectify the condition. The following procedure may serve as a guide:

1. The counselor should consult confidentially with a professional colleague to discuss the nature of a complaint to see if the professional colleague views the situation as an ethical violation.
2. When feasible, the counselor should directly approach the colleague whose behavior is in question to discuss the complaint and seek resolution.
3. If resolution is not forthcoming at the personal level, the counselor shall utilize the channels established within the school, school district, the state school counseling association and ASCA's Ethics Committee.
4. If the matter still remains unresolved, referral for review and appropriate action should be made to the Ethics Committees in the following sequence:
    ◆ state school counselor association
    ◆ American School Counselor Association
5. The ASCA Ethics Committee is responsible for:
    ◆ educating and consulting with the membership regarding ethical standards
    ◆ periodically reviewing and recommending changes in code
    ◆ receiving and processing questions to clarify the application of such standards; Questions must be submitted in writing to the ASCA Ethics chair.
    ◆ handling complaints of alleged violations of the ethical standards. At the national level, complaints should be submitted in writing to the ASCA Ethics Committee, c/o the Executive Director, American School Counselor Association, 1101 King St., Suite 625, Alexandria, VA 22314.

ASCA NATIONAL STANDARDS FOR STUDENT ACADEMIC, CAREER, AND PERSONAL/SOCIAL DEVELOPMENT (COMPETENCIES AND INDICATORS)

Legend: AA-1.1 = Academic Domain, Standard A, Competency 1 and Indicator 1

◆ ACADEMIC DEVELOPMENT

Standard A: Students will acquire the attitudes, knowledge and skills that contribute to effective learning in school and across the life span.

A:A1 Improve Academic Self-Concept
A:A1.1	Articulate feelings of competence and confidence as learners
A:A1.2	Display a positive interest in learning
A:A1.3	Take pride in work and achievement
A:A1.4	Accept mistakes as essential to the learning process
A:A1.5	Identify attitudes and behaviors which lead to successful learning

A:A2 Acquire Skills for Improving Learning
A:A2.1	Apply time-management and task-management skills
A:A2.2	Demonstrate how effort and persistence positively affect learning
A:A2.3	Use communications skills to know when and how to ask for help when needed
A:A2.4	Apply knowledge and learning styles to positively influence school performance

A:A3 Achieve School Success
A:A3.1	Take responsibility for their actions
A:A3.2	Demonstrate the ability to work independently, as well as the ability to work cooperatively with other students
A:A3.3	Develop a broad range of interests and abilities
A:A3.4	Demonstrate dependability, productivity and initiative
A:A3.5	Share knowledge

Adapted from Campbell, C. A., & Dahir, C. A. (1997). *Sharing the vision: National standards for school counseling programs.* Alexandria, VA: American School Counselor Association.

©American School Counselor Association. Reprinted by permission.

Standard B: Students will complete school with the academic preparation essential to choose from a wide range of substantial post-secondary options, including college.

A:B1 Improve Learning

A:B1.1   Demonstrate the motivation to achieve individual potential

A:B1.2   Learn and apply critical-thinking skills

A:B1.3   Apply the study skills necessary for academic success at each level

A:B1.4   Seek information and support from faculty, staff, family and peers

A:B1.5   Organize and apply academic information from a variety of sources

A:B1.6   Use knowledge of learning styles to positively influence school performance

A:B1.7   Become a self-directed and independent learner

A:B2 Plan to Achieve Goals

A:B2.1   Establish challenging academic goals in elementary, middle/junior high and high school

A:B2.2   Use assessment results in educational planning

A:B2.3   Develop and implement annual plan of study to maximize academic ability and achievement

A:B2.4   Apply knowledge of aptitudes and interests to goal setting

A:B2.5   Use problem-solving and decision-making skills to assess progress toward educational goals

A:B2.6   Understand the relationship between classroom performance and success in school

A:B2.7   Identify post-secondary options consistent with interests, achievement, aptitude and abilities

Standard C: Students will understand the relationship of academics to the world of work and to life at home and in the community.

A:C1 Relate school to Life Experiences

A:C 1.1   Demonstrate the ability to balance school, studies, extracurricular activities, leisure time and family life

A:C1.2   Seek co-curricular and community experiences to enhance the school experience

A:C1.3   Understand the relationship between learning and work

A:C1.4   Demonstrate an understanding of the value of lifelong learning as essential to seeking, obtaining and maintaining life goals

A:C1.5   Understand that school success is the preparation to make the transition from student to community member

A:C1.6   Understand how school success and academic achievement enhance future career and vocational opportunities

◆ CAREER DEVELOPMENT

Standard A: Students will acquire the skills to investigate the world of work in relation to knowledge of self and to make informed career decisions.

C:A1   Develop Career Awareness

C:A1.1   Develop skills to locate, evaluate and interpret career information

C:A1.2   Learn about the variety of traditional and nontraditional occupations

C:A1.3.   Develop an awareness of personal abilities, skills, interests and motivations

C:A1.4   Learn how to interact and work cooperatively in teams

C:A1.5   Learn to make decisions

C:A1.6   Learn how to set goals

C:A1.7   Understand the importance of planning

C:A1.8   Pursue and develop competency in areas of interest

C:A1.9   Develop hobbies and vocational interests

C:A1.10 Balance between work and leisure time

C:A2   Develop Employment Readiness

C:A2.1   Acquire employability skills such as working on a team, problem-solving and organizational skills

C:A2.2   Apply job readiness skills to seek employment opportunities

C:A2.3   Demonstrate knowledge about the changing workplace

C:A2.4   Learn about the rights and responsibilities of employers and employees

C:A2.5   Learn to respect individual uniqueness in the workplace

C:A2.6   Learn how to write a resume

C:A2.7   Develop a positive attitude toward work and learning

C:A2.8   Understand the importance of responsibility, dependability, punctuality, integrity and effort in the workplace

C:A2.9   Utilize time- and task-management skills

Standard B: Students will employ strategies to achieve future career goals with success and satisfaction.

C:B1   Acquire Career Information

C:B1.1   Apply decision-making skills to career planning, course selection and career transition

C:B1.2   Identify personal skills, interests and abilities and relate them to current career choice

C:B1.3   Demonstrate knowledge of the career-planning process

C:B1.4   Know the various ways in which occupations can be classified

C:B1.5   Use research and information resources to obtain career information

C:B1.6   Learn to use the Internet to access career-planning information

C:B1.7   Describe traditional and nontraditional career choices and how they relate to career choice

C:B1.8   Understand how changing economic and societal needs influence employment trends and future training

C:B2   Identify Career Goals

C:B2.1   Demonstrate awareness of the education and training needed to achieve career goals

C:B2.2   Assess and modify their educational plan to support career

C:B2.3   Use employability and job readiness skills in internship, mentoring, shadowing and/or other work experience

C:B2.4   Select course work that is related to career interests

C:B2.5   Maintain a career-planning portfolio

Standard C: Students will understand the relationship between personal qualities, education, training and the world of work.

C:C1 Acquire Knowledge to Achieve Career Goals

C:C1.1   Understand the relationship between educational achievement and career success

C:C1.2   Explain how work can help to achieve personal success and satisfaction

C:C1.3   Identify personal preferences and interests influencing career choice and success

C:C1.4   Understand that the changing workplace requires lifelong learning and acquiring new skills

C:C1.5   Describe the effect of work on lifestyle

C:C1.6   Understand the importance of equity and access in career choice

C:C1.7   Understand that work is an important and satistying means of personal expression

C:C2 Apply Skills to Achieve Career Goals

C:C2.1   Demonstrate how interests, abilities and achievement relate to achieving personal, social, educational and career goals

C:C2.2   Learn how to use conflict management skills with peers and adults

C:C2.3   Learn to work cooperatively with others as a team member

C:C2.4   Apply academic and employment readiness skills in work-based learning situations such as internships, shadowing and/or mentoring experiences

◆ PERSONAL/SOCIAL

Standard A: Students will acquire the knowledge, attitudes and interpersonal skills to help them understand and respect self and others.

PS-A1 Acquire Self-Knowledge

PS-A1.1   Develop positive attitudes toward self as a unique and worthy person

PS-A1.2   Identity values, attitudes and beliefs

PS-A1.3   Learn the goal-setting process

PS-A1.4   Understand change is a part of growth

PS-A1.5   Identify and express feelings

PS-A1.6   Distinguish between appropriate and inappropriate behavior

PS-A1.7   Recognize personal boundaries, rights and privacy needs

PS-A1.8   Understand the need for self-control and how to practice it

PS-A1.9   Demonstrate cooperative behavior in groups

PS-A1.10 Identify personal strengths and assets

PS-Al. 11 Identify and discuss changing personal and social roles

PS-A1.12 Identity and recognize changing family roles

PS-A2 Acquire Interpersonal Skills

PS-A2.1   Recognize that everyone has rights and responsibilities

PS-A2.2   Respect alternative points of view

PS-A2.3   Recognize, accept, respect and appreciate individual differences

PS-A2.4   Recognize, accept and appreciate ethnic and cultural diversity

PS-A2.5   Recognize and respect differences in various family configurations

PS-A2.6   Use effective communications skills

PS-A2.7   Know that communication involves speaking, listening and nonverbal behavior

PS-A2.8   Learn how to make and keep friends

Standard B: Students will make decisions, set goals and take necessary action to achieve goals.

PS-B1 Self-Knowledge Application

PS-B1.1   Use a decision-making and problem-solving model

PS-B1.2   Understand consequences of decisions and choices

PS-B1.3   Identity alternative solutions to a problem

PS-B1.4   Develop effective coping skills for dealing with problems

PS-B1.5   Demonstrate when, where and how to seek help for solving problems and making decisions

PS-B1.6   Know how to apply conflict resolution skills

PS-B1.7   Demonstrate a respect and appreciation for individual and cultural differences

PS-B1.8   Know when peer pressure is influencing a decision

PS-B1.9   Identify long- and short-term goals

PS-B1.10   Identify alternative ways of achieving goals

PS-B1.11   Use persistence and perseverance in acquiring knowledge and skills

PS-B1.12   Develop an action plan to set and achieve realistic goals

Standard C: Students will understand safety and survival skills.

PS-C1 Acquire Personal Safety Skills

PS-C1.1   Demonstrate knowledge of personal information (i.e., telephone number, home address, emergency contact)

PS-C1.2   Learn about the relationship between rules, laws, safety and the protection of rights of the individual

PS-C1.3   Learn about the differences between appropriate and inappropriate physical contact

PS-C1.4   Demonstrate the ability to set boundaries, rights and personal privacy

PS-C1.5   Differentiate between situations requiring peer support and situations requiring adult professional help

PS-C1.6   Identify resource people in the school and community, and know how to seek their help

PS-C1.7   Apply effective problem-solving and decision-making skills to make safe and healthy choices

PS-C1.8   Learn about the emotional and physical dangers of substance use and abuse

PS-C1.9   Learn how to cope with peer pressure

PS-C1.10   Learn techniques for managing stress and conflict

PS-C1.11   Learn coping skills for managing life events

SCHOOL COUNSELOR PERFORMANCE STANDARDS

School counselor performance standards align with the ASCA National Model and contain basic standards of practice expected from counselors. Personnel delivering the school counseling program are evaluated in the areas of program implementation, program evaluation and professionalism. All too often, school counselors are evaluated using an instrument designed for teachers or resource professionals. These school counselor standards accurately reflect the unique training of school counselors and their responsibilities within the school system. Although used for performance evaluation, the standards are also an important tool in the school counselor's own self-evaluation and will help focus personal and professional development plans. It is suggested that school counselors and administrators work within their individual systems to design appropriate evaluation and/or appraisal tools that meet their district governing board and bargaining unit policies. It is recommended that administrators evaluate school counselors every year. An evaluation should include individual comments as well as a rating system for how well the school counselor is meeting required performance standards.

School counselor standards are:

Standard 1: Program organization
Standard 2: School guidance curriculum delivered to all students
Standard 3: Individual student planning
Standard 4: Responsive services
Standard 5: Systems Support
Standard 6: School counselor and administrator agreement
Standard 7: Advisory council
Standard 8: Use of data
Standard 9: Student monitoring
Standard 10: Use of time and calendar
Standard 11: Results evaluation
Standard 12: Program audit
Standard 13: Infusing themes

Standard 1: The professional school counselor plans, organizes and delivers the school counseling program

1.1 A program is designed to meet the needs of the school.
1.2 The professional school counselor demonstrates interpersonal relationships with students.

1.3   The professional school counselor demonstrates positive interpersonal relationships with educational staff.

1.4   The professional school counselor demonstrates positive interpersonal relationships with parents or guardians.

Standard 2: The professional school counselor implements the school guidance curriculum through the use of effective instructional skills and careful planning of structured group sessions for all students.

2.1   The professional school counselor teaches school guidance units effectively.

2.2   The professional school counselor develops materials and instructional strategies to meet student needs and school goals.

2.3   The professional school counselor encourages staff involvement to ensure the effective implementation of the school guidance curriculum.

Standard 3: The professional school counselor implements the individual planning component by guiding individuals and groups of students and their parents or guardians through the development of educational and career plans.

3.1   The professional school counselor, in collaboration with parents or guardians, helps students establish goals and develop and use planning skills.

3.2   The professional school counselor demonstrates accurate and appropriate interpretation of assessment data and the presentation of relevant, unbiased information.

Standard 4: The professional school counselor provides responsive services through the effective use of individual and small-group counseling, consultation and referral skills.

4.1   The professional school counselor counsels individual students and small groups of students with identified needs and concerns.

4.2   The professional school counselor consults effectively with parents or guardians, teachers, administrators and other relevant individuals.

4.3   The professional school counselor implements an effective referral process with administrators, teachers and other school personnel.

Standard 5: The professional school counselor provides system support through effective school counseling program management and support for other educational programs.

5.1   The professional school counselor provides a comprehensive and balanced school counseling program in collaboration with school staff.

5.2   The professional school counselor provides support for other school programs.

Standard 6: The professional school counselor discusses the counseling department management system and the program action plans with the school administrator.

6.1   The professional school counselor discusses the qualities of the school counselor management system with the other members of the counseling staff and has agreement.

6.2   The professional school counselor discusses the program results anticipated when implementing the action plans for the school year.

Standard 7: The professional school counselor is responsible for establishing and convening an advisory council for the school counseling program.

7.1   The professional school counselor meets with the advisory committee.

7.2   The professional school counselor reviews the school counseling program audit with the council.

7.3   The professional school counselor records meeting information.

Standard 8: The professional school counselor collects and analyzes data to guide program direction and emphasis.

8.1   The professional school counselor uses school data to make decisions regarding student choice of classes and special programs.

8.2   The professional school counselor uses data from the counseling program to make decisions regarding program revisions.

8.3   The professional school counselor analyzes data to ensure every student has equity and access to a rigorous academic curriculum.

8.4   The professional school counselor understands and uses data to establish goals and activities to close the gap.

Standard 9: The professional school counselor monitors the students on a regular basis as they progress in school.

9.1   The professional school counselor is accountable for monitoring every student's progress.

9.2   The professional school counselor implements monitoring systems appropriate to the individual school.

9.3   The professional school counselors develops appropriate interventions for students as needed and monitors their progress.

Standard 10: The professional school counselor uses time and calendars to implement an efficient program.

10.1   The professional school counselor uses a master calendar to plan activities throughout the year.

10.2   The professional school counselor distributes the master calendar to parents or guardians, staff and students.

10.3   The professional school counselor posts a weekly or monthly calendar.

10.4   The professional school counselor analyzes time spent providing direct service to students.

Standard 11: The professional school counselor develops a results evaluation for the program.

11.1   The professional school counselor measures results attained from school guidance curriculum and closing the gap activities.

11.2   The professional school counselor works with members of the counseling team and with the principal to clarify how programs are evaluated and how results are shared.

11.3   The professional school counselor knows how to collect process, perception and results data.

Standard 12: The professional school counselor conducts a yearly program audit.

12.1 The professional school counselor completes a program audit to determine the degrees to which the school counseling program is being implemented.

12.2 The professional school counselor shares the results of the program audit with the advisory council.

12.3 The professional school counselor uses the yearly audit to make changes in the school counseling program and calendar for the following year.

Standard 13: The professional school counselor is a student advocate, leader, collaborator and a systems change agent.

13.1 The professional school counselor promotes academic success of every student.

13.2 The professional school counselor promotes equity and access for every student.

13.3 The professional school counselor takes a leadership role within the counseling department, the school setting and the community.

13.4 The professional school counselor understands reform issues and works to close the achievement gap.

13.5 The professional school counselor collaborates with teachers, parents and the community to promote academic success of students.

13.6 The professional school counselor builds effective teams by encouraging collaboration among all school staff.

13.7 The professional school counselor uses data to recommend systemic change in policy and procedures that limit or inhibit academic achievement.

PROGRAM GOALS FOR ADULT PARTNERS IN THE DAP MODEL

In a comprehensive school counseling program, counselors have primary responsibility for the growth and development of the student partners of the Domains/Activities/Partners Model. But the ASCA National Model mandates that counselors also work toward systemic change, meaning counselors must also work systemically and holistically to address the systems in which our students are embedded. We must be aware of the needs of all partners in the education of young people. A comprehensive school counseling program, therefore, will also include systemic work with all the adult partners of the DAP model: parents and caregivers, teachers, administrators, other student services professionals (school psychologists, nurses, and social workers), and community colleagues (community mental health professionals, physical health professionals, social service and law enforcement professionals, employers, etc.).

For the work done with our adult partners, goals must be defined that will guide these interactions and provide outcomes that can be measured. This appendix contains some ideas for goals for adult partners, which could become part of the comprehensive school counseling program. These goals are presented here as a beginning for discussions, and should be modified based on local needs and priorities as established by the professional school counselor, in consultation with advisory groups. See Chapters 5 and 6 for a discussion of advisory groups and the program design process.

◆A. GOALS FOR ALL ADULT PARTNERS

Goal A.1 All partners will understand the developmental needs of students from a holistic perspective.

Goal A.2 All partners will understand the systemic elements of families, schools, and communities that facilitate student development.

Goal A.3 All partners will understand the systemic elements of families, schools, and communities that impede student development.

Goal A.4 All partners will understand the academic development process of students and will understand strategies to help students in that process.

Goal A.5 All partners will understand the career development process of students and will understand strategies to help students in that process.

Goal A.6 All partners will understand the personal/social development process of students and will understand strategies to help students in that process.

Goal A.7 All partners will understand their role in the development of students.

Goal A.8 All partners will demonstrate basic strategies for communicating with students in developmentally appropriate ways.

Goal A.9 All partners will understand the role of the other partners in the developmental process of students.

Goal A.10 All partners will understand the role of the school counselor and the role of comprehensive school counseling programs in the developmental process of students.

Goal A.11 All partners will feel comfortable approaching the school counselor with questions or concerns about students, families, schools, human development, or other topics.

Goal A.12 All partners will find the school counselor helpful in answering those questions and/or resolving those concerns about students, families, schools, and so on.

Goal A.13 All partners will understand the role of schools in educating young people for life, learning, and working.

Goal A.14 All partners will feel a part of the school community and the larger community and will share responsibility for, responsibility to, and will respond to the needs of those communities.

◆ B. GOALS FOR PARENTS AND CAREGIVERS

Goal B.1 Parents/caregivers will feel welcome in the school environment.

Goal B.2 Parents/caregivers will feel included and invested in the work done with students in the comprehensive school counseling program.

Goal B.3 Parents/caregivers will understand the crucial effects that family can have on the development of young people.

Goal B.4 Parents/caregivers will acquire strategies for creating a healthy family environment for students.

Goal B.5 Parents/caregivers will foster positive interactions between families, schools, and the community on behalf of students.

◆ C. GOALS FOR COLLEAGUES IN THE SCHOOLS

Goal C.1 Colleagues in the schools will understand the philosophy of developmentally appropriate education.

Goal C.2 Colleagues in the schools will feel included and invested in the work of the school counselor in the comprehensive school counseling program.

Goal C.3 Colleagues in the schools will understand the critical effect that schools can have on the development of young people.

Goal C.4 Colleagues in the schools will understand the need for an environment of respect in the school.

Goal C.5 Colleagues in the schools will acquire strategies for promoting an environment of respect in the school.

Goal C.6 Colleagues in the schools will foster positive interactions between families, schools, and the community on behalf of students.

◆ D. GOALS FOR COLLEAGUES IN THE COMMUNITY

Goal D.1 Colleagues in the community will feel welcome in the school.

Goal D.2 Colleagues in the community will feel included and invested in the work of the school counselor in the comprehensive school counseling program.

Goal D.3 Colleagues in the community will understand the critical effect that neighborhoods and communities can have on the development of young people.

Goal D.4 Colleagues in the community will understand that civility and respect in the community will have a profound impact on the climate of the school.

Goal D.5 Colleagues in the community will acquire strategies for creating that environment of civility and respect in the community.

Goal D.6 Colleagues in the community will foster positive interactions between families, schools, and the community on behalf of students.

Index